World Yearbook of Education 1987

VOCATIONAL EDUCATION

*Edited by John Twining (Guest Editor),
Stanley Nisbet (Associate Editor) and
Jacquetta Megarry (Series Editor)*

**Kogan Page, London/Nichols Publishing
Company, New York**

Previous titles in this series

World Yearbook of Education 1981
Education of Minorities
Edited by Jacquetta Megarry, Stanley Nisbet
and Eric Hoyle
Subject Adviser: Ken Eltis

World Yearbook of Education 1982/83
Computers and Education
Edited by Jacquetta Megarry, David R F Walker,
Stanley Nisbet and Eric Hoyle

World Yearbook of Education 1984
Women and Education
Edited by Sandra Acker, Jacquetta Megarry,
Stanley Nisbet and Eric Hoyle

World Yearbook of Education 1985
Research, Policy and Practice
Edited by John Nisbet, Jacquetta Megarry and Stanley Nisbet

World Yearbook of Education 1986
The Management of Schools
Edited by Eric Hoyle and Agnes McMahon

First published in Great Britain in 1987 by Kogan Page Limited
120 Pentonville Road, London N1 9JN

British Library Cataloguing in Publication Data

World yearbook of education — 1987
    1. Education — Periodicals
    370'.5   L16

  ISSN 0084-2508
  ISBN 1-85091-219-X

First published in the USA 1987
by Nichols Publishing Company
PO Box 96, New York, NY 10024

Library of Congress Cataloging in Publication Data

Main entry under title:
World Yearbook of Education: 1987
    1. Education — Periodicals

    ISBN 0-89397-262-2
    LC Catalog No. 32-18413

Printed and bound in Great Britain
by Anchor Brendon Ltd, Tiptree Essex

Contents

List of contributors

Introduction

John Twining

Summary: Vocational education, worldwide, is rich and diverse. The students range in age from those who are at school full-time, those emerging into the world of work and those studying for a trade, a profession or to be entrepreneurs, to those seeking, updating or changing careers and those preparing for retirement. The aims of their studies range from basic numeracy, language and survival skills, through competence at work, to professional qualifications at postgraduate level. The content of vocational education is the 'hidden hand' behind most aspects of everyday life. Everything we do is affected by commerce or industry, and behind commerce and industry is a massive chain of vocational competence which is normally based on vocational education.

It is useful to distinguish vocational education from general education on the one hand and vocational training on the other. My preference is for a broad concept of vocational education as a 'dual mandate' to develop the individual both in the interests of self and of employment. There is an inherent conflict between these two elements, and the way in which it is resolved may well be a question of political philosophy or national or local culture. Differences in the way in which vocational education has developed in the countries described in this *World Yearbook* are often due to varying national cultural factors, which are part of the exciting diversity of vocational education. More can be learned from comparative studies than from those confined to one country only.

Yet vocational education is perhaps the least studied and understood sector of education, partly because few of those who administrate or write about vocational education have been through a vocational education system, partly because the market is comparatively small, but largely because, of all sectors of education, vocational education is subject to constant change in response to the pressures of technology, the nature, content and availability of employment, and attitudes to learning and to work.

This common element of change, together with other strands, unites the widely different developments described in this volume.

Dissatisfaction with industrial performance has led the United Kingdom to a greater degree of experimentation at national level than many other developed countries and it is therefore a useful 'laboratory' for studying different approaches, but those in Britain can learn from other countries just as well as other countries can learn from developments here.

Vocational education, worldwide, is rich and diverse. The students vary more than in any other sector of education. They range in age from those who are still at school full-time, through those emerging into the world of work and those studying for a trade, a profession or to be entrepreneurs, to experienced workers seeking updating or who are changing careers, and to those preparing for retirement. At the bottom end the aims of their studies may be basic numeracy and language or survival skills for industrial or agricultural societies. The majority are seeking to develop competence in manufacturing, maintenance or services, including commerce and office work. At the top end, studies can lead to professional status, often with qualifications at postgraduate level.

The combination of diversity of students and study aims with the 'hidden hand' of content (see below) has led to the adoption of many different modes of delivery. Full-time courses often closely resemble those of schools or universities. In some countries part-time courses predominate (eg the 'day release' pattern which prevailed in UK vocational education from the 1950s until the 1980s). In some countries there have been long traditions of evening classes or 'night school'. There are innumerable short courses, often for updating adult knowledge, many different approaches to self-study, and the growing recognition that much learning takes place informally or at the workplace.

The hidden hand

The content of vocational education is the 'hidden hand' behind most aspects of everyday life, at least in the developed world. Imagine a family at home. Grandfather is sitting in an armchair (dependent on *furniture manufacture* and *upholstery*) reading a newspaper (dependent on *journalism, paper production, printing ink, printing*). Grandmother is watching *television*. The young son is playing with *toys* on the *carpet*, which covers the *floor*. A book case (*book binding, paper making, printing, joinery*) has a vase (*glass manufacture*) of flowers (*horticulture*) on it. A piano (*musical instrument manufacture*) stands in the corner. And so on through every room of the house. Mother is checking the electricity bill against a meter reading, and the daughter is doing homework. Outside, father is washing the car. We take for granted *building construction, plumbing* and *interior decoration* (even do-it-yourself is supported by *paint* and paintbrush manufacturers). We rely unthinkingly on *food manufacture, transportation* and *energy industries*. The kitchen, the garage, the garden, all depend on work supported by vocational education. In the UK, for example, there are vocational courses leading to qualifications in all the subjects printed in italics, and hundreds more.

When an electricity bill drops through the letterbox in the UK, it is the end product of a computerized accounting system, based on readings taken from an instrument which records electricity consumed in lighting, heating or the use of manufactured appliances. Mains electricity has been brought to the point of consumption by wires and a mass of components which have had to be installed to a high standard to ensure safety. A complex distribution system, which is monitored to even out peaks and troughs in demand, has delivered the electricity from the power station, which itself has converted energy sources into a consumable form. Each energy source, whether it be coal, oil, gas, nuclear power or hydroelectricity, is in turn dependent on a massive chain of vocational competence which almost always includes the contribution of vocational education.

Do we need definitions?

The pervasiveness of commerce and industry in virtually every aspect of our lives is a matter of fact. The boundaries between what is vocational *education* and what is vocational *training*, and between what is *vocational* education and what is *general* education, are matters for debate. Probably no definitions will be universally valid. However, attempts are frequently made to draw such boundaries because in many countries they can influence who does what and who pays for what. In Britain, for example, some have suggested definitions related to the location of learning: what takes place in industry is *training*, what takes place in schools and universities is *general education*, and what takes place in post-school institutions other than universities is *vocational education*.

But this definition is no longer valid in the UK, given the Technical and Vocational Education Initiative (TVEI) (described by Pignatelli in Chapter 4), and arguably never has been valid in such subject areas as shorthand and typing, catering and hairdressing. The development of open learning opportunities, particularly self-study, 'learning by appointment' and 'outreach', has also tended to cut across this type of definition by location. In any case, there are differences between one country and another, depending on who is considered responsible for different aspects of learning and the accreditation of competence, the type and number of institutions a particular country can afford, and how far compulsory school education is given a vocational bias (discussed by Hughes in Chapter 1, Pignatelli in Chapter 4).

So should we not concentrate on what is learned, and not where it is learned or what label we attach to the process of learning? Is it still worthwhile trying to distinguish vocational education from training on the one hand, and general education on the other? I believe it is, at least in broad terms, if only because to evade doing so can make things so much worse. Failure to distinguish between *general* education and *vocational* education can lead to perceptions from employers that *all* education is irrelevant to economic needs. In turn these perceptions can communicate themselves to their employees, especially the less ambitious, and may affect their motivation to learn anything which is not of immediate and obvious application. 'Vocational' is often taken to mean 'work related'; this is fine provided the 'work' is not always equated with the *immediate* task — but all too often this is exactly what happens.

Equally, failure to distinguish between vocational *education* and vocational *training* has led many educationists in the UK automatically to use the adjective 'narrow' when *anything* vocational is being considered. This tendency is exacerbated by government 'newspeak' in the mid-1980s of VET — Vocational Education and Training. But similar tendencies of undervaluing vocational education can be found in societies as different as the USSR (Marsh, Chapter 6), the Netherlands (van der Putten and Frissen, Chapter 10), and the USA (Ashmore, Chapter 12). I regard as intellectual arrogance the perception that all vocational education is 'narrow'.

Take, for example, electrical circuitry. Design of an electrical circuit normally requires a higher level of intellectual skills than its installation. The same person who does the installation, however, may also be responsible for fault-finding if the circuit is not functioning correctly; this activity may require the application of considerable knowledge and of intellectual skills which are moving close to those of design, especially if the circuit is a complex one. These higher intellectual skills are likely to be developed, and the knowledge (often based on principles not of obvious immediate application) gained, through 'education' rather than through 'training'. In terms of general education, electrical circuitry can be compared to grammar. It is as fundamental to energy distribution as grammar is to speech, but the consequences of failure are more serious. An ungrammatical sentence may be understood; a faulty electrical circuit may not work at all, or may cause fire or fatality.

My own preference is for a broad concept which recognizes that vocational education has a 'dual mandate' to develop the individual both in the interests of self and of employment. If we tip the balance too far in the interests of self, then we cross the boundary into general education; if we tip it too far towards employment then we cross the boundary into vocational training. But this concept is a servant, not a master; there will always be room for argument, blurred edges and commonsense decisions. I have applied the concept fairly broadly in the chapters of this *World Yearbook*.

Cultures

There is an inherent conflict between the elements of the dual mandate. Its implementation always requires a compromise. The way in which this conflict is resolved may well be a question of political philosophy or of national or local culture — the influence of culture is surprisingly strong in vocational education. Although *commercial* education is clearly influenced by national legislation, currency and language, it might be thought that *technical* education would be culture-free. Ohm's Law is surely Ohm's Law in Alaska or in Zimbabwe. In practice, however, if we were able to visit all the 20 or more countries mentioned in this *World Yearbook* we would find that the learning of Ohm's Law and its applications was affected by a mixture of geography, history, tradition, language, employment opportunities, attitudes, government initiatives, institutional structures, and even the constitutional or legal way in which institutions are organized.

To take an example: the success of the electrical wiring course (including its associated theory, such as Ohm's Law) provided by the Allama Iqbal Open University in Pakistan (see my Chapter 14) has depended on

- ☐ job opportunities in the Gulf states (a *tradition* of young males from the rain-fed areas of the Punjab who migrate temporarily for work) and as a result of the village electrification programme (*government initiative*)
- ☐ learning opportunities provided in Urdu by a prestigious national distance learning institution (*language*, *institutional structure*, another *government initiative* overcoming the *geographical* problems of distance)
- ☐ hands-on work based on cheap materials bought in the bazaar (*tradition* of a 'no-waste' culture) together with the use of educational institutions for materials when they are closed to their normal students on Fridays (a process eased by Muslim attitudes to education).

In contrast to Pakistan, entry to the electrical installation trade in Britain has for years been largely controlled by agreement between the employers and the relevant trade union, with a formalized apprenticeship (and now a traineeship) and an essential educational qualification, now supplemented by a trade test set by the Construction Industry Training Board.

Vocational studies may also be affected by attitudes to and perceptions of learning, of work and of personal progress. Contrast, for example, Ashmore's Chapter 12 on individual entrepreneurship in the USA, or Curtis's Chapter 15 on institutional entrepreneurship in Canada, with Engelhard and Kreuser on West Germany in Chapter 5, Marsh on the USSR in Chapter 6, van den Putten and Frissen on the Netherlands in Chapter 10. To take other examples from Pakistan: I visited a small shop in a township on the Grand Trunk Road, a graveyard for buses, lorries and cars. The elderly illiterate owner made his living by repairing and rebuilding vehicle radiators with pliers and solder. His specialization was indeed narrow, his workmanship exquisite. Again, in a small lock-up shop in a Lahore bazaar I saw a ten-year-old boy winding armatures of electrical motors. This was his sole skill, as it was of his father, and had been of his grandfather before him. Contrast that with the current Western European philosophy of flexibility, job changes, multi-skilling (eg Johnson, Chapter 2; Longden, Chapter 3) and with Ford's insights on Japan in Chapter 20.

Even where industry and educational institutions may have started with similar roots, the influence of different national cultural factors makes blatant or subtle changes in the way in which vocational education develops. These differences can operate on a macro scale; as Johnson reports in Chapter 2, the European Economic Community (EEC) has abandoned attempts to create a common vocational education and training pattern across its member states. England and New Zealand may have started with similar traditions, but Longden in Chapter 3 and Imrie in Chapter 9 show how they have grown apart. Differences can also operate on a micro scale; attempts in England to arrange collaboration of institutions in different local authority areas are exceptionally difficult, even where the political composition of those authorities is the same.

These differences, particularly at national level, are part of the exciting diversity of vocational education. More can be learned by comparative studies than by those confined to one country only. This is one justification for this volume. We can learn from each other, even if the total transfer of systems, structures, institutions or even the sharing of learning material is impossible because of cultural differences.

Another justification for the publishers to devote a *World Yearbook* to vocational education is that, compared with other sectors of education, it is less studied and less well understood. The bibliography contains a high proportion of government-sponsored reports, policy papers and laws, but few seminal works of academic authority. There are several reasons for this. First, few of those who administer or write about vocational education have been through the system themselves; in some countries the senior teaching posts require qualifications which cannot yet be obtained normally by those who follow a vocational education route. The market for published studies is also comparatively small. Probably the most potent reason of all is that, of all the sectors of education, vocational education is the least insulated from the pressures of technological change, both directly and also indirectly through changes in the nature, content and availability of employment, and in attitudes to learning and to work. It is very easy to get out of date.

Change

So, despite differences in culture, one current common thread for vocational education, worldwide, is that it is subject to immense change. This change affects

☐ educational institutions – these are being amalgamated in the Netherlands (van der Putten, Chapter 10); and becoming aware of the need to market their services (Curtis, Chapter 15). Banthiya (Chapter 16) describes how what was originally a traditional teacher training college has become an instrument of change and has itself adopted new processes to achieve this. Ayot (Chapter 13) describes the way in which 'village polytechnics' established by local community initiatives come increasingly under central control as their need for resources outstrips what the local community can provide.

☐ educational structures – the West German structure, which is well rooted in history, is being adapted because of major changes in demography, employment and technology (Engelhard and Kreuser,

Chapter 5). In Brazil (Romiszowski, Chapter 7) and East Asia (Waitt, Chapter 8) the needs of developing industry make it urgent to introduce new approaches.

☐ educational patterns — in particular, modular structures are becoming increasingly popular (Pignatelli, Chapter 4; Romiszowski, Chapter 7; Ashmore, Chapter 12; Twining, Chapter 14) and warrant the in-depth treatment given by Roberts in Chapter 18.

☐ assessment — common threads can be seen in New Zealand (Imrie, Chapter 9), India (Banthiya, Chapter 16) and in the UK, where Ward (Chapter 19) also does a study in depth.

☐ information technology — at once a cause of change and a means of handling it comes through in several different national studies (Marsh, Chapter 6; Romiszowski, Chapter 7; Twining, Chapter 14; McCallum, Chapter 17). A scenario for the future is given by Knutton in Chapter 21.

The knowledge gap

Many perceive the gap between the developed and the developing world in terms of wealth, but the knowledge gap is as great and is increasing just as rapidly. This knowledge gap may relate to industrial plant. Lack of foreign exchange for spare parts may keep plants out of commission, but lack of maintenance knowledge may have led to the breakdown in the first place. This particular gap is likely to widen as microprocessors are included in more and more equipment being imported into developing countries. But the knowledge gap does not only apply to industry. In some agricultural societies the pressure of population makes it urgent that crop production is increased, and although there are other factors such as lack of fertilizers or lack of water, it is often lack of knowledge which is the biggest drawback (Garforth, Chapter 11).

The concept of the knowledge gap is important because it should be less difficult and costly to transfer knowledge than to transfer wealth, and the knowledge thus transferred may itself be a generator of wealth. Such a means of overcoming the 'north-south' divide would alone justify paying greater attention to the study of vocational education.

In any event, it is necessary to start somewhere. The main constant in vocational education is change. One must understand the changes which are taking place and the reasons behind them before one can undertake any helpful study relating to content or the way in which different disciplines are best learned in different cultures. This specific aspect of the knowledge gap is wide even between developed countries.

Because of consistent failure to invest in vocational education from the 19th century through to the 1950s, there are few countries in the world where dissatisfaction with industrial performance has been so great as in the United Kingdom. This has led, in turn, to a greater degree of experimentation at national level (chronicled by Longden in Chapter 3) than in many other developed countries in which earlier, more substantial investments had created better systems (though even these are now subject to pressures to change). This range of experimentation, which covers the whole field of vocational education from school days to updating, makes the UK an exceptional 'laboratory' for studying different approaches. One field where it is premature to cite the British example is in 'mainline' craft and technician education, which looks as if it is soon to be subject to further experimentation and change. Here we can learn from the Netherlands and West Germany, from the Soviet Union, Malaysia, Korea and New Zealand. Perhaps in return others can learn from British experiments and initiatives and perhaps also we can all learn from Japan — the model learning society, which Ford views through Australian eyes in Chapter 20.

Even if, as Knutton suggests in Chapter 21, the world is on the way to becoming a global village as a result of information technology, the local cultural differences will remain. Nevertheless, the urgent need to learn from each other, and particularly from each other's innovations, will increase. The authors in this *World Yearbook* between them offer important contributions to that need.

1. General education and its relationship to vocational education: an Australian study

Phillip Hughes

Summary: A major impetus for the current major reconsideration of general education in Australia has been the changing situation with respect to employment and, in particular, the very high incidence of youth unemployment. The paper looks briefly at major periods of change in Australian education and concludes that the current situation will bring changes at least as significant as those in any period of Australian history.

While there is substantial agreement on the need for change, there are still major differences as to the proper directions. It is clear that one effect of recent changes will be greatly to increase the retention of pupils in secondary education. This change will make even more crucial the nature of the programmes to be provided in secondary education. While one pressure is for the period of general education to be more vocational and more practical, this is seen as an incidental response even in terms of vocational needs. Two other types of role are seen as being as important as the vocational role itself, and the implications of these are developed.

Current issues for general education in Australia

A period of major reconsideration

The current reconsideration of education in Australia is not so much of vocational education as of the implications of vocational needs for general education. This emphasis is strongly linked with the structural changes in employment, particularly with high youth unemployment. It is leading to a major reconceptualization of general education — that part of education seen as necessary and relevant to the whole generation. A major part of this reconceptualization will be directed towards the curriculum for the period of compulsory education.

The school curriculum is an explicit expression of the values of a particular society. It represents those aspects of its culture which a society selects for emphasis through education. Many institutions play a role in the transmission and the development of culture, including the family, religious institutions, the media and the arts. Only the school, and in particular the state school, has the responsibility of imparting a selected common core of culture to everyone, plus that of transmitting specific aspects of culture to various groups in society.

The processes by which these selections are made are complex, only partly explicit and involve a variety of agencies, groups and individuals. Teachers play a central role, since their action and inaction mediates any decisions made elsewhere. Students also play a crucial role, since their actions, choices, motivations and expectations finally define the curriculum, in the sense that the curriculum is what happens in schools. Parents also play a part, now seen as more important than it used to be, since their influence has been shown to shape the attitude of students. These are internal factors. There are also important external factors: the influence of society, of culture, of technology and of ideology. These operate in many ways, through deliberate decisions of governments and other bodies, through employment policies and patterns, through technological change, through group and individual values.

Australian society is now at a period when the effects of such influences, and the desirable directions of future change, are being reconsidered. That reconsideration is of a fundamental kind, equivalent in importance to other major periods of educational change in Australian history.

Major periods of change

In the earliest period of education in Australia — the early 1800s — the separate schools operated more or less independently. Though schools received government financial support, there was no effort to determine school programmes or to obtain competent teachers. The programmes reflected a common view that anything beyond a limited literacy was unnecessary and probably unsafe for society. The inadequate education and training of teachers ensured that nothing more was possible. The earliest change, occurring in the 1830s, was when the content and sequence of these limited courses began to be specified and inspectors were appointed to supervise them. A limited control began to develop through regional boards of education.

The controversy as to whether public education should be religious or secular led to the next major change. A long-standing debate was settled for a substantial period in the 1870s by the decision that the various states of Australia should exercise control over education, which was to be 'free, compulsory and secular'. In this period state systems began to develop, first of all universal primary education, then systems for training teachers, then the development of universities, selective secondary education and finally technical education. Though disturbed by wars and economic upheavals, the systems had developed the essentials of their present forms by the 1930s.

The pattern was clear. Primary education for six years was the period of general education. Courses were clearly specified. Teachers were trained to teach those courses and inspectors tried to ensure that they did so. A small proportion of the more successful students continued on to secondary school, with the main purpose of preparing for university education. Others went on to technical schools and thence to work. Still more left primary school to go straight to work. The pattern of education mirrored the pyramid of employment in society: a few at the top, a larger section of semi-skilled workers and a much larger group of unskilled workers.

The 1939-45 war, after causing a period of artificial stability in education, led to a major time of change. There was a sense in which the war was seen as being a prelude to a more open, equitable and free society, and schools were seen as a major means to this. At the same time, the pattern of employment was changing drastically, with reductions in the need for unskilled workers, and more than compensating demands for higher levels of skills in employment. The education pattern reflected these changes, with a dramatic expansion of secondary education, from a level of 10 per cent staying on in Grade 10 to one of nearly 100 per cent. Yet the emphasis of secondary education remained broadly the same, with academic studies and the ladder to higher education seen as the goal. The continued demand for employment and for higher educational levels for employment served to disguise the fact that for 50 per cent or more of students, secondary education was an unsatisfying experience, which confirmed in them a self-concept of failure. Yet the outward features of the period were an unprecedented demand for education, and it enjoyed a high social and political priority.

The period since 1970 in Australian education has been one of unprecedented contrasts, even of paradox. It began as a period of considerable activity in education, accompanied by massive increases in expenditure. There was a mood of optimism: the long struggle against shortages of personnel, buildings and other resources seemed to be in the past. That optimism was to be remarkably short-lived; it gave way to an atmosphere of doubt and questioning. It is paradoxical that the fundamental approach to education in a period of shortages was one of optimism: as those shortages began to disappear through an unprecedented increase in resources, the mood appeared to be one of pessimism or, at best, uncertainty.

Major features of the period may be identified as follows:

☐ an increased involvement of the national government in education;

☐ a clear identification of needs in education and an explicit statement of values;

☐ a significant commitment of finance to specific programmes in education;

☐ the involvement of the national government in curriculum development;

☐ a growing emphasis on school-based curriculum development as an aspect of school-based decision making;

☐ the beginnings of real participation in decisions by teachers, parents and students;

☐ a reduction in external controls, partly through a reduced use of external examinations;

and, later:

☐ an intense debate on the nature of education, including the achievement of public accountability, the satisfactory development of
minimum 'basic skills' and the perceived dichotomy between 'open
education' and 'traditional education';

☐ a deeper concern about the education of girls, and particularly
the broadening of opportunities for girls, springing from the
feminist movement and from other social pressures;

☐ the growth of unemployment, particularly youth unemployment,
and the consequent concern for the school-work interface;

☐ the recognition that Australia is now a multi-cultural society with
an obligation to recognize the validity and worth of a variety of
cultures;

☐ the more obvious impact on education, and on society as a whole,
of pressure groups espousing particular causes;

☐ the potential impact of information technology, including computers, not only on the processes and purposes of education, but
on the structure and values of society.

These later issues are at the forefront of the current reconsideration.

The need for constructive responses

Uncritical acceptance of change is as harmful as uncritical rejection. Our
hopes must rest on the possibility of a careful and sustained effort to
select from and shape future options in ways that make changes work to
benefit our society. This requires constructive responses which take
account of the issues to be faced, which consider possibilities realistically
and which seek to make the best of available choices.

For the current situation, we shall consider three groups of issues that
are directly relevant to society and indirectly relevant to schools.

1. The implications of continuing change, of which the most obvious
   example is the development of the new technologies: these will
   continue to alter the possibilities in our society, and thus force on
   us a process of re-evaluation of our purposes. In this area, one
   striking example is in the changing employment structure. The
   present situation is one of increased demand for skilled workers
   and greatly reduced demand for unskilled workers. The net effect
   is a reduced demand for quantity of work and an increased demand
   for quality. One option is to accept a society with two broad classes:
   one which has highly skilled work and an effective control of
   production and key decisions, and one which experiences an uneasy
   mixture of unskilled work and welfare benefits. Another option is
   for a substantial restructuring of employment on a more equitable
   basis. This is a choice for societies to make, but the outcome
   strongly affects schooling.
2. Greater interdependence: economic changes in one country are felt

in varying ways in many other countries, though often with equal strength. This is merely one example of the interdependence, political and economic, which exists between and within nations. None of our societies can shield itself from the influences of other societies' actions and decisions, whether or not these are deliberately directed towards such effects. Again this is a social issue, but of importance to schools in that it must influence both the content and the purposes of teaching.

3. The decisions we make as individuals on matters such as health, politics and ecology now have a much greater impact. For example, in health our decisions on diet, exercise, drugs and general style of life are now the key factors in our well-being. Similar patterns operate in other aspects of our life, giving a much enlarged importance to reasons for our decisions and the procedures by which we make them.

It is in the context of such issues that general education is being re-evaluated. When we turn to the specific impacts of such issues on schooling, it is difficult to avoid the feeling that re-evaluation must lead to substantial and basic changes. This is not because schools are doing less satisfactorily than they were, but because styles and responses which were once appropriate and effective have become less so. This mismatch between what schools are doing and what individuals need for their own and their society's well-being can only grow worse if this brief analysis of the nature of change is valid. The re-evaluation currently taking place in general education necessarily reflects also society's own re-evaluation of its purposes. Schools cannot of themselves solve social issues, but they need to recognize the impact those issues make upon them, and to develop constructive responses.

Bases for curriculum change

The necessity for change in the general curriculum in Australia is a matter of wide agreement. The directions of that change are not so easily agreed.

Educational changes in the past, at least the major ones, have followed on social changes. The introduction of primary education followed the need for a more literate society. The increase in the demand for professional and clerical skills led first to a selective secondary education and then to a universal secondary education.

The most emotive issue suggesting change currently springs from the situation with respect to youth employment. The *Quality of Education Review* (Karmel, 1985) pointed out that between 1966 and 1984 the number of full-time jobs for the 15-19 age group fell from 615,000 to 418,000; the review predicted that by 1982 the number of such jobs would fall further to 200,000. In the same period the number in the age group rose from 1,038,000 to 1,290,000. Thus, at a time when there is a population increase of over 250,000 young people, the full-time jobs available for them are reduced by 415,000. In summary, this means a change from 60 per cent in full-time jobs to a low figure of 16 per cent. At the beginning of the period, the proportion in education, part-time employment and unemployment totalled 40 per cent of the age group; at the end of the period that proportion is predicted to be 84 per cent. The figure for youth unemployment, as at November 1985, is 25 per cent.

This situation is putting enormous pressures on schooling. Because the part-time work available is only temporary in nature and does not lead to career employment, the real options for 80 per cent of the age group are for some form of education, or for unemployment. Unemployment is clearly not an acceptable option from any point of view. For young people, work is still the first priority in their life choices. It is seen as the recognition of independence and adulthood and holds a symbolic import-ance far beyond its financial implications. For society generally, youth unemployment represents a wasting of its most precious resource, a wasting that is costly in human and social terms as well as financial.

The most obvious answer is to increase the retention of pupils in secondary education, a figure which has remained very low in recent years in comparison with many countries. While almost the complete generation survives until year 10, there is a heavy dropout rate between years 10 and 11, and further loss before the end of year 12. In 1982, the apparent grade retention rate into year 11 was 57.4 per cent; by 1984 this percentage rose to 65.5; the comparable figures for year 12 were 36.3 per cent for 1982 and 45.0 per cent for 1984. This is a sub-stantial increase, which might imply that the problem could solve itself in due course. In statistical terms this might well be so. The *Quality of Education Review* (Karmel, 1985) presents the following picture for 1982 (actual) and 1992 (projected).

	1982 Actual[a]	1992 Scenario
	Thousands	Thousands
Full-time education	565	755
Full-time employment	390	200
Training: apprentices	100	100
Kirby trainees	—	75
Looking for full-time work	105	30
Other[b]	130	130
Total population	1,290	1,290

(a)   ABS Cat. No. 6227.0; Department of Employment and Industrial
      Relations, Apprenticeships Statistics 1972-73 to 1981-82.
(b)   Main components are: persons not in education and not in labour force
      (50,000); persons not in education but in part-time employment (34,000);
      persons in permanent defence forces and in institutions (28,000)

Table 1. *Activities of persons aged 15 to 19 years: actual, 1982*
and projected, 1992

This drastically reduces the numbers looking for full-time work, partly through a new government-sponsored scheme, the Kirby traineeships, and partly through a substantial increase in the numbers retained in full-time education, an increase of 190,000. As will be apparent from the above, these increases will be almost entirely at the years 11 and 12 levels, though not necessarily in the standard forms of secondary education. What is implied for the period is almost a doubling of the year 12 retention. In this case, the possible solution of one problem is at the expense of creating another or, more correctly, worsening another problem. That problem relates to the actual and the perceived usefulness of secondary education, not only at years 11 and 12 but also for the earlier period.

It is clear from the retention statistics that a substantial proportion of year 10 students do not think it is worthwhile to continue on to year 11. What does not emerge directly from those statistics is that many students express substantial dissatisfaction with their courses at year 10 level and earlier. A longitudinal study by Power (1983) showed that for both the 1970 and 1980 generations of year 10 students, 50 per cent indicated either moderate or severe dissatisfaction with schooling. This picture is confirmed by a study carried out first by Anderson and Beswick in 1972 and repeated by Anderson and others in 1979 (Anderson *et al*, 1980). The responses for year 10 and years 11 and 12 students were rated for expressed alienation from school: the levels of alienation for year 10 and for years 11 and 12 in traditional high schools were at the 60 per cent level. Only for students in separate secondary colleges did the levels for alienation fall to 30 per cent. Figures similar to these are reported by writers for other countries, eg by Törsten Husén for Europe (Husén, 1979).

If Australian students are to stay on in school, the levels of dissatisfaction are likely to rise. Even if they were to remain at their present levels, they are a matter of concern for those who have to plan courses and those who have to teach them. Increased retention is not an answer in itself to the problems of young people, which are indeed associated mainly with the unemployment level.

Responses to this situation vary. In the employment field, employers become more selective, and their selection criteria take the shape of higher educational requirements. These may be general, in the form of more years of education, or they may be specific, in the demand for higher levels of basic skills. Students and parents, formerly seeing education as a direct access to work, express disenchantment when the link fails to function. Formerly unexpressed dissatisfactions become substantial complaints. For their part, teachers feel aggrieved as they see themselves being blamed for a shortage of jobs, a shortage they would explain in terms of structural changes in employment, and not a lack of appropriate skills.

The time when young people can act as responsible adults is postponed by the need for increased schooling, probably to a minimum of 12 years. This seems unlikely to improve, as the entrance to more satisfying work will depend on more, and better focused, education. The lack of opportunity to work early is linked with a lack of opportunity for other decisions.

The reduction in an obvious connection between education and work is a major factor in poor motivation for learning.

The all-embracing term 'alienation' is used to cover a wide range of negative attitudes arising from this lengthened period of dependency. These may range from outright hostility and disruptive action to a more passive dissatisfaction and lack of interest and to truancy and dropping out. Even in many able students, it emerges as a determination to play the game by the defined rules, but to see that game as irrelevant to genuine concerns.

Another type of response to the situation is to see if secondary studies can be changed to forms seen to be more practical and useful. Studies performed over the past decade in Australia show a surprisingly high level of agreement on perceived roles of secondary education. In an article for *Australian Education Review*, Collins and Hughes (1982) surveyed 22 such studies carried out in Australia over the last 10 years. There was a considerable consistency in the results. These may be summarized as follows:

☐ Students, parents and teachers all agree in defining a broad scope for secondary education. The scope includes

basic skills — mathematics and communication
health understanding — the requirements for healthy living
personal awareness — the development of the individual
social awareness — understanding of important social issues
practical orientation — useful knowledge and skills
socialization — relating effectively and easily with others
academic orientation — the traditional academic subjects
aesthetic orientation — interest in/feeling for the arts.

☐ The order listed above indicated the priority in terms of importance seen by the three groups.
☐ The areas seen as achieved best, in relation to their importance, were basic skills, socialization and academic orientation.
☐ The areas seen as falling below the desired achievement level, in respect of assessed importance, were health, personal development and social awareness, practical orientation and aesthetic orientation.

This would argue for a dual role for schools: an instrumental role involving perceived usefulness to the individual both as an individual and as a member of society, and a developmental role, which sees the person developing as an individual and as one capable of playing a responsible role in society.

The low standing of academic studies among secondary students is one of the reasons many people have urged that schools should be more practical in their emphasis, perhaps even vocational in form.

However, this is generally recognized as inadequate from two points of view. Most obviously, a strictly vocational education in the form of preparation for particular vocations is inadequate even for its own limited purposes. Vocational patterns and requirements are changing too quickly and too unpredictably for it to be sensible for schools to prepare people for specific jobs. This would be a very inadequate vocational preparation. The needed base must be broader and more adaptable so that students develop the ability to acquire skills as needed.

There is a more important reason why this approach is inadequate. Work is a major priority in the lives of young people. The working role is one of the most important roles in our society. It is not, however, the only important role. It is equally important that schools prepare their students as citizens and as individuals. These needs are clearly identified by our earlier analysis. They also emerge in the priorities listed for secondary education above. It is this broader question, the form of general education needed for these roles, that has become the issue, rather than vocational education.

Directions for future change

The Australian responses to needs in secondary education have been at both national and state levels. While there has been a substantial increase in the number and substance of these responses, they are part of a concern that has gone on longer and has a broader geographical base.

A number of American reports have carried out analyses and put forward solutions. Prominent among these are *A Place Called School* (Goodlad, 1984); *Horace's Compromise* (Sizer, 1984); *High School: A Report on Secondary Education in America* (Boyer, 1983); and the National Commission on Excellence in Education's *A Nation at Risk: The Imperative for Educational Reform* (Gardner, 1983). These all argued for an agreed common curriculum for general education, while differing on the constitution of the common section, and how it would be presented.

In Europe, similarly, there has been a series of reports with a like emphasis. In Britain, Her Majesty's Inspectors (HMI) published the Curriculum 11-16 Working Papers, known as 'the red book' (HMI, 1977). At the same time in Scotland the Munn Report, *The Structure of the Curriculum* appeared (Munn, 1977). A variety of initiatives was taken by the European ministers of education, culminating in a number of reports. Typical of these was the report by Margaret Marshall, *The Compulsory Secondary School* (1983). Two publications by David Hargreaves continued the sequence: the first (Hargreaves, 1983) is a scholarly account of the situation of comprehensive secondary education, and the second (Hargreaves, 1984) is a detailed report to the Inner London Education Authority (ILEA) indicating how secondary schools should be organized. The pattern of a broad common curriculum is proposed, with a substantial compulsory element.

It is against this background that the Australian initiatives need to be seen, as there is a consistency in the general thinking in the three strands of development. This consistency springs less from an imitation of other educational structures or of some common model than from social analyses noted in a particular culture, identifying needs which turn out to be common and which invite similar remedies. The report of the Schools Commission in 1979, *Schooling for 15 and 16 Year Olds* (Schools Commission Project, 1979) first took up the issues, including that of unemployment, and linked them to the need for a *general* reappraisal of secondary education, rather than a response to particular issues.

> '. . . in their general orientation most schools lag in their adjustment to the needs of the full range of students for the last two decades of the twentieth century.' (Schools Commission, 1979)

This needed 'adjustment' was taken up by a number of state initiatives. The first four of these were in South Australia (Keeves, 1982), in the Australian Capital Territory (Steinle, 1983), in New South Wales (Swan and McKinnon, 1984), and in Western Australia (Beazley, 1984). All adopt the position that high unemployment and the changing nature of work are only some of the factors leading to rising post-compulsory age retention rates. It is the full range of factors and the fact of the retention change itself which provide the rationale for change. The reports identify four main issues: broadening the curriculum, changing the certificate pattern, the future of the external examination pattern, and the necessary administrative and organizational structures.

In terms of our focus here, the emphasis will be on the suggested curriculum pattern. All reports saw the extension of attendance to year 12 as becoming the norm and saw the need for a common base for that curriculum. Thus Keeves recommended recognition of four areas of 'foundation learning': language, science, mathematics and social learning. Beazley speaks of seven areas: language and communication, social studies, mathematics, science and technology, physical and health education, vocational and personal awareness, practical and creative arts. It is easy in looking as such lists to see them as representing broad differences, but in fact the strongest impression is one of broad agreement on a number of principles which will be summarized below.

☐ Secondary education should be for the whole age group, although not necessarily in one continuous pattern. Its emphasis should be to provide value and purpose for all, and not only to select and prepare a minority for tertiary education.

☐ Every student should receive a broad general education including skills of oral and written communication, quantitative and logical reasoning, the capacity to solve problems individually and in groups, and the other skills required to participate successfully in modern society.

☐ A primary purpose of schools should be towards developing knowledge, skills and attitudes for a society which has both a common cultural framework and yet recognizes a diversity of cultural contributions.

☐ There will be continuing mandatory elements in the curriculum to achieve these common ends, together with increasing options, to enable real choice and the development of responsibility. This might mean, for example, up to two-thirds of the first four years of the secondary curriculum being common to all pupils.

☐ Schools will have considerable freedom within the suggested framework to plan programmes and sequences of study, to provide the greatest degree of continuity and coherence consistent with keeping open choices for study and vocations. A variety of organizational forms will be of use in such planning:

- linkings of primary and secondary schools in different ways;
- grouping secondary schools in particular clusters;
- linking secondary and technical schools;
- increasing the interchange and liaison between education and work;
- utilizing small 'building blocks' (modules) to give sequence and structure to courses while providing greater diversity of opportunity;
- using short courses for enrichment, remediation and bridging;
- providing a variety of organizational patterns for year 11 and 12 students, recognizing the need for greater freedom and responsibility.

☐ The curriculum may retain its traditional subject names, but will be planned to ensure that the skills, knowledge and attitudes identified as desirable will be specifically catered for under these various headings.

☐ Teaching and learning methods are at least as important as the decisions on content and the ways of organizing content in the achievement of these purposes.

☐ The community has the right and responsibility to participate in the decisions on curriculum for schools, and in particular on what it is important for all students to know and be able to do.

The reports mentioned above dealt either with the whole span of education (cf Beazley, 1984) or with the area of secondary education as a whole. More recently there has been additional attention to the period of post-compulsory education. The Blackburn Report in Victoria (Blackburn, 1985) focused specially on this area, and the need to build a variety of links between the period of general education, kindergarten to year 10, through the post-compulsory phase, equivalent to years 11 and 12. The emphasis, broadly described, is to provide links to technical and further education (TAFE), to work and to higher education, rather than only the latter. The characteristics are described in the following excerpt.

'This Review points to a new direction for the education of young people in the post-compulsory years of schooling. Major changes have been suggested in curricula, certification and the structures of schooling. These changes are intended to enable post-compulsory provision to have the following characteristics:

☐ It must be such that more students want to participate in and see purpose in it.
☐ It must be designed within a comprehensive curricular rationale defining a range of options and common studies to which all students should have access to the maximum degree possible.
☐ It must include significant, practical, work-related studies within a framework of continuing general education.
☐ It must not be so rigidly tracked into 'academic' and 'non-academic' streams that it excludes students from participating in both.
☐ It must promote equity in participation in schooling.
☐ It must give all students access to a common and significant credential.
☐ It must lead into all forms of post-school study and into employment and citizenship.
☐ It must have demonstrated relevance to major issues of the contemporary world and to the concerns of students entering it as adults.
☐ It must relate theory to its applications where appropriate and locate ideas in a social and historical context.
☐ It must allow for participation of varying kinds — discontinuous and part-time as well as continuous and full-time.
☐ It must be conducted in ways which move decisively over the two years away from those appropriate to early adolescence towards those operating in task-centred adult associations.' (Blackburn, 1985)

This is a sizeable agenda for any society. It is not, however, an optional agenda. The choices will be made by us, explicitly, or they will be made for us, by forces we choose to ignore.

References

Anderson, D S et al (1980) Schools to Grow In: An Evaluation of Secondary Colleges Australian National University Press: Canberra
Beazley, K Chairman (1984) Education in Western Australia Government Printer: Perth
Blackburn, J Chair (1985) Ministerial Review of Postcompulsory Schooling: Report, Volumes 1 and 2 Melbourne
Boyer, E (1983) High School: A Report on Secondary Education in America Harper and Row: New York, NY
Collins and Hughes, P W (1982) Where junior secondary schools are heading The Australian Education Review 16
Committee on Higher Education (1963) Higher Education (The Robbins Report) HMSO: London
Gardner, D P Chairman (1983) A Nation at Risk: The Imperative for Educational Reform United States Government Printer: Washington, DC
Goodlad, J (1984) A Place Called School: Prospects for the Future McGraw-Hill Book Company: New York, NY

Hargreaves, D (1983) *The Challenge for the Comprehensive School: Culture, Curriculum and Community* Routledge and Kegan Paul: London

Hargreaves, D *Chairman* (1984) *Improving Secondary Schools: Report of the Committee on the Curriculum and Organization of Secondary Schools* Inner London Education Authority (ILEA): London

Husén, T (1979) *The School in Question: A Comparative Study of the School and its Future in Western Society* Oxford University Press: Oxford

Her Majesty's Inspectors (of Schools) (1977) *Curriculum 11-16: Working Papers: A Contribution to Current Debate* HMSO: London

Inner London Education Authority (ILEA) (1984) *Improving Secondary Schools* (The Hargreaves Report) ILEA: London

Karmel, P *Chairman* (1985) *Quality of Education in Australia: Report of Ministerial Review Committee* Australian Government Publishing Service: Canberra

Keeves, J *Chairman* (1982) *Education and Change in South Australia: A Final Report* Government Printer: Adelaide

Marshall, M (1983) *The Compulsory Secondary School: Adolescents and the Curriculum* Report to the Standing Conference of European Ministers for Education, Thirteenth Session: Dublin

Munn, J (1977) *The Structure of the Curriculum in the Third and Fourth Years of Scottish Secondary School* HMSO: Edinburgh

Power, C (1983) *Satisfaction with High Schools* Flinders University: South Australia

Schools Commission Project (1984) *Schooling for 15 and 16 Year Olds* Launceston Teachers Centre: Launceston, Australia

Scottish Education Department (SED) (1977) *The Structure of the Curriculum in the Third and Fourth Years of the Scottish Secondary School* (The Munn Report) HMSO: Edinburgh

Sizer, T (1984) *Horace's Compromise: The Dilemma of the American High School* Houghton Mifflin Company: Boston, MA

Steinle, J *Chairman* (1983) *The Challenge of Change: A Review of High Schools in the ACT* Australian Government Publishing Service: Canberra

Swan, D and McKinnon, K (1984) *Future Directions of Secondary Education: A Report* New South Wales Education Department: Sydney

2. Transition from school to work in Wester Europe

Ron Johnson

Summary: Education and training for young people in Western Europe is in the throes of traumatic change. Unemployment and the transformation of those jobs that remain has highlighted the need to look afresh at how young people are helped to prepare for adult life.

Four key issues tend to dominate the discussion: the *relevance* of education and training to working life (and to other aspects of life in an uncertain world); the need for *flexibility* on the part of people (young and old); the need to improve people's ability to make reasoned *choices* about education and employment, and who will pay the *cost* of this education and training.

These factors are causing the current diversity within Western Europe to diminish as countries share their experiences and seek to create open, dynamic, relevant and cost-effective education, training and (more slowly) guidance systems, to help young people through the turbulent teenage years.

Introduction: review and reform

Since the early 1970s there have not been enough jobs to go round for school leavers. The nature of the employment market is undergoing irreversible changes. Young people seem to leave school unprepared for this new situation, where employment is scarce and the labour market is complex and unstable. This situation is causing employers, parents and politicians to revise their views about what kind of education and training young people should receive and how and where this should be done.

Stopgap methods introduced in the early 1970s to deal with youth unemployment are giving way to longer-term developments. The methods used have themselves brought about changes in attitudes towards education and training, as new approaches to helping young people to learn – and to motivate them to learn – have been devised.

The focal point for discussion is the transition from school to working life. As many young people find it difficult to get jobs, it might more properly be called the transition from school to adult life. Although each country is unique, there are a number of common threads.

In Western Europe, serious discussion about this transition is dominated by four key issues: relevance, flexibility, choice and costs. The problem is that measures taken to deal with one of these issues frequently produces difficulties in one of the other areas. For example, measures such as a full-time basic training year may increase the flexibility of the trainees, but the actual programmes may seem of less direct relevance to employers — and sometimes to the youngsters themselves. Such measures may helpfully delay the choice of occupation for youngsters, but they also increase training costs.

Those who seek to develop policies and plans for training have therefore to confront a number of dilemmas. The education and training systems and the cultures of the various countries in Western Europe vary markedly, and it is not therefore surprising to find that they have dealt with these problems in different ways.

Four key issues

Universal education in Europe began less than two centuries ago — less than one century ago in some countries. This universal education was and is to a large extent utilitarian, in that it prepares young people to take their place in society. However, the extent to which vocational subjects and skills are included in the curriculum varies considerably from country to country.

Within Western Europe, the *relevance* of the education and training provided for young people has been a recurring theme, but the dramatic rise in unemployment in the early 1970s, coupled with the recognition that modern work and society will require young people — and adults — to be more adaptable, has sparked off a reappraisal of learning needs.

The validity of vocational education and training which is narrowly directed towards a single occupation has been seriously questioned, and in its place has come a demand for *flexibility* — training which enables young people to acquire a foundation on which alternative occupational competences can be built, and which will enable them, if necessary or desirable, to change occupations at a later date.

This starting point can, however, lead in different directions. In some countries, particularly in Sweden, it has led to a heavy emphasis on very broad vocational educational curricula, whereas in others (notably in West Germany) the result has been experiment within the apprenticeship system, with common foundation training years each covering groups of related occupations.

It is a mistake, however, to think that merely broadening the base of learning somehow makes young people more flexible. It has some effect, but flexibility is more closely related to how people learn and their attitudes towards acquiring more skills. The programmes where success has been obtained in helping disadvantaged young people to develop confidence and competence have concentrated on showing them how to learn and to experiment with a range of strategies.

When seeking to group together topics to produce broader education and training programmes, the usual approach — and the one which works —

is to do this on a strictly pragmatic basis which makes sense to employers and to young people. This is the practice in West Germany, Denmark and France.

A related concern has been the need to help young people to *choose* appropriate career paths, and to relate their education and training options to these careers. For many young people in Europe, it is unrealistic to talk about 'careers', when all they can expect is a period of unemployment or a first job. Again, a pragmatic grouping of topics which makes sense to young people and to employers enables trainers to put together programmes which both capture the interest of young people (a prerequisite of effective learning) and also gain the support of employers.

Young people who fail to find a suitable education or training route are especially at risk. This group, who used to take the low-paid work which has largely disappeared, have been the subject of many special programmes mounted in different ways in the different countries of Europe. Many of these special programmes which started out as 'make-work' schemes have developed into training programmes.

The support of employers is essential for any effective scheme concerned with the transition from school to working life. Employers' support is needed financially and in terms of information and practical help to educators, trainers and careers counsellors. The question of *cost* and who pays for this transitional training has been tackled in various ways in different countries.

In essence there are three 'interest groups' concerned with the transition from school to work: that is, three groups of people who stand to gain if it is successfully undertaken. The prime group is of course the young people themselves. If this initial training is done well, they will acquire knowledge, skills, understanding and attitudes that will help them throughout their lives, particularly in the early years after leaving school. Secondly, employers will gain if they are able to recruit and retain capable and flexible people and, thirdly, society gains by having positive, able and constructive citizens.

The question then is how the cost should be spread across the three beneficiaries. In general, the formula which is emerging in different forms across Europe is that the young people 'pay' by receiving a comparatively low wage during the traineeship period. The government (which might be national, federal or regional) provides a proportion of the education/training costs, and employers pay the rest. The systems for fixing the trainee wages and the level of governmental support are particularly well developed in France and in the Federal Republic of Germany.

This formula applies readily to young people undergoing traineeships or apprenticeships where learning at work is interwoven with learning off-the-job (eg in apprentice colleges). This is commonly referred to as 'alternance training'. However, there are very real financial problems for young people who opt for the full-time education route: this generally involves considerable sacrifice.

Whereas in many Western European countries schemes for bridging the school to work transition have been part of the natural development of national education and training systems (eg Belgium, Denmark, the Federal Republic of Germany, France and the Netherlands), in other countries a much more radical approach has been required. Indeed, new systems of vocational education and training are being created virtually *ab initio* (in Italy and the United Kingdom, for example).

European diversity

In terms of the transition from school to work, Western European countries fall into three broad groups (see Table 1). In some countries the emphasis is on full-time education and training for the 16 to 18 year olds, eg Belgium, France, Greece, Italy and Sweden. In Denmark and the Federal Republic of Germany, the emphasis is on the apprenticeship system. In other countries there is a mixture of routes with no bias towards either full-time study or apprenticeship.

	Dominant youth training system
Belgium	Full-time study
Britain	Neither form is dominant
Denmark	Apprenticeship
France	Full-time study
Germany	Apprenticeship
Greece	Full-time study
Ireland	Neither form is dominant
Italy	Full-time study
Luxembourg	Neither form is dominant
Netherlands	Neither form is dominant
Sweden	Full-time study

Table 1

Thus in respect of vocational training for teenagers Sweden represents one extreme (full-time courses) and West Germany the other (apprentice-ship-dominated). It is notable, however, that in both Denmark and the Federal Republic of Germany, one year of full-time study is becoming more widespread as part of the initial vocational training.

In each European country a significant proportion of young people — the academically able — remain in full-time education after the official school leaving age (see Tables 2 and 3). In Germany a significant number of the academically able young people leave the full-time education system at about 18 years of age to take an abbreviated apprenticeship before returning to continue their academic studies in college or university. Such young people have a thorough grasp of practical matters as well as a sound grounding in theory.

In most countries, vocational education (full-time or part-time) and apprenticeship training run alongside (full-time) academic education for

	School-leaving age (ie compulsory full-time education)	Lower secondary schools[1]
Belgium	14	Selective
Denmark	15	Comprehensive
France	16	Comprehensive
Germany	15/16	Selective[2]
Greece	14	Comprehensive
Ireland	15	Selective
Italy	14	Comprehensive
Luxembourg	15	Selective
Netherlands	16	Selective
Sweden	16	Comprehensive

Notes

1. These terms are not strictly applicable in countries other than Britain; here the term 'comprehensive' indicates that up to the age of about 14, 15 or 16 (lower secondary level) the young people study in the same kind of school, whereas 'selective' means that there are different kinds of schools. These sometimes approximate to the former English grammar and secondary modern schools, but some are quite different, eg with a much more vocational bias.
2. The provision of comprehensive schools varies from *Land* to *Land*.

Table 2

the over 16 year olds. In France, for example, both full-time vocational training and apprenticeship training are available for the 16 to 18 year old age group. Sweden, however, aims to provide full-time courses for every one of its 16 year olds. In Germany, where there is still a heavy emphasis on the apprenticeship system, about 60 to 70 per cent of school leavers become apprentices. In France, the aim is to give every youngster at 16 the opportunity either to continue in full-time general education up to university standard or to follow a vocational course (full-time or by apprenticeship) leading to skilled worker status.

The lack of reliable statistics and the variety of definitions used means that comparative statistical data must be used with extreme care. In the Federal Republic of Germany reliable statistics are collected, but here again it is necessary to be careful over definitions: for example, the apprenticeship system covers almost every kind of job the 16 year old can embark on — in commerce and the public service, as well as in engineering and construction skills.

Vocational studies begin at about age 13 in Belgium, Luxembourg, Ireland and the Netherlands. In Luxembourg, young people can opt at this stage to continue with general education (academic), or to take vocational or 'complementary' education (essentially life skills and pre-vocational studies). In France, pupils receive a general introduction to vocational subjects at age 11 to 13. Technical subjects can begin in earnest at age 13 to 14, when young people can decide to concentrate to some extent either on technical and vocational subjects or on academic subjects. In Greece, vocational studies can commence at age 15.

	% of 16 age-group			% of 17 age-group		
	F	P	N	F	P	N
Belgium	78	3	19	64	6	30
Denmark	48	20	32	29	13	58
France	75	10	15	54	6	40
Germany	50	35	15	33	46	21
Ireland	60	9	31	29	4	67
Italy	55	11	34	40	9	51
Luxembourg	50	29	21	37	19	44
Netherlands	84	6	10	64	13	23
United Kingdom	60	7	33	32	12	56
Europe	61	15	24	41	18	41

Notes
1. F means full-time education or training, P means part-time training and
   N means not attending education or training courses to any extent.
2. These figures should be treated with caution for the reasons explained in
   the text. The situation has also changed dramatically since 1978. The data
   is quoted from *Vocational Training*, the Bulletin of the European Centre
   for the Development of Vocational Training, Berlin, 1980.

Table 3. *Participation in education/training[1] at age 16 and 17 in 1978[2]*

In some countries it is thus possible to leave full-time education at 16
with a vocational certificate (in France, Luxembourg, Belgium, Ireland
and the Netherlands), whereas in other countries (Italy, Germany and
Denmark) there is no such opportunity. The age at which compulsory
full-time education ends varies from country to country (Table 2) and,
in Germany, from *Land* to *Land*. It should be noted that part-time
attendance at a school or college is compulsory for young workers up to
the age of 18 in Germany and in the Netherlands. For the most part, this
part-time education is integrated into the apprenticeship in Germany.

The Swedish model — full-time education

The Swedish integrated upper secondary school aims to give students a
more uniform starting point for their subsequent educational and vocational
activities. A new reform of this system is currently under way. Under the
system instituted in 1972, about 85 per cent or so of the young people
enter the upper secondary school at 16 years of age to take one of the
(currently 25) 'lines' of study. Originally there were 22 lines, 5 concerned
with arts and social studies, 3 concerned with economic and commercial
studies, and 14 with technical and scientific studies.

Courses typically last from two to four years, and sometimes include
substantial periods of practical work (in engineering and construction,
for example). There was initial disquiet on the part of employers who felt
that this education was no substitute for vocational training, although the
young people who emerged were more 'rounded', enquiring and, it was
hoped, flexible. Over the years the employers have come to accept this

system, along with the necessity to provide training for young people when they have completed their upper secondary school studies. Generally speaking, young people require training within industry for a further year before they attain skilled worker levels.

A career education and guidance programme based on the schools helps young people approaching 16 years of age to have a reasonable understanding of the way various industries work, the kinds of jobs that are available and the qualifications needed to get such jobs.

The reforms currently being implemented are intended to push this process of integration further, with more academic material for the technical stream students and more practical and technical work for the academic students, especially in the first six months in the upper secondary school.

The West German model — apprenticeship

West Germany is a federation of eleven *Länder* (singular, *Land*), one of which is West Berlin. Formally, co-ordination of vocational training is the responsibility of the Federal Government. As far as education policy and planning are concerned, however, the role of the Federal Government is limited, as each *Land* has the primary responsibility for education within its borders. Co-operation is secured through the Standing Conference of Education Ministers from the *Länder*. Employers' organizations and trade unions play a major role in regulating vocational training within this framework.

Currently, about two-thirds of the young people who attain school leaving age take up an apprenticeship. Under the traditional system each apprentice will have a contract with an employer within the framework of Federal law. The trainees generally start at age 15 and are compelled by law to attend classes at a vocational school (run by the *Land*) for at least a day a week. In some occupations trainees can attend for up to two days a week. The trainees are also trained within the firm to a nationally agreed and prescribed syllabus.

The apprenticeship system is well established and highly regarded, especially by employers and parents. The object of this initial training is defined by the Vocational Education and Training Act 1969 as

'to provide through a systematic training programme a broadly conceived basic preparation for an occupation and the necessary technical abilities and knowledge to engage in a skilled form of occupational activity. Initial training shall also enable a trainee to obtain the necessary occupational experience.'

The training contract for each trainee must be registered with the appropriate Chamber (where the employer is registered, as he must be by law) and the training will then be monitored by the Chamber, which will also conduct the final tests for the award of skilled worker status. The training and testing must conform to nationally agreed standards. Each traineeship must relate to an officially recognized occupation, and some years ago these were reduced in number to about 450.

However, this training must not be thought of as narrow or restrictive. Although it is difficult to generalize over such a wide range of occupations, on the whole the vocational education component is broad but relevant and the traineeship system encourages young people to take a measure of responsibility for their own learning and work. Furthermore, there is ample evidence that most of those who complete this training continue to learn and can be readily retrained as the requirements of industry and commerce alter.

In-firm training is conducted under the supervision of an appropriately qualified person (usually a qualified *Meister*, that is, a master craftsman or the equivalent in industrial, commercial and administrative occupations). Firms without such qualified personnel are not allowed to take on apprentices. The length of the contract varies with the occupation: three years is the most common. The traineeship can be shortened in some cases where the youngster has previously undertaken appropriate studies at the upper secondary level.

Those who do well in their skilled worker tests and examinations may proceed by further education and training either towards the *Meister* qualification or towards technician level.

Experiments have been conducted with a basic training year, where trainees receive training related to a whole group of occupations. The idea is to help students to (a) identify, understand and evaluate the general relationships between work, the economy and society and their own position in working life and society; (b) make more informed career decisions; (c) be occupationally mobile; and (d) be equipped to meet the specific demands of occupational training.

The French model — controlled experimentation

In France it is still the full-time education route which is favoured by parents for their teenager, but employers and the government appear to have rediscovered the importance of a skilled workforce. Over recent years there has been a determined attempt to improve the quality of full-time vocational education (which now includes work experience) and also to promote apprenticeship training. The vocational certificates (which cover about 300 trades) can be obtained by either route and entitle the young employee to the wages of a skilled worker at the basic level.

There are now 'modules' through which young people can obtain a credit on passing each part of the course. This means that youngsters who do not complete the entire vocational certificate can still achieve a number of credits which demonstrate their abilities in certain areas. At each stage there are practical as well as written tests in the vocational courses. Apprentices are obliged to continue with general and social education.

Employers and trade unions are linked with the authorities in determining the content of the training and they are also actively involved in the trade testing procedures in the apprenticeship system. However, there is an uneasy tension between broadening the youngsters by increasing their general education, as opposed to helping them to become flexible by 'polyvalence', that is, basic training programmes embracing material relevant to two or more occupations. Employers generally favour polyvalence, whereas trade unions and educationists tend to favour more general education.

There has also been a concerted effort over the last decade or so to re-energize the apprenticeship system within France, and to provide training opportunities for disadvantaged young people. These measures were given added impetus by the report prepared by Professor Bertrand Schwarz (1981).

In France, as in Sweden, the system is dominated by the education ministries, so that the tendency towards more general education seems to hold sway, in spite of the evidence that young people who are less able academically are motivated to learn by practical job-related training, and not by traditional schooling. Apprentices in France, as in the United Kingdom, are impatient with academic subjects which do not seem to help them to do better on the job.

Problems and trends

In France and Italy more power is being given to regionally elected bodies in the sphere of vocational training, and it will be interesting to see how the influence of these regional bodies will develop. As mentioned above, the system in West Germany is already regionalized, with the *Länder* Governments and local employers and trade unions playing a major role. In Italy the regionally elected bodies are more responsive to local labour market needs in their vocational training provisions, and early indications are that the same will apply in France, particularly in relation to apprenticeships. It is ironic that while France, Germany and Italy are strengthening the vocational training role of their regionally elected bodies, the United Kingdom is weakening the role of locally elected bodies in this sphere.

Perhaps the most significant change is the way in which the gap between vocational training and education is narrowing in Europe. Within Belgium, the new law introduced in 1983 making part-time attendance at an educational establishment compulsory up to 18 years of age has had a marked effect on vocational education and training. At the same time the importance of academic subjects is being emphasized. In Denmark the youth unemployment position continues to give cause for concern, and new initiatives have been made to increase the number of training places in private firms.

In France, school syllabuses originally intended to act as a preparation for vocational education or apprenticeships have, in the event, been mainly remedial in nature. There has also been a marked movement towards 'culture technique', the introduction of technology into virtually all aspects of the education system to familiarize young people with technical products and the demands of a competitive world.

In common with many European countries, Ireland introduced in 1984 a social guarantee for school leavers and young unemployed people — offering them an opportunity of a place on a full-time programme of training and/or work experience. Ireland has also played a major part in the Europe-wide transition projects co-ordinated by IFAPLAN from Cologne. In Ireland the main emphasis is on helping young school leavers with poor job prospects, unemployed school leavers, and girls and women with poor job prospects.

Italy is still trying to cope with what is seen as the failure of the state education system to prepare young people for working life. Reform is very slow to come to fruition, and the results of the new regional training initiatives are not yet clear. In the Netherlands, vocational education and training for the transition period is still in a state of flux: what is clear is the acceptance by government, industry and educational institutions of the need for co-ordinated action and a joint responsibility to make progress.

In the Federal Republic of Germany, increasing numbers of young people are remaining in full-time education, and at the same time many young people are claiming that they are unable to find apprenticeship places with companies. Instead they are turning to the full-time courses at vocational schools, in particular the basic vocational training year which should count as the first year of an apprenticeship. There is, however, still a reluctance on the part of many employers to recruit these young people on to their apprenticeships.

The Commission of the European Community continues to press for improved training in this transitional period, and strongly favours the 'alternance' pattern in which learning off the job is interwoven with learning on the job, as well as preferring a two-year programme for each young person, leading to a recognized vocational qualification. However, earlier attempts at harmonizing vocational training across Europe have now given way to the concept of mutual recognition and transparency — that is, understanding what a particular qualification means in practical terms.

Conclusions

Although there is a good deal of sharing of experiences across Europe, each country is working out its own solution to the problems of young people in transition. The solutions depend on the historical and cultural context in each case, and on the existing legal and institutional structures. There is no universal model that can be applied to every country: the answer appears to depend on pragmatic solutions that can gain the support of governments, employers, trade unions, educationalists, parents and, above all, the young people themselves. Such solutions must take full account of the variegated needs of the young people concerned, their abilities and their aspirations.

The main trends that can be identified are that *all* young people need a firm foundation of learning in the teenage years — and this must include an ability to go on learning throughout life. For many young people a vocational context for learning is vital to motivate them to learn. Young people need help in understanding themselves, their strengths and weaknesses, their aspirations, and their likes and dislikes. They also need to understand the world in which they move as young adults.

There is another key factor that older folk — especially politicians and civil servants — must come to terms with. Although young people will be regarded, rightly, as learners during their teenage years, they nevertheless require and must be granted a measure and a sense of independence and freedom of action. Indeed, without this they are effectively denied the conditions and experiences they need to mature into responsible citizens.

Many of the current education/training and financial support systems urgently need reform. They often present a 'qualifications jungle' through which young people must fight their way, with the added complication of discriminatory financial support which distorts free choice. These systems hinder young people from making informed and free choices, and all too often prevent them from developing their full potential.

In the main, these problems have been identified and steps taken to deal with them. But progress is fitful, and often painfully slow.

References

House of Lords Select Committee on the European Communities (1984) *Youth Training in the EEC* Report H L 282 HMSO: London

Schmitt, R J *et al* (1984) *Vocational Training Systems in the Member States of the European Community: CEDEFOP Guide* European Centre for the Development of Vocational Training: Berlin

Schwarz, B (1981) *The Integration of Young People in Society and Working Life* Report for the Prime Minister of France: Paris. English version published by European Centre for Vocational Training: Berlin

3. School to work in England and Wales

Jack Longden

Summary: Concern about, and development in, the transition from school to work led to the creation of secondary education after 1900 and the rise of further education. Since the 1950s the implications of the 1944 Education Act and the rapid changes in technology have effected changes in manpower, skills, and industrial organization. Public concern about the inadequacy of training in industry has increased. The Industrial Training Act of 1964, and the developments which it engendered, led to the formation of the Manpower Services Commission (MSC). Many experiments in vocational preparation and changes in the structure of further education have been introduced, culminating in major proposals by the MSC for a New Training Initiative. This has extended training opportunities to all young people for the first time, with special implications for curriculum design. Recent developments in vocational preparation and qualifications suggest the need for new modes of learning and trends which link school and college more closely with the world of work.

Introduction

The most usually accepted concept of an ideal society is one in which each person, regardless of class, ability, or disability, enjoys gainful employment which produces sufficient value to confer a comfortable standard of living, together with enough leisure time to enjoy it. Work, with its scope for individual success and the development of personal skills, brings a sense of satisfaction and security and a dignity which are unique. Leisure alone is not enough. In economic terms a nation can only be sustained by the product of work and its natural resources. The more limited natural resources become, the greater the significance of work. The Methodist work ethic and the determined, if not ruthless, exploitation of opportunity and labour, were at the root of Britain's leadership in the industrial world for at least a century and a half. The waning of this leadership has much to do with attitudes towards work.

The public provision of education in Britain has been dominated by two influences. Firstly there is the concept, derived from the older universities, that education is valuable in itself, that it can be imperilled by too close a contact with its direct applications, and that it is essentially elitist: for the purpose of identifying and crediting the most able.

Secondly there is the political philosophy of *laissez-faire* inherent in British life since the Reformation. This dictated that education was essentially voluntary and the responsibility of the individual. In fact, throughout most of the 19th century the churches, often in rivalry, were the chief providers. In Germany there was at least partial provision of compulsory education from about 1720 and similar provision in France from 1882. In Britain it was the Fisher Act of 1918 which firmly established state schools and a universal minimum leaving age. It is this minimum which establishes further education as a distinct stage of development based upon proper preparation, yet it was and still is characterized by voluntarism and uncertainty, despite ample evidence of the national and personal disadvantage which this produces.

For those able to acquire a private or grammar school preparation there has for many years been access to the universities and to training for vocations such as the church and the armed forces. For the bulk of the population, increasingly affected by the rise of industry, further education began with the Mechanics' Institutes, established by 'self-help' or public subscription from about 1800.

Often established by groups of artisans, these institutes provided books and instruction for 'self-improvement'. They led to the need for examinations as an index of capability, and voluntary joint bodies were set up to provide and regulate them. The Union of Lancashire and Cheshire Institutes was formed in 1829 and the City and Guilds of London Institute in 1878. Enlightened employers became concerned about British backwardness and visited the Continent (Swire Smith, 1877), and in 1889 the School Boards were empowered to promote technical education. Despite endowment and subscription from the public and from far-sighted industrialists, attendance remained essentially a personal part-time responsibility on top of a 50-hour working week. Reports like the Hadow Report of 1926, and increasing concern about the inequalities in secondary education, resulted in an increase in the numbers attending grant-aided grammar schools from 30,000 to over 400,000 between 1902 and 1939. Nevertheless the percentage receiving a structured secondary education (in the sense of a curriculum planned for specific attainment) was only about 15 per cent and the secondary technical schools catered for about 3 per cent of boys and 2 per cent of girls.

Post-school attendance for further education, especially among craftsmen, was by 1939 negligible by day and very uncertain by evening study. It was not unusual for less than a score of craftsmen to qualify annually in mechanical engineering or textiles in a major town or city. The effect of this at the start of the 1939-45 war was well-nigh fatal. When new technology and new high-production processes were necessary for national survival there were insufficient craftsmen with the right types and levels of skills. Special intensive schemes had to be set up to produce technicians holding appropriate Higher National Certificates in six months instead of the usual part-time two years. This was in spite of the fact that the national certificate system had been established in 1921. The unsatisfied requirement for education linked to the needs of industry consequently emerged as a crisis factor in a time of grave national emergency.

The 1944 Education Act made education compulsory to the age of 15 and reformed the socioeducational structure by abolishing elementary schools and establishing universal secondary education. By 1955 there were 5,124 secondary schools, of which 1,180 were grammar schools, 3,550 secondary modern schools, and 338 technical/bilateral schools. The grammar school curriculum had little or no technical content. The modern schools adopted the 'pure' concept of educational purpose and even prohibited the use of qualifying examinations which could connect with progression into employment. They were frequently badly equipped and staffed for any kind of technical development. The secondary technical schools, which were specially intended to prepare children for entry into working life, and had more suitable equipment and aims for this, accounted for less than 7 per cent of all establishments. The lesson had not been learned.

Change in the 1950s, 1960s and 1970s

By 1954, industry was formally complaining to the City and Guilds of London Institute that its main engineering schemes did not provide the practical development of workers needed in industry, and a revision was begun. The Carr Report (Ministry of Education, 1958) revealed that training for the engineering industry was in a confused, even chaotic, condition and self-evidently inadequate for modern needs. As engineering was among the best organized of industries from a training aspect, the general situation was clearly much worse.

The next decade seemed full of portents of change. The Newsom Committee was formed in 1961 and reported in 1963 (Department of Education and Science, 1963). It advised raising the school leaving age to 16, a step which was not taken for another 10 years. It reported gross inequalities in opportunity and in educational treatment and the apparent neglect of potential ability and of disadvantage, and all this 20 years on from the 1944 Act. Strangely, it dealt only in passing and in general terms with the issue of vocational preparation, which it pronounced 'a dangerous but indispensable word'. The issue of 'school to work' was not mentioned in its principal recommendations.

The Robbins Report on Higher Education appeared in 1963 (Committee on Higher Education, 1963). It proposed that a university level education should be available to all those able and willing to benefit by it. It made no attempt to match the output of the system to the demand for graduates by the national economy, or to the practical needs of the society which would have to pay for it, or to make it purposeful in terms of job opportunity. Therefore at both ends of the educational spectrum, the vital links between attainment, qualification, and vocation were not a serious part of forward thinking and planning.

In the meantime, other developments were emerging under pressure of technical change within industry. In 1961 the Ministry of Education white paper *Better Opportunities in Technical Education* categorized the labour force within a technologist/technician/craft/operative structure in which the operative was regarded as unskilled (Ministry of Education, 1961). The City and Guilds of London Institute had begun to modify its examination schemes accordingly. The issue of wastage in the national certificate system had been publicly exposed by Dr Ethel Venables. The effects of poor preparation for further education and poor correlation with the realities of working life were at last causing concern. The Henniker-Heaton report of 1964 showed that only 30 per cent of boys and less than 8 per cent of girls got day release for further education after leaving school (Department of Education and Science, 1964). The Haslegrave Committee on technician education was being set up.

A government white paper of 1962 (Cmd. 1892) announced proposals for industrial training. The Industrial Training Act of 1964 led to the establishment of 26 Industrial Training Boards (ITBs) for the major industries. Each had statutory responsibility to prescribe training schemes (and, technically, further education). They had no powers of enforcement except by making financial grants from funds raised by levies on employers. The Act set up a central training council which could co-ordinate and influence, but not control, the activities of the boards. These ITBs did a great deal to bring form and structure to training processes on a wide front and increased the professionalism available for training. They improved but ossified traditional ideas about training and who should be trained. They failed to cope, therefore, with organic changes occurring in technology and in the manning of the workplace and were considered administratively burdensome by employers. Apart from better definition of standards of entry to certain occupations they did little to improve the links between schools and work. By 1974 this structure was being dismantled and responsibility passed to a government-financed statutory body — the Manpower Services Commission (MSC).

The regional boards which administered the new Certificate of Secondary Education (the CSE) appeared reluctant to link the qualification firmly to vocational entry points. The top grade of CSE was equated with the Ordinary level of the General Certificate of Education (GCE) with assumed progression to higher education, which was itself so ill-connected with vocational trends. The Haslegrave Report of 1969 (Department of Education and Science, 1969) and the formation of the Technician Education Council in 1973 redirected attention towards the elitist end of the spectrum and away from new and quite dramatic shifts taking place in manpower structures and skills. By 1974 unmistakable trends could be extrapolated from manpower statistics and from perceived changes in industrial structure. Improved technology was rapidly reducing labour-intensive operations in both manufacture and ancillary services. The number of traditional craftsmen employed in engineering and process industries fell by 60 per cent or more within ten years. The increase in technicians was only about 20 per cent of a smaller base number. Hence there was a radical decline in the numbers receiving substantial training. A wide range of occupations emerged, requiring new types and levels of skill. These did not and do not fit into conventional employment, training and career progression structures, or into the assumptions which had begun to underpin ideas about preparation for school-leaving and entry into working life, or into established programmes of further education.

Other sociological trends have emerged to complicate the scene. Improved living standards, access to consumer technology, mass communication, shorter workloads, improved health levels and, above all, increased expectations have caused a massive shift of labour from manufacturing to service occupations to which traditional skill and work patterns do not apply. Most significantly, over 60 per cent of the working population no longer aim to enter fixed occupations via traditional apprenticeships. These occupations are not seen as carrying any social or financial advantages. It has become common for people to accept and make use of change; to move from one occupation to another, often right across technical boundaries, and to seize opportunities as they arise. These opportunities come from new developments in the workplace, from new industries, and from the changing distribution of jobs. The profitable new skills are the ability to learn and adapt quickly, to comprehend and live with new technology (not necessarily to understand its detail), to handle terminology and respond to instructions, and to work comfortably with the functions of microtechnology and computer science.

There is a special effect of the reduction of the age of majority to 18. About 25 per cent of the school population will expect to enter occupations in the professions, as technicians, or other extended-skill categories which they accept will require preparation extending into their early twenties or beyond. They anticipate eventual socioeconomic rewards which justify the effort and the waiting, although that is now doubtful in many apprenticeships. The rest of the population increasingly expects to attain maturity at 18, that is, to receive an adult wage to match their legal and community obligations. The whole pattern of assumptions about transfer from school to work is put into disarray by this factor. A new qualification at 17-plus, constructional links between school programmes and traditional further education courses, and structured patterns of progression have little meaning for the bulk of school leavers. Paradoxically our slowness to match educational and vocational needs since 1944 may now be an advantage, because we are not as tied to rigid training/educational structures as some other European countries are. Our basic needs are

1. to retain a clear but flexible pattern of preparation
2. to adopt a controlled but infinitely variable 'roll-on/roll-off' system which will serve the bulk of the population throughout life, and
3. to pay concomitant attention to those with special needs.

The 1980s

By 1980 the Central Training Council and all but seven of the Training Boards had been dissolved. These lost their autonomy and became the responsibility of the Manpower Services Commission (MSC). Its responsibilities now include aspects of vocational education and it has considerable autonomy and financial authority, being directly accountable to government ministers. It still has to cope with two established facets of national policy and attitudes. The first is that local authorities have been vested with responsibility for education since 1888 in the belief that their independence is essential to the quality of education. The second is the voluntary principle in training and personal development. Ten years of corporate responsibility for training over whole industries under the Industrial Training Act did not change this approach.

In 1978 the MSC and the DES had jointly experimented with a system of unified vocational preparation aimed at the bulk of school leavers who would not receive any substantial training on entering employment and needed help in getting a job. It was successful in that it confirmed that there was a new need to be met and that new techniques must be designed in order to meet it.

In 1981 the MSC announced a New Training Initiative (Department of Employment, 1981) which had three long-term objectives:

1. to develop and modernize skill training, including apprenticeships, so that it accommodates young people at various ages and with different educational attainments, and enables them to acquire agreed standards of skill and provide a basis for progression;
2. to provide an initial training for *all* young people entering employment and to acknowledge that, for the majority of young people, these needs are not being met at the moment;
3. to open up widespread opportunities for adults whether employed, unemployed or returning to work to acquire, update or increase their skills and knowledge during the course of their working lives.

Action on the first and most traditional objective has scarcely begun. In simple terms it involves the reform of long-established practices in which both employers and trade unions have deep labour relations problems.

The second objective is a new, major and unprecedented national commitment to give every young person the opportunity of a planned and structured basic training. This is to be done through a national Youth Training Scheme started on a one-year basis in 1984 for those who are 16 years or over. It has aroused intense support and intense opposition linked with national and industrial politics. It had to be implemented quickly and with little in the way of experience or precedent on which to base its structure. It has succeeded sufficiently for it to be made into a two-year system which will therefore carry the majority of young people from school-leaving age to the age of majority. The content and style of the scheme aim to give trainees adaptable and transferable skills, the ability to cope with real and changing workstyles, and a capability for personal and social responsibility. It clearly describes, perhaps for the first time, a necessary balance in the development of personality and directly useful skills, and the idea that suitability for employment and for life is a joint responsibility of employer and community. It is strange that the obligations it lays upon employers are not dissimilar to those of the Statute of Apprentices of 1658. It is a momentous development which has begun to enforce new thinking about the nature of secondary and further education and how they are connected. It is consistent with the British tradition in that there has been no provision for a concurrent and correlated review of educational schemes, perhaps because educational change is managed by a number of separate bodies and a Department of Education and Science which has little prescriptive control over development.

In 1983 the MSC offered financial inducement to secondary schools to join an experimental scheme: the Technical and Vocational Education Initiative (TVEI) (see Chapter 4). This was to set up learning programmes which bridged schools, colleges and employers, and brought about their joint involvement. In 1986 it was confirmed that it will continue as a regular part of the school curriculum if required. The government has decided to replace the GCE and CSE examinations with a single qualification by 1989, and implementation has begun. The Youth Training Scheme will have its own form of certification with facility for recognizing various forms of educational achievement. The Business and Technician Education Councils have been amalgamated and are rationalizing technician qualifications. The universities and polytechnics are being pressed to take increasing cognizance of job opportunities and needs, and financial pressures have been applied in the regulation of grants.

In April 1985 the MSC and the DES set up a joint working group to carry out a review of vocational qualifications. The Interim Report of the review expressed concern at the lack of pattern, correlation and defined purpose in existing post-school qualifications. It is proposed that all qualifications should be framed around five objectives — comprehensibility, relevance, credibility, accessibility and cost-effectiveness (MSC, 1985). It is hoped that this will at least remove ambiguity in relating educational attainment to work.

However, it is also consistent with tradition that take-up by young people of the Youth Training Scheme is entirely voluntary and the scheme is heavily dependent upon the goodwill of employers to provide work experience and training for persons who are not employees. This demands learning schemes which embody strong motivation for both learner and employer. They must therefore connect closely with the employer's business and with a range of occupations and technologies never before considered, much less provided for, in learning schemes. The most serious problem in curriculum design and planning of learning is that of keeping up with changes in technology and with the methods and manpower structures of industry and business. The normal practice in curriculum design has been to define a range of job skills or techniques, to outline

the training processes needed, and then to construct an educational
scheme and tests based on the information content of the job skills and
techniques. This establishes a pattern of courses with narrow scope and
low flexibility. Any individual who does not fit an available scheme gets
learning of low relevance. It is difficult and expensive to revise such
schemes to keep pace with change or to provide as many schemes as there
are different jobs. The alternative is to design schemes which suit a wide
range of jobs and have a content which will adapt easily to the specific
needs of the individual and the occupational factors involved. If these
factors change, even in the short term, then the learning system is re-
aligned and adapts to the new conditions. Within limits of operational
and financial practicality this enables learning programmes to be tailored
to the needs of companies, individuals and training systems.

The trades principles system

By 1986, there was only one such learning system in a tried, tested and
operational form. This is the trades principles system developed by the
Yorkshire and Humberside Association for Further and Higher Education
(1982) in conjunction with employers and other industrial and business
interests (Longden, 1986). It will provide about 22 basic schemes which,
by adaptation, can cover about 80 per cent of all known occupational
areas. Its design features are intended to ensure that it is not invalidated
by technological change, so that the serious problem of matching education to its applications can be overcome. It also provides new levels of
motivation and a new approach to qualification and progression which
aligns well with the main objectives of the Review of Vocational Qualifications. It uses learning methods which include learning in the workplace
and a properly structured and controlled partnership between educators/
trainers, employers and learners, of a kind which has seldom if ever existed
before. The system can be used on both sides of the school leaving age.
It is only through such partnership that transition from school to work
can realistically be arranged.

Trades principles has its problems. It requires the education service
to be open to a participation in active planning and involvement by
'outsiders'. It requires employers to plan and execute training and learning
carefully and constructively in partnership with others, and to have regard
for the wider issues involved in personal development. It requires employer,
educator and learner to accept that a learning programme must be seen to
be profitable in real terms to each partner. These requirements reveal a
need for new techniques in presenting and managing a completely different
occupational concept. But the potential of any acceptable general learning
system of this kind is exciting, since it will be adapted for use in schools,
further education, vocational preparation (like the Youth Training Scheme)
and for adult training — the third strand of the New Training Initiative.
If one system can bridge these needs, then the economies in curriculum

development, staff development, management and a smooth transition from school to work could prove a major achievement.

In 1984 a proposal was published for a Certificate of Pre-Vocational Education (CPVE) (Joint Board for Pre-Vocational Education, 1984). The proposal is to 'establish a framework that will permit the development of courses that are demonstrably relevant to the needs of young people as emerging adults and prospective employees'. The programmes of study provided are

1. to form vocational interests
2. to develop competences applicable to jobs and adult life, and
3. to extend general education and *inter alia* to encourage and guide progression.

There have to be alternative programmes to suit different abilities and learning styles. Each will, in its different way, convey core studies by focusing them through vocational topics. It is conceived as a 16-plus system which will embrace existing qualifications and the new examination at 17-plus. It is not yet clear how the proposal will link with the new qualification at 16-plus or how it can apply to the majority outside the range of existing schemes, or how it will relate to the review of vocational qualifications.

The MSC has the power to intervene in the transition from school to work, and therefore in the affairs of schools, colleges and employers, albeit within the context of the present voluntary system. So far it has stimulated or precipitated much significant movement in thinking and intentions. In the conditions of a free and unregulated society it has moved us much closer to a rational process of vocational development, but it has also aroused all the emotions and reactions enshrined in national habits and attitudes and in many long-standing vested interests. Perhaps real progress towards a sensible transition from school to work, and life-long personal development opportunities for everyone, has just begun.

References

Committee on Higher Education (1963) *Higher Education* (The Robbins Report) HMSO: London

Department of Education and Science (DES) (1963) *Half Our Future: Report of the Central Advisory Council for Education (England)* (The Newsom Report) HMSO: London

Department of Education and Science (DES) (1964) *Day Release: Report of a Committee set up by the Minister of Education* (The Henniker-Heaton Report) HMSO: London

Department of Education and Science (DES) (1969) *Report of the Committee on Technician Courses and Examinations* (The Haslegrave Report) HMSO: London

Department of Employment (1981) *A New Training Initiative: A Programme for Action* Cmnd 8455 HMSO: London

Joint Board for Pre-Vocational Education (1984) *The Certificate of Pre-Vocational Education* City and Guilds of London Institute and Business and Technician Education Council: London

Longden, J (1986) *Learning with Profit. The Application of the Tradec System to the Youth Training Scheme and Beyond* Yorkshire and Humberside Association for Further and Higher Education: Leeds

Manpower Services Commission (MSC) (1985) *Review of Vocational Qualifications in England and Wales: Interim Report of Joint Manpower Services Commission/ Department of Education and Science Working Group* Manpower Services Commission: Sheffield

Ministry of Education (1961) *Better Opportunities in Technical Education* Cmnd 1254 HMSO: London

Smith, Sir S (1877) *Educational Comparisons: Remarks on Industrial Schools in England, Germany and Switzerland* Simpkin, Marshal & Co: London

Yorkshire and Humberside Association for Further and Higher Education (1982) *The Principles and Practice of Trades Education* YHAFHE: Leeds

4. The Technical and Vocational Education Initiative and Scottish educational developments

Frank Pignatelli

Summary: The introduction of the Technical and Vocational Education Initiative (TVEI) into the educational provision available in schools and colleges in the UK was greeted with suspicion and mistrust by educationists. In Scotland especially there were reservations, based on a wish to resist any compromise of the Scottish tradition of broad-based education and a firm desire to eschew vocational education at a time when two major educational programmes were being developed which would offer balanced education to all young people from 14 to 18 years of age.

On closer examination, the aims and criteria of TVEI were seen to be consistent with those of the Scottish national programmes and therefore a decision was taken to become involved in promoting TVEI project proposals. The structure, content and philosophy of the educational programmes for 16-18 year olds in Scotland were specifically seen as particularly appropriate vehicles for developing responses to TVEI. Paradoxically, however, the very determination of Scottish educationists to ensure a firm place for national educational programmes within TVEI project proposals has led to increasing concern about vocationalism in the Scottish school curriculum, particularly for the younger school population.

In 1982 the government introduced a pilot scheme to stimulate the provision of technical and vocational education for 14-18 year olds in the education system in England, Scotland and Wales. The scheme, the Technical and Vocational Education Initiative (TVEI), encouraged the development of different projects within national criteria and guidelines.

In 1983 the Scottish Education Department (SED) issued an Action Plan setting out proposals for improving the quality and co-ordination of the educational provision made for the 16-18 age group in Scotland. The plan proposed the development of a modular curriculum which would allow young people to move freely within courses and between institutions, taking advantage of the availability of credit accumulation and credit transfer.

Background

Scotland came late to the Technical and Vocational Education Initiative. This was not in any way an indication of an inability to respond in a

timely way to the invitation from the Manpower Services Commission
(MSC) to participate in this potentially exciting, innovative and well-
funded initiative. Rather it was an indication of what has been termed
'Caledonian caution', a concern to ensure that participation in the
initiative would not compromise Scottish educational developments, or
breach educational principles which had been established in Scotland
as a result of the experiences gained in attempting to introduce vocational
elements into the curriculum of Scottish schools during the 1960s.

Throughout the 1960s in Scotland, attempts had been made through
the Brunton Report (SED, 1963) to see the vocational perspective as the
core around which the curriculum should be organized. Experience proved
that this approach was too simplistic, and towards the end of the 1960s
wider definitions of the vocational perspective were beginning to
command support in Scotland. In England, the Department of Education
and Science published the Henniker-Heaton committee report on day
release (DES, 1964). This stressed the complementary nature of general
and vocational education and gave momentum to the changing perspectives in Scotland.

More recently, developments in Scotland have taken forward the
lessons of the 1960s and the early 1970s. In particular there was the
final report of the planning committee of the Education for the Industrial
Society project *An Education for Life and Work* (Consultative Committee
on the Curriculum, 1983). This was developed by individual authorities
throughout Scotland over the late 1970s and early 1980s, and the report
clearly outlines the attempts which have been made to achieve a balance
between the vocational emphasis and the broader curriculum in Scottish
schools.

Even more important in this context has been the national support and
collaboration given to the government's proposals for 14-16 year olds in
Scotland, which have among their aims the provision of a single certificate
for all pupils after four years of secondary schooling. These Standard Grade
proposals emanated from the report of the committee set up to consider
the structure of the curriculum in the third and fourth years of Scottish
secondary schools (SED, 1977). These proposals were put forward in the
context of a range of areas of study or modes, based broadly on the range
of traditional subjects of study and very similar to the 'areas of experience' outlined in the so-called 'Red Books' produced in England by
the Schools Inspectorate over the years 1978-83 (DES, 1979, 1981, 1983).
Like the HMI reports, the Scottish proposals were an attempt to combine
balance, choice and flexibility in the curriculum. Again like the HMI
recommendations, the Scottish proposals did not include technical and
vocational modes in any explicit way. Indeed, debate has continued in
Scotland on the desirability of proposing a technological mode in the
framework put forward. Based on previous experiences and on the
traditions of Scottish education, however, the consensus has been that,
particularly at the compulsory stages of schooling, an emphasis should
be maintained on general education, recognizing always that the

opportunities for technological education exist in abundance within the overall curriculum framework proposed. Developments in post-compulsory education and the involvement of Scottish schools and colleges in the Manpower Services Commission's (MSC) Technical and Vocational Education Initiative have created tensions in relation to the maintenance of a balance between general and technical/vocational education.

The context of change

In January 1983 the government published plans for reforming the framework of education and training for young people aged 16-18 in Scotland. The document *16-18s in Scotland — An Action Plan* set out principles, detailed proposals and a timetable for introducing a new system of courses and qualifications for this age group (SED, 1983).

The Action Plan highlighted shortcomings in the existing system and pointed to the need for a new framework for education. Along with the existing provision of academic school-based courses this framework included:

1. New courses based upon a collection of learning units or 'modules', usually of 40 hours' duration.
2. A new national 16-18 certificate for students and trainees taking the new courses.
3. A range of points of entry to and exit from education and training with greater freedom of choice for young people, leading to the realization of the idea of education as a lifelong process.
4. Better opportunities to change areas of study, with recognition given for earlier achievement.
5. Closer links between schools and among schools, further education colleges, community education centres and all other agencies involved in the education and training of young people.

Implementation of the new arrangements began in August 1984, and the system was to develop gradually over a period of years. It heralded a move towards the development of new post-16 years courses having a more pronounced vocational emphasis and involving closer co-operation among the various providers of education. Given the clear direction of developments in England and Wales following the publication of the New Training Initiative (Department of Employment, 1981) and the priority accorded to the development of structured education and training for 16-19s following the Macfarlane report (DES, 1980), Action Plan developments in Scotland gained wide and ready support.

At that time in Scotland there was a strong belief that schools and colleges needed to adjust more quickly and in appropriate ways to changes in technology and in society, and must be prepared to respond to the requirements of the more diverse population in the senior stages of school education. There was also the recognition of a need for further education and training to be able to respond quickly to changes in technology and to help young people use their knowledge and skills in a flexible way. Long-standing agreements and practices which had led to separate patterns of traineeship and apprenticeship had to be reviewed to cater for changing industrial conditions. The new educational framework outlined in the Action Plan was the proposed solution, designed to take account of the needs of all young people, reflecting current occupational requirements and providing a sound base on which to build for the later acquisition or updating of skills and knowledge to meet the challenges of the future.

Against the above background, Scottish authorities were invited to make bids for funding for project proposals under the Technical and Vocational Education Initiative (TVEI).

When the approach to consider participation in TVEI came, there was a general consensus in Scotland that the TVEI principles and criteria were consistent with those already set out for the new Scottish courses for 14-16 year olds and for 16-18 year olds. In particular it was noted that in TVEI:

1. initiatives would be developed through local authorities working within a framework of national criteria and guidelines
2. courses would lead to nationally recognized qualifications
3. courses would be for young people across a wide range of ability, including young people with special educational needs
4. courses would include general education, pre-vocational education and work experience from age 15 onwards
5. courses would encourage broadly based skills and competencies including initiative, problem-solving abilities and other aspects of personal development
6. young people's participation would be voluntary
7. courses would be progressive and link effectively with subsequent training/educational opportunities
8. equal opportunities would be available to young people of both sexes
9. arrangements would be made for regular assessment, performance discussion and careers and educational guidance.

In January 1984, therefore, the education committee of the Convention of Scottish Local Authorities agreed to recommend participation of authorities in TVEI, subject to the acceptance of safeguards designed to protect Scottish educational developments.

The interaction of TVEI and Action Plan

Early in the design of TVEI projects it became clear that courses leading to nationally recognized certificates would be required in order to attract support from parents and young people and in order to command the respect of employers and other users.

Across the UK the preparation of proposals for external scrutiny by the MSC led to a rapid public realization of the patchwork nature of courses and certification for 14-18 year olds. The range of certifying bodies — educational, professional and industrial — and their inter-relationship had become highly complex. Arrangements for vocational qualifications, while maintaining certain worthwhile features such as credibility, diversity and stability, had nonetheless revealed weaknesses as the pace of change increased, as the need for the application of knowledge and understanding grew, and as demand for the availability of opportunities for progression was voiced. Recognizing that a coherent system for the assessment and certification of vocational competence was an important factor in achieving the adaptability and competitiveness required of young people leaving school, in 1985 the government set up a national review group which commended a major reform of examination and certification systems in vocational education and training (MSC, 1985). There is no doubt that the decision to set up the review group had been substantially influenced by the difficulties experienced by local authorities in developing coherent and acceptable TVEI proposals.

In Scotland, several factors were causing concern to drafters of TVEI project proposals. TVEI had been described as a programme aimed at improving the preparation of young people for the world of work, helping them to use their skills and knowledge to solve real-world problems and designed to emphasize the development of personal qualities such as initiative, motivation, enterprise and problem-solving skills. By promoting these activities, industry's confidence in the curriculum of schools was expected to be established.

There was a clear need for credible, flexible courses which would allow Scotland to maintain the balance of general and vocational education, particularly at the 14-16 stage, and yet would develop curricular strengths and promote the bridging of education between schools and further and higher education implicit in TVEI planning. The Scottish Action Plan offered a number of features which provided solutions to these problems. However, Action Plan had been designed for 16-18 year olds involved in courses of non-advanced further education. It had never been designed for 14-16 year olds for whom a quite separate programme had been developed: the Standard Grade programme. Notwithstanding the potential difficulties of allowing 14-16 year olds access to the Action Plan programmes of study, the pressures were such that a decision was taken to permit such a move. All young people involved in TVEI were given access to the range of courses and certification available through the Scottish Action Plan.

The strengths of Action Plan in relation to TVEI

One of the main strengths of Action Plan is the flexibility offered by its modular structure. The plan is based on a model which breaks down

traditional courses into units of study or modules so that students can
progress from module to module and take modules from other areas of
study, gaining credit as they progress. On a cumulative basis, students
receive a single national certificate recording their attainments in the
various general and specialist modules which they complete wherever they
study — in school, college or in MSC placements. Clearly such a flexible
system supports the approaches being developed in relation to TVEI
programmes, in particular the need to ensure progression throughout the
four-year programme, the need for the programme to be capable of
adapting to the changing needs of employers and society, and the need
for the programme to be capable of linking effectively with subsequent
training and educational opportunities.

Within Action Plan, individual modules have been designed to be
general or specialist in nature. This approach ensures that within a
student's individual programme there will be opportunities for a broad-
based educational experience linked to a more specialized consideration
of certain areas. No matter what the composition of the individual
programme, however, it is important that it should include a range of
fundamental components such as language and communication, number,
personal development, problem-solving, planning and manipulative skills —
all key elements of TVEI programmes.

Clearly such an approach to curriculum planning and design offers
excellent opportunities for modification and adjustment to suit changing
circumstances, based as it is on flexibility. The system is responsive to
demands and can anticipate needs; it can also accommodate retraining
requirements, all within its present structural design.

But perhaps the greatest strength of Action Plan in relation to TVEI
is the range of areas of study available to students. Some 2,000 modules
are available covering the areas of interdisciplinary studies, business and
administration, distribution, food services and personal services, engineering, the built environment, caring, industrial processing, land and
sea-based industries and pure and applied sciences (Scottish Vocational
Education Council, 1985). Such a range offers wide opportunities for
young people to become involved in programmes of study designed to
promote skills and develop knowledge which will enhance their attractiveness to employers and bridge the move from school to further and higher
education more easily.

However, the availability of these opportunities has created pressure
on the Scottish education system generally and has again raised the spectre
of vocationalism, particularly in relation to the younger age group for
whom Action Plan modules were never intended. In an attempt to ensure
that TVEI would not compromise Scottish educational developments nor
breach firmly established educational principles, Scottish educationists
have consequently insisted on a prominent place for Action Plan curriculum structures and assessment procedures in TVEI programmes. There are
some in Scotland whose 'Caledonian caution' leads them to believe that
such approaches have distorted educational provision for the younger

school population and that only by great vigilance and conscious action will the balance between general and technical/vocational education be maintained in Scotland.

References

Consultative Committee on the Curriculum (1983) *An Education for Life and Work: Report by the Planning Committee of the Education for the Industrial Society Project* HMSO: Edinburgh

Department of Education and Science (DES) (1964) *Day Release: Report of a Committee set up by the Minister of Education* (The Henniker-Heaton Report) HMSO: London

Department of Education and Science (DES) (1979) *Curriculum 11-16: Working Papers by HM Inspectorate — A Contribution to Current Debate* HMSO: London

Department of Education and Science (DES) (1980) *Education for 16-19 Year Olds: A Review undertaken for the Government and the Local Authorities Association* Chairman: N Macfarlane HMSO: London

Department of Education and Science (DES) (1981) *Curriculum 11-16: A Review of Progress* HMSO: London

Department of Education and Science (DES) (1983) *Curriculum 11-16: Towards a Statement of Entitlement* HMSO: London

Department of Employment (1981) *A New Training Initiative: A Programme for Action* Cmnd 8455 HMSO: London

Manpower Services Commission (MSC) (1985) *Review of Vocational Qualifications in England and Wales: Interim Report of Joint Manpower Services Commission/ Department of Education and Science Working Group* MSC: Sheffield

Scottish Education Department (SED) (1963) *From School to Further Education* HMSO: Edinburgh

Scottish Education Department (SED) (1977) *The Structure of the Curriculum in the Third and Fourth Years of the Scottish Secondary School* (The Munn Report) HMSO: Edinburgh

Scottish Education Department (SED) (1983) *16-18s in Scotland: An Action Plan* HMSO: Edinburgh

Scottish Vocational Education Council (SCOTVEC) (1985) *The National Certificate* SCOTVEC: Glasgow

5. Pressures on vocational training in the Federal Republic of Germany

Dorothee Engelhard and Kurt Kreuser

Summary: In the Federal Republic of Germany, vocational training relies substantially on the dual system which involves learning at two places: the firm and the vocational school. Learning on the job is organized on the basis of a contract between the employer and the trainee, and the learning in vocational school takes place on a part-time basis. In addition, vocational training is possible in full-time vocational schools. The legal basis for the training of young persons is the Vocational Training Act (1969).

Since 1977 the vocational system has had to cope with the following developments:

☐ demographic change from 1955 to 1964
☐ young people's changing attitudes to education
☐ economic developments.

In 1977, 585,000 young persons were asking to be trained on the job; in 1984 this number had increased to 764,000. Employers could not satisfy this demand. In 1977 they were able to offer 584,000 places; in 1984 they offered 727,000.

Because of economic developments, young people stay longer in the educational system. About 50 per cent now start their vocational training when they are 18 or older. The training on the job has to be supplemented in certain vocational fields by training centres which have the capacity to teach more complex processes than are possible in the smaller companies.

The system

In the Federal Republic of Germany most young people start out in their vocational career with a job in the workplace and concurrent attendance at a part-time vocational school (*Berufsschule*). These two linked places of learning form the basis of the dual system of vocational training. Vocational qualifications can also be obtained through

☐ courses at a full-time vocational school (*Berufsfachschule*)
☐ courses leading both to vocational qualifications and to higher education.

The spectrum of vocational training is wide, covering around 450 occupations.

Legal basis

There are three important federal laws applying to vocational training:

The Vocational Training Act, covering also the planning and statistics of vocational training and the work of the Federal Institute for Vocational Training.

The Works Industrial Relations Act, giving the works council — the representatives of a company's employees — the right of co-operation regarding in-company vocational training.

The Youth Labour Protection Law, providing special protection regulations for trainees and young employees.

The Vocational Training Act (1969) comprises initial training, further training and vocational retraining. The form of German vocational training — with its basis of learning by doing, and with the employer as its central element — means that the regulations governing it also have a labour law component. For instance, the relationship between employer and trainee is based on a civil law training contract which is subject to the legal principles and provisions governing contracts of employment.

The consequence of this is general freedom to contract. The employer can decide whether he wishes to take on trainees and with whom he will conclude a training contract. The same applies to the young people. Neither for employers nor for young people is there an obligation to train. Nor are the young people directed into specific occupations: the labour offices merely give vocational advice and help to find training places for prospective trainees in one of the following occupations: industry and commerce, crafts, agriculture, public services, and the various independent professions.

The craft trades sector is governed by rules under the Crafts Code, supplementing the Vocational Training Act.

The Vocational Training Act does not apply to vocational training schools, for which the individual states of the Federal Republic (*Länder*) are responsible.

The dual system

For the process of training, the dual system is the traditional mode of vocational education and is provided on the job and in vocational schools. Practical vocational training is given at work — the trainee is introduced, helped and trained by the training employer. This training is backed up by theoretical and general education provided in vocational schools. For each trainee the practical and theoretical work needs to be harmonized. There are official guidelines on the interrelation of curricula in both places of training.

Most young people start their 'dual training' at 15 or 16 years of age after completing nine or ten years at school (full-time compulsory education). They generally have their final certificate from secondary school. There are no special conditions for admission.

Training normally takes three years. It is organized in such a way that the trainees first acquire basic skills and knowledge. This is being done increasingly in a basic vocational training year either in full-time form or in co-operative form. In 1983, 6.6 per cent of those starting their training in the dual system had had this specific form of preparation (Report on Vocational Training, 1985a).

Co-operative basic vocational courses have become particularly necessary in the field of industrial training, due to its increasingly complex character. In particular, what are known as basic skills have to be imparted, independently of production, in separate training courses. During this first year the trainees become acquainted with the underlying principles of several related vocations. They attend school for two days a week and for the remaining time they are trained on the job. In the second and third years they specialize in their chosen job with the company they had their initial contract with.

Full-time basic vocational courses take place in vocational schools and last for one year. Basic knowledge and skills for related jobs are taught. After that year the training on the job within the dual system is started.

Those in the traditional dual system start with their in-company training, together with the compulsory 8 to 12 hours' instruction at vocational schools, right from the beginning.

IN-COMPANY TRAINING

In factories, enterprises, plants, workshops, laboratories, offices or shops, trainees are meant to learn through their work how to solve increasingly difficult problems step by step on their own. The jobs they have to become acquainted with and must complete are laid down in a general training syllabus, and in many cases also in a company training syllabus based on it. The way in which the skills and knowledge are imparted differs according to the field of training and the size of the company.

In a large company the trainees become acquainted with various areas of the work in accordance with a training syllabus drawn up for them. For instance, in the commercial sector they start out in accounts, progress through various administrative departments and then come to the purchasing or sales department. In the industrial or scientific area the first stop is frequently a training workshop or a training laboratory. After this they enter a variety of workshops, production plants or laboratories. Under the instruction of full-time or part-time teachers they apply what they have learned and increase their skills and knowledge.

Many companies, particularly the medium and large-size enterprises, provide additional training courses for their trainees over and above the vocational school classes.

Persons training in a small company are placed in the care of an experienced member of staff. Under the supervision of the owner of the firm, the master craftsman or an instructor, the trainee becomes familiar with the different jobs and can in time complete part-jobs independently. This in-company training is often supplemented by training courses in an off-the-job group training centre. By these means the trainees also get to know jobs that do not arise in their firm, but which are included in the general training syllabus.

TRAINING IN VOCATIONAL SCHOOL (OFF-THE-JOB TRAINING)

All young people have to attend a vocational school during their period of training. Their employer is obliged to give them time off, without wage deduction, for the time required for classes. It is the task of vocational schools to supplement in-company training. About 60 per cent of the instruction is specific to the occupation for which the student is being trained (*Vocational Training*, 1983). The vocational school teachers are expected however, over and above this, to advance their students' general education.

Vocational schools are divided according to branches of trade. There are, for instance, vocational schools for business, industry, home economics and agriculture. Students are grouped in classes according to their year of apprenticeship and receive instruction for a single occupation or for several related occupations.

FULL-TIME VOCATIONAL COURSES

Vocational education can also take place in specialist vocational schools (*Berufsfachschulen*). These institutes provide full-time instruction. The students spend one to three years, depending on the subject taken and the objectives envisaged. Most of these schools supply basic vocational training together with general educational subjects. Examples can be found in the two-year commercial school of advanced business studies. They prepare young people with lower-level or intermediate-level secondary school leaving certificates for a business profession. The students can then enter working life straight from the vocational school. However, many young people do an additional business training course in their companies, under the dual system. Three-year specialist vocational training schools also deal with all the aspects of training for specific occupations — particularly in places or regions where there are not enough available training places under the dual system and also in professions for which the dual system does not provide instruction (eg youth and community work or child-care occupations).

There are other full-time vocational schools which contribute to a differentiated educational system and increase the possibilities of obtaining further qualifications (ie *Fachoberschulen*, *Berufsaufbauschulen*, *Fachschulen*).

In addition to all the above there are two types of school which offer both a vocational qualification and a college or a university entrance qualification (*Kollegschule*, *Berufliches Gymnasium*).

RESPONSIBLE AUTHORITIES

Certain vocational training duties have been transferred by legislation to the chambers of industry and commerce; of crafts; of agriculture and of the various independent professions.

The chambers, which all enterprises within a certain section of the economy and the independent sectors (eg doctors and solicitors) are required to join and pay contributions to, are self-governing bodies. They come under the legal supervision of a higher state authority (the Ministry of Economic Affairs).

Chambers, as representing the employers' side, supervise the practical part of the training process. It is their duty in particular to inspect the companies' conditions of training and to check whether training is carried out in accordance with laid-down regulations. They also conduct interim and final examinations.

TRAINING REGULATIONS

The basis for in-company training is provided by training regulations. There is a complicated system through which they are developed and updated. The Federal Institute for Vocational Training plays a decisive role. It submits proposals to employers, unions, federal and local authorities. When an agreement has been reached the responsible ministry (eg the Federal Ministry of Economic Affairs) promulgates the training code.

These associated responsible bodies (federal government, state government, chambers, unions, local authorities) require an elaborate system of co-ordination at different levels of responsibility, sensitive to the slightest disturbance. Nevertheless, this way of proceeding does guarantee that everyone involved in vocational training can have a part in its organization and structuring, and that solutions achieved in co-operative work are then also put into joint practice.

Quantitative development

Since 1977 there has been an increase from 585,000 juveniles to 764,000 in 1984 applying for the regular 'dual' (on-the-job plus vocational school) training (Report on Vocational Training, 1985b). There are three main reasons for this:

1. demographic change from 1955 to 1964: the birth rate started to climb in 1955 and reached its peak in 1964 (*Berufsbildung*, 1984)
2. young people's changing attitudes to education
3. economic developments.

These reasons will be dealt with in turn.

Demographic change

Since the beginning of the 1970s there has been an increase in the 15 and 16 year olds leaving general secondary schools in order to take up vocational training. This demographic trend will go on even after 1980 because the age group concerned is shifting towards the 17 and 18 year olds. In 1984 nearly 50 per cent of those applying for the 'dual' training were 18 years old (Report on Vocational Training, 1985c). Therefore it is only since 1982 that a slight decline of school leavers can be observed.

Young people's attitudes

At the beginning of the 1980s young people started to change their educational attitude. Vocational training became more attractive. In 1980 about 60 per cent of the 15 and 16 year olds chose a vocational training; in 1984 this percentage had increased to 74 (Report on Vocational Training, 1985d). If one considers young people's formal education it becomes obvious that trainees in general are better educated (Table 1).

Year	General Secondary School	Intermediate Secondary Technical School	Senior Grammar School
1970	79.7	18.8	1.3
1982	55.2	38.0	6.8

Source: Report on Vocational Training, 1984: 32

Table 1. *Formal education of trainees (percentage)*

This development can be partly attributed to a greater differentiation and flexibility within the German school system, which has — for historical reasons — developed three branches: secondary and senior grammar schools, intermediate secondary technical schools and general secondary schools. After four years of primary school, pupils attend one of these school types. Table 2 shows the different tracks young persons undergo before they start their vocational training in the dual system. The trainee's higher age is thus largely due to his longer and better education.

Worth mentioning within this development is the increase in those holding a university or college entrance qualification. At the beginning of the 1970s about 95 per cent of those with the requisite entry qualifications (Abitur) actually started a university or college education; in the mid-1980s this percentage tended to be less than 80. A growing number have preferred to train vocationally before they start their university or college education.

Since 1982 the decline of 15-16 year old school leavers entering vocational training has been gradually compensated for by an increasing number of those holding university or college entrance qualifications. In 1982, 17 per cent of juveniles asking to be vocationally trained had a university or college entrance qualification; in 1985 it was probably 30 per cent (*Bund-Länder Commission*, 1985).

The occupational sectors preferred by young persons in this group in 1983 were: industry and commerce (10.7 per cent); agriculture (13.7 per cent); and independent (14.2 per cent) (Report on Vocational Education,

General secondary school without leaving certificate	General secondary school with leaving certificate	Intermediate secondary technical school	Senior and specialized grammar school	Basic vocational training year	Full-time vocational training school
3.0	39.9	31.7	8.4	6.6	9.4

Source: *Berufsbildungsbericht*, 1985e: 38

Table 2. *Formal education of 'dual' system trainees in 1983 (percentage)*

1985). The occupations they chose were mainly: merchant banker, industry merchant, trade and foreign trade merchant, tax and economic adviser, clerical merchant, gardener, insurance broker, dental technician, joiner and medical assistant.

The craft sector is less challenging for those holding a university or college entrance qualification. In 1983, 4.3 per cent of those who started their 'dual' system training had such qualifications (Report on Vocational Education, 1985). But even in this sector a rising tendency can be observed: in 1984, 5 per cent belonged to this group (Trainee Statistics, 1985). Most of those entering the craft sector have had their secondary education in a general secondary school. In 1984 the percentage was 58 (Trainee Statistics, 1985).

Within the craft sector changes are also becoming apparent. In 1984, due to the recession in the building trade 3.6 per cent less than in 1983 asked for a contract in this vocational field. The trend has been similar in the food industry, where a reduction of 5.7 per cent has taken place. Vocational opportunities in the field of merchant bankers has expanded by 3.7 per cent between 1983 and 1984, largely because of an expansion in the jobs of wholesale and export clerks. The vocational field of clothing has grown most remarkably (up 10.8 per cent from 1983 to 1984) (Trainee Statistics, 1985). Within the vocational field of metalwork, only a few occupations, eg machine fitter, toolmaker, chassis maker and electrician, attracted young people. Some of the more traditional occupations within this field are of lesser interest to young people: blacksmith or vehicle mechanic, for instance.

Economic developments

Due to economic developments and the high level of unemployment young people are changing their outlook on their future working life. In 1973 only 1.4 per cent of those unemployed were at the same time untrained. By 1984 this percentage had risen to 18.7 (*Bund-Länder Commission*, 1985a: 10). Young people who at the beginning of the 1970s were immediately absorbed through the labour market are nowadays willing to be trained in order to avoid unemployment.

The rising unemployment in academic careers has induced prospective students to begin with a vocational training in order to have a subsequent choice between continuing in that vocation and switching to a university or college education.

Although the number of school leavers is decreasing, the demand for training places has not yet stabilized because companies cannot offer enough training places for all young people who apply for one. The unsuccessful applicants are more likely to be those who left general secondary school without a final certificate. Moreover, the demand does not decrease, because school leavers from vocational full-time schools and those with a university or college entrance qualification have to be catered for. Table 3 shows the percentages and absolute numbers in 1980 and 1984 and the prospective development in 1985.

Year	Total	Direct transfer from general schools		Transfer from vocational school and re-applicants		Transfer from senior grammar school	
Year	(thousands)	(thousands)	%	(thousands)	%	(thousands)	%
1980	667	475	57.4	167	20.1	25	12.0
1984	764	428	54.5	256	31.8	80	28.2
1985	746– 764	409	54.5	254– 262	32– 33	83– 93	28– 31.5

Source: *Bund-Länder Commission*, 1985b: 9

Table 3. *Demand for training places*

Problems and perspectives

As employers can decide whether they wish to take on trainees and choose with whom they will conclude a training contract, politicians try to persuade them to satisfy the demand. With an enormous effort employers have increased their offer from 584,000 places in 1977 to 727,000 in 1984 (Report on Vocational Training, 1985). To give an example – in the crafts sector in 1983 every second company took on trainees; in 1973 only one company in three did this (Alex, 1983).

Due to this policy each juvenile will, in one way or another, have a training, and will not be unemployed during this period. The problem of unemployment only becomes acute when the young person has finished training. In fact in 1985, 500,000 under the age of 25 were unemployed, which means an unemployment rate of 9.6 per cent. The real rate is probably higher, due to the so-called 'silent reserve' which consists of those who have become resigned to joblessness and do not any longer appear in the statistics, or those who are engaged in recurrent education programmes.

Companies cannot give them regular working contracts because they already train more workers than they actually need. Towards the end of the 1980s, however, the labour market will urgently need those skilled workers. In the meantime an attempt is being made to keep them up to date through recurrent education programmes or special programmes (ABM) which are financed by public money.

In the long run it is very likely that those who left the general secondary school without a leaving certificate and have been refused a training place one or more times will join the ranks of the unemployed. In times of economic growth, jobs for unskilled workers were in abundance, but through the recession these workers were the first to be dismissed. Since then the technical challenge has brought about qualitative and structural changes in the setup of the economy which give reason to believe that unskilled workers will only be needed on a much smaller scale than in the past.

Another group is increasingly hit by unemployment. It is made up of skilled workers who have specialized in jobs which are no longer needed, because structural changes have occurred (in mining and quarrying, ship construction, the foundry sector, and so on), or who have been trained for jobs where the job profile has changed (printer, traditional clerk, designer, painter, bricklayer).

Increasing employment can be expected in jobs which depend in one way or another on modern technologies.

Structural changes caused by technical development require a vocational system which is flexible enough to adapt to changed economic, social and technological circumstances. The dual system should — despite its structural variety and complex organization — be capable of satisfying the changing demands of the labour market.

These demands involve broader vocational qualifications. Knowledge is preferred to skills. The individual does not deal so much with products, machines or procedures, but with planning and thinking in bigger systems. In order to cope with electronics or data processing, abstract thinking is required. Jobs, profiles and qualifications are changing. Revised and new training regulations are therefore crucial for employers and instructors if they are to train young persons in accordance with the requirements of the labour market.

Due to the increasing complexity of work, companies find it difficult to integrate trainees into the working process in such a way that they learn the vocational basics laid down in the training regulations. Trainees cannot see, cannot imitate and practise what has to be learned. Therefore medium and large-sized enterprises provide additional training workshops or training laboratories. Companies in the craft sector are usually smaller and therefore do not have the capacity to install such laboratories.

Basic vocational training years and off-the-job group training centres (which are financed by chambers, professional associations and company federations) have been set up with the intention of supplementing the training on the job. Both provide basic skills and knowledge in an occupational field which serves several associated trades. It is easier in these institutions to implement technical processes than it would be in smaller specialized companies.

In none of the trade branches — agriculture, commerce and industry, craft trades, public services and others — is it intended to exclude the core of the dual system — the training on the job — and to replace it by school-like institutions. At the same time it is recognized that certain technical developments can only be explained in supplementary courses or laboratories.

In conclusion, there are three main challenges for the vocational system in the Federal Republic of Germany:

☐ to accommodate the high number of juveniles asking for training places

☐ to train juveniles for those jobs which the labour market is demanding

☐ to adapt the training process to technological changes.

Within the dual system this seems possible. Employers are independent and can react in accordance with the principles of a free market economy. The Vocational Training Act is the instrument for bringing together the responsible authorities to devise the training regulations. Delays should be avoided. Further development of the basic vocational training year and the training centres should guarantee the necessary integration of technical material into the training process.

References

Alex, L (1983) Education and Qualified Labour Demand (Ausbildung und Fachkräftebedarf) *Berufsbildung in Wissenschaft und Praxis*: 181

Bund-Länder Commission for Educational Planning and Research Promotion (Bund-Länder-Kommission für Bildungsplänung und Forschungsförderung) Short- and Medium-Term Possibilities to Secure Training Places (*Kurz- und mittelfristige Möglichkeiten zur Sicherung von Ausbildungsplätzen*) (1985) BLK: Bonn

Bund-Länder Commission for Educational Planning and Research Promotion (Bund-Länder-Kommission für Bildungsplänung und Forschungsförderung) Future Job Prospects of Graduates (*Künftige Perspektiven von Hochschulabsolventen im Beschäftigungssystem*) (1985a) BLK: Bonn

Report on Vocational Training (Berufsbildungsbericht) (1985) *Grundlagen und Perspektiven für Bildung und Wissenschaft* 7 Der Bundesminister für Bildung und Wissenschaft: Bonn

Trainee Statistics (*Lehrlingsstatistik*) (1985) Deutsches Handwerksblatt (10): Bonn

Vocational Training in the Federal Republic of Germany (*Berufsbildung in der Bundesrepublik Deutschland*) (1984) Bundesinstitut für Berufsbildung: Berlin

Vocational Training — Investment for the Future. The Dual Training System in the Federal Republic of Germany (1983) Carl Duisberg Gesellschaft eV: Cologne

6. Learning a trade in the USSR

Derek Marsh

Summary: Uniform vocational training in a country as large and as diversified as the USSR is the result of a centralized system. As a Marxist-Leninist state, vocational training is designed to meet the needs of a planned, state-owned economy and to instil in young people the work ethic of the Communist Party of the Soviet Union (CPSU). Any description of that system has to take these two aims into account.

Vocational training in basic craft skills begins at school, and is developed throughout compulsory education and in legally required collaboration with enterprises in industry, commerce and services. For those students not proceeding immediately to higher education at the universities or technical institutes (and not entering unskilled employment), trade training is largely compulsory between the ages of 15 and 18 and leads to a trade diploma in one of the 1,500 recognized crafts across the 14 branches of the Soviet economy. The major workhorse of the system is the special professional technical school (SPTU) of which there were some 7,600, with 3.8 million students, in 1983. Annually SPTUs produce 2 million skilled and semi-skilled workers for industry.

Despite a comprehensive training system and a radical review in 1984, there remain many internally voiced criticisms that the economy regularly fails to achieve its targets of both quantity and quality. Nevertheless, the system has much to recommend it to Western countries seeking to close the gap between education and vocational training.

Note: As a Briton who has spent some time studying a particularly interesting type of Soviet educational institution, I have included both factual information and personal impressions in this chapter. I have dealt principally with the SPTU, an upper secondary school which combines general secondary education with training for a particular vocation, but I have also commented on vocational training as a whole in the USSR. Many Russian terms relating to education do not have an exact counterpart in English. In this chapter English approximations have largely been used for the sake of comprehension and readability. Readers interested in precise use of Russian terminology can follow it up in the glossary in Zajda, 1980, whose definitions have largely been used where it has been important to employ a Russian concept.

Introduction

The USSR is vast: 22 million square kilometres stretch 12,000 kilometres from west to east, and 4,000 from north to south. Speaking 70 different languages, its 271 million people live in 15 union republics, 20 autonomous republics, eight autonomous regions and ten autonomous areas. Dense urban and industrial areas lie within sparsely populated countryside ranging from fertile to arctic and desert regions. National languages, traditions and customs are avidly retained, but the most powerful influences are those from Russia, Ukraine and Byelorussia, accounting for some 200 million people. It is, therefore, a complex and varied country which faces issues of integration and communication. The problem of administrating such diversity is partially solved by a centralized bureaucracy which provides a uniform and controlled system.

There is a duality within the governance of the USSR between the Communist Party of the Soviet Union with its own organizational structure, and the state's structure. The two systems meet at the top in the sense that the CPSU determines all policy, and the state administers it.

The overriding values and moral codes of the USSR are those of Marxist-Leninist principles. Within this framework, education plays a vital role, with explicit tasks to perform in the development of effective workers and citizens, as shown in the policies and processes of vocational training.

The constitutional and conceptual frameworks of vocational training

Vocational training is designed to achieve political, economic and social aims. The Constitution of the USSR says that three of the aims of the state are:

> 'to lay the material and technical foundations of communism, to perfect socialist social relations and transform them into communist relations, and to mould the citizens of a communist society'.

'Socially useful work' and its results determine status in this society, to be achieved by combining material and moral incentives and encouraging innovative and creative attitudes towards work (Article 14, *The Constitution of the Union of Soviet Socialist Republics*).

Differences of class, or rural and urban areas, and of mental and physical work have to be eliminated. Hence, free education and training is available for all, providing communist education and promoting intellectual and physical development of youth who must be trained for work and social activity (Article 25). Such education is both moral and aesthetic (Article 27). Article 40 guarantees employment for pay in accordance with the quantity and quality of work, and the right to choose a trade or profession in accordance with the individual's inclinations, abilities, training and education, 'with due account of the needs of society'. Whilst Article 45 provides the right to such free education, Article 59

obliges compliance with socialist conduct. Article 67 also obliges everyone
to be concerned with rearing children, to train them for socially useful
work and to develop them as worthy members of a socialist society.

These fundamental laws have been reflected consistently in the
development of vocational training since 1919, when Lenin instituted
compulsory training for certain trades and crafts and established a Chief
Committee for Vocational Training to manage, co-ordinate and control at
central government level the work of various departments to provide
skilled workers for the economy. Basically, the same structure still exists.
Factory apprentice schools were introduced after 1919, but there was no
uniformity in training across the USSR. It was subordinated to the needs
of individual factories. Not enough skilled workers were being provided
for a growing industrial-based economy and vocational training was too
narrow, lacking the essential broad base provided by extensive general
education.

These criticisms can still be heard today. The Decree on State Labour
Reserves of 1940 provided for three basic types of school (which still
remain in existence) to train in three main groups of skills: for the heavy
industries, for the railways and in all basic craft skills. Vocational schools
were reorganized to enable transfer from the eight-year general school
into trade training courses varying in length between one and three years.
In 1968 post-school courses were extended by a year and contained a
larger element of general education. In 1977, when compulsory ten-year
schooling was introduced, guidelines set out to improve instructional
quality and to unite more closely the processes of trade and general
instruction. In 1981, at the 26th Congress of the CPSU, the first steps
were taken towards the present system, introduced in 1984 to coincide
with the state's next five-year plan. This emphasized the role of the
SPTU (*Srednie Professionalno Technicheskoe Uchilishche*) as the main
source of skilled workers for the economy, and the development of
Lenin's ideas on a unified labour and polytechnical education (*poli-
technicheskoe obrazovanie*). In order to understand the context of the
SPTU it is helpful first to consider the way in which education and
vocational training are administered.

The central administration of education and vocational training

Public education in the USSR is the responsibility of two ministries
(for Public Education in the USSR, and for Higher and Specialized
Secondary Education in the USSR), and the State Committee for Vocational Training in the USSR.

The Ministry for Public Education is responsible for pre-school establishments and for compulsory education at primary and secondary levels.

The Ministry for Higher and Specialized Secondary Education controls
all tertiary level institutes of higher education (VUZs) including universities, polytechnics, monotechnics and other institutions which train
to non-degree level for semi-professional vocations.

The State Committee of the USSR for Vocational Training has responsibilities for technical vocational schools and associated institutions. It has governmental status equal to that of the two Ministries and is responsible to the Council of Ministers of the USSR. The principal role of the Committee is to develop and manage the training system for the manpower required as the Soviet economy develops. Departments handle training methods; moral and political education (*vospitanie*); textbooks; liaison with republic committees, and dealings with the state enterprises. In order to control the uniform policy for vocational training throughout the USSR, the Committee also develops and elaborates curricular and teaching methodology, conducts research into problems bearing on vocational training, and is responsible for liaison at all levels between training schools and local industry, financing the system, teacher training and staff development, inspection to ensure quality, drafting regulations, administering them and deciding upon the structure of the various trades recognized as requiring qualification.

At present there are some 1,500 such trades, divided into 14 categories related to the various 'branches' of the economy: for example, general engineering (42 trades), construction (45 trades), electrical industries, transport, textiles, light engineering, food, general services, agriculture and natural resources (mining, oil, water, forestry, etc).

In the Soviet Union there are over 7,500 vocational schools (SPTUs, PTUs and VPTUs — see below) with 3.8 million students aged between 15 and 18 (in 1986 this had risen to 4 million) being trained in the 1,500 different trades, producing each year some 2 million skilled and semi-skilled workers. The 1981-86 five-year plan called for 13 million graduates of the system; by 1984 the total output has reached 7.3 million. There are also some 2,100 agricultural schools with 1 million students, annually providing 680,000 skilled and semi-skilled agricultural workers, engineers and specialists. The system employs some 340,000 teachers and instructors.

Vocational training is carried out in:

1. SPTUs — secondary special professional technical schools (*Srednie Professionalno Technicheskoe Uchilishcha*). Most students have completed grade 8 general education and undertake a three-year course for trade training diplomas and general education to the level of *Attestat* (matriculation). The 1984 reforms emphasized the role of the SPTU which, unlike the old PTUs (see below) contain compulsory general education. The annual intake will rise from 1 to 2 million according to economic needs.
2. Secondary vocational schools (PTUs), which admit only grade 8 leavers and offer one- or two-year courses with little general education and which students complete on a part-time basis when they are in employment. These are being phased out in favour of SPTUs.
3. Part-time evening schools (VPTUs) where students, while working, can qualify for a trade diploma and complete their secondary education.

The Committee is also responsible for liaising with the two ministries for vocational training in secondary schools and for special courses of vocational training in the tertiary institutions, as well as for ensuring orderly arrangements for progression from general secondary school to SPTU, and thence in a few cases to higher education. In particular, the teacher and instructor training, retraining and updating for the SPTUs is carried out in the tertiary institutions.

Structure and progression

Compulsory education starts at the age of six with grades 1 to 4 in elementary school. This is followed up by going to either so-called 'incomplete secondary schools', catering for grades 5 to 8, or the 'complete secondary schools' which continue through to grade 10. Children can leave either type of school at grade 8 to take low-grade employment as unskilled workers or to enter an SPTU. Students at 'complete secondary schools' may stay on to pass their Attestat at 17 to 18 years (grade 10) and then take a competitive entrance examination to enter higher education, or enter an SPTU.

The reforms of the 1980s have given greater emphasis to the development of the complete secondary schools, and to encourage entrance to SPTU from grade 10. As yet, however, only a minority of pupils do this. Those entering at grade 8 take a three-year SPTU course and those at grade 10 a one-year course. At one SPTU which I visited, 650 of the 700 students had entered at grade 8 and 50 at grade 10. Given that the grade 8 students were on a three-year course, this implies a proportion of slightly less than 20 per cent entering from grade 10. The proportion may be increased, as it has been found that those who enter SPTU after a full secondary education to grade 10 require less training (I was told half as much) to become fully effective in industry when in turn they leave the SPTU.

An SPTU is run by a director, appointed by the State Committee, together with two deputies: one in charge of vospitanie (moral and political education), the other running technical training and production processes. There is also an administrative and technical secretary responsible for the administrative and support staff. There are three kinds of teaching staff: teachers and senior teachers, who deal with the academic, theoretical and general educational studies; instructors, who run the practical trade training in the workshops; and tutors, who look after the welfare and organized extra-curricular activities of students, most of whom live in hostels attached to the SPTU. Academic staff are grouped into 'commissions' headed by a chairman, while instructors work directly to a senior instructor.

The curriculum

The three-year SPTU course comprises some 5,000 hours of instruction of which 2,400 hours are for academic work, including social studies, a course of Marxist-Leninist principles, since communist ethics 'define the context of educational work at the vocational schools'. Indeed, throughout the whole educational system these two strands of *obrazovanie* (education or schooling) and *vospitanie* ('upbringing or character training in schools, embracing moral, social, cultural aspects of schooling' Zajda, 1980) coexist. Soviet psychology maintains that young people learn and develop within the context of structured intervention by adults and that three factors determine development — heredity, the environment, and social interaction. The environment of the school is seen as compensating for what may be lacking in the home, and is deliberately constructed to instil communist etiquette and conduct (*povedenie*). The implementation of this crucial element of Soviet education is ensured by its central control.

In the classroom the result is step-by-step instruction, frequent testing (usually objective-type), rote learning, repetitive processes, centrally produced textbooks, a heavy reliance on audiovisual aids (also centrally produced), and the practice of introducing innovative methods of teaching only after rigorous research to prove their effectiveness. There is little or no opportunity for individual teachers to show their initiative by matching their style and content of teaching to the particular group of students in front of them.

A vocational element in education starts in elementary school. The subject of 'labour training' systematically introduces children to work from grade 1. Grades 1 to 4 concentrate on basic handcraft skills with a variety of materials and produce, for example toys, visual aids for use in school, or carry out simple school maintenance and horticulture.

While at general secondary school every child has the opportunity to master a craft skill. Grades 5 to 9 study and practise working with wood and metal, electric technology, technical drawing and analyse the main branches of the public economy of the USSR. Grade 8 emphasizes working in teams to produce goods in school workshops, local enterprise or in the local SPTU. The 'complete secondary schools' have introduced a programme of closely integrated theory and its application to work, which includes an increasing amount of time spent working on special production lines within local enterprises, on the lines of the model operating in the German Democratic Republic.

All schools are required by law to work with a patron base enterprise (*shefy*) to develop labour training. Local Soviets decide on the local need for skills, and hence what each school will offer. Profits from goods are reinvested in the school. Concurrent with labour training, systematic vocational guidance has been instituted for which the State Committee for Labour and Social Affairs is responsible, by organizing guidance in schools and centres across the USSR. One effect of this vocational guidance is that all young people who are not able to get into higher education and thus 'escape their fate' are virtually earmarked for the local factory or other enterprise from their early teens, and the trade they are trained in at the SPTU will largely depend on the labour requirements of that enterprise rather than on personal choice.

What is taught in relation to each trade at SPTUs is decided centrally by the State Committee through the All-Union Scientific Centre for Methods of Vocational Training. The centre works with the National Committee for Labour Affairs to produce lists of trades, associated jobs and job descriptions, to develop the relevant curricula and to produce textbooks and audiovisual aids. The 'plan' and the 'programme' are the two main documents which govern all training. An SPTU curriculum for mechanical engineering is shown in Table 1; those for other trades would follow similar patterns in the allocation of hours.

SPTU Curriculum (Mechanical Engineering)

Areas of study and subjects	Total number of hours during three-year training period
Vocational area of study including:	2,564
industrial training on machinery	2,110
special processes	231
tolerance and technical measurements, mechanical engineering: materials and technology, technical drawing, fundamentals of economics	233
General educational area of study including:	2,386
Russian language and literature	217
mathematics	322
history	239
physics and astronomy	312
chemistry	191
a foreign language	114
social science, geography, biology	189
aesthetic education, physical culture, etc.	802
Total:	4,950

Table 1. *Allocation of hours in a sample SPTU curriculum*

Table 1 illustrates how the curriculum lists the subjects to be taught and allocates the number of teaching hours to them; the associated syllabus details the content of each subject and the step-by-step sequencing of each topic within a subject.

The broad training consists in the first year of the special technologies of the industry or service, safety, technical drawing and familiarization with equipment and processes used in the factory. In the second year the emphasis shifts more to vocational and practical training in the workshops which simulate the production line, while in the third year increasing time (up to three days a week) is spent working in the factory, under supervision, on production of goods. The All-Union Scientific Centre has been developing a single document which contains a set of 'core skills' on which to concentrate for the maximum transfer of learning and the teaching methods for each skill. Meanwhile, the All-Union Research Institute for Vocational and Technical Training is concerned with developing model curricula for future trades, such as computing (informatics) and automation technologies.

In June of the final year students sit the state examination for their Diploma in Vocational Training after which, if successful, they are awarded the badge of their trade. They have to pass in both general education and trade training. If they fail, they take on unskilled work and may return later to complete their studies. All students are guaranteed a job. Perhaps 10 per cent take advantage of the special preferences given to SPTU students to go directly into higher education institutions.

Extra-curricular activities

A significant factor throughout all Soviet education is the role played by youth organizations in the education of young people up to the age of 25. Between 7 and 10 years, most children join the Octobrist Movement, and at 9 or 10 years the Pioneer Movement. At 17 many young people join the 42 million strong All-Union Young Communist League (Komsomol); the SPTUs I visited in 1983 claimed a 96 per cent Komsomol membership. The movements provide extra-curricular activities, summer and work camps, hobby circles and class self-management. Members serve in socially useful roles within schools (for example as prefects) and take part in decision making within the institution. It is important for the student to obtain a good Komsomol report, which may determine entry into higher education.

Most SPTU students live in hostel accommodation. There are no fees to pay, and uniforms, textbooks, accommodation and three meals a day are provided free. Cut-price public transport is available and there are allocations of free tickets to concerts, theatres and other cultural activities. Students earn roughly 30 per cent of the going rate for their trade, which they retain and which increases in line with their competence. They have two weeks' holiday in the winter and six in the summer, the so-called 'fifth term' in which many participate in unpaid voluntary work in projects often organized by the Komsomol.

An important aspect of student life is self-management. At one level there are duties related to manning reception, serving meals, cleaning, tidying and maintenance, organized by student self-governing councils. At a more important level, self-government has a legal status in that students have the right to discuss improvements in academic process, ideological work, student progress, discipline and life in the school. Students participate with staff and with the SPTU academic council in making decisions concerning the payment of allowances to students who do not meet the prescribed criteria and staff who may not reach the high standards of competence required of them.

Benefits of the system

Those in countries with *ad hoc* and fragmented approaches to training and education may feel that the Soviet system has many beneficial aspects.

1. The legal requirement in many trades for a qualification as a licence to practise implies achievement of a known standard.
2. The centrally controlled syllabuses and single award-making body maintain a consistency of provision and standard of required achievement.
3. Vocational training is relevant to the economy it serves because of the integration of schools with economic enterprises within its locality.
4. General education is now seen to be as important as skills training since it provides the basic flexibility of workers in coping with future change.
5. Students are progressively introduced into the world of work, its obligations, duties and realities, and they develop the social and mental skills to enable them to cope with the transition from school to work.
6. Students see their training as relevant to their future work and as providing a route to further training and higher education if they so wish and can meet the entry requirements.
7. Student assessment is continuous, rigorous, and reinforces learning.
8. New curricula and teaching methods are introduced only after rigorous research to establish their validity.
9. The dual system of teachers and instructors in the schools maintains up-to-date knowledge and skills within the trades.
10. In-service training and staff development processes are readily available, systematic, rigorous and compulsory.
11. The quality of performance of teaching staff is regularly monitored and where necessary remedial action is taken.
12. There is considerable use of audiovisual aids in the classroom and the quality of materials provided is extremely high.

The integration of vocational training with industry, commerce and agriculture is another goal which other countries are striving to attain. One major achievement of the Soviet reforms is the legally enforced system of enterprise patronage (*sheftsvo*) for vocational schools, thus ensuring a relevant and cost-effective training system which is not deprived of funds, materials and staff as the economy fluctuates. However, such financing simply shifts funds on paper from one part of the socialist economy to another, so that the true cost-effectiveness is difficult to ascertain. Nevertheless, although much of the system is self-financing, the amount of money spent on training represents a significant proportion of national income.

Probably the most significant factor is central government control.

The Committee for Vocational Training has the same influence as those ministries concerned with public and higher education. All are backed by laws which confer authority and power to construct a unified system integrated with national policymaking.

Issues and problems

Performance standards

The resources put into vocational training are not, however, reflected in the quality of its output. Despite the care, the intensive training and insistence on high standards of achievement in even low-level skills, there is a large gap between training and its effects as reflected in the real world. Buildings are poorly constructed, service in shops and hotels minimal, and country life seems relatively untouched by the modern world of the city although 25 per cent of the working population is involved with agriculture. Consumer goods are scarce and shoddy, and life in the bleak landscapes of high-rise apartments can only be described as dreary.

This poor performance partly stems from causes outside vocational education. The management skills and process of Soviet production across the economy have recently been critically reviewed. From 1986 a new mode of management has been introduced to increase efficiency, quality and the technical level of production. In essence, enterprises have been given more autonomy and must try to run themselves on a self-financing basis. The result of these reforms may not only improve the performance of Soviet industry, but may also make it more attractive and interesting as a place to work.

The higher educational sector has also been criticized. Its effectiveness has been called into doubt, as managers believe that its graduates are generally incapable of doing their jobs on appointment. The past success of the system has created its own problem: with a shortage of skilled and qualified labour, employing bodies could not insist on quality. With the development of a more technologically based economy, the old strictly-defined curricula have failed to keep up to date, and critics have pointed out that in some areas it has taken ten years to develop new courses, by which time they are already obsolete for industry's needs.

Attitudes to vocational education

Nevertheless, some of the problems of Soviet industry can clearly be traced to vocational education. For example, it does not provide the same opportunities as higher education for upward social mobility. Despite the image of a classless society, upward social mobility into the privileged intelligentsia and party officials (*apparatchiks*) derives primarily from the universities and other VUZs; vocational training in the SPTUs runs a poor third choice. The lower abilities and lack of demonstrated attainment of SPTU entrants are reflected in the low percentage who go on to higher education, despite the privileged entry accorded to them by VUZs. For 60 years the USSR has tried both to improve the status and image of vocational training (which is, after all, fundamental to belief in the dignity of labour) and to direct more young people into it through quota systems and vocational guidance. The reforms of 1984 simply reinforce guidelines first laid down in the 1940s.

Because of this lack of upward mobility, most young people do not want to attend the SPTUs, where often they are trained in a trade which they do not intend to pursue; research has shown that the productivity of 'reluctant' workers was only 65 per cent of that of the willing. As a result, a system of mentors has been introduced in which some 4 million skilled workers, in collaboration with the Young Communist League, help novices master their jobs and instil a healthy set of work ethics.

Control of employment

Another aspect of vocational training is that it is a means of controlling the labour pool. Officially, unemployment does not exist in the USSR. This is partly because the economy cannot meet all the demands made of it; there is, as yet, no surplus capacity. There are indeed not enough skilled workers available to meet workforce needs. This may be partly accounted for by the virtually compulsory education of all young people up to the age of 19 which is followed by military service; the alternative of unskilled work and part-time study for the early school leaver is unattractive. The major part of the age range in which there is massive unemployment in the West is thus effectively taken out of the labour pool. Vocational training, together with higher education, effectively controls the annual input of young people into the labour pool according to the capacity of the economy to accept them.

Political education

One of the costs of Soviet vocational education is the politicizing process. The pressure to conform to 'socialist norms' laid down by the CPSU with its membership of 18 million (about 6 per cent of the population) envelops young people in powerful propaganda. Undoubtedly, vocational training could be more efficient — if less time were spent on political education — and more interesting if less centrally controlled. But pressure, competition and conformity seem to be part of communist society. Deviation from the norm brings both subtle and crude retribution. The result is an observable joylessness and lack of spontaneity.

Quality and motivation

Internal evidence, derived from the preliminary discussion for the 27th CPSU Congress in 1986, identifies how the vocational system has failed to meet expectations of high quality production by a motivated workforce.

Industry, particularly the light industry sector, has been criticized for not meeting fully or quickly enough the reforms introduced in 1984. First Secretary Gorbachev, when Chairman of the School Reform Society, demanded an increase of 150 to 200 per cent in the number of apprentices, and had construction begun on 60 new SPTUs and improvements on another 160. There is also no doubt that the general level of educational attainment has risen: from 1979 to 1982 the number of school leavers with a completed secondary education has risen from 50 per cent to 80 per cent. However, the links between the SPTUs, schools and industry have had to be strengthened and developed to create more work collectives.

The Trade Union Congress of the USSR, through its Committee for Youth Affairs, has been even more critical, pointing out that only two-thirds of young people under training have their skill level raised within the first two years of work. A survey of 10,000 young people in the Moscow and Volvograd areas showed that one-third changed their trade one or more times, explaining why so many are unable to obtain higher-graded craft skills. One of the major problems of industry has been the low level of skills in the workforce, holding back both growth and productivity. Reducing manual jobs by 20 per cent would release 25 million jobs. The first 5 million have already been realized, thus making people available for retraining, upgrading and promotion to more skilled craft jobs in the production ladder.

High technology

Vocational training has not as yet had to handle high technology. There is little evidence of basic computer literacy in the SPTUs, or of particularly complex machinery used in factories. The long-running rigidity of training, organized in a way to reflect the arbitrary division of the economy into branches, may militate against flexible retraining and against a planned lessening of reliance on labour-intensive processes.

There are indeed compelling needs to modernize and automate production. The Soviet Academy of Sciences has thus formed a new department of informatics, computer technology and automation. During 1985 some 50,000 computer engineering rooms were established in secondary schools. All children in grades 9 and 10 (15 to 17 year olds) will learn the rules and methods of problem-solving and of making rapid calculations on Russian-built microcomputers in the new subject of 'informatics' (this includes hardware, software, algorithms, mathematical modelling, image identification and the programming languages of BASIC and FORTRAN). The SPTUs have included in their programme the compulsory 'ABC of Information and Computing Science' and central authorities have already provided a curriculum and a teachers' guide.

In 1985 thousands of teachers attended summer school and 20,000 graduates were assigned from VUZs and industry to work in schools. All teacher training courses now include a compulsory computer literacy course, and in many areas district teaching and production centres for groups of schools have been established as the process of automation increases in industry. Since 1981, over 2,600 automated process systems have been introduced in the steel, cement and chemical industries alone. With a zero growth in the labour market it is planned to use some 100,000 robots, to add another 400 automated production lines to the economy and to introduce 300 computer-aided design systems (CADs).

It will be interesting to observe how information technology, which elsewhere in the world is leading to greater individualization and 'downloading' of learning, will thrive in the centralized Soviet system of vocational education.

References

Brine, J, Perrie, M and Sutton, A eds (1980) *Home, School and Leisure in the Soviet Union* George Allen & Unwin: London

Constitution of the Union of Soviet Socialist Republics (1984) Novosti Press Agency Publishing House: Moscow

Learning a skill: training young workers in the USSR (1983) *Socialism: Theory and Practice* 7: 73-78

Lisovsky, V (1983) *Soviet Students: Questions and Answers* Novosti Press Agency Publishing House: Moscow

Lunacharsky, A (1981) *On Education: Selected Articles and Speeches* Progress Publishers: Moscow

Marsh, D T (1984) *Vocational Training in the USSR: Further Education Staff College Information Bank 2023g* Bristol

Soviet Weekly 2204-2308 May 1984 - September 1986: London

Vocational Training in the USSR (1982) Novosti Press Agency Publishing House: Moscow

Weaver, K (1981) *Russia's Future* Praeger Special Studies: New York, NY

Zajda, J (1980) *Education in the USSR* Pergamon Press: Oxford

7. Information technology in Brazil

A J Romiszowski

Summary: This chapter presents a case study of an approach to adult technician retraining through modular, individualized, courses which utilize information maps as a format for the organization and presentation of content and a microcomputer-based management system as a means of evaluation, diagnosis and advice to learners, as well as rapid and flexible access to appropriate training materials.

Although developed for electronics technicians and implemented in Brazil, the system may be a model for upgrading/recycling courses in many other subject areas and most other countries, both developing and developed.

New technology: bane or blessing?

Educators in Brazil view the new technologies with mixed feelings:

'The advanced nations, with their elevated level of socio-political development, large investment potential, efficient infra-structure and extensive industrial capacity, absorb the "information revolution" into their operational context, understanding that the mastery of this new technology is decisive for maintaining their leadership and status.

'In the case of developing countries, where the political and cultural dimensions are under-developed in comparison to economic growth, the incorporation of new technology tends to increase the "gap", transforming the nation into a production sub-system of the developed world.

'Our capacity to govern the direction of this revolution will depend on the familiarity we have with the techniques involved and the control we have over the resultant social effects.' (EMBRATEL — Project CIRANDA, 1982)

This quote is taken from an official Ministry leaflet, which introduced a project that has grown into a nationwide computer users' network, with educational and cultural objectives. That such a network should be officially sponsored, that the idea sprang from the Ministry of Communications and not the Ministry of Education, and that the network is operated by the country's telephone company (rather than by schools or universities) is indicative of the trends that I shall attempt to analyse and illustrate in this chapter.

I shall start by looking at how the telecommunications and micro-electronics revolutions have developed in Brazil and shall then examine some case studies of how the skilled labour shortage is being tackled.

The telecommunications revolution of the 1970s

In a country the size of Brazil, communications are of prime importance. However, due to unco-ordinated foreign investment over the years, the country found itself in the early 1970s on the brink of a telecommunications revolution but with over 200 separate privately owned telephone companies, with no standardization of equipment or systems and no effective inter-city or international network. A state-owned company, EMBRATEL, was set up to provide the long-distance communications within the country by means of a network of microwave booster stations and internationally by means of satellite communications. Soon it was possible to make long-distance phone calls with excellent quality of communications — so long as you made your call from the EMBRATEL office. Very few of the private local companies were connected to the network.

In the mid-1970s the government formed another company, TELEBRAS, as a holding organization, empowered to tax all telephone services and use the money to buy out the private operators. By 1977, Brazil had a national system comprising 25 state-based telephone companies, all linked into the EMBRATEL long-distance network. This rapid progress was not without its difficulties, given the variety of telephone equipment and communication systems installed in different regions. It was said that Brazil could serve as a scaled-down model of the world's telecommunications system — no manufacturer of note and no technique of importance was without its representation in one or other of the private companies that were taken over, not to mention the variety of skills and methods of work that had been transferred from the countries of origin. TELEBRAS set about the task of welding this variety into a coherent system. Two important parts of this work were accomplished with UN assistance: a project to set up and develop a powerful research and development centre in Campinas, São Paulo State, and a project to develop standardized work methods and training systems to be implemented in all 26 of the new companies (Romiszowski and Machado, 1978).

As a result of these and other stimuli, Brazil entered the 1980s as an important manufacturer of telecommunications equipment and an exporter to other Latin American countries of both the hardware systems being developed at Campinas and the training know-how developed alongside.

The microelectronics revolution of the 1980s

With the 1980s, the micro revolution has arrived in full force. In Brazil the large mainframe computer market was dominated by the multinational giants. IBM, for instance, had local manufacturing facilities capable of supplying all local needs, and profited from low labour costs to export efficiently to the rest of the continent. However, this and other similar operations were no more than assembly lines using nearly 100 per cent imported components. In line with the trend to nationalize all new technologies and to restrict imports severely, the government launched the 'reserved market' policy, which restricts the microelectronics industry to Brazilian-owned companies. This *Reserva do Mercado* was instituted for a period of eight years, considered to be a sufficient amount of time to allow a national microelectronics and computer industry to grow without the feared competition of the multinationals.

We are not yet out of the eight-year period, although there are signs that with recent government changes the policy may be modified or indeed abandoned. However, more than half the intended period has passed and we have indeed seen some phenomenal growth of local industry. The reserved market served as an excuse to develop products which were more or less copies of foreign technology, without incurring most of the normally associated development costs and yet, in a market totally protected against imports, being able to charge well in excess of foreign prices. The expected proliferation of 'clones', based on Apple, TRS, Sinclair and principally IBM technology, appeared on the market, as did a host of 'pirate' software. The early boom in sales encouraged many entrepreneurs to enter this sector and although some have burnt their fingers in the process, the Brazilian microelectronics industry has in five years grown from miniscule proportions to enter the world's top ten in terms of turnover and manpower employed. There are signs that some parts of the industry are maturing, forming joint ventures with foreign patent holders or indeed investing in the development of new products. Other sectors of industry are hungry for control systems, tele-processing systems and all the other specialized products made possible by microchip technology.

All this adds up to a powerful new industry, the only one to grow vigorously over the last few years of economic depression. The main factor holding back even faster growth is the acute shortage of skilled labour.

Education's slow reaction

It suddenly became fashionable to discuss the question of computer studies and new curricula in both the vocational and non-vocational sectors of the educational system. As microcomputers became plentiful, at least in the shops and the homes of the affluent, interest also developed in the potential use of the computer as an educational *tool*. Educational journals began to carry articles on foreign applications of CAI (computer-aided instruction) (Romiszowski, 1983a, 1983b). Conferences and seminars began to give space to the topic (ABT, 1983). However, little was done to put the computer to use in the schools. The state schools were not able to invest their near-zero resources in equipment which carried what was by international standards a much inflated price-tag. Private schools in some cases went ahead, but their progress was hampered by the scarcity of locally applicable courseware and their efforts were seen by the public sector as one more example of the growing gap between the haves and the have nots. By and large, the early stages of the nation's computer literacy programme were furnished by private enterprise — myriads of short courses on principles of computing, BASIC, Visicalc or whatever, offered by small night schools, usually owned by one or other of the growing number of computer stores: 'Buy your micro here and receive free tuition . . .'.

The Ministry of Education tried to impose some order by setting up a government organization (CENIFOR), empowered to approve and finance educational research and development projects in this field and also to control the quality of educational courseware put on the Brazilian market (Lima, 1984a, 1984b). Unfortunately, as is so often the case with government organizations, there has been more talk and paperwork than stimulation of progress. Much time was spent on discussing and establishing criteria by which to judge and evaluate educational courseware, but to date no effective action has been taken to increase the amount of courseware available. Some five long-term research projects have been sponsored (MEC, 1983), all based in renowned universities, but to date no large-scale effects of this research have filtered down to the school system as a whole (Peixoto, 1984; ABT, 1985).

Industry's role in promoting tele-informatics education

The rapidly expanding telecommunications and microelectronics industries could not afford to wait for the educational system to catch up with the new technologies. They acted in two ways — by internal training to satisfy immediate manpower needs, and by exerting their influence on the two vocational training institutions, SENAI and SENAC, to offer relevant vocational education of satisfactory quality. The first to act on a large scale were the state-owned telecommunication companies, which since the 1970s had been suffering acute technical staffing problems. Both TELEBRAS and EMBRATEL devoted considerable resources to the development of internal training courses — many in modularized form, administered at a distance. Very soon, EMBRATEL realized that one manpower problem holding back progress was not the lack of highly specific technical knowledge and skills in the relatively small number of designers and engineers, but a general lack of understanding and 'feeling', in all employees, about telecommunication and computer concepts and possibilities. What was needed was 'total immersion' in a simulated 'informaticized society' — computer literacy by daily exposure. This viewpoint gave birth to 'Projeto CIRANDA', an attempt to link all key EMBRATEL personnel in a microcomputer network that would be used on a daily basis to carry out all manner of business — professional, social, educational and cultural. In time, the CIRANDA network was made available to many groups outside EMBRATEL and has become one of the key catalysts of computer literacy and educational courseware utilization in Brazil. We shall examine this project in more detail later on.

The mushrooming small entrepreneurial companies could not invest in developing tailor-made in-company training. They had to rely on the state vocational education system. This includes the National Service for Industrial Learning (SENAI) and the National Service for Commercial Learning (SENAC), two institutions which run networks of technical training colleges and are supported by a special tax levied on local industry. As local enterprise pays the bills and is represented on the governing bodies, it was not very long before pressure was applied to supply the forms of training that were now becoming of paramount importance. SENAC has set up a network of centres that cater for the *user* of new technology (especially the electronic office) and SENAI has moved to set up the microelectronics technician training programmes we shall be describing below.

Project CIRANDA: the 'teleinformaticized community'

The background to 'Projeto CIRANDA' has already been given. Technically speaking, it is nothing more than a network of microcomputer users linked to a central mainframe computer via the telecommunications network of EMBRATEL. Its interesting aspects are the way it was set up and how it is run today.

Initially the project was set up for EMBRATEL personnel. All employees were offered the opportunity to acquire the necessary equipment on very favourable interest-free terms. The microcomputer used was the PROLOGICA-CP500, a Brazilian-built version of the first TRS-80 computer, which could be linked by means of an appropriate modem to the network via the normal EMBRATEL telecommunications channels and a specialized data communication service. Many thousands of these computers were thus sold and linked up. A significant portion of them soon changed hands, for a smart profit margin, so that a considerable number of enthusiastic computer users, not necessarily EMBRATEL employees, were soon making use of the services offered. To ratify the existing state of affairs, EMBRATEL in a very short time opened the network to many non-employees, so that CIRANDA became the first and largest computer users' network in the country (EMBRATEL, 1982).

The services offered cover a wide range of interests and are designed to involve all members of the user's family. They include electronic mail; a teletext service of useful, regularly updated information; a register of network members and their interests; a news bulletin; a library of applications software that may be downloaded to individual micros; a classified advertisement service; a classified index to medical and other community services for every part of the country; a library of educational courseware, and a teleconferencing service which is used, among other things, for administration of the network on a truly democratic model. This last service is perhaps the most unique aspect of CIRANDA. Each member of the community may propose motions or suggestions and each member may vote on these issues in a method of participation modelled on ancient Athens. Even governing representatives are voted in by computer networking. The aim is to make the computer a regular and indeed indispensable tool of everyday life and thus by natural means achieve the necessary level of computer literacy which will guarantee the intelligent use of this new technology.

The SENAI project: hi-tech on a low budget

I have described the CIRANDA project in some detail because, although it is not a 'hard' vocational education project, it is a spin-off from some very hard, but not completely successful training activity in the telecommunications industry. It is a somewhat novel approach to the development of a general level of literacy in a new technology which is essential for its efficient and intelligent utilization. Another reason for mentioning CIRANDA is that it has served as one of the chief catalysts in the process of introducing new technology into the educational system. The CIRANDA project has for some years now been collaborating with a small but increasing number of schools and colleges, making equipment available on loan or on special purchase terms and furnishing free access to the educational software and other informational materials (EMBRATEL, 1983). There is no reason why the CIRANDA network could not play an important role in some future *vocational distance-education* system. The SENAI project that I shall now describe in some detail could well be a candidate, or at least a model, for such a system.

The project's background

Although SENAI is a national organization, it is decentralized at the individual state level in order to respond better to local needs. Financing is also decentralized, local industry contributing to local technical schools. As the state of São Paulo is by far the most industrialized, and is a leader in microelectronics and telecommunications, it is natural that it should have been the first to attempt to fill the gap of skilled technicians in the maintenance and design of digital logic circuits and equipment.

In December of 1983 an electronics project, composed of no less than 16 subprojects, was launched. Three of these subprojects involved the development of modular training courses designed to update the knowledge and skills of technicians already employed in the industry

(SENAI, 1984). As the project intended to use modern educational technology to teach modern electronic technology, the assistance of my company, SISTECH, was sought during the instructional design stages of the three courses. The course design described here is an attempt to get the most out of the relatively limited resources available, while creating a model that could be technologically extended in the future.

The modular training courses

The modular structure of these three training programmes was dictated by the characteristics of the target population and their disparate needs, identified in the early stages of analysis. Each programme is composed of several modules of about two weeks in duration. Trainees may enter the programme at any point that is suited to their present needs and skills.

Each module has both a theoretical and a practical component, emphasis in the latter being placed on simulation of the tasks actually performed in the industrial context. The theoretical component is thoroughly documented in the form of structured, or 'mapped' materials, suitable for both initial learning and later on-the-job reference. These materials are developed in accordance with the rules and suggestions of the information mapping (IM) system of structured writing* (Horn, 1974), together with some additional rules developed especially for this project.

In addition to the use of these 'maps', trainees are encouraged to make full use of other materials available in the training centre library, especially articles in specialist journals — often the most up-to-date sources of information in a fast-developing field such as microelectronics.

The instructional materials

The system of writing was designed to incorporate features that make it especially useful for the authoring of computer-based textual material. One of these features is the organization of the information in 'maps'. A map presents, in structured format, all the information deemed necessary on one specific topic. The title of the map clearly indicates the topic in question, thus facilitating the reader's access to relevant information. The information that is presented is closely analysed and classified into types (eg definition, example, application, common synonyms, relation to other topics, etc). Each different type of information is presented in a separate and clearly marked-off 'block' (paragraph) and is identified by a descriptive subtitle that, once more, facilitates the reader's selection of relevant information. The material may be read in a flexible, non-linear manner, adapted to the user's needs and learning style.

Another characteristic of this system that is of especial value in the SENAI project is the facility with which mapped materials may be

* The names 'information mapping' and 'infomaps' are registered trade marks of Information Mapping Inc, Lexington, Massachusetts. The system was originally developed by Robert Horn and his associates (Horn, 1974).

updated or modified. The requirement for flexible, non-linear use implies that each block of information must be written in such a way that it makes sense on its own, when removed from the context of the material that immediately precedes and follows it. This feature, coupled with the division of the material into relatively short maps that deal with only one topic (or aspect of a topic), facilitates the processes of modification and updating of the content.

Yet another characteristic that we are exploiting in the SENAI project is the use of clear map titles as indicators of the key words that may be used to relate a given map to a given book chapter or article available in the library.

Integrating the library into the system

As outlined above, trainees are expected to make extensive use of the library for a variety of reasons. They may use this resource to follow up topics of individual interest that go beyond the objectives of the module, or to gain further technical knowledge on topics dealt with in condensed form in the course, or to review concepts that were not fully understood in classroom sessions, or simply to access reference data which they do not need to learn but which is nevertheless necessary for the execution of practical assignments. The librarians have the task of indexing the existing materials in such a way that useful study prescriptions may be offered to individual trainees.

In order to perform this task, the librarians require a structured set of keywords that, as a whole, define the subject area in question (in our case, digital electronics and its applications). This keyword set is provided by the authors of the mapped materials, who take great pains to analyse the subject thoroughly and structure the maps so as to include all relevant keywords in the map titles and subtitles. This knowledge structure serves as a guide to trainees when using the materials and as a classification tool for librarians when indexing other related materials available.

Computer-managed control and evaluation

The evaluation of the practical activities is generally based on the instructor's observations of the trainees and the analysis of their final reports. These observations are, however, only one part of the total evaluation and control system. Entry into a particular laboratory activity is controlled by a pre-test which checks the trainee's mastery of prerequisites that should have been learnt in preceding modules or units. These tests are currently administered in normal printed paper format. However, the items are listed in a classified item bank in the database, together with cumulative data on the use made of specific items, error frequencies and so on.

Thus the database enables the same test to act both as a prerequisite test to control entry into laboratory activities and as a post-test that provides both summative and formative data to the instructor and other interested parties. For example, materials developers may access the database in order to identify areas that require revision, instructors may use it as a powerful aid to diagnosis and treatment of specific individual learning difficulties, and training administrators and client organizations may request a range of summative reports on the progress and overall outcomes of the training programmes.

The system specification

The system runs on a 6502 8-bit Apple-compatible micro, with a Z-80 card running the CP/M operating system. The relational database management system used is D-Base II. The system includes the following:

- ☐ a series of database files for registering students, enquiries regarding the status of students, etc;
- ☐ a library database, organized on the basis of keywords that are linked to the structure of the mapped instructional materials (as described earlier);
- ☐ a means of *identifying/classifying* test items and the use made of them (we do not store the full text of the test items in the system, due to limited storage capacity and to difficulties associated with the graphics content of many of the items);
- ☐ a means of generating prescriptions based on the performance of individual students on a specific module or part of a module, indicating relevant maps/library materials.

With regard to the mass storage needs of the system, we are using a 10-megabyte hard disc. This, as indeed are all the hardware components of our system, is Brazilian-manufactured.

In summary, therefore, our system has many, if not all, of the characteristics of most systems for the computer-based management of instruction. One characteristic currently absent from our system, which many other systems (designed to run on much more powerful hardware) generally have, is the ability to store the test items and thus generate tests or offer online testing capabilities. This is outside the storage capabilities of our present hardware. Given the requisite expansion of storage, however, the D-Base II software would be capable of handling this. On the other hand, the system does offer the rarely met and perhaps unique capability of integrating systematically developed instructional materials with other resources not so developed, knitting the combination into a system in which one set of materials complements and enriches the other. Due to this capability, the system immediately ceases to be totally bound by some set of pre-specified learning objectives, or by some predetermined set of learning sequence and strategy alternatives.

The system described and currently in operation can be characterized as economical, practically feasible and largely adequate for the requirements of the parent institution. It is seen to be economical in that it uses only readily available hardware and software, of specifications that may now be obtained 'over the counter', as it were, in a growing number of countries that have even quite young microcomputer industries. It is seen to be practically feasible, from the experience of SENAI, São Paulo, in managing to take the described project from initial conception to full-scale implementation in a matter of months (the project team was modest in number and largely new to projects of this nature). It is seen to be largely adequate by SENAI, designed as it was to meet the specific philosophy and set of constraints which govern the mode of operation of the institution.

The vocational training system of the future

The system installed at SENAI can be considered an experimental model, capable of many further enhancements. In an earlier paper (Arce and Romiszowski, 1985) the technical details are more fully explained, as is the possibility of extending the computer management facility by operating on a local network serving several remote schools from one larger database stored in a minicomputer with the adequate memory capacity. This earlier paper also outlines in more detail how the information maps may be readily transformed into electronic format for online access, given the requisite power and memory in the hardware. A later paper (Romiszowski, 1985) gives more detail on the instructional design principles employed and the importance of the knowledge structure created by the maps' authors as part of any future 'expert teacher' or 'adviser' system on digital electronics. I argue there that the SENAI system is indeed a simulation of an expert system for the teaching of electronics, where the maps form the structured *knowledge base* and the instructor when acting as evaluator and guide is performing the role of the *inference engine*. The data collected in the database may be used to document (and later transform into a heuristic program) the best teaching tactics of the best instructors we have.

Here, however, I would like to close by emphasizing yet one more extremely practical development that such a system may undergo. Given that SENAI is a national body, with hundreds of technical schools spread over an area somewhat larger than the whole of Europe, and given also that in a very short time all these schools will be offering *some* vocational training at *some* level on *some* aspects of digital logic and microcomputers; given further that the SENAI network of schools is not the only group of institutions that are interested in offering such training, and given finally that the structure of the knowledge base and the layout of the information in the maps makes them useful in most related courses, whatever the specific objectives, it would seem to make sound economic sense to network the information nationwide: through CIRANDA, for example.

Not only is it probable that in this day and age the distribution costs *via* electronic data networking would compare quite favourably with the printing of perhaps thousands of copies of a manual of several hundred maps (only a fraction of which would be used by any one student) but the learning management system may also be made available to remotely located users (both instructors and 'lone' students). The greatly increased usage and data flow would enable the more accurate adaptation and revision of the system to serve a variety of target student groups better, taking into consideration the students' own suggestions of improvements to content, examples or exercises.

In its present state of development, our knowledge base resembles an electronic encyclopaedia, rather like the Grolier service already offered in the USA. Unlike the Grolier electronic encyclopaedia, ours is limited to a tightly defined subject area and goes into much more depth, but just like the Grolier service it would adapt to the needs and interests of the user, presenting general overviews or detailed studies as requested, cross-referencing automatically and so on.

At a more advanced state of development, we may be able to offer to the interested public at large a truly efficient (if only 'artificially intelligent') expert tutor/adviser on digital electronics. Our tutor may be limited to theoretical subject matter, or may even be able to guide and test us through some simple home experiments using a standard kit of parts — after all, we could wire up our circuit designs and test them out with a computer-controlled multimeter, so we do not even have to type in our readings to let the 'expert tutor' know how well we have performed in practice.

Before we get too carried away with ideas, let us just remember that in the new technology game, this morning's pipe dreams often turn out to be this afternoon's reality. And we can often *simulate* the future systems we would like to have, using simpler technologies, and people as actors, so that we are ready with our ideas and plans when the hardware and resources we need finally catch up. The vision conjured up here of an individualized, distance education system for specific subject areas of vocational courses (not necessarily the whole of vocational education, but by no means only digital electronics), is not far from a technical reality. The components of the system all exist separately. All that is required is to knit them together in an intelligent manner — and here I am not referring to the artificial intelligence of the one-subject expert system, but the true intelligence of the creative, innovative instructional designer.

Although such a system may enhance any vocational education programme, it would particularly benefit developing countries such as Brazil where needs are particularly urgent, traditional instructional resources scarce, trainee populations scattered and very varied as to the level of preparation, and distances are very large indeed.

As our opening quotation implies, successful absorption of the new technological revolution depends on our social, political, cultural and educational preparedness. In order to gain the necessary 'familiarity with the techniques involved' and to 'control the resultant social effects', we require both vocational and non-vocational education on all aspects of 'tele-informatics'. And what better way to gain knowledge *about* something than to *work with it*? As in the CIRANDA project, let us use new technology to learn about new technology. As in the SENAI project, let us plan ahead to use the technologies available in such a way that we start learning about the technologies which are still around the next corner.

References

ABT (1983) *Working paper for the discussion group on computers in education, at the 1983 Seminar on Educational Technology of the Brazilian Association for Educational Technology* Associacao Brasileira de Tecnologia Educacional (ABT): Rio de Janeiro

ABT (1985) *Working paper for the discussion group on computers in education, at the 1985 Seminar on Educational Technology of the Brazilian Association for Educational Technology* ABT: Rio de Janeiro

Arce, J F and Romiszowski, A J (1985) Using a relational database as a means of integrating instructional and library materials in a computer managed course *Proceedings of the 26th ADCIS International Conference* Association for the Development of Computer-Based Instructional Systems, Western Washington University, Bellingham: Washington, DC

EMBRATEL (1982) *Projeto CIRANDA: a Primeira Comunidade Teleinformatizada do Brasil* EMBRATEL, Ministerio de Comunicacoes: Rio de Janeiro

EMBRATEL (1983) *Unindo Esforcos: Empresa e Escola (Convenio EMBRATEL/ Centro Educacional de Niteroi)* EMBRATEL, Ministerio de Comunicacoes: Rio de Janeiro

Horn, R E (1974) *Course Notes for Information Mapping Workshop* Information Resources Inc: Lexington, MA

Lima, M C M A (1984a) Informatics and education (Informatica e educacao) *Tecnologia Educacional* 56: January/February 1984 ABT: Rio de Janeiro

Lima, M C M A (1984b) A informatica educativa no contexto do Ministerio de Educacao e Cultura *Tecnologia Educacional* 59: July/August 1984 ABT: Rio de Janeiro

Ministerio de Educacao e Cultura (MEC) (1983) *Projeto 'EDUCOM'* MEC: Brasilia

Peixoto, M do C L (1984) O Computador no Ensino de Segundo Grau no Brasil *Tecnologia Educacional* 60: September/October ABT: Rio de Janeiro

Romiszowski, A J (1983a) Introduction to an annotated bibliography on computers in education (Computador na educacao: o que ha para ler?) *Tecnologia Educacional* 54: September/October ABT: Rio de Janeiro

Romiszowski, A J (1983b) The computer in education: how to get started on a shoestring (Computador na educacao: como comecar com o minimo de recursos) *Tecnologia Educacional* 55: November/December ABT: Rio de Janeiro

Romiszowski, A J (1985) Applying the new technologies to education and training in Brazil. In Rushby, N and Howe, A eds (1985) *Aspects of Educational Technology* (XIX) Kogan Page: London/Nichols Publishing: New York, NY

Romiszowski, A J and Machado, N H S (1978) Developing a large-scale modularized training system for Brazilian telecommunications. In Brook, D and Race, P eds (1978) *Aspects of Educational Technology* (XII) Kogan Page: London/ Nichols Publishing: New York, NY

SENAI (1984) *Comunicacao/SENAI* 58: July/August. Newsletter describing the 16 electronics training projects developed in 1983-85.

8. Technician education in East Asia: South Korea and Malaysia

Ian Waitt

Summary: Korea and Malaysia are two parallel rising trading powers. The need for more technicians in their growing industries is accepted although, particularly in Korea, the local concept of a technician is not necessarily the one understood in Western Europe. In Korea technician status is acquired through on-the-job training after leaving technical high school or through attendance at an institution of higher education. Production technicians are usually high school graduates and engineering technicians generally graduates of junior technical colleges. There is a constant push to upgrade institutions, and six of the junior technical colleges have become 'open universities'.

In Malaysia, where there was formerly little need for technician education, action is well under way to produce 20,000 technicians a year by the 1990s. This will be achieved by expansion of vocational skills linked to the creation of polytechnics.

The particular dynamics of the two countries and their different cultural backgrounds have led them to tackle the need for technicians in rapidly developing industry in quite different ways. The common ground is that each country has considerable national energy, determined goals and self-confidence. The different ways in which they are achieving their aims are appropriate to their own perceptions of their goals.

Introduction

It is increasingly assumed in the West that the countries of the Pacific basin will grow yet further, and that by the turn of the century they will have altered the focus of the world politically and economically, if not socially. The main current Asian imitators and competitors to Japan are Taiwan, Singapore, Hong Kong and South Korea. Among the prime aspirants to join their ranks is Malaysia.

South Korea

Korea's rise continues to be phenomenal. A closed, traditional, Confucian 'hermit kingdom' until the latter part of the 19th century, Korea suffered particularly forceful occupation by Japan from 1911 to 1945. The country became a source of cheap labour and a dumping ground for the

Japanese. Education was denied to all but an elite. Korean customs, central to a traditional society, were subjected to attempted eradication. The end of occupation was followed by the devastation of the Korean War and the division of the country. To the homogeneous population of Korea the partition of 'Han Gu' is a tragedy greater than, in its time, the division of Christendom to a European. ('Han Gu' means the 'Great Country'; its indivisibility is a central part of a cultural ethic in which country, people and heaven are united in a balanced whole.) At the end of the Korean War, there was scarcely a building left standing in Seoul; most of the population was illiterate, and the Republic of South Korea had no natural resources other than its people. The resources lay in the north, controlled by the continuingly brutal regime in Pyongyang. There is still no peace treaty. Border skirmishes continue (including northern attempts to tunnel through border territory). The armed forces consume a disproportionate amount of the south's wealth.

Thirty years after the armistice which concluded formal hostilities, South Korea is the world's fifteenth largest exporter; illiteracy has been virtually eradicated; and a quarter of the population of 41 million inhabit the concrete high-rise modern city of Seoul. The average GNP growth was over 8 per cent between 1962 and 1982. Despite the world recession, the growth figure is currently around 7 per cent. Per capita income is about a quarter of that of the UK.

The prime reasons for Korea's remarkable growth are similar to those found in Japan: traditional Confucian attitudes and government direction of industry. Whereas the predominant official religion of the country is Christianity, Confucian ethics predominate, even though younger generations retain less respect for traditional attitudes and values than do those aged over 45. Great respect is accorded to education; there is widespread national belief in hard work (working in Korea entails longer working hours than even the most workaholic Europeans are usually happy to tolerate); group co-operation, hierarchy, order and a deep national pride continue to produce an enthusiastic, dedicated and easily manageable workforce. The exploitation of these attitudes is well illustrated by the Saemul Undong movement which has produced breathtaking agricultural reform. Village collectivism was used as the base for adult literacy programmes, coupled with the provision by government of resources and technology according to the development plans of the villages: as a community showed that it could grow and use resources effectively, so further resources were supplied.

South Korea has enjoyed continuity in government — 20 years under the Presidency of Park Chung-Hee, followed by the Presidency of Chun Doo-Whan, unbroken since 1979, complemented by continuity of policy: an unswerving determination to promote long-term economic expansion. Although opposition parties currently have a majority in the national assembly it is wholly unlikely that any progressive political liberalization will deflect economic policy. The threat of the North not only demands political and military defence, causing and justifying the maintenance of the world's fourth largest standing army; it also entails the need for an ever-expanding economy. Like Japan, Korea has endeavoured to spread wealth throughout the population, and also like Japan has produced a type of government-industry corporate state. The mixture of flexibility and respect for authority which can be exercised and utilized by government and industry in a context of order and cultural predictability has allowed the weathering of political and energy crises. Progress is maintained, and is complemented by international development funding. Korea is the world's fifth largest debtor nation. The provision of aid reflects the facts of international politics. Korea also has the ability to repay its loans.

Korean industry followed the original Japanese model. Some 20 large industrial groups, primarily engaged in heavy industry — steel, chemicals and shipbuilding — arose with government support. The construction industry has diversified from being the engine of the reconstruction of the country and the stimulator of the domestic economy to international project contracting, largely in the Middle East and in developing countries. A relatively new motor car industry, again heavily directed by government, has already made impressive inroads into Europe and the USA. It is rare in Korea to see any vehicle not made in the country. The restrictions of choice are more than compensated for by national pride. Although textiles continue to generate large exports, the government has only fairly recently given attention to small- and medium-sized companies, in the predictable context of high technology. Government control of industry, apart from transport, electricity and some of the steel industry, is indirect. It is exercised through control of capital for investment and incentive-led policy. Companies are consequently encouraged to develop for export in various sectors. A key part of President Chun's international policy is concerned with opening up and consolidating export markets. Government ministers are frequently drawn from industry, and frequently return to it.

The industrial strategy to provide for rapid growth, as well as equipping the army and physically modernizing the country, was to promote export-led heavy industry, which could in turn supply cheap production for the home market. The domestic economy was held in check by import restrictions and taxation or disincentives to industry for marketing at home. The price for this policy has been that of insularity. Foreign companies have usually to conclude joint venture agreements to operate in Korea, and these have often been dogged by problems, although efforts are now being made for smoother operation.

Access to new technology has been difficult to acquire. As policy has begun to change to accommodate the needs and desired development of new technology industries, so the position of technical education has become more important.

Confucian values accord the educator and the educated enormous status. There are 110 universities (including engineering colleges of university status) in a country of 41 million people. Below these, usually linked or associated on the USA model, are numerous junior colleges. All offer degrees or associate degrees. Following the USA model, a Korean degree from a good university — the standard is variable — approximates to around A level standard in the UK, with the significant difference that education is for breadth rather than depth. Apparent equivalence can therefore be misleading. An able Korean graduate has the rough equivalence of something approaching 13 A levels. A good Korean masters' degree approximates to completion of a UK first degree. Learning is also Confucian: memorizing is the key; research usually means the gathering of comparative data; theory has higher status than practice; and breadth of study rather than depth produces flexibility. The high status of the professor — in university or college — means that it is at best difficult to effect curriculum change.

While the great Korean research institutes such as the Korea Advanced Institute of Technology, the recently established Korea Institute of Technology and the Seoul National, Yonsei and Korea Universities compare with any institutions of learning in the world, thereafter the tail is long. Below the elite, there are large gaps. Until the end of the 1970s, this did not matter. *Industry retrained the graduates to fit its purposes*, looking less for technical competence than for breadth of education, adaptability, and suitability for employment.

To understand Korean technical education, it is necessary to appreciate that parents will willingly pay for post-school education, that the great majority of school leavers demand further education, that possession of a degree is a social imperative, and that outside the great institutions there was, until recently, restricted contact between education and industry. Thus the technical high school graduate (who will have operated computer numerically controlled machines) and the high school graduate will both participate in something akin to a complex lottery for a university place. Many misfits occur. Many of those studying at technician level in a junior college of 'open university' would often wish if at all possible to gain a degree as an engineer. Since industry often initially employs university graduates and college graduates at the same level (the process is one of progression from the shop floor to whatever part of the company is ultimately appropriate), the person educated to the notional technician level (in effect, a watered-down university level) finds employment difficult: the company will prefer a university graduate, even if his actual level is that of a technician, and call him an engineer. Resultant technician-level graduate unemployment, while an issue, is no disaster when the economy is sufficiently expansionist to absorb the slack elsewhere. Compulsory military service also delays entry to employment, and adds further experience which increases employability.

However, the need to give attention to small- and medium-sized firms — which do not have the resources of the large corporations to retrain graduates — and the demands of the expectation for expansion of high technology are now altering the picture. In one sense this is wholly unexceptionable in that it is the needs of industry which are shaping the provision of technical education. In another sense it is revelatory: Korean heavy industry development required foreign engineering design.

Diversity has always required attention to quality maintenance in that new procedures entailed workforce retraining. Like other East Asians, Koreans have distinct learning patterns (attention spans, for example, are very much greater than in the West) and their formidable work rate helps ensure achievement, even if mistakes are made in the process. To be dismissive would be to make a very grave error. The demands are new, but it would be surprising if they were not met.

A further complication has arisen in that labour-intensive industry has been affected by rising wage levels, which have affected export costs. The desired compensatory shift to capital-intensive industry and industries of high technology is inhibited by restrictions in research and development. Major international funding has been acquired to stimulate science and technology development and research in education, linked to industry. While this development is targeted for higher education, Korea's educational system, as illustrated, will be utilizing some of this funding at technician level.

In 1981 Korea's industrial structure was: farming and fishery, 35 per cent; mining and manufacturing, 25 per cent; and tertiary industry, 40 per cent. By 1991, it is expected that the proportions will be 25 per cent, 30 per cent and 45 per cent respectively. The engineering colleges, new technological institutes, and open universities and junior colleges are intended to produce the technologists and the technicians to support this shift.

Korea's formal education system is composed of a basic six years of compulsory primary education followed by three years of middle school and a further three years of high school, academic or vocational. To be employed as operatives, those in receipt of primary education only must attend training institutes or gain apprenticeships. There are 283 institutes of vocational training with the capacity to produce over 60,000 operatives and semi-skilled workers annually. Middle school graduates in receipt of subsequent one-year intensive vocational training at one of the 23 institutes under the Ministry of Labour's agency, the Korea Vocational Training and Management Agency (VOTMA), are classified as semi-skilled workers. Skilled worker status is achieved after several years of industrial experience and completion of VOTMA upgrading courses, or else by completion of a three-year course at a VOTMA institute. VOTMA also provides master craftsman training, and instructor training.

Technician status (with the caveat that a Korean technician approximates only generally to the Western European concept of a technician) is acquired through on-the-job training after leaving technical high school, or through attendance at an institution of higher education. The usual Korean distinction is that a production technician is a high school graduate, and an engineering technician a graduate of a junior technical college. However, as noted above, a considerable number of technician posts are filled by graduates of the four-year engineering colleges. The two-year junior technical colleges (JTCs), annually enrolling some 100,000 students, are intended to produce middle-level technicians. Much of Korea's education is provided by private institutions. There has been a (government-encouraged) growth of JTCs, with many institutions attempting to cater for various desired specialisms. JTC graduates are largely employed ultimately as engineering or laboratory technicians, but their salaries are much lower than engineering graduates. This has helped to fuel the desire for status and a degree further; JTC graduate unemployment is adversely affected by competition from university/engineering college graduates: and the situation worsened in that JTC curricula are often watered-down versions of university curricula.

Two major steps have been taken to address this problem. One is the establishment of the new prestigious Korea Institute of Technology, under the Ministry of Science and Technology, and the other the establishment of 'open universities'.

There are six open universities, all of which are upgraded JTCs. Their mission is to provide continuing education for all, at Korean university level, on an open-access basis, and to train technologists (ie equivalents of Western European higher technicians) according to industrial needs. The openness is defined as possession of minimum admission requirements, regardless of age or sex. Admissions are divided equally between freshman and junior levels: the former requires at least one year of industrial experience after leaving high school, and the latter either graduation from a JTC or transfer equivalence. The system began only in 1982, partially supported by international funding, and has been attended by uncertainties, particularly regarding the curriculum, role, and linkage with industry. One of the open universities has modelled its curriculum on that of the UK Technician Education Council, and reports success. Funding, equipment, industrial liaison, curriculum, teacher training and practical work, however, all remain considerable issues for all the open universities.

All open university applicants must pass basic examinations, of which English and mathematics are compulsory. Fees are low and determined according to the number of credits (courses). Self-managed learning is possible. Intriguingly, in an overall system where at school level the curriculum is centrally devised and otherwise adapted from university models, the open university curricula are being established through 'industry-education co-operative committees'. The system is too young yet for judgements to be passed, but determined efforts are being made to grapple with the very serious problems which have beset Korean technician education. Necessity, in the form of the economic imperative, is bringing considerable change to a traditional, conservative, status-conscious educational system.

The four-year engineering colleges, all confusingly of university status or functioning as parts of universities, annually enrol some 140,000 students. Six of those colleges are designated to meet the needs of local industry.

Educational change in Korea is difficult to achieve because of the professional conservatism enforced by Confucianism. Yet government pressure, economic imperatives, hard work, and appreciation of the need to change are bringing rapid developments. The potential clash between the traditional and the new is at its most obvious in technical education. However, as Korea has so successfully undertaken development throughout its economy in the last 30 years, it seems likely that by 1991 the harnessing of technician education to determined industrial needs will have been achieved. The rapidity of development and change in Korea also means that this chapter may be overtaken by events by the time of publication.

Malaysia

One of the most intriguing dashes for development is being undertaken by Malaysia. Although relatively economically secure, Malaysia's particular problems have helped inspire a radical approach to desired growth, in which technician education is a key element.

The staples of Malaysia's economy are exports of rubber, tin, and palm oil. However, despite local acquisitions, many of the plantations and mines are under foreign ownership; there has also been considerable penetration of the domestic market by Japan and Korea. Constitutionally, the federation of states is marked by a divide between the relatively developed peninsular Malaysia (West Malaysia) and the resource-rich, underdeveloped Sabah and Sarawak (East Malaysia). The new economic policy, begun in the early 1970s, signalled a massive attempt at social and economic engineering. Traditionally, the Malay community held political power but was agrarian-based; the Chinese dominated business and industry; and the Indian (Tamil) community engaged mainly in clerical occupations. Direct state intervention, through the establishment of Malay trading corporations on the Japanese and subsequently Korean models, provision of loan and equity finance, was intended to increase Malay participation in the economy. Similar affirmative action was undertaken to increase Malay presence in public service. One result has been to increase the public sector presence in the economy to such a proportion that the government has determined to halt its growth. A consequence for education is that, as all teachers are public sector employees, at the very time that technical education is being required to expand, manpower resources are having to be reallocated from existing stock.

Since his accession in 1981, Prime Minister Datuk Seri Dr Mahathir Mohamad, as well as attempting to limit public sector growth via privatization and recruitment restriction, has emphasized a 'look east' policy. This is complemented by continuing linkages with the Western world, despite interruptions caused by the UK's dramatic raising of overseas student fees in 1981 (which caused wholly understandable large-scale resentment in Malaysia) and doubts concerning either the quality or price of overseas education offered by other developed nations. Currently there are 56,000 Malaysians studying overseas, and 52,000 in Malaysian universities. 'Look east' means especially learning from Japanese and Korean models, while retaining Malaysian approaches. The policy has entailed fostering the growth of heavy industry, production of the Proton Saga — the 'national car' — with Japanese co-operation, and promotion of large trading companies, staff training in Japan and Korea, and planned investment in steel, cement and petrochemicals.

To support desired industrial growth, both in manpower and the creation of a greater domestic market, the government requires a major population increase. A current population of some 15 millions is to be expanded to 70 millions by the year 2100. This solution, prompted by the unlikelihood of Malaysia being able to emulate Japan and Korea as major world exporters, presupposes the expansion of the domestic market, including the development of East Malaysia (in which oil is expected to have major importance). As with Korea, the impetus to the building and construction industries is intended further to support and enforce domestic expansion.

The policy pressures on education are therefore considerable. Despite the foundation of higher education establishments in Malaysia, overseas study, particularly in the UK, remains a traditional route with graduates returning often to public service. Technician education has been restricted in that there was formerly little need for it. Assisted by international funding, planning and action are well under way to move from the current production of technicians of around 4,000 a year (2,000 per year in 1982) to 20,000 per year by the 1990s. A massive development and training exercise is being undertaken, complicated by the inevitable possible contradictions of major educational and economic planning in national contexts. It would be remarkable if industrial growth, infra-structure development, and technician manpower production exactly coincided. Some wastage is therefore inevitable, as are mismatches. The officials in the Technical and Vocational Education Department of the Ministry of Education, and the educational administrators in the technical education system have a complex and difficult task before them. One obvious example of the problems to be faced is that while new institutions are being sited and developed in areas targeted for industrial growth, the industries are not yet all in development areas. Distance from relevant industry makes industrial liaison, let alone industrial experience, more than usually difficult to achieve satisfactorily.

Technician education is to be provided by the expansion of vocational schools linked to the creation of polytechnics, the model for which is the polytechnic at Ipoh, founded in 1969. This expansion is accompanied by similar development at the vocational and skilled worker levels through industrial training institutions under the Ministry of Labour.

While the scale of planned activities and their contexts may appear to be somewhat daring, any doubts must be set against Malaysia's economic performance during the last decade or so. Per capita income at around US $1,870 is among the highest in South-east Asia (about three-quarters that of Korea). Growth has been maintained at about 5.5 per cent per annum in the last decade. Agricultural improvement has offset periodic declines elsewhere in the economy. Manufacturing growth has been accompanied by diversification in exports (electronic goods, petroleum, natural gas, and palm oil). Unlike Japan and Korea, Malaysia operates an open economy. Domestic consumption has been led towards an import substitution pattern. Political stability has allowed firm government direction and fixed policies which, while allowing deficits due to international recession, have maintained progress towards desired long-term economic goals. However, while sharing some of the cultural factors of other East Asian countries, Malaysia is distinct in many respects. 'Look east' has produced models, but a more relaxed cultural base gives Malaysia a distinctly different overall approach.

Heavy international borrowing has been used to finance development as well as to finance continuing industrial expansion during recession. Technician education straddles the crossroads of expenditure restraint in the public services and locally and internationally financed major expansion.

The school system has recently been simplified, leading to two distinct secondary educational routes: academic and vocational. The vocational schools provide introductory skills training and produce semi-skilled graduates for the employment market; the industrial training institutes and other skill training institutes and centres prepare school leavers for industrial employment and upgrade the skills of employed workers. Technician education is mainly provided by the polytechnics. Unlike Korea, most education is directly provided under the public service. There are two polytechnics functioning fully, and two others soon to come into full operation. It is further planned to have three more polytechnics, one of which will be in East Malaysia, in operation by 1989. About 60 per cent of current entrants are sponsored by employers — mainly government departments. Certificate courses, arranged on a sandwich pattern involving industrial placement, are of 27 months' duration. The desired expansion is likely to result in the operation of two-session days. Other institutions also produce technicians, but the prime focus for development is the polytechnics.

As well as the obvious major investments in plant and equipment, the prime developmental need has been in staff training. While core staff for the new systems have been drawn from the existing polytechnics and vocational schools, it has also been necessary to provide overseas training — in management, and in technical skill upgrading, acquisition or development — for teachers currently employed in technical education. The curriculum is being updated or devised by external consultants in collaboration with polytechnic and ministry staff.

Among the more obvious complications are those of polytechnic teachers' salaries, in that competition from higher salaries in industry or for engineers in other government departments means that it is necessary to upgrade other existing staff. Industrial liaison is crucial to any technician education system, but it is made complex both by distance and the need to persuade industry at local level to support the national initiative, and also offers the danger of staff poaching. Senior staff in the polytechnics are young and dedicated. The present benefits of energetic application may turn to problems when staff grow old together. The inheritance of English as the common language has now been superseded through the national policy of Bahasa Malaysia as the language of instruction. While productive of cohesion and national identity, the price of Bahasa is greater difficulty for younger teachers sent to the West for skill upgrading, and in curriculum restrictions caused by the shortage of technician level reading material. This circumstance tends to support student reliance on teachers, a particular difficulty where recruitment and output pressures result in the operation of large classes (over 25,000 qualified applicants sought the 2,000 available places in 1984 alone). However, Malaysia is building from the base established in 1969 and is particularly conscious of quality in education, so it is unlikely to succumb to lower standards in order to produce technicians in bulk.

The development of technician education through a policy planned to mirror industrial expansion offers particularly exciting prospects. Given Malaysia's record and the determination of its government, it is likely that the results will be important. It is easy to note obvious current difficulties. But the cultural forces and peculiar dynamics of the Pacific basin are relevant. The rise of Japan and the achievements of Korea, Taiwan and Singapore are being echoed by particular variants from elsewhere in the region. The Malaysian example — and probably subsequently that of Indonesia — will be especially interesting. Determination, partnerships in planning, application, and adherence to stable and expansionist economic strategy produce results. Most salutary for educationists too, perhaps, is the firmness of the governments discussed here in harnessing education to desired economic goals.

Conclusion

Korea in North-east Asia and Malaysia in South-east Asia can be seen as two parallel and complementary rising trading powers. An analogy can be drawn with the relationships between Britain, North America and Germany in the 19th century and the relationships now between Japan, Korea and Malaysia.

The power of Japan is unlikely to decline quickly, but it is reducing some of the trading bases which stimulated its growth (textiles, shipbuilding). More obviously, Korea is replacing Japan as an exporter of certain manufactured items. Malaysia appears to be the sole South-east Asian nation capable at present of mounting resistance to Japan within its region. The process will take longer than Korea's remarkable acceleration of growth over some 35 years, and is obviously vulnerable to societal and global change.

Korea's need for development partnerships is less than Malaysia's and its self-confidence demonstrably greater. Whereas currently Malaysia seeks joint educational development and has begun a determined internal growth process, Korea's emphasis is on political protection balanced by trade agreements. A simple lesson is that nations which currently ignore either country will probably rue the omission by the end of the century.

Whatever 'experts' anywhere may think, it is a commonplace that any country invariably runs itself to its own level of acceptable general internal satisfaction. Thus, Korea's particular dynamic has brought it to its current remarkable achievements. Education is a major factor in that dynamic: whether by positive contribution (Confucian study productive of theoretical depth and enforcement of the work ethic) or negative effect (apparent lack of practical application in technical education), *this actually does not matter*. Apparent failings are compensated for by other means, the driving forces being national energy, determined goals, and self-confidence.

In Malaysia, racial differences can be seen to make very positive contributions. Each community is tempered and constrained by the other; economic policy is designed to harness those energies in the national interest, directing potential internal conflict towards national external goals.

Technical education content therefore is better seen as within national and economic processes: the message is the medium.

I have not discussed cultural perspectives at any length. However, technical education is also an application of science, and cultural beliefs and philosophy underlie and dominate scientific enquiry. Certain connections emerge between culture and technical education development in both countries. Korea balances Confucian logic with energy and national identity, viewing all processes within a holistic view of life. A new computer centre, or a renovated hotel, may be celebrated with an ancient, symbolic ceremony. Malaysia is more diverse culturally and shows other characteristics, one being the balance of nationalism, Islam and Chinese business applications: as the Chinese must learn Bahasa Malaysia to succeed in official life, so the Bumiputra entrepreneurs have to acquire business skills. If we then ask the ultimate educationist's question of 'where does the curriculum come from?' we may arrive at conclusions complementary to the economic data and predictive statements offered above.

Education is nothing if it is not about growth. Both Korea and Malaysia demonstrate a determination to achieve such growth. Readers from countries which are not experiencing growth on the Korean and Malaysian scale, or do not aspire to it, may be well advised to learn from these examples. They should consider whether their criticisms say more about their own perspectives than about any general principles and processes of technical education.

9. Technician education in New Zealand

Brad Imrie

Summary: This chapter reviews the development of technician education and training in New Zealand and discusses the work of the Authority for Advanced Vocational Awards (AAVA), the national body responsible for course and assessment requirements for technician qualifications. The AAVA responsibilities for prescriptions, examinations and for validation are described with reference to the New Zealand system of 22 technical institutes and community colleges.

Future trends for technician education and training are discussed in the context of national policy for the development of science and technology. Attention is drawn to the urgent need to plan for a more extensive and better quality technician workforce. Co-ordination of the interests of government departments, employers and the technical institute system is necessary if constructive action is to replace previous suspicions and even hostility. Current and future developments are outlined which could transform the structure of vocational education in New Zealand and change the nature of technician training. Consideration is given to experience in other countries to draw attention to some possible strategies and directions for the future.

Introduction

The structure of the vocationally qualified workforce in New Zealand has developed since the Second World War. Vocational education and training for the technician in New Zealand continues to progress, but legislative and policy provisions are not always co-ordinated, partly due to lack of awareness and lack of information.

This chapter considers past and future developments and provides a context for identifying some current problems. Positive action is needed to improve the provision of technician training, both as opportunity for the school leaver and as an essential requirement for the development of a New Zealand economy that incorporates a changing blend of primary production, manufacturing, service and information industries.

After the Second World War it was clear that, for post-war industrial development, the professional (ie graduate) engineers (trained overseas) needed a force of skilled tradespeople. Provision for formal training in the trades came with the passing of the Apprentices Act (1948) and the Trades Certification Act (1948), and the establishment under the latter

Act of the New Zealand Trades Certification Board. Offenberger (1979) notes that, 'At this stage, recognition of the role of the technician in the workforce was not widespread in New Zealand', and quotes Beeby (1956) as Director of Education:

'New Zealand is backward in the provision of training for technicians and, indeed, in the very recognition of this most important category.'

The NZ Institution of Engineers, while clearly recognizing that many graduates did (and still do) technicians' work, required university training for its professional membership and rejected the recommendation of the Consultative Committee (1949) to institute part-time diploma courses of professional standing in the technical colleges (Offenberger, 1979).

During this period there had been a limited form of technician development to meet the needs of particular government or public sector organizations for tradespeople with a broader understanding of the principles of technology. The first New Zealand qualification for such people was established by the Post and Telegraph Department in 1946 as the 'Certificate in Radio Technology' (CRT) derived from the UK course for a Technician's Certificate in Broadcasting. Thus the initial two groups (engineers and tradespeople) had developed into a three-level system in response to the needs of (engineering) industry.

The continuing development of industry required a technician level of competence provided by appropriate vocational education and qualification. The new qualification (the New Zealand Certificate) came into being with the establishment in 1955 of the Controlling Authority for the New Zealand Certificates in Engineering. There were then four levels or categories of technical qualification: Trade Certificate, Technicians Certificate, New Zealand Certificate and Degree. The Controlling Authority then became the Technicians Certification Authority (TCA) in 1960 and, in 1966, the TCA introduced the 'Radio Technicians Certificate', which replaced the CRT. Throughout this development there seemed to be different levels of requirements for all groups, and a clear distinction could be made between the engineering technician (with a Technicians Certificate) and the technician engineer with a New Zealand Certificate (McBride and Imrie, 1985).

In 1980 the TCA was reconstituted as the Authority for Advanced Vocational Awards (AAVA), and during the 1980s the AAVA has initiated vigorous and comprehensive development of prescriptions, assessment and validation to continue to meet the needs of industry and commerce at a time when the pace of change is increasing. The NZ Certificate holder can be variously described as a technician builder, technician engineer, technician manager, technician scientist, and so on. The Technicians Certificate still meets a need and demand.

Here is a summary of vocational qualifications and their relevant organizations:

Trade Certificate Advanced Trade Certificate	NZ Trade Certification Board
Technicians Certificate (3 stages) (Intermediate Certificate)	Authority for Advanced Vocational Awards
New Zealand Certificate (5 stages)	Authority for Advanced Vocational Awards
New Zealand Diploma	Authority for Advanced Vocational Awards
Degree	Universities

The intermediate certificate, for students registered for the NZ Certificate, recognizes satisfactory completion of all subjects of the first three stages of the NZ Certificate.

The diploma in the technical institute system is developing as an important qualification, and responsibility for its standard is currently shared by the Technical Institutes Association and by the AAVA. The AAVA considers that, for professional purposes, the NZ Diploma is approximately degree-level equivalent. Unfortunately there has been a wide variation of standard of the diploma as a qualification used by the New Zealand universities, with approximately four levels of diploma ranging from undergraduate to postgraduate. The university system is currently considering appropriate rationalization.

Current developments

In New Zealand, therefore,

'. . . technicians are sub-professionals who have been trained by a combination of study and concurrent work experience to a level part-way to a professional qualification, but with a bias toward practical application.' (Offenberger, 1979: 5)

The Colombo Plan Staff College for Technician Education (1982) has produced a most useful publication on technician education which refers to the Training Services Agency (TSA, 1976) for consideration of the abilities required by technicians:

□ proficiency in the use of scientific method and in understanding basic principles in physics, chemistry and the biological sciences as appropriate;
□ facility with mathematics;
□ understanding and facility in the use of materials, equipment and apparatus;
□ communication skills including the ability to record, analyse, interpret and transmit facts and ideas orally, graphically or in writing.

The formal functions of AAVA include:

'To set standards, approve curricula, and prescribe courses and syllabuses for advanced vocational awards; and to conduct examinations, and to appoint examiners, moderators, supervisors and assessors for the purposes of these examinations.

'To approve teaching institutions as being suitable to conduct prescribed courses, and to accredit approved teaching institutions to conduct examinations to a national standard.' (Vocational Awards Act, 1979: 6-7)

The policies and procedures which enable the Authority to fulfil its functions are determined by a board widely representative of education, training and user groups. Much of the advice on which the Authority bases policy decisions is formulated by course committees established by the Authority. These have a membership drawn from the occupational groups which are relevant to the subjects or courses within its responsibility. There are four such committees covering course interests under the following headings:

building
commerce
engineering and draughting
science.

In 1985 the Authority had a full-time staff of 17 (including a full-time chairman and director) to maintain and develop a national system of vocational courses and awards which comprised:

12 three-stage, part-time Technicians Certificate (TC) courses
44 five-stage, part-time NZ Certificate (NZC) courses
4 NZ Diploma courses (post-NZ Certificate).

For these vocational awards approximately 400 subject syllabuses or prescriptions are provided for teaching in a TI system consisting of 13 polytechnics or technical institutes and 9 community colleges, most of which opened on 1 April 1986.

In addition to providing course and subject prescriptions, the Authority is the examining body responsible for approximately 200 subject examinations for stage 3 and stage 5 subjects. In 1984 approximately 7,400 students sat these examinations at centres all over New Zealand and throughout the South Pacific. In general, for the assessment of student performance, examinations contribute 60 per cent and coursework (assessed internally by tutors) 40 per cent to the overall subject result for all AAVA subjects. Stages 1, 2 and 4 of the certificate courses are entirely internally assessed by the technical institutes and community colleges.

At these vocational institutions there are various types of courses offered; in 1983, student numbers for all NZC and TC certificate courses (Department of Education, 1984) were:

Types of courses	1983	
	NZ Cert	Tech Cert
Part-time courses	7,420	392
Correspondence courses	4,576	1,461
(Technical Correspondence Institute)		
Block courses (full-time study, part year)	1,954	1,404
Full-time, one-year courses	1,354	
Total	15,304	3,257

It is of interest to note that the NZ Technical Correspondence Institute (TCI) was the first senior technical institution to be formed and has its origins in the establishment of the Technical Correspondence School in 1946 (Offenberger, 1979).

The aim of the Authority's certificate courses is to provide an approved qualification or vocational award of national standing which signifies satisfactory completion of a programme of study *and* work experience so that the certificated technicians are immediately productive in subsequent work, ie they are able to do the job properly. Accordingly, the Authority awards certificates only to students who have

1. enrolled in a technical institute (or approved institution) and completed the subject requirements for a particular certificate;
2. satisfied the work experience requirements of the Authority, including completion of three years' suitable work experience.

It is the Authority's view that, for each student, suitable work experience provides the vital and individual context for effective study of vocational subjects *and* for the development of appropriate attitudes and understanding.

Validation

In 1983, as provided by the Vocational Awards Act (1979), the Authority extended its functions of prescribing and examining to include that of validating, ie approving and recognizing courses developed and provided by teaching institutions or other organizations. For this purpose the Authority introduced a new set of awards or 'national qualifications' (AAVA, 1983) to provide for the certification of technicians (or their equivalent) seeking to practise in a wide range of vocations up to a level comparable with a university first degree or a technical institute diploma. The following broad banded relationships apply between the national qualifications and the Authority's own awards:

NZ diploma	National diploma
NZ certificate	Advanced national certificate
NZ certificate (stage 4)	National certificate
Technicians certificate	Ordinary national certificate

By the end of 1984, the first two courses had been validated: they were (a) Advanced National Certificate in Technical Education (Secondary Teachers College, Auckland), and (b) Ordinary National Certificate in Beekeeping (National Beekeepers Association in conjunction with the Bay of Plenty Community College). Other submissions in process of validation include such topics as beauty therapy, business studies, electronic data processing, leather technology, and radiography.

Thus from the initial provision of the first NZ Certificates for technician engineers a wide range of certificates has been developed in response to industry requests to provide appropriate courses and qualifications for technician builders, technician scientists, technician draughtsmen and equivalent technician managers in the general area of business and commerce. Subjects have been developed by groups of experienced representatives of industry and education and presented for teaching as syllabuses supplemented by notes for the tutor.

Prescriptions

In 1983, the Authority decided that subjects should be presented as 'prescriptions' for teaching, learning and assessment. Current policy involves a five-yearly review of each subject, existing subject syllabuses and tutor notes being revised or rewritten as appropriate. The principal elements of a prescription are as follows:

1. For each subject, major topic areas are identified which represent the scope or coverage of the subject, as statements of general objectives. For each topic area, subtopics are represented as outcomes to specify content depth and levels of learning skills. Statements of outcomes take the form of (for example):

   a. what the student should know after completing the subject;
   b. what the student should be able to do after completing the subject.

2. These statements of objectives and outcomes provide the structure for a complementary assessment prescription based on the following two-tier model (Imrie *et al*, 1980) for assessment of student performance at different levels.

Level of learning	Assessment words	Level of assessment
*RE*call	define, describe	
Comprehension	explain, distinguish	tier 1 (minimum essentials)
Application	apply, comment	
Problem solving	analyse, evaluate	tier 2 (development)

Note:
This *RECAP* model (Imrie, 1984a) provides a two-tier assessment structure for course work as well as examination. At the tier 1 level, where the outcomes are described in terms of 'minimum essentials', the satisfactory attainment level for student performance could be 80 per cent, ie at the level of competency or mastery.

At the tier 2 or developmental level, what is being assessed are abilities to
analyse problems, produce solutions and evaluate the quality of the solution.
Essay or report writing is an example of this type of problem solving.

In addition, each prescription indicates the proportions of coursework
and end of course examination contributing to the overall subject assessment of student performance (in general 40:60); also such matters as
timetabled hours, resources such as texts, and evaluation procedures to
improve the prescription in the light of the first year of teaching.

Accordingly the AAVA subject prescription is a comprehensive document summarizing all principal considerations relating to the quality of
teaching, learning and assessment for a vocational subject in the context
of work experience. As such, each prescription is based on wide consultation with appropriate user groups in industry, commerce and public
service, and provides the essential framework for the participation of
tutor, student and examiner.

Current problems

For some considerable time there has been widespread policy neglect of
the value and role of technicians. This will be discussed with reference to
specific examples.

Demand and lack of supply

The technician of the future must be able to cope with change and be
adaptable to retraining and updating (Colombo Plan, 1982). In a discussion of the context for technician education, Weir (1980) emphasizes
change and concludes that knowledge industries will provide the greatest
industrial demand for technicians. He quotes Brannen (1975):

'... knowledge jobs are increasing in number; they are spread
between industries but are likely to be most concentrated within
large organisations and within the most advanced section of the
economy and institutions which service these (as for example,
education). Workers must be able to acquire rapidly new and different techniques over the course of their working lives.'

In 1984, Naisbitt drew attention to a major shift in the USA from an
industrial society to an information society. He considers that this transformation, which has been in process for nearly 20 years, is one of ten
megatrends indicating the direction in which the USA and other developed
countries are moving.

The relevance to New Zealand is that 'it is quite possible for a single
country to be in various states of agricultural, industrial, and information
societies simultaneously.' It is therefore necessary to provide both established and developing industries with technicians who are 'multi-skilled'
and able to adapt and apply skills to do the job properly. In so doing

technicians interact with people as well as information and there are skills involved. Naisbitt considers that basic reading and writing skills are needed 'more than ever before'. However, from his study of national and state reports he concludes that

> 'As we move into a more and more literacy-intensive society, our schools are giving us an increasingly inferior product. Scholastic Achievement Test scores have been going down each year for more than a decade. For the first time in American history the generation moving into adulthood is less skilled than its parents.'

As Naisbitt points out, information becomes knowledge only when it is organized to be accessible. With scientific and technical information now increasing at the rate of 13 per cent per year or doubling every 5.5 years, the technician must be able to adapt to the implications of an information society. As technology systems become more complex with the assistance of microprocessors, Naisbitt also identifies a future scarcity of technicians to operate and maintain these systems.

In New Zealand, a study of trends in the future demand for skilled people in the engineering industry (Department of Labour, 1984) referred only incidentally to technicians and concentrated on tradespersons. Staff responsible for the major energy projects are looking only at the construction phase; no consideration seems to have been given to future requirements for technicians for operation and maintenance.

It has also been noted that having too many graduates and too few technicians will mean that an increasing number of scientists will be doing technicians' work. But 'they are not trained for technicians' work; they are not very good at it and not very happy doing it' (Studt, 1971).

More recently Duncan (1984), as a chemistry professor and chairman of the New Zealand Futures Trust, considered options for New Zealand's future and noted:

> 'An aspect of this is our lop-sided science education. Although it has been recognised for over ten years, we still produce far too few technicians and far too many (especially non-science) graduates. Graduates may find that their job expectations are not met. Technicians are not found in anything like sufficient numbers for efficiency and effectiveness in industry, government science and even university science laboratories.
>
> 'But more technical training will be needed in universities and polytechnics. For as always, it is the way we exploit technology which will determine our future, and unless we train people with the necessary skills our resources will not be used efficiently or effectively.'

The current output of technicians just maintains a ratio of 1:1 for technicians:technologists in engineering and 0.8:1 for technicians:scientists. The survey by Taylor (1980) of the supply and demand for technicians and professional engineers (1976-82) estimates a 'most likely' supply total of approximately 6,500 professional engineers in 1982. A corresponding assumption for the total number of professional scientists is 6,000 (approximately). However, not all of these engineers and scientists will be engaged directly in research and development.

To enable the most efficient use to be made of professional expertise, improvements are required in the ratio of technicians to engineers and scientists. Ratios of 2:1 for technicians to engineers and about 1.2:1 for technicians to scientists have been recommended (McCallion and Britton, 1978).

In 1984 the National Research Advisory Council (NRAC) published a 'Science and Technology Plan: the first steps' (NRAC, 1984) which was intended to assist government in assessing its role in stimulating science and technology in both the private and public sectors. The 165-page Plan has only a single reference to technical institutes as part of an independent set of provisions for post-secondary education. To redress this imbalance and to emphasize that technicians will be indispensable for a national initiative to succeed in improving research and development in science and technology, a paper (Imrie, McCallion and Thomas, 1985) has been prepared for the NRAC. It shows that, for a modest growth (3 per cent) of research and development, the number of technicians qualifying annually in 1983 will have to increase by a factor of 2.5 by the year 2000. There is already serious shortage because policy and planning have been neglected by people who do not understand and are not aware of the vital significance of technicians in a national economy and of the national need for vocational education to produce technicians and provide opportunity for school leavers.

In other countries such lack of planning is noted as a lack of understanding and co-operation between industry and technician institutions, with the result that industry claims that the products of technician education systems do not fulfil its manpower requirements (Colombo, 1982). In New Zealand itself in 1984, the NZ Employers Federation published a discussion paper on the 'Employer Approach to Vocational Training' and claimed that technical institutes provide for less than 10 per cent of industry's training requirements. However, the section of only five paragraphs assigned to the role of technical institutes and examining authorities also asserted that courses in technical institutes are 'excessively dominated by examination prescriptions'. Such assertions without justification are unacceptable and irresponsible. Probably due to absence of consultation, the paper showed little awareness of technician training and the functions of the Authority for Advanced Vocational Awards, but rather confusion with the role of the NZ Trades Certification Board (TCB) and apprenticeship training.

Again, in 1985, the Employers' Federation made the same assertion in its discussion paper 'Tertiary Education and the Path to Work'. Although this time there was explicit reference to AAVA (and consultation), the assumptions were in error and again indicated confusion with TCB. It would seem that repetition of opinion is to be the print substitute for information.

Also in 1985, the NZ Planning Council published a planning paper on 'Young People, Education and Employment' (Catherwood, 1985). There was discussion of apprenticeships, no discussion of technicians and the only two references to the NZ Certificate as a post-secondary qualification were both wrong.

Even the OECD (1983) examiners, in their review of NZ policies for education, briefed by the Department of Education, did not seem to be sufficiently aware of technician education to mention the work of an authority established as the national body responsible for setting standards, prescribing courses and work experience, and conducting examinations for advanced vocational awards.

Current problems therefore relate to years of neglect, lack of awareness and an absence of the policy co-ordination by employers, government and the TI system, essential for development of the appropriate quantity and quality of NZC technicians.

Future developments

Late in 1985 it was possible to write optimistically about some affirmative actions and initiatives which are evident, although the outcomes would not be fully perceived for at least a year. The initiatives are being taken by the Minister of Education in conjunction with Ministers of Employment, Maori Affairs, and Science and Technology. The OECD (1983) Examiners expressed (diplomatically) a commonly held view about the inequality of school experience when they stated:

'For the young woman or man who is not going to university, the curriculum and values of existing secondary schools appear to need some adaptation to the available forms of education and training in non-university tertiary institutions, and subsequent employment in industry and commerce.'

In 1984, the Minister of Education (Mr Marshall) established a Committee of Inquiry into Curriculum, Assessment and Qualifications in forms 5 to 7 (ages 15 to 17). The first report (Ross, 1985) noted that

'The persistence of the University Entrance examination in form 6 has introduced undesirable constraints on the curriculum of schools and seriously hindered schools from providing a well-balanced education for its students at this level.' (p 8)

The committee recommended that Sixth Form Certificate should be the sole national award in form 6, beginning in 1986; and there is no doubt that curriculum *and* assessment will now develop the vocational relevance appropriate to the needs of the 85 per cent of school leavers who will not end up in universities or teachers' colleges. The committee has also proposed a secondary board of studies which recognizes, for the first time in the school system, the right of the TI system (including AAVA and TCB) to be represented and to be consulted.

This is consistent with the AAVA submission to the Committee of Inquiry, and it is highly significant in that the sixth form (and the fifth form to some extent) will provide the interface for vocational education and work experience for school leavers.

In 1985 the Ministers of Education, Employment and Maori Affairs issued a discussion paper on education and training for the transition from school to work. The paper *Skills for Young People* (Ministers, 1985) proposes a system concept (designated ACCESS) which provides school leavers with access to education, guidance and training in skills for life and work. This paper foreshadows a government green paper which will deal with the training requirements of the general workforce and the institutional arrangements needed for them to be met.

The Vocational Training Council (VTC) was established by act of parliament in 1968 to make recommendations on training to the government and industry, to undertake research and to promote systematic training throughout New Zealand. The VTC Act 1982 transferred primary ministerial responsibility for the VTC from the education to the labour portfolio, while still retaining the links with the Minister of Education and the education system. In 1985, for the first time, not only has VTC budgeted for research into the shortage of technicians (and into the use of educational technology in training), but there has even been informal discussion between the paid officers of VTC and AAVA.

Similar informal discussions have taken place between officers of the Authority and the Department of Labour, the Employers' Federation, and the Department of Education, in an attempt to close the gap between reality and rhetoric.

Finally, for this brief summary, the Minister of Education, in response to the Ministers of Trade and Industry and of Science and Technology, has asked the Authority to investigate the achievement of reciprocal recognition of technician level qualifications between New Zealand and Australia.

Positive action

Various initiatives have been taken by the Authority for the development of the training and role of the technician in New Zealand. Mention has been made of the recent introduction of the validation function of the Authority. It has sought to make submissions to inquiries, reviews, discussion papers and draft legislation, and must continue to do so.

The Colombo Plan publication (1982) refers to current practice in New Zealand and also includes a pertinent and detailed view of the education and training of technicians. The reference to New Zealand is to vertical mobility, which is the opportunity for an apprentice to commence part-time study for an NZ Certificate halfway through an apprenticeship. Then, with an NZ Certificate (and high grades) the technician becomes eligible for direct entry to the second professional year of an engineering degree course (for example) and can complete the degree in two years of full-time study instead of the usual four.

The Authority will continue to develop links between these sectors of tertiary education and training but the major development required is in the area of technician training. The principal objective of technical education is to equip technicians with a broad portable qualification which will provide an adequate foundation for change of occupation and the ability to learn from experiences. It is this vocational mobility which is the more important objective (Imrie, 1984b).

Deeds not words

This chapter has been written with the pessimism of knowing what needs to be done and knowing that the resources will not be provided to do the job properly. The value of a full-time chairman (first appointed 1 November 1984) has already been established, but it is likely that interventionist restructuring will specify a part-time chairman. The value of a full-time director with educational ability has been demonstrated and the first permanent appointment was made in 1985. For professional assistance in the continuing development of a national system of technician training, there is currently limited provision for *one* tutor on secondment. This level of investment in courses, prescriptions, assessment and qualifications for the future technicians of New Zealand is totally inadequate and politically irresponsible.

In a paper addressing vocational options for school leavers it is argued (Imrie, 1985) that much can and should be learned from the experience of other countries. In a report on 'The Future of Vocational Education and Training' (OECD, 1983) it was noted:

'Governments have often made decisions about trade, economic policy, investment or regional development, and sometimes even education, without taking vocational education and training into account, so that it has not become part of overall public policy.'

Developments in other countries should be studied to evaluate the principles and procedures which would enable New Zealand to optimize vocational education opportunities for school leavers. There is clearly interdependence between the areas of responsibility of government, employers and the technical institute system for the future of school leavers and of New Zealand. The sharing of responsibility requires co-ordinated interaction and the experience of Portugal is relevant (OECD, 1983):

'To establish liaison between the Ministries of Education and Labour and to guarantee the co-ordination of their various activities, a Permanent System to co-ordinate Education and Work (SAPETE), composed of officials of the two Ministries, has been set up by ministerial decision. It aims to develop and make the maximum co-ordinated use of the existing human and other resources of the Ministries of Education and Labour in the framework of vocational education and training and of information and counselling services.' (p 35: 69)

In Scotland there have been radical changes in vocational education: in 1985 the Scottish Vocational Education Council was established and the 16-plus Action Plan with a module-based National Certificate for pre-vocational education was introduced (see Pignatelli, Chapter 4).

In New Zealand, the Minister of Education has translated his words into action with a major investment in continuing education in 1985, with further investment promised for 1986. It remains to be seen whether the investment and the co-ordination with other government departments will focus sufficiently on the need and demand for technicians. By any measure the investment return could be spectacular for the future of New Zealand.

References

Association of Teachers in Technical Institutes (ATTI) (1984) *Development Policies* Annual Conference of the NZ ATTI

Authority for Advanced Vocational Awards (AAVA) (1983) *The AAVA 'National' Qualifications* Authority for Advanced Vocational Awards: Wellington

Beeby, C E (1956) Address to the Senate of the University of New Zealand *in* Offenberger

Brannen, P (1975) *Entering the World of Work* HMSO: London

Catherwood, V (1985) *Young People, Education and Employment* Planning Paper 23 NZ Planning Council: Wellington

Colombo Plan (1982) *Aspects of Curriculum for Technician Education* Colombo Plan Staff College for Technician Education: Singapore

Department of Education (1984) *Education Statistics of New Zealand* Department of Education: Wellington

Department of Labour (1984) *Engineering Industry (A Study of Trends in the Future Demand for Skilled People)* Department of Labour: Wellington

Duncan, J (1984) *Options for New Zealand's Future* Victoria University/ANZ Bank: Wellington

Employers' Federation (1984) *Employer Approach to Vocational Training* NZ Employers' Federation: Wellington

Employers' Federation (1985) *Tertiary Education and the Path to Work* NZ Employers' Federation: Wellington

Imrie, B W (1984a) AAVA Assessment of Student Performance M Circular 84/4 Authority for Advanced Vocational Awards: Wellington

Imrie, B W (1984b) *Technical Education and Training, AAVA Policy: Current Topics and Future Development* Invited paper presented at the Biennial Conference of the NZ Institute of Draughtsmen: Wellington

Imrie, B W (1985) *Vocational Options for School Leavers in New Zealand* Papers of the Fourth World Conference on Co-operative Education: Edinburgh

Imrie, B W, Blithe, T B and Johnston, L C (1980) A review of Keller Principles with reference to mathematics courses in Australasia *British Journal of Educational Technology* 11: 2

Imrie, B W, McCallion, H and Thomas, R F (1985) *Providing Technicians for Research and Development* Paper prepared for the National Research Advisory Council: Wellington

McBride, E F and Imrie, B W (1985) Technician training — on the right track *New Electronics*: October

McCallion, H and Britton, G A (1978) *A Survey of Engineers in New Zealand Engineering and Manufacturing and Processing Industry* Technical Manpower Training Committee: March

Miller, R M *ed* (1971) *Technician Training* Report of the National Study Conference, Massey University

Minister of Education (1984) *Education, the Economy and Social Equity* Address to the Economic Summit Conference, Wellington

Minister of Education (1985) Address to the Annual Conference of Association of Teachers in Technical Institutes (22 May 1985): Upper Hutt

Ministers of Education, Employment and Maori Affairs (1985) *Skills for Young People* A discussion paper on transition education and training. Ministers of Education, Employment and Maori Affairs: Wellington

Naisbitt, J (1984) *Megatrends* Warner Books: New York

National Research Advisory Council (NRAC) (1984) *A Strategy for Science and Technology* Discussion Paper NRAC 84 257 National Research Advisory Council: Wellington

Offenberger, H (1979) *The Making of a Technician: A Study of New Zealand Certificate Holders* New Zealand Council for Educational Research: Wellington

Organization for Economic Co-operation and Development (OECD) (1983) *The Future of Vocational Education and Training* OECD: Paris

Ross, J A (1985) *Implications of the Removal of the University Entrance Examination from Form 6* First Report of the Committee of Inquiry into Curriculum, Assessment, and Qualifications in Forms 5 to 7. Department of Education: Wellington

Studt, F E (1971) New Zealand's requirement for science technicians *in* Miller, R M (ed) *Technician Training* Report of the National Study Conference, Massey University

Taylor, J B C (1980) *The Supply of and Demand for Technician and Professional Engineers (1967-82)* Technical Report April 22: Department of Mechanical Engineering, University of Canterbury: Canterbury, NZ

Training Services Agency (TSA) (1976) *Technicians: A Possible Basis for a TSA Programme* TSA: UK

United Nations Educational, Scientific and Cultural Organization (UNESCO) (1974) *Revised Recommendations Concerning Vocational Education adopted by the General Conference of United Nations Educational, Scientific and Cultural Organization (UNESCO)* UNESCO: Paris

Weir, A D (1980) A context for technician education *in* Heywood, J (ed) *The New Technician Education* Society for Research in Higher Education, Surrey University: Guildford

10. Higher vocational education in the Netherlands

Marijke van der Putten and Paul Frissen

Summary: This chapter deals with higher vocational education (HBO) in the Netherlands, with particular emphasis on higher technical education — a subset of HBO.

In 1986 a new law comes into effect which will bring HBO fully into the higher education system, and in 1987 a new funding system is being introduced Also in 1987, an operation to bring about scale expansion, concentration and specialization should be completed. The aim is to have a limited number of large HBO institutes with different types of fields of study at each one.

The background to this government policy includes the decline in student numbers, the need to economize on government expenditure, the altered demand for education, the increase in unemployment, and the tense relationship between education and the job market.

Government policy is taking the form of institutional differentiation in higher education; increased competition, variation and quality; a 'corporate' approach involving scale expansion and strengthening of management; deregulation, and more general regulation.

As a result of the changes there are unresolved conflicts between different types of higher educational institution (universities and HBOs), between the advocates of specialized institutions and of those catering for a wide range of subject sectors, and between the pedagogical 'cultures' of different sectors. While large multi-sectoral institutes have much to commend them in financial terms, one less happy consequence would be a weakening of the professional links with particular vocational fields. There are also unresolved issues of staffing and management.

Introduction

The Dutch educational system

Education in the Netherlands is compulsory from the year a pupil attains the age of 5 years 6 months until the age of 16 (Compulsory Education Act, 1900, recently amended in 1975 and 1984). So nowadays pupils are obliged to attend some form of full-time education for 10 years.

After primary education (age 4-12) there are four directions:

- □ junior secondary vocational education (LBO) (4 years)
- □ junior general secondary education (MAVO) (4 years)
- □ senior general secondary education (HAVO) (5 years)
- □ pre-university education (VWO) (6 years).

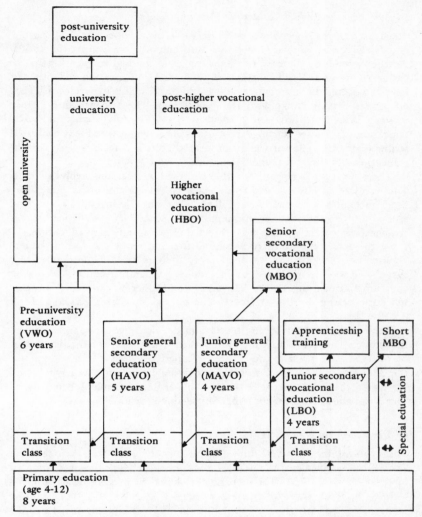

(Source: Ministry of Foreign Affairs, The Kingdom of The Netherlands)

Figure 1. *The Dutch educational system*

Pre-university or senior general secondary education is a requirement for entry into higher vocational education (HBO). Sometimes senior secondary vocational education (MBO) also offers the possibility of attending higher vocational education. For example, after finishing the theoretical stream of the senior secondary technical school, one can start in the first year of a higher technical school (see also van Kemenade, 1981).

Higher vocational education: some facts and figures

The Dutch term 'Hoger Beroeps Onderwijs' (higher vocational education) is a fairly recent one. It only came into common use during the 1960s. At the same time there were increasing calls for higher vocational education to be made legally distinct from secondary education and either to have it covered by its own separate Act or to make it part of a higher education system along with the universities. These ideas came mainly from within education itself. And it was primarily higher technical education (a subset of higher vocational education) which protested strongly when in 1969 it was incorporated after all in the new Secondary Education Act (known as the 'Mammoth' Act).

There were two reasons for this protest. One reason involves status. The standard of HBO is held to be equal to that of university education; legal recognition is therefore called for (van Wieringen, 1976). And secondly, government involvement with secondary education is far stronger, more detailed and more direct than with university education.

In the 1970s the ministry published the first reports and green papers concerning the possibilities and impossibilities of a higher education system. It was decided first to introduce a separate Act to cover higher vocational education. On 19 May 1981 the Higher Vocational Education bill came before the Lower House. The bill has now been passed and will become law.

Table 1 gives a list of the sectors inside higher vocational education, the student numbers and the number of institutes. As regards student numbers — past, present and future — Table 2 provides information about the admission of students to higher vocational education as a whole and to higher technical education (HTO) in particular. Table 3 provides information about government expenditure on education.

Higher Technical School (HTS)

The roots of the higher technical schools go back to the 19th century. They were established by private foundations. The first one was founded in Rotterdam in 1851. The demand for skilled people whose capabilities were in between those of manual workers and those of middle management increased sharply around 1900. In 1933 the Netherlands had 11 senior secondary vocational technical schools. At this time a choice could be made from five departments: architecture, civil engineering, mechanical engineering, electrical engineering and shipbuilding engineering. In the 1960s government policies were aimed at the introduction of a new level of technical course: the middle vocational technical school. The 'old' MVTS was renamed higher technical school (HTS).

The number of students rose from 2,500 in 1940 to about 28,000 in 1984 (full-time students). Nowadays one can choose between 20 specializations. The smallest HTS has some 400 students, the biggest 2,200. In 1984 there were 31 institutes, although not every HTS caters for all the specializations. Subsidies are allocated on the basis of the number of

Sectors	HBO student numbers*		
	Full-time day education	Part-time education	Total
Higher Technical Education (HTO)	28600	2700	31300
Medical and Chemical Analysis Education (HLO)	5600	1300	6900
Higher Nautical Education (HNO)	2700		2700
Higher Health Care Education (HGZO)	17300	3600	20900
Higher Agricultural Education (HAO)	5600		5600
Higher Economics and Book-keeping Education (HEAO)	16500	2300	18800
Primary Teacher Training Colleges (PA)	5600		5600
Basic Education Teacher Training Colleges (PABO)	2700		2700
Teacher Training Courses (LERO)	20600	16000	36600
Higher Human Relations and Social Science Education	19900	10600	30500
Arts Education (KUO)	13200	3900	17100
Special Sectors (BL)	5900	140	6040
Total	144200	40540	184740

*Figures rounded off to nearest hundred (Rhobos, 1984)

(Source: HBO Council, 1985: 15)

Table 1. *Sectors in higher vocational education (HBO)*

students. Some specializations are in such great demand that institutes have to restrict student admissions.

The majority of schools are independent, with independent boards, managements and premises, and are financially independent (van der Putten, 1981).

Recent developments in government policies

There are currently three major developments taking place at a rapid pace which will greatly affect systems of higher vocational education (referred to as 'HBO' for the remainder of this chapter).

The first one is the HBO Act, which will become law on 1 August 1986. This new law provides higher vocational education with its own legal and policy-making framework and disconnects higher vocational education from the secondary education system. As a result of the new law, HBO will become an independent component of the higher education system, alongside and not inferior to university education. In anticipation of this, the Minister presented the HBO sector with proposals for a new funding system in November 1984 (Ministry of Science and Education, 1984). Discussions about this are still in progress. It is intended that

		Higher vocational education (HBO)	Higher technical school (HTS)
Actual	1980	51315	7477
	1981	53824	7704
	1982	54824	8014
	1983	55069	8434
Estimates	1984	56406	8884
	1985	57952	9051
	1986	58868	9327
	1987	60383	9691
	1988	61323	9929
	1989	61563	10040
	1990	60834	9922
	1991	59106	9617
	1992	57087	9208
	1993	55061	8780
	1994	53541	8383
	1995	52026	8072
	1996	51208	7862
	1997	50656	7736
	1998	50476	7689
	1999	50138	7644
	2000	49614	7580

(Source: HBO Council, 1985, pp.209-210)

Note: The figures for HBO include those for HTS

Table 2. *Admission of students to HBO and HTO*

this new funding system will come into force in 1987. The new system will basically mean that the method of financing HBO will be more or less the same as for university education. There will be a system of lump-sum financing based on input and output (yield) figures. The institutes will be given greater freedom to spend the lump sum allocated.

The third and probably most radical development is the process of scale expansion, specialization and concentration in higher vocational education, started in September 1983. (For the rest of this chapter this process is referred to as the STC operation.) At that time the Minister presented what was known as the STC green paper to HBO (Ministry of Science and Education, 1983). In February the HBO Council[1] was put in charge of process co-ordination. It is hoped to complete the operation in August 1987. At the time of writing, August 1985, the operation is only two months behind schedule.

The main aim of the STC operation is to bring about a qualitative (broadening of pedagogical responsibilities) and quantitative (increasing

1. The HBO Council is the national advisory and consultative body for higher vocational education. Its tasks are: to develop higher vocational education and to advise and consult with government.

	1970	1975	1980	1981	1982
Actual expenditure	8535	17694	25802	26892	27436
As % of national income at contemporary market prices	8.1	9.3	8.5	8.5	8.4
Expenditure for higher vocational education	–	1072	1732	1773	1835
Expenditure at 1980 prices	20388	24367	25802	25910	Not available
Actual expenditure per head of population	651	1288	1816	1882	1913
Expenditure at 1980 prices	1435	1715	1816	1824	Not available

(Source: CBS, *Statistisch Zakboek, 1984*: The Hague)

Table 3. *Government expenditure on education in million guilders*

the size of the institutes) strengthening of HBO. The objective is to reduce the present 384 institutes to a small number of multisectoral institutes. In concrete terms this means that:

1. institutes with fewer than 600 students will disappear;
2. a student roll of at least 2,500 students is required in order to be eligible for funds for research and services;
3. there is a single competent authority, under which a central board should see to the day-to-day management.

Every newly formed institute will have to meet certain conditions about geographical concentration. Which HBO institutes will amalgamate is a matter of choice and negotiation.

Contrary to all pessimistic expectations, the STC operation has given rise to great activity within higher vocational education. There is not one institute that is not at least at the discussion stage with another one. In many cases amalgamation negotiations are being held between the most diverse HBO institutes, and at a very fast pace. Sometimes clusters of over ten schools are having discussions with one another; in other cases only two or three schools are involved (HBO Council, 1984 and 1984-1985).

Background to government policy: social developments

For many years the largest item in the government budget in the Netherlands has been expenditure on education, though now and again this has been exceeded by expenditure on social security. It is therefore not surprising that as part of the general reduction in government expenditure, education, including higher education, has been considerably affected by the spending cuts. In fact, these economies tend mainly to take the form of restrictions on increases in government spending.

In the education sector the cuts have mainly taken the form of salary reductions of teaching staff. Besides this the pupil:teacher ratio has been altered so that institutes receive less financial support for the same student numbers. The objective of the STC operation described above is also to achieve reductions in costs by amalgamations of institutes and rationalization of specialization.

The target for cuts is 12 million guilders in 1986, 40 million guilders in 1987 and 68 million guilders in 1988 (HBO Council, 1983).

Another important point, to some extent related to these figures, is the drop in the number of students, which is now noticeable in higher education, though its drastic effect on this sector of education will become particularly evident in the 1990s (Acherman, Brons and Kuhry, 1981-1982; Bevers, Bouhuis and Gobbits, 1981). Due to the direct coupling between student numbers and financing, this means a considerable reduction in funds for HBO institutes.

The decline in student numbers can be attributed primarily to a shrinkage in the standard source of students: those who have finished pre-university and senior general secondary education. No doubt an increase can be expected in the demand for higher education by women, part-time workers, the unemployed and elderly people. But the net result will be a fall in the number of students (Acherman *et al*, 1981-1982; Bevers *et al*, 1981; Kodde, 1983; van Lieshout, 1984).

However, the extent to which even this new demand for higher education can be met depends largely on how capable higher education institutes prove to be in matching their supply to this demand (Frissen and van Hoewijk, 1985).

One of the aims of the STC operation is to allow a more flexible reaction to such changes in the demand for higher education. In other words, on the one hand the quantitative reduction in the demand for education as a result of demographic developments has to be assimilated; on the other hand reorganization will make it easier for higher education to react to the qualitative changes in the demand for education by providing an appropriate educational supply (van Lieshout, 1984; Gevers, 1984).

The need to economize on government spending on education is not the only result of the economic recession. Evidence of the recession can also be found in the increase in unemployment among higher education graduates (Bronneman-Helmers, 1984; Ritzen, 1982 and 1983). This applies particularly to those specializations which depend on the public sector for jobs, since this sector is being cut back. In addition to this, graduates from HBO institutes will also encounter more competition from university graduates (Ritzen, 1983; de Grip, 1984).

This has created tension in the relationship between education and the job market. Unemployment in general, and unemployment among higher education graduates in particular, forces us to consider the question of whether courses should be maintained irrespective of the job prospects they offer. One of the background reasons for the STC operation at any rate is to bring about a better match if possible between the educational supply and the demand for types of graduates on the job market. This may necessitate the reallocation of assets between specializations by way of amalgamation and concentration, and/or an increase in flexibility in the courses on offer within a particular specialization, for example by introducing modular education.

Options and considerations in government policy

After years of discussions concerning the relationship between university education and HBO — the two components in Dutch higher education — the government appears to have opted for amalgamation and restructuring *within* each component before any closer co-operation, let alone integration between the two components, can even be considered. This has now been official policy for quite some time (as an example, see Ministry of Science and Education, 1975).

Though it is true that HBO has now become part of higher education, both legally and as far as policy-making is concerned, within this higher education system the aim appears to be not so much integration as institutional differentiation. At any rate, the result of the STC process will be a variety of HBO institutes, certainly in size if nothing else. Meanwhile, in 1984, the Open University was formed alongside existing university education. The restructuring of this latter form of higher education into a four-year first phase and a number of postdoctoral specializations has also been settled.

This means that the direction of development is on the one hand towards a single system of higher education and on the other hand towards greater differentiation within that system (see also van Lieshout, 1984).

Evidently the government wishes to stimulate competition within the system (Veld, 1985). HBO is being given the opportunity to strengthen itself by means of amalgamations and specialization, so as to become an equal component of the higher education system.

This differentiation may also be a solution to the qualitative changes in educational demand. Greater variety in educational supply, in a different institutional form as well, is a prerequisite for a vigorous higher education system. Greater competition and more variety can thus be regarded as roads leading to an improvement in the quality of the system (Frissen, 1985).

These objectives are to be achieved by expanding the scale of HBO institutes. It would appear from the STC operation that large institutes with different specializations are considered to be more capable of competing with university education, generating variety themselves and thus providing higher quality (Gevers, 1984).

Specialization within large institutes and the concentration of fields of study into a limited number of institutes are intended to ensure a macrocosmically effective structuring of the educational supply. The larger size of institutes, which will then inevitably be multisectoral, is a prerequisite for effective use of funds by the creation of economies of scale. At the same time magnitude is a precondition for flexibility in educational programming at the individual institutes.

The emphasis on scale expansion is evidence of a more corporate attitude towards the management and administration of HBO institutes (Gevers, 1984). The turbulent social developments taking place call for HBO institutes which are large enough to be able to evolve new activities at the correct moment, without being hindered in this by being too dependent on one or more fields of study and the social sectors linked to them.

An expansion of scale also requires a strengthening of the management within institutes (see also Ministry of Science and Education, 1984a). This strengthening is needed so that strategic policy can be conducted (Duncan, 1982; Keller, 1983). Strategic policy is necessary so as to be able to foresee social developments and react accordingly by adjusting educational supply to demand.

Finally, it is important that the implementation of the STC operation is being left to the HBO Council. Central government determines the basic premises and boundary conditions, while an HBO institution itself co-ordinates the process. This specification choice for the implementation of the policy fits in with efforts to deregulate and generalize the system, a goal which is also evident in other policy activities in the field of higher education (Ministry of Science and Education, 1985).

Although the Dutch educational tradition is one of strict regulation and detailed involvement by central government, so that a certain amount of scepticism is called for, the STC operation would appear in this regard to represent something of a break with the past.

Implications of government policy

Government policy on higher vocational education has certain implications, which we will describe on three levels:

1. implications for the HBO system and other forms of higher education;
2. implications for the higher technical education sector;
3. implications for individual HBO institutes.

Implications for the HBO system and other forms of higher education

For the higher education system as a whole, the policy's objective is the equality of the three components: HBO, university education and the Open University. This equality, which is to be achieved mainly by strengthening HBO, increasing its independence, expanding its scale and increasing its freedom, is necessary on two grounds. Firstly, the three forms of higher education differ in both input and output. They aim at different categories of students in terms of origin, characteristics and aspirations. They also train people for different vocational segments in social sectors.

Secondly, equality is necessary to facilitate competition. Only if they are equal can the components of the higher education system compete with one another and thus achieve an improvement in quality (Veld, 1985).

For this view to be successful, however, it is fundamental that this policy must not be entirely dominated by considerations of spending cuts. HBO must be given a genuine opportunity to become an equal partner or competitor to the other components in the higher education system (Gevers, 1984). One aspect which must not be left unmentioned is the possibility that HBO has to develop other activities in addition to normal education. Examples of this might include research and market-oriented services. This requires not only financial resources, but more importantly scope for policy-making and deregulation, for example in the sphere of the legal status of staff. For the moment a certain amount of scepticism is justified here (Kickert, 1985).

Whether these policy developments will result in a sufficient variation in educational supply (another policy aim) is a question that must for the moment remain unanswered. One result will probably be institutional variation: the traditional university education, the Open University and HBO.

Nothing definite can yet be said about the variation and the flexibility required to achieve this within and between these components. Thus, for example, some might ask whether differences created by the new specializations within HBO are greater than its differences from the specializations within university education and within the Open University. For some HBO specializations, for instance for technical subjects, integration with comparable courses in university education would probably be preferable to co-operation with other types of HBO courses (van Lieshout, 1984). The possibility of this being a subsequent phase in the restructuring of higher education cannot be ruled out.

As a matter of fact, the measures announced for the whole of higher education (Ministry of Science and Education, 1985) give higher education institutions greater autonomy, so that they have greater policy-making freedom in programming the educational supply.

Developments in the direction of cross-links between sectors in higher education cannot therefore be excluded in advance.

Implications for the higher technical education sector

The implications of government policy for the higher technical education sector cannot as yet be determined with absolute certainty. We can, though, formulate a number of expectations and questions.

Since the 1960s, higher technical education has advocated increased co-operation with its counterpart in university education, the technical universities. Now that a political decision has been made to give HBO a greater degree of independence by means of legislation and the STC operation, this will undoubtedly have consequences for the hoped-for co-operation.

There continues to be a tendency towards a single system of higher education in spite of other developments in, say, West Germany and certain dissenting views, notably from technical universities (Christiaans, 1985). As far as higher technical schools are concerned, however, the STC operation will represent a delay in their aim of co-operation with university education.

The HTS will now find itself in a multisectoral HBO institute. This may be an institute with a wide variety of specializations, or an institute in which 'hard' specializations are concentrated: economics and commerce, medical/chemical analysis, nautical, agricultural and engineering studies. Some writers advocate this way of clustering just 'hard' specializations because of their relationship to one another (van Andel, 1984).

If the clustering is a broader one, then the growth of more intensive co-operation between similar specializations within the cluster cannot be ruled out.

In either case, however, the HTS will be forced to relinquish some of its former character. What significance this will have for any possible co-operation with technical universities is as yet unclear.

The STC operation will also affect other developments in higher technical education. The emphasis on large-scale institutes and integration (a single management, a single board, many specializations) conflicts with the need for differentiation. Differentiation is required so that a specialization can be correctly co-ordinated with the vocational area and developments going on there. The HTS is characterized by increasing differentiation in specializations and by vocational areas. Thus internal integration is necessary in order to increase manageability and to prevent departments from becoming isolated and conservative (Lawrence and Lorsch, 1967).

The progress of integration with other courses imposed by the government policy complicates this tension between integration and differentiation within a specialization.

The STC operation may also affect developments in higher vocational education generally, and in higher technical education in particular, towards a less rigid link between specializations and vocation. These developments are still extremely uncertain. The structure of the HTS is characterized primarily by the domination of systematic factual knowledge, by an atomistic curriculum, by a year group system and by an educational process dictated by the final examination (van der Putten, 1981). In terms of educational supply, however, there has been a gradual increase in the attention given to personal and social education (Mertens, 1981). This development could be stimulated by the STC operation.

This links up with the discussion which is currently going on about the structure of higher education in subjects which are derived, on the one hand — as in the case of HBO — from occupations, and on the other hand — as in the case of university education — from academic disciplines.

Various authors have their doubts about whether specialization is organizationally and pedagogically the most suitable unit, given the demands made on vocational courses.

An alternative proposal is for a system in which the composition of study programmes is based chiefly on the student's own choice (Aarts, 1985; McDaniel, 1985; Academic Council, 1983).

Government policy — the STC operation and the proposed measures to grant greater autonomy to higher education institutes (Ministry of Science and Education, 1985) — tends towards this alternative proposal.

Implications for individual HBO institutes

A number of implications of government policy for the standard of HBO institutes can also be mentioned. The main method being used to strengthen HBO is expansion of scale by means of amalgamation. This means that the amalgamation is being enforced from outside. It can hardly be said that it is a voluntary move. Experience with amalgamations in other sectors of education indicates that a great deal of time and energy is required to get teachers to work enthusiastically in a new situation that has come about by coercion. A stable teaching situation is only re-established after a number of years have elapsed.

It has also been found from other sectors that compulsory large-scale innovations such as amalgamations leave very little energy over for pedagogical innovations. Many people in HBO and many policy-makers expect the STC operation to generate pedagogical changes as well. However, the amalgamation itself will draw away so much attention that there will be little scope left for this.

It is therefore unwise to defend within an institute the amalgamation resulting from government policy with pedagogical arguments regarding greater options for students, wider experimentation potential, more rapid adaption to meet new developments, and so on. The most important thing to teachers is what the amalgamation will mean for their employment situation and terms of employment. Only when these matters have been clarified will it be possible to deal with content-related aspects of the working situation and only at the final stage will there be energy for co-operation processes (van den Berg and Vandenberghe, 1981).

A major problem for institutes during an amalgamation is that there is often no conception of the pedagogical system of the new institute. And this is necessary, since the master plan of a new educational institute is based on:

1. a conception of the pedagogical situation;
2. an organizational structure which is so arranged that the educational system can achieve its goals optimally (Marx, 1975).

In the absence of a conception regarding the educational system of the new institute, many discussions during amalgamation processes will chiefly concern organizational matters.

Partly as a result of this type of problem, a tendency can currently be discerned in amalgamation processes to create federative co-operation ties. These then constitute the first step in the direction of the integration of different institutes to form a single institute, with a single board and a single management, as envisaged in the government policy.

But it is not easy to integrate specializations which often have such widely differing approaches, even cultures. HBO institutes usually derive these cultures from the vocational sector at which the specialization is aimed (Lawrence and Lorsch, 1967; Knip, 1982). This similarity as regards culture is also often a prerequisite for effective co-ordination between education and the job market. Disparities will often make it difficult for graduates to find work (Knip, 1982).

Now that different specializations will have to co-operate, problems of this nature cannot be ruled out. Moreover, the culture difference between specializations is itself an impediment to co-operation.

Conclusions

The STC operation is still in full swing. Inevitably, therefore, the implications outlined above will often be in the nature of expectations and questions. All the same, it is clear that the operation will have extremely far-reaching consequences.

Although the process was set up by the ministry, applying a rational planning approach, and its co-ordination has been entrusted to a single national body, the HBO Council, its course and outcome will be far more in the nature of the garbage-can model (Cohen, March and Olsen, 1972): complex, haphazard, differing from situation to situation and dependent on fluctuations in the balance of power.

An important feature of HBO courses, and certainly of higher technical education as well, has always been the close relationship with the corresponding vocational field. This vocational field supplies the course with its identity, especially as far as cultural aspects are concerned. This identity is a precondition for effective co-ordination with the job market and enables adjustments to be made to meet new developments in the environment.

Such reactions to new developments in the environment are not entirely problem-free processes. The question is whether the policy developments — legislation, the STC operation and the new funding system — will make this any easier. The intention of creating large-scale multi-sectoral institutes in particular makes it very difficult to maintain the institute's own professional identity.

There is certainly something to be said in favour of large-scale institutes because of the cost aspects; but the opposite is true when differentiation and flexibility are considered (Hover, 1983).

As far as the HBO institutes are concerned, the STC operation will have far-reaching consequences for management. Following the amalgamations the management of a particular field of study will have some part in managing the new institute. But to some extent the managerial duties will remain on the level of the 'old' institute. This will certainly mean a lengthening of lines of communication and decision-making procedures. The middle management in a school performs an extremely important function here.

Add to this the participation council introduced in 1983, in which all sections of a school are involved in joint consultation and, in some cases, in joint decision-making in the school's affairs, and we have briefly outlined the complicated consultation and decision-making structure. When in addition the new funding system comes into force and the proposals to increase schools' autonomy become reality, the management in an HBO institute will be faced with a task as complex as it is challenging.

Finally, a certain amount of scepticism may be expressed concerning the objective as formulated by the government to bring about greater autonomy for higher education institutes (Ministry of Science and Education, 1985). The tradition of a high degree of regulation in Dutch education and the maintenance of staff numbers in the central government apparatus give rise to suspicion for the moment.

However, this is not an excuse for institutes simply to neglect using the policy-making freedom being offered. On the contrary, wherever an institute can conduct its own strategic policy it should do so. The turbulent developments in the environment make this inevitable.

References

Aarts, J F M C (1985) *Features of specializations in higher education: a problem definition (Kenmerken van studierichtingen in het hoger onderwijs: een probleemstelling) in* Aarts and Wijnen (1985)

Aarts, J F M C and Wijnen, W H F W eds (1985) *Specializations in Higher Education (Studierichtingen in het Hoger Onderwijs* Swets and Zeitlinger: Lisse

Academic Council (Academische Raad) (1983) *A Convergent Model for Higher Education (Een Convergent Model voor het Hoger Onderwijs)* Staatsuitgeverij: The Hague

Acherman, J A, Brons, R and Kuhry, B (1981-1982) De ontwikkeling van het aantal studenten in het wetenschappelijk onderwijs (The development of student numbers in university education) *Universiteit en Hogeschool* 28: 6: 321-339

Andel, S I van (1984) On the grass between the tiles (Over het gras tussen de tegels) *Higher Vocational Education in Variety by Context (Hoger Beroepsonderwijs in Verscheidenheid naar Samenhang)* HBO-Raad/VUGA: The Hague

Berg, R van den and Vandenberghe, R (1981) *Educational Innovation in Shifting Perspective (Onderwijsinnovatie in Verschuivend Perspectief)* Zwijsen: Tilburg

Berkel, H J M van, Bax, A E and Holleman, J W eds (1985) *Quality of Higher Education: Control and Improvement (Kwaliteit van Hoger Onderwijs: Bewaking en verbetering)* Versluys: Amsterdman

Bevers, J A A M, Bouhuis, P A J and Gobbits, R (1981) *Results of the preliminary investigation: Te verwachten mutanten in de vraag naar c.q. het aanbod van hoger onderwijs in de komende decennia* (Expected changes in the demand for and supply of higher education in the coming decades) Staatsuitgeverij: The Hague

Bronneman-Helmers, R (1984a) Developments and outlooks (Ontwikkelingen en vooruitzichten) *in* Bronneman-Helmers (1984b)

Bronneman-Helmers, R (1984b) *The Job Market for Higher Education Graduates (De Arbeidsmarkt voor Hoger Opgeleiden)* SCP: Rijowijk

Christiaans, H H C M (1985) WO en HBO-kenmerken in het technisch hoger onderwijs (Features of university education and higher vocational education in technical higher education) *in* Aarts and Wijnen

Cohen, M D, March, J G and Olsen, J P (1972) A garbage can model of organizational choice *Administrative Science Quarterly* **17**: 1: 1-25.

Duncan, J G (1982) A marketing perspective *in* Squires (1982)

Frissen, P (1985) De overheid en kwaliteitsbewaking in het hoger onderwijs (The government and quality control in higher education) *in* van Berkel *et al* (forthcoming)

Frissen, P and Hoewijk, P M T van (1985) De universitaire onderwijs organisatie: omgeving en beleid (University education organization: environment and policy) *in* Frissen, van Hoewijk and van Hout (forthcoming)

Frissen, P, Hoewijk, P M T van and Hout, J F M J van eds (1986) *De Universiteit: een Adequate Onderwijsorganisatie?* (The University: an Effective Educational Organization?) Het Spectrum: Utrecht/Antwerp

Gevers, J K M (1984) Van visionair bestuur en vaderlijk beheer (Of visionary administration and paternal management) *in Hoger Beroepsonderwijs in Verscheidenheid naar Samenhang* (Higher Vocational Education in Variety by Context) HBO-Raad/VUGA: The Hague

Grip, A de (1984) Onderwijs en arbeidsmarkt (Education and job market) *Intermediair* **20**: 21

HBO Council (HBO-Raad) (1984) *HBO Council's View of the Green Paper on Scale Expansion, Specialization and Concentration in HBO* (*Standpunt HBO-Raad over Nota Schaalvergroting, Taakverdeling en Concentratie in het HBO*) HBO: The Hague

HBO Council (HBO-Raad) (1984-1985) *Scale Expansion/Specialization/Concentration Reports: Various Issues* (*Schaalvergroting-Taakverdeling-Concentratie-Berichten*) HBO: The Hague

HBO Council (HBO-Raad) (1985) *Almanak 1985* (Almanac 1985) HBO: The Hague

Hout, J F M J van, Frissen, P and Hoewijk, P M T van eds (1985) The University: an Effective Educational Organization? (*De Universiteit, een Adequate Onderwijsorganisatie?*) Symposiumverslag: Nijmegen

Hover, C (1983) Schaalvergroting: meer mensen, meer problemen, meer kosten (Scale expansion: more people, more problems, more costs) *HBO-Journaal 6* **2**: 34-37

Keller, G (1983) The management revolution in American higher education *Academic Strategy*

Kemenade, J A van ed (1981) *Education: Management and Policy* (*Onderwijs: Bestel en Beleid*) Woltes-Noordhoff: Groningen

Kickert, W J M (1985) Quo vadis, hoger onderwijs? Huidige beleidsontwikkelingen en mogelijke toekomstverkenninge (Quo vadis, higher education? Present-day policy developments and possible future explorations) *Bestuur* **4**: 14-25

Knip, H (1982) Organization Studies in Education (*Organisatiestudies in het Onderwijs*) SVO: Harlingen

Kodde, D A (1984) Wie kiest er voor hoger onderwijs? (Who's for higher education?) *Research Memorandum 8401* University of Nijmegen

Lawrence, P R and Lorsch, J W (1967) Managing differentiation and integration *Organization and Environment* Harvard University Press: Boston

Lieshout, W C M van (1984) The time is ripe (De tijd is rijp) *in* Lieshout (1984a)

Lieshout, W C M van (1984a) Higher Vocational Education in Variety by Context (Hoger Beroepsonderwijs in Verscheidenheid naar Samenhang) The Hague

McDaniel, O C (1985) De indeling van het hoger onderwijs en de criteria voor de toekomst (The structure of higher education and the criteria for the future) *in* Aarts and Wijnen (1985)

Marx, E C H (1975) *De Organisatie van Scholengemeenschappen in Onderwijskundige Optiek* (The Organization of School-Groups from a Pedagogical Viewpoint) Tjeenk Willink: Groningen

Mertens, F J H (1981) Het praktijkjaar van het hoger technisch onderwijs (The practical year in higher technical education) *Stages in een Beroepsopleiding* (Practical Periods in Vocational Education) PhD Thesis, Amsterdam

Ministry of Science and Education (Ministerie van Onderwijs en Wetenschappen) (1975) A possible long-term development and first moves in the coming years (Een mogelijke ontwikkeling op lange termijn en aanzetten in de komende jaren) *Higher Education in the Future* (*Hoger Onderwijs in de Toekomst*) Staatsuitgeverij: The Hague

Ministry of Science and Education (Ministerie van Onderwijs en Wetenschappen) (1983) Scale Expansion, Specialization and Concentration in Higher Vocational Education (*Schaalvergroting, Taakverdeling en Concentratie in het Hoger Beroepsonderwijs*) Staatsuitgeverij: The Hague

Ministry of Science and Education (Ministerie van Onderwijs en Wetenschappen) (1984a) *Meer over Management* (More about Management) Staatsuitgeverij: The Hague

Ministry of Science and Education (Ministerie van Onderwijs en Wetenschappen) (1984b) Towards a New Funding System for HBO (*Naar een Nieuw Bekostigingssysteem voor het HBO*) Staatsuitgeverij: The Hague

Ministry of Science and Education (Ministerie van Onderwijs en Wetenschappen) (1985) A different administrative method (Een andere besturingswijze) *Higher Education: Autonomy and Quality* (*Hoger Onderwijs: Autonomie en Kwaliteit*) Staatsuitgeverij: The Hague

Putten, M J T A van der (1981) Ontwikkelingen in het onderwijsbeleid en het functioneren van het Rijksschooltoezicht Hoger Technisch Onderwijs (Developments in educational policy and how the higher technical education school supervision functions) *Beleid en Toezicht* (Policy and Supervision): Nijmegen

Ritzen, J M M (1982) Hoger opgeleiden in de knel (Higher education graduates in a spot) *Research Memorandum 8205* University of Nijmegen

Ritzen, J M M (1983) Geen werk voor hoger en semi-hoger opgeleiden? (No work for higher-education and further-education graduates?) *Hoger Onderwijs* **1**: 2: 43-46

Squires, C ed (1982) *Innovation through Recession* Society for Research in Higher Education: Guildford

Veld, R J in 't (1985) Opening van het symposium (Opening of the symposium) *in* Hout, Frissen and Hoewijk (1985)

Wieringen, A M L van (1976) Een onderzoek naar de taak en plaats van het hoger beroepsonderwijs in het Nederlandse schoolwezen (An investigation into the role and position of higher vocational education in the Dutch school system) *De Identiteit van het Hoger Beroepsonderwijs* (The Identity of Higher Vocational Education) Tjeenk Willink: Groningen

11. Agricultural extension services in the anglophone countries of Southern Africa

Chris Garforth

Summary: This chapter is about public systems of advice and support for farmers in Southern Africa. Within the countries of this region there are great variations in scale of farming, commercial orientation and farming systems. Publicly funded extension services are generally designed to serve the small-scale farmers, who are in the majority. A basic premise has been that farms could be far more productive with the adoption of improved agricultural practices and crop varieties. More recently, the limitations of this view — and the varying suitability of the practices recommended — have been recognized. Field-level extension workers formerly concentrated their efforts on a relatively few 'progressive' farmers. Because of the failure to influence the farming practices of the majority of farmers, extension workers assist groups of farmers to identify local problems and potential, and plan extension, technical and training support to meet local needs. Women are at last being recognized as farmers in their own right and extension programmes are being adjusted accordingly. Agricultural research procedures are being developed which will produce recommendations more relevant to local environments and the realities of small-scale farmers. Educational media are used extensively to support extension and training: the introduction of formative research into their design has improved their relevance and effectiveness. The training and visit system of agricultural extension is now being introduced in ways which complement, rather than replace, existing approaches.

Introduction

Arguably the most important vocational education in Southern Africa is the 'in-service' or 'on-farm' education provided by the public agricultural extension services for working farmers. The English-speaking countries of Southern Africa remain largely agricultural. Although mining and manufacturing industry make increasing contributions to national economies, these activities employ a relatively small proportion of the labour force. The overwhelming majority of people in the region still rely on agriculture for their subsistence and for their cash incomes; and the cash crops of Zimbabwe, Malawi and Swaziland and the cattle of Botswana remain vitally important sources of foreign exchange. Even within the non-agricultural sectors, relatively few people have made a complete break with agriculture. Civil servants, industrial employees and others working in urban areas may own cattle, or employ people to farm their land for them, or provide cash and inputs to members of their family who work the family farm. Agriculture pervades the personality, perceptions and economies of most families in the region.

It follows that vocational training and non-formal education for those working in agriculture is an important aspect of educational provision. Although there is an increasing emphasis on the teaching of agriculture in primary and secondary schools (particularly in Zimbabwe and Swaziland, which have made considerable investments in school agriculture in recent years) most of this educational work is the responsibility of agricultural extension services. Their broad aim is to enable farmers to make the best use of the resources of land, labour, capital and knowledge available to them in the interests both of their families and of the national economy. This involves the provision of technical information, advice and training. It also involves education on environmental processes and their implications — particularly soil erosion, which has been seen as a serious problem since the introduction of the plough into the region in the 19th century. Extension agencies also offer technical services, which vary from country to country but may range from the hire of tractors and the sale of day-old chicks to assistance in designing soil conservation measures on individual farms.

Agricultural extension and training are not provided exclusively by government agencies. There are many local initiatives which have been started by enterprising individuals, by churches and by other non-government organizations. In Lesotho, for example, the Thabe-Kupa Ecumenical Centre Farm Institute was established near Roma by the Lesotho churches in response to the problem of unemployment among primary school leavers. Beginning with a two-year course in intensive, commercially oriented agriculture, activities soon expanded to offer continuing extension support to students once they had established themselves as independent farmers.

School leaver unemployment was also the stimulus behind the Brigades movement in Botswana, one of the most important developments in vocational training in the region. Due largely to the initiative of Patrick van Rensburg and the leaders of the Bamangwato tribe, the Brigades have grown from small beginnings at Swaneng Hill School in 1965 to become a national movement in which young people can gain apprenticeship-type training in a range of vocations, from farming to building, and tanning to carpentry (van Rensburg, 1974).

In the more fertile areas of Zimbabwe, which were taken over in the 19th century by European settlers and became a highly productive and commercialized enclave within the agricultural economy, larger-scale farmers often rely more on technical advisers from suppliers of seed, equipment, fertilizer and pesticide, and from crop processing companies, than on government extension services (Kennan, 1980). Tobacco companies in Malawi and Zambia have their own teams of advisers working with smallholders to recruit new growers and to maintain production and curing quality.

Diversity of provision reflects the great variations in agriculture within and between the countries of the region. (This is due largely to variations in climate and soils, from the harsh environment of the Kalahari Desert where cattle compete with mining companies and bushmen for scarce water resources, to some of the most productive land in Africa. It is also in part, however, a legacy of colonial history and commercial exploit-ation.) Between the lush plantation of sugar cane with its sophisticated machinery and irrigation and employing hundreds of labourers, and the subsistence farm on the Kalahari fringe from which a woman and her children derive a precarious living under the constant threat of drought, there is a wide spectrum of farm types, with very different extension and training needs. Export crops give way to food crops; mechanized farms of several hundred hectares give way to smallholdings of five hec-tares or less, worked with an ox plough or a hoe; crops give way to cattle.

Most farmers in the region, however, operate small-scale holdings; and it is towards the needs of these farmers that government extension services are generally directed. The exception is Zimbabwe, where before inde-pendence two separate extension services were established: one for the white, commercial farmers, and the other for black farmers in the communal areas (formerly 'tribal trust lands').

Agricultural extension in Southern Africa began from the premise that existing farming practices were not only inefficient but in some cases threatened the long-term viability of the very soils on which farmers depended. The yields of food crops were seen to be much lower than could be obtained with more modern farming techniques. To increase productivity would mean more foodstuffs on the market for the growing urban population; while the introduction of new crops to smallholders (cotton and tobacco, for example) would boost the national economy. The strategy that emerged throughout the region was the introduction of improved farming practices on individual farms, backed up by legislation to prevent the destruction of farming resources. The improved tech-nology was to come initially from imported views on how farming ought to be done (crop rotation, manuring, effective ploughing and weed control), but increasingly from agricultural research conducted within the region.

In Zambia, the early colonial Department of Agriculture established eight agricultural field stations in the 1940s, at which extension staff (totalling 24 at that time) organized field days, held demonstrations and offered recommendations to farmers in the vicinity on crop rotation, the use of oxen as draught animals and other improvements (Maimbo, 1982). Extension began earlier in Zimbabwe, with demonstration plots estab-lished from 1926 within the 'tribal' areas to show the benefits of manuring and crop rotation (Kennan, 1980).

From these early, localized efforts, all countries in the region have developed a network of field-level extension workers (variously called agricultural demonstrators, agricultural assistants, commodity demon-strators and field assistants) backed up by supervisory staff and specialists to whom they can turn for advice on specific farm enterprises or problems. Farmer (or 'rural') training centres offer residential courses of a few days to farmers. These extension and training activities are reinforced by farm broadcasting and the production of visual and audiovisual aids by specialized units within the ministries of agriculture.

The demise of the 'progressive farmer'

In the early days, extension workers were encouraged to identify and work closely with a small number of farmers who were willing to be taught new farming methods. The Pupil Farmer Scheme in Botswana had its counterparts in Malawi and Zimbabwe. Under the Botswana Scheme, an extension worker recruited a few 'pupil farmers' who, over a period of a couple of years, would be trained in a package of improved farm practices and new enterprises. They were also offered access to credit and the inputs they needed. Gradually, the pupil farmers were to become 'improved' and, finally, 'progressive' farmers. On reaching that stage, farmers would become virtually independent of the extension worker, who would then be free to recruit another set of farmers into the scheme. Furthermore, the improved performance of the progressive farmers would serve as a demonstration and an incentive to other farmers to take up the improved practices.

Part of the thinking behind such a 'progressive farmer' strategy was that enterprising individuals should be taken out of the subsistence sector, away from 'traditional' farming, and transformed into commercially oriented farmers. This was institutionalized in Zimbabwe through the establishment of 'African purchase areas', in which farmers from the tribal trust lands could at first lease and then buy freehold plots of land. They could then move out, physically as well as technologically, from the subsistence-based farming of the tribal trust lands. Conditions were stringent. An applicant needed to have had two years of formal training in agriculture, or a Master Farmer's certificate, and some capital. The option to purchase the farm was dependent upon satisfactory farm husbandry during the initial two-year lease period.

Progressive farmer schemes proved very expensive in scarce manpower and not particularly effective in promoting the widespread uptake of new farming practices. In Zimbabwe in the early 1970s, the African purchase areas had a ratio of 1 frontline extension worker to 34 farmers, compared to a ratio of 1 to 524 in the tribal trust lands (Bembridge, 1972; Mungate, 1983). In Botswana, 90 per cent of extension worker time was being devoted to the 7 per cent of farmers enrolled in the Pupil Farmer Scheme (Kingshotte, 1979): once enrolled, few farmers were graduating as independent 'progressive' farmers. The majority of farmers were left untouched by extension.

There was a further source of disillusion with these approaches. Once most of the countries in the region became independent in the mid-1960s (the obvious exception being Zimbabwe, which did not achieve that status until 15 years later), agricultural development became seen as much more than a contribution to the growth of the national economy: it was now seen as an important means to directly improve the standard of living of the majority of the region's population. A progressive farmer approach was no longer tenable on equity grounds.

Changing roles for extension workers

The failure of progressive farmer approaches to bring widespread benefits to smallholders was only one of the factors that prompted a number of changes in the way agricultural extension was organized and practised during the 1970s. Another was the increasing fragmentation of extension activities. Each new agricultural specialism or project generated its own cadre of field-level specialists. In Botswana before the 1975 reorganization the Ministry of Agriculture was divided into ten specialist Divisions, each reporting directly to the permanent Secretary, and each with its own specialist staff in the field attempting to work directly with farmers. The farmer was faced with a potentially bewildering array of advisers, each with a particular specialist axe to grind — from chickens and maize production to soil conservation and co-operative development.

The principle that a cadre of extension workers with a general agricultural training should form the point of contact between ministries of agriculture and farmers has now been generally accepted. This cadre can see the farm — its resources, its mixture of crop and livestock enterprises, its problems and potential — as a whole, rather than through the narrow perception of a specialist. The specialist divisions now provide in-service training, technical support and advisory backup to the field-level staff. In Zambia, for example, all services to the farmers are co-ordinated through the office of the district agricultural officer. If farmers require specialist advice or assistance which the agricultural assistant cannot provide, he can call on the services of specialists at district or provincial level. In Botswana, as elsewhere, this has involved a considerable re-organization: the 10 divisions were replaced in 1975 by three departments (animal health, agricultural research and agricultural field service), with the department of agricultural field services responsible for all extension work other than livestock health. The specialists of the pre-1975 divisions were brought under the umbrella of this latter department (Kingshotte, 1979). The status of the agricultural demonstrator as the main point of contact with farmers has consequently been enhanced.

The role of field-level extension workers has changed in another important respect: they are now expected to provide extension services to *all* farmers in their area — and between them they now cover the entire agricultural areas of their respective countries — rather than the favoured few. In Botswana, a farmer record card was introduced to help agricultural demonstrators get to know the circumstances of all the farm families in their areas. (The relatively favourable ratio of extension workers to farmers in Botswana of 1:200 made this at least a feasible target, which it would not be elsewhere in the region where ratios can be over 1:500.) Over a period of a few years, agricultural demonstrators were expected to collect household and farm data for every family in the area and to update the record card whenever appropriate. As well as providing useful information as a basis for working with individual farm families, the cards taken together were to be a basic database for the planning and monitoring of extension activities in the area (Kingshotte, 1979).

Women in agricultural extension

One major category of farmers which agricultural extension has tended to ignore until recently is women. It has taken male-dominated extension services, influenced as they have been by American and European concepts of the farm family with its male farmer and female housewife, several decades to wake up to the reality that women do more than half of the farming work in the region. In many cases — over 30 per cent of rural households in Botswana and parts of Malawi — households have no adult males for much of the year: women run the home *and* the farm. Even farm work that in the past was regarded as 'man's work', such as ploughing in Botswana, is now done by women. But women, even in male-headed households, have always played an important role in farm decision making. In some areas, women are responsible for cultivating food crops, while their menfolk grow industrial crops for sale.

Extension for women used to be equated with home economics — food preparation, nutrition education, sewing, knitting and child care. Courses in these subjects were run at Farmer Training Centres and in Malawi, a separate farm home economics section, staffed by women, was established. Agricultural training for women was usually limited to vegetable gardening and possibly small-scale poultry production. Male agricultural extension workers tended to work exclusively with men. This gender bias in agricultural extension is not peculiar to Southern Africa (Berger *et al*, 1984) but the relative prominence of women in agriculture in the region makes it particularly serious.

This problem has been approached in different ways. In both Malawi and Botswana, women's extension advisers were appointed at either national or regional level in the 1970s to explore how agricultural extension services could be made more responsive to the needs of women, and more accessible to women farmers. Both countries now have senior officers at national level within the Ministry of Agriculture with overall responsibility for ensuring that the extension and training needs of women are met. In Malawi, the approach has been to broaden the remit of the farm home economics section (now renamed the women's programme section) to include agriculture. In the field, farm home assistants act as subject matter specialists at sub-district level. There is thus a separate cadre of extension workers responsible for women's affairs, serving as specialist backup to the frontline male extension workers. In Botswana, on the other hand, female agricultural demonstrators are trained and posted on the same basis as men (Bettles, 1980). However, they are few in number and tend to gravitate towards posts within regional or national headquarters because of the isolation they experience within an almost exclusively male extension service and the difficulties of establishing their credibility with male farmers. The orientation of residential training courses has also been tackled, albeit in a small way. Two of Botswana's rural training centres have tried to develop agricultural curricula of particular relevance to rural women (Higgins, 1984).

Where extension activities have been geared specifically towards women, they have often found a more enthusiastic response than similar activities among men. This has been claimed in respect of women's clubs in Zimbabwe (Plowes, 1980) and seems to have been the case with women's groups on training courses in the integrated farming pilot project in Botswana (Bettles, 1980).

From individual farmers to groups

The need to bring extension services to all farmers demanded a re-think of extension methods. Extension advice could not be offered to all farmers on an individual basis. There has consequently been a growing emphasis on working with groups of farmers. It is more economical for an extension worker to spend an hour with a group of 10 or 15 farmers than with a single farmer. However, this is not the only reason for advocating group approaches to extension. Groups also offer an environment in which discussion and mutual reinforcement can promote more effective learning and problem-solving; while for many farming activities, particularly in smallholder agriculture, a group is a more appropriate entity for taking action than an individual farm (Garforth, 1982). Soil conservation, for example, or the purchase of an item of machinery that would be uneconomic for a single person to own, make more sense when they become group activities.

There has for long been a group element in extension work in the region. Field days and demonstrations have always been designed for groups of farmers. Extension workers have been encouraged to establish farmers' committees and to use these as a point of contact with farmers in the area. In Zimbabwe, master farmers formed local groups, which were affiliated to provincial master farmers' associations: these associations provided training courses, regular newspapers and other services to their members and were the beginnings of an autonomous extension and training service run by farmers for farmers (Bates, 1980).

But by and large, groups were used as a mechanism for making predetermined information available to larger numbers of farmers than could be reached by individual contact. The past ten years have seen innovations in group extension methods in the region which imply a new role for extension and a more balanced relationship between extension workers and farmers. In the communal areas of the Midlands province of Zimbabwe, each extension worker is responsible for an area containing about 550 farm families. These are all regarded as members of farmers' groups — with 50 to 90 families per group, and group membership being determined on a geographical basis. The groups, through elected committees, play an active role in planning extension and training programmes in their areas and in setting their own farming objectives (in terms of yield increase, adoption of new practices, acquisition of new equipment, and so on). The extension worker supports the process of group development through the various stages of mobilization, organization, training, resource support and replication (Vaughan-Evans and Madebvu, 1986). As well as providing a structure within which training received by group leaders and representatives is passed on to other group members, extension activities and technical advice are becoming much more relevant to local needs, aspirations and potential.

It is in Botswana that group extension has been developed most thoroughly as an alternative to progressive farmer approaches. Extension workers have been trained to identify existing and potential groupings, based on social relationships or common interests, which they have then encouraged to work together to plan group projects. The Ministry of Agriculture makes money available in the form of grants to match funds which the group raises itself towards the financing of its projects. This approach, when introduced in the mid-1970s, seemed to unlock a tremendous reserve of initiative, leadership and innovative potential which had lain dormant under previous extension approaches (Willett, 1981). Hundreds of groups were formed and projects identified. Instead of being solely purveyors of new technology, extension workers have become facilitators of group development and activity. This new role, however, requires a shift in attitudes, perceptions and methods for extension workers. Pre-service and in-service training curricula have had to be adjusted to support the change in extension approach (Russell, 1986). More emphasis has been placed on communication techniques, group dynamics and social research skills (Odell, 1977).

Fortmann (1984) suggests, however, that where extension workers suffer from low morale and receive inadequate encouragement and support from their superior officers, the policy changes have had little impact on practice. The lack of any formal accountability of the extension workers to the communities they serve further reduces their incentive to implement the new approach.

Identifying relevant technology

The new emphasis on local initiative, however — the involvement of farmers' groups in extension planning, for instance, and the proliferation of day training centres in Malawi which complement the residential training centres by offering non-residential courses of specific local relevance — has given additional impetus to a review of how agricultural technology is developed. The suitability for small farmers of agricultural practices developed on well-equipped research stations in climatic conditions and on soils very different from their own has frequently been questioned. At the same time, farmers' own expertise in experimentation is at last being recognized (Richard, 1985). Various attempts have been made to involve farmers in the formal testing of research findings under small farm conditions, but tensions between the research designs and protocols of scientists and the realities of small-scale farming have led to disappointing results. Recently, however, Zambia and Malawi have introduced on a national scale an innovatory approach to identifying research priorities and producing agronomic recommendations that are locally relevant. In Zambia, adaptive research planning teams are being set up in each province. These teams, comprising an agronomist, a farming systems analyst and a research extension liaison officer, are responsible for testing recommendations on smallholders' farms and adapting them to suit conditions within the province (Roling, 1982). In Malawi, adaptive research teams were being introduced in 1984 within the eight agricultural development divisions into which the country is divided under the National Rural Development Programme (Chirambo, 1985).

Media in agricultural extension

Educational media have been used in the region for many years to support agricultural extension and training. Farm broadcasting is well established in Malawi, Zambia and Botswana. Mobile units take films, slide sets and puppet shows around the rural areas to support the local activities of extension workers. Magazines, newsletters, flipcharts, leaflets and posters are produced for extension staff and for farmers. Video is now being used in Zimbabwe. Media production tends to be centralized at national level, largely on grounds of economies and the shortage of skilled personnel. In Malawi, however, extension aids units are being established within the Agricultural Development Divisions: these are in a better position to design locally relevant visual and audiovisual aids.

In farm broadcasting, a variety of formats is used, including farmers' music requests interspersed with short items of agricultural news and information, soap operas, magazine programmes, field recordings of interviews and discussions with farmers, and panel discussions among agricultural experts. In Zambia, the farm forum has been a feature of agricultural broadcasting for many years: the extension worker meets with a group of farmers on a regular basis specifically to listen to the radio programme, to discuss with them the issues it raises, and to reach with the farmers some decisions on how they should use the ideas put across in the broadcast. Other countries have not attempted to organize radio listening to such an extent; but in Botswana the radio forum concept contributed to the design of an intensive ten-week campaign in 1976 to explain, and canvass views on, a major reform of grazing land policy. In 1979, a similar approach was adopted for the provision of non-formal education to communities in the west of the country which were relatively isolated from agricultural extension workers. Research in the area indicated educational priorities; audio cassette programmes were produced and supplemented by magazines, study guides and flipcharts; volunteer group leaders were recruited from within the communities and trained in the use of the materials; and over a six-month period groups met, listened to the cassettes, discussed the material, sent in questions and comments to the Ministry of Agriculture, and attended demonstrations held in the area. The groups' questions were answered in regular farm broadcasts (Byram and Garforth, 1980).

Media communication can be extremely cost-effective, provided it conveys relevant information, in a comprehensible way, and reaches large numbers of people. Perraton (1983) has shown the low unit cost of making an hour of agricultural broadcasting available to an individual farmer in Malawi — only 0.1 per cent of the cost of an hour's visit from an extension worker. Questions of relevance and comprehensibility have been tackled in Malawi and Botswana by the incorporation of formative (or action) research into the production of media for agricultural extension. Action research units have been established in the extension aids branch and agricultural information services respectively. Through their background research into farmers' knowledge, attitudes and practices in relation to agricultural topics, their pre-testing of draft media and their evaluative studies, the relevance and effectiveness of audiovisual, broadcast and printed extension aids have been enhanced (Garforth, 1986).

Training and visit

Finally, no chapter on agricultural extension would be complete without reference to the Training and Visit (T&V) system, which has had a profound effect on extension practice in the past ten years. Introduced within World Bank assisted projects in a number of Asian countries in the mid- to late 1970s, T&V is designed to improve the flow of relevant technical information to farmers while at the same time offering better management, supervision and training of extension workers. Field-level extension workers meet with groups of contact farmers on a regular fortnightly schedule to pass on information and training which they themselves have received at fortnightly training sessions. At these sessions, subject matter specialists deal with any problems or questions encountered by extension workers during the previous two weeks (Benor, Harrison and Baxter, 1984). The contact farmers are then supposed to pass on their knowledge and training to other farmers.

Doubts have been expressed about the applicability of T&V to Africa given the variability, even within local areas, of cropping patterns, the scale of individual farms, and the timing of operations. However Zambia, Zimbabwe and Malawi have introduced elements of T&V into their extension services in ways which demonstrate the versatility of the system. In Malawi, under the 'block extension approach' which is now being commended to agricultural development divisions by the Ministry of Agriculture, field assistants divide their areas into a number of geographical blocks, each containing between 30 and 100 farm families. Each block is allotted two days of the field assistant's time each month: one day for the training of farmers and one for follow-up visits to farmers' fields. Within the block, a plot is made available for demonstrations and a 'block house' serves as a local training centre (Chirambo, 1985). The group approach in Midlands province of Zimbabwe described earlier has been developed in the context of a T&V system introduced under the National Agricultural Extension and Research Project (Vaughan-Evans and Mandebvu, 1986). In Zambia, T&V had been introduced into two of the eight provinces by 1979 without any major organizational changes in the extension service (Maimbo, 1982). It has proved a useful way of increasing contact between extension workers and farmers, improving the in-service training and supervision of extension workers, and introducing an element of accountability to the farmers they serve.

The trends of the past 15 years, then, have been towards universal access by farmers to extension services, improved management, supervision and training of extension workers, better media support, greater local participation in the planning of extension activities and in determining training needs, and greater care in identifying and refining appropriate agricultural technology. The next few years will show whether these changes can help to achieve the sustained increases in agricultural production, combined with an equitable distribution of the benefits of agricultural development, to which the countries of the region aspire.

References

Bates, D B (1980) Important innovations introduced by agricultural extension to the tribal farmer over the last twenty years *The Zimbabwe Science News* 14: 7: 187-190

Bembridge, T J (1972) *Extension in a Rhodesian Purchase Land Area* Unpublished MSc dissertation, Reading University: UK

Benor, D, Harrison, J and Baxter, M (1984) *Agricultural Extension: The Training and Visit System* World Bank: Washington, DC

Berger, M, Delancey, V and Mellenchamp, A (1984) *Bridging the Gender Gap in Agricultural Extension* International Centre of Research on Women: Washington, DC

Bettles, F M (1980) *Women's Access to Agricultural Extension Services in Botswana* Women's Extension Unit, Ministry of Agriculture: Gaborone, Botswana

Byram, M and Garforth, C (1980) Researching and testing non-formal education materials: a multi-media extension project in Botswana *Educational Broadcasting International* December: 190-194

Chirambo, S (1985) *Factors affecting the Rate of Adoption of Agricultural Innovations with Special Reference to Northern Malawi* Unpublished MSc dissertation, Reading University: UK

Fortmann, L (1984) *The Performance of Extension Services in Botswana* Network Paper 20, Agricultural Administration Network, Overseas Development Institute: London

Garforth, C (1982) Reaching the rural poor: a review of extension strategies and methods *in* Jones and Rolls (1982)

Garforth, C (1986) Universities, educational research and the development of media for non-formal education: lessons from agricultural projects in Africa and SE Asia *in* Smawfield (1986)

Higgins, K M (1984) *Curriculum Development and Citizen Education: A Case Study of a Farmer Training Programme for Women in Botswana* Institute of Adult Education, University of Botswana: Gaborone

Jones, G E ed (1986) *Investing in Rural Extension: Strategies and Goals* Elsevier Applied Science Publishers: London

Jones, G E and Rolls, M R eds (1982) *Progress in Rural Extension and Community Development, vol. 1: Extension and Relative Advantage in Rural Development* John Wiley and Sons: Chichester

Kennan, P B (1980) Agricultural extension in Zimbabwe, 1950-1980 *The Zimbabwe Science News* 14: 7: 183-186

Kingshotte, A (1979) *The Organisation and Management of Agricultural Extension and Farmer Assistance in Botswana* Discussion Paper 1, Agricultural Administration Unit, Overseas Development Institute: London

Maimbo, P (1982) *An Analysis of the Training and Visit System as an Additional Approach to Agricultural Extension in the Central Province of Zambia* Unpublished Diploma dissertation, Reading University: UK

Mungate, D T (1983) *Agricultural Extension: Philosophy and Practice, with Special Reference to the Small-Scale Commercial Areas of Zimbabwe* Unpublished MSc dissertation, Reading University: UK

Odell, M J ed (1977) *Group Formation: Senior Agricultural Officers' Workshop. Final Report and Course Materials* Ministry of Agriculture: Gaborone

Perraton, H (1983) Mass media, basic education and agricultural extension *in* Perraton, Jamison, Jenkins, Orivel and Wolff (1983)

Perraton, H, Jamison, D T, Jenkins, J, Orivel, F and Wolff, L (1983) *Basic Education and Agricultural Extension: Costs, Effects and Alternatives* World Bank: Washington, DC

Plowes, D C H (1980) The impact of agricultural extension in the eastern tribal area of Zimbabwe *The Zimbabwe Science News* 14: 7: 197-200

van Rensburg, P (1974) *Report from Swaneng Hill: Education and Employment in an African Country* Dag Hammarskjold Foundation: Uppsala, Sweden

Richard, P (1985) *Indigenous Agricultural Revolution. Ecology and Food Production in West Africa* Hutchinson: London

Roling, N (1982) Alternative approaches in extension *in* Jones and Rolls (1982)

Russell, J A A (1986) Extension strategies involving local groups and their participation, and the role of this approach in facilitating local development *in* Jones (1986)

Smawfield, D ed (1986) *International Academic Interchange and Cooperation in Higher Education* International Education Unit, University of Hull: Hull

Vaughan-Evans, R H and Mandebvu, F G (1986) Group activity and involvement of peasant farmers in disseminating technology in the Gweru Region of Midland Province, Zimbabwe *in* Jones (1986)

Willett, A B J (1981) *Agricultural Group Development in Botswana* (4 vols) Government Printer: Gaborone

12. Vocational education in the USA as a vehicle for the entrepreneurial spirit

Catherine Ashmore

Summary: It is now commonplace that small businesses in the USA have generated very large numbers of new jobs. Since 1976, the National Center for Research in Vocational Education has been developing strategies for vocational education's involvement in small business creation. The main goal of entrepreneurship education is to provide a broader look at career options and to identify ways to reach these options. It can also help students gain a better understanding of the problems of employers.

The National Center has designed a five-stage model based on the premise that skills and attitudes for successful business development are not learned at any one place or time, and that the earlier young people begin to learn such skills the more likely they are to become successful entrepreneurs. The National Center's Program for Acquiring Competence in Entrepreneurship (PACE) covers 18 major topics which provide the management basics for most small businesses. These 18 topics can be introduced at three levels: at the point at which the student would not be ready to start a business but could be thinking along these lines as a career option while still at school; for students who want to acquire more in-depth knowledge, ideally for planning a business to be started some time in the future; and for the person who is ready to start a business. Even if the students do not become entrepreneurs as a result of these programmes, they will have absorbed something of the dynamic entrepreneurial spirit which is so important to the American economy.

Are entrepreneurs born with the ability to be successful in business? Or do they 'become entrepreneurial' through their lifelong experiences? These questions lead to quite different answers in the education of the entrepreneurs who will build the jobs of our future. Those who support Albert Shapero's (1982) philosophy that the characteristics of entrepreneurs are attained through education, experience, and individual personal choice can also see the merit of exposing vocational students to the possibilities of starting their own businesses some day.

The vocational programmes in the United States encompass a complex system of courses in the public high schools, area vocational high schools, two-year colleges, technical institutes, and adult education settings. This complexity is based on the responsibility that each state has in designing a customized vocational training programme which considers the needs of the community and the area's students. There were almost three million high school graduates in 1982. About three-quarters of all young people in the USA finish high school, and slightly less than half of these enter a degree programme in a college or university. About 23 per cent of students in their late teens can be expected to earn a bachelor's degree, 7 per cent a master's degree, and about 1 per cent a doctorate. Although a significant percentage of high school graduates pursue some form of higher education, the majority (54 per cent) begin looking for employment immediately after high school (National Center for Educational Statistics, 1983). Regardless of the education they pursue, the major reason vocational education exists and succeeds is the need for everyone to find work expertise leading to employment opportunities.

Vocational education at the federal and state levels has taken the lead in a new movement to provide students with a greater understanding of their career options. One of the newest of these career options is the possibility of becoming self-employed rather than unemployed or employed by others. Once an individual considers self-employment and the competencies needed for it, starting a business that will also employ others becomes the next logical step. After all, Ford Motor Company and Sears Roebuck did not begin as huge corporations. The successes of Henry Ford and Richard Sears, the founders of the companies, came from their courage in turning ideas into reality and making the most of their opportunities.

Economic need for job creation

A study by Birch (1979) at Massachusetts Institute of Technology concluded that about two-thirds of US employment growth came from businesses with 20 or fewer employees. Most of these companies were less than five years old. The US Small Business Administration (SBA) reports that in 1981 and 1982, at the height of economic recession, small independent firms created 2,650,000 new jobs, more than compensating for the 1,664,000 jobs lost by large industry in the same period (US Small Business Administration, 1984).

The US Bureau of Labor Statistics predicts that the 40 occupations with the largest projected job growth between 1982 and 1995 will be largely in service industries — the type of business most easily started because of relatively small investment needs (*Monthly Labor Review*, 1983). Many of these same occupational needs are also being addressed by skill-building programmes in vocational education. If vocational education is to provide complete follow-through on skill-building programmes, it should also help its graduates find employment to use their skills and expertise.

It is common for vocationally trained students to be employed in small businesses — both because many skilled occupations are more often found in smaller businesses and because large corporations prefer their own training programmes. Regardless of the reason, the opportunity exists for vocationally trained students to gain experience in small business management — a valuable opportunity for the potential entrepreneur.

Vocational education

Federal legislation since 1963 and corresponding state legislation have supported a nationwide system of training programmes in high schools, two-year colleges, and community-based adult settings. Although occupational outcomes of all programmes are highly diverse, and often customized to business needs and employment opportunities, they have been characterized as 'entry-level training' by many. This attitude has led to educational snobbery — an unspoken assumption that vocational courses are for 'less able' students. When vocational training has led to career success for young people, accelerated upward mobility, and paycheck superiority, it has been a surprise to the educational community. Perhaps such positive results emerge because vocational educators have been unwilling to accept the preconceptions of others who suggest that some people are born to be managers and some are only able to handle entry-level career opportunities. The successes of vocationally trained entrepreneurs speak for themselves. Many vocational educators have taught students what they need to enter and advance in all types of work — including how to start businesses of their own. But entrepreneurship education has only recently been considered an integral part of vocational education.

Since 1983, it has been the policy of the US Department of Education to include entrepreneurship education and training in all vocational programmes both for high schools and adult programmes (Ross, Ashmore et al, 1984). The policy states that:

'It is the policy of the US Department of Education to encourage the inclusion of entrepreneurship as an integral part of vocational and adult education and to support all endeavors which serve to increase the capacity of vocational and adult education to deliver education for entrepreneurship.

'In keeping with this policy, the Office of Vocational and Adult Education will:

1. Give leadership in the development of entrepreneurship education.
2. Encourage the introduction of entrepreneurship concepts, essentially for career consideration, into all instructional programs in vocational and adult education.
3. Advocate the expansion of instructional programs specifically for entrepreneurship, especially at the post-secondary and adult levels of education.
4. Collaborate and cooperate with national associations and federal agencies concerned with the small business environment, including those which provide special assistance to women and minorities.

5. Identify and disseminate information about exemplary practices in entrepreneurship education.
6. Provide the states with suggested strategies for the promotion and implementation of entrepreneurship education.
7. Advocate the concept that the potential for entrepreneurial success is not limited by reason of age, sex, race, handicapping condition, or place of residence, and give special attention to those underrepresented in entrepreneurial fields, namely, women and minorities.
8. Maintain a communications network with various audiences in the public and private sectors in order to advance entrepreneurship education at state and local levels.
9. Document the scope of activities and achievements in entrepreneurship education.'

States have been slower to support this concept because it involves a major change in their announced goals for entry-level training in vocational education. However, a number of states have recognized the economic importance of job creation to their own future and have moved towards leadership in the entrepreneurship education movement. Vocational education programmes, serving approximately 30 per cent of the high school population, could have a major impact on new business startups in the USA as a result of the new focus on entrepreneurship education as a programme component.

Since 1976 the National Center for Research in Vocational Education has been developing strategies for vocational education's involvement in the small business creation movement. The National Center recognizes that there are a number of different ways people prepare for work. It recognizes that not all students will choose to become their own boss as a career option, but that all vocational students will contribute to the success of the community's entrepreneurs with their skills and work attitudes.

Entrepreneurship education options have a number of different outcomes for students, depending on the time devoted to the topic and the business background students bring to the programme. Objectives for a variety of programme options may include any of the following:

☐ *Career planning.* Students should understand their opportunities to start a business or become self-employed some time in their career. Generally, most students are not ready for this at graduation; however, they should see ways in which they can eventually move towards this option, if they so decide.
☐ *Business understanding.* Whether a person owns a business or is an employee, it is helpful to the operation for the person to understand all the functions of a business. Entrepreneurship education in the public schools will give all students a stronger business base.
☐ *Application of skills.* Entrepreneurship education may serve as a vehicle for students to see ways to become employed with the skills

they are acquiring in a vocational programme. It provides a method of exploring all the ways in which these job skills may be applied to community business needs.

☐ *Community understanding*. Students may use the entrepreneurship education programme to study entrepreneurs in the community, to perceive opportunities for new businesses in the area, to learn of the suppliers available, and to analyse the demographics that would contribute to the success of selected small business ventures.

☐ *Self-understanding*. Acquaintance with the life story of successful entrepreneurs can help students think about their personal attributes and lifestyle choices. It is important to look at both the positive and negative factors in a person's psychological makeup before choosing entrepreneurship as a career.

☐ *Orientation to change*. Students will learn to look for changes that may lead to business opportunities in the future. Entrepreneurs seem to have a single-minded drive to try the 'new' and stay ahead of others.

☐ *Creativity*. Entrepreneurship education encourages all kinds of innovative thinking related to new products, new services, changes in demographics, new technology, societal change, and community needs. Creating a business on paper that might be started in the community is an excellent exercise in such business creativity.

The ultimate goal of entrepreneurship education is thus to provide a broader look at career options and to identify ways to reach these options. Also, all students can, through entrepreneurship study, gain a better understanding of the problems of employers.

Lifelong learning model

The National Center's five-stage model was designed to show the lifelong development process desirable for encouraging successful small business creation. It is based on the premise that skills and attitudes necessary for successful business development are not learned at any one place or time. In fact, the earlier young people can begin to learn such skills, the more likely they are to be successful as entrepreneurs. Arthur Lipper III, in the October 1985 newsletter of the International Council of Small Business, maintains that learning to plan is the major missing ingredient for most entrepreneurs (Lipper, 1985).

The five-stage model supports different student outcomes for programmes at each stage (see Figure 1). Stage 1 may take place anywhere from kindergarten upward. It suggests that being your own boss may be a motivation for learning basic skills and the benefits of the free enterprise system. Stage 2 is designed to teach an understanding of the management skills one must develop to run a business. This stage is considered important for all vocational students and could be described as basic business skills needed to increase productivity. Stage 3 represents the

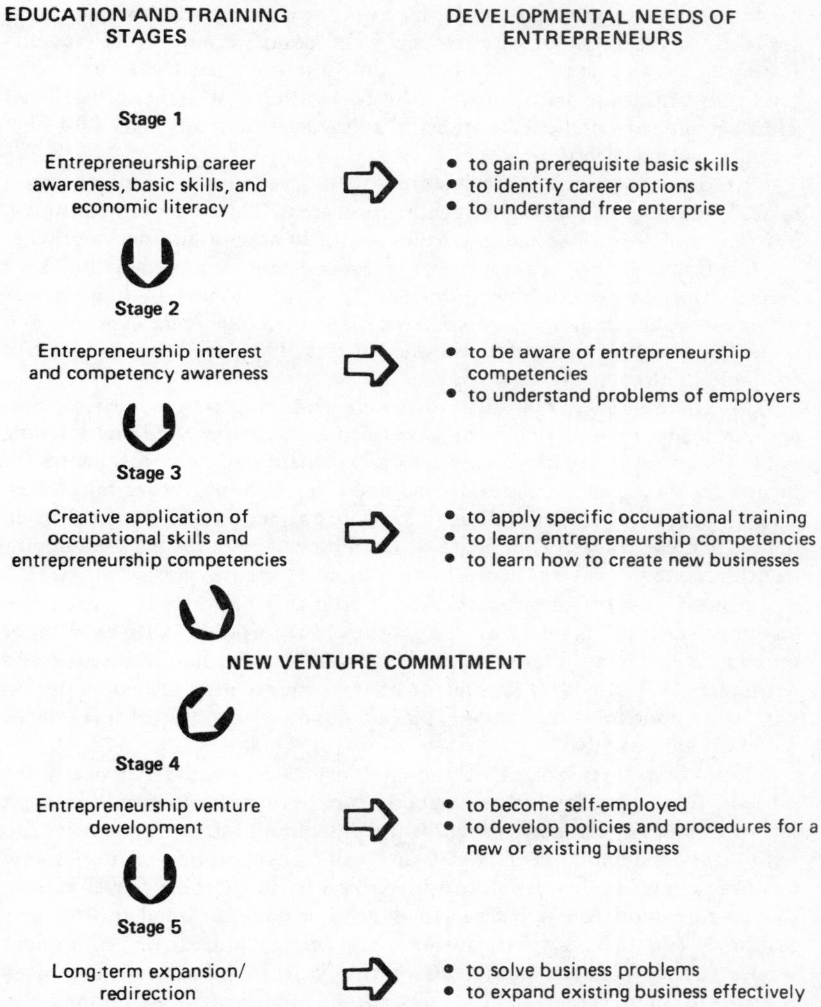

**EDUCATION AND TRAINING
STAGES**

**DEVELOPMENTAL NEEDS OF
ENTREPRENEURS**

Stage 1

Entrepreneurship career
awareness, basic skills, and
economic literacy

- to gain prerequisite basic skills
- to identify career options
- to understand free enterprise

Stage 2

Entrepreneurship interest
and competency awareness

- to be aware of entrepreneurship
  competencies
- to understand problems of employers

Stage 3

Creative application of
occupational skills and
entrepreneurship competencies

- to apply specific occupational training
- to learn entrepreneurship competencies
- to learn how to create new businesses

NEW VENTURE COMMITMENT

Stage 4

Entrepreneurship venture
development

- to become self-employed
- to develop policies and procedures for a
  new or existing business

Stage 5

Long-term expansion/
redirection

- to solve business problems
- to expand existing business effectively

Figure 1. *A framework for lifelong entrepreneurship education*

next level of development, generally found in advanced high school vocational programmes or in two-year colleges. It provides more in-depth understanding of the competencies needed to become a successful entrepreneur. It also encourages the student to dream a bit — to plan a business that might be started using acquired vocational skills.

At this level, vocational marketing education programmes prepare their students to create a business on paper and compete with other students in the state and in the nation for the best entrepreneurial plan. The youth organization Distributive Education Clubs of America (DECA) sponsors an entrepreneurs' contest that involves as many as 2,000 high school students each year.

Vocational agriculture programmes help students to explore farm-related businesses they might start in rural areas. This approach to finding jobs for rural youth has had important results in community development.

Vocational home economics programmes see entrepreneurship as a logical addition to teaching homemaking skills. Home-based businesses often use home economics competencies for their technical expertise and allow homemakers to work from their homes. They are thus able to care for their children at the same time.

The trades, taught through the trade and industrial education programmes, are natural fields for new business activity. Students learning such trades as carpentry, electronics, cosmetology, car mechanics or health technologies are natural candidates for starting future businesses. Young people need to be able to be subcontractors and contractors in many of these trades. They need to learn how to look for business opportunities related to their skill areas and to market their expertise.

Business and office programmes offer many opportunities for small business startups as well as for working in corporate offices. Use of computers leads to many service businesses for other businesses and consumers. Knowledge and skill in office systems may provide a person with the expertise to be the much-needed partner for a local inventor or technical entrepreneur.

These first three stages of the lifelong learning model concern the schools. Education for future entrepreneurs has been almost non-existent in our public educational system in the past. Emphasis in business courses within this system has been largely on working for corporate America, and business expertise has been considered primarily a college-level course. Career role models emphasized in education have included mostly professionals (doctors, lawyers, authors, teachers or nurses) or government service (police officers, politicians or firefighters). Educators have often considered such career fields as restaurant management, plumbing, and retail fashion shop operation as second-class occupations. Yet the reality of chances for success in these areas has been largely overlooked. Entrepreneurship education can be a vehicle for exploring the real opportunities in our society and making a decision based on greater exploration of the world of entrepreneurs — our small business community.

The last two stages of the lifelong learning model address the continuing need for helping entrepreneurs to get a business started and to keep it running successfully. These are not the roles for our public education programmes for young people at school. But there has been, and will continue to be, a great need for such assistance from adult educators. It has been estimated that one-half of the new businesses in the United States fail in the first two years (US Small Business Administration, 1984). In the absence of entrepreneurial skill education in the public schools, these last two stages of the model have carried the entire responsibility for support systems for our entrepreneurial society.

National Entrepreneurship Education Consortium

The necessity to encourage entrepreneurship education opportunities in the public school system was recognized in the development of the National Entrepreneurship Education Consortium.

In its first two years of operation, the consortium has gained commitment from 22 state directors. Commitment from the state vocational director of vocational education was the key to each state's support for entrepreneurship education. Each state is represented by a liaison member of its staff, who works co-operatively with other states on key issues of interest to all states. Consortium members meet twice a year to share ideas and programme activities. At these meetings there is an opportunity to go far beyond sharing ideas to a level of consensus on issues and co-ordination of initiatives for the benefit of a number of state members. In this way, duplication of efforts is avoided and sharing new ideas and information is encouraged.

Collaboration on one or two activities a year is an expected outcome for all state members. In the first two years the states contributed to a major publication which will be available from the National Center for Research in Vocational Education: *The Economic Value of Entrepreneurship Education* (Ross and Kurth, 1985). The study outlines those economic factors which suggest that small business development makes good economic sense for the future. The advancement of new ventures has recently grown in national acceptance as a concept in economic development. This document points out these economic opportunities and then defines the need for entrepreneurship education to support national entrepreneurial spirit. This publication will serve to communicate the need for entrepreneurship education to educational policy makers, who need to understand why vocational education is an appropriate vehicle for entrepreneurship education.

Communication between individual states and the National Center, as well as communication among all states and other entrepreneurship education networks, is key in making the consortium effort a success. The National Center's central role is to encourage this communication. A news release system, called the New Venture Network, is designed to collect success stories, programme ideas, meeting announcements, and other newsworthy items. Figure 2 is one example of over 200 news releases

New Venture Network   For Immediate Release

NATIONAL ACADEMY FOR VOCATIONAL EDUCATION TO OFFER
SPECIAL ENTREPRENEURSHIP WORKSHOP

Interested in helping your students learn how to run their own small businesses successfully? If so, be sure not to miss the National Academy for Vocational Education's latest workshop on entrepreneurship!

On October 18-19, 1983, the National Academy will present "Infusing Entrepreneurship Education: Strategies for Vocational Education" at the National Center for Research in Vocational Education in Columbus, Ohio. Designed to provide vocational educators with the opportunity to examine the latest in materials and programs on entrepreneurship education, the workshop will help participants learn how to---

*describe essential elements of entrepreneurship education;

*identify approaches for program implementation and improvement;

*select materials that are appropriate for a given program; and

*assist others in planning for program implementation and improvement.

The cost of the workshop is $125. For additional information, write or call---

        The National Academy for Vocational Education
        The National Center for Research
            in Vocational Education
        The Ohio State University
        1960 Kenny Road
        Columbus, Ohio 43210
        (800) 848-4815 toll free
        (614) 486-3655 (in Ohio and outside the continental U.S.)

##

THE NATIONAL CENTER
FOR RESEARCH IN VOCATIONAL EDUCATION
THE OHIO STATE UNIVERSITY
1960 KENNY ROAD · COLUMBUS, OHIO 43210

NEWS ON ENTREPRENEURSHIP EDUCATION
The National Center for Research in Vocational Education

Figure 2. *News release example*

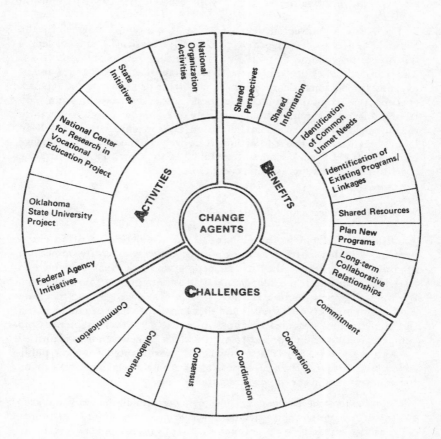

Figure 3. *The agenda for action for entrepreneurship education*

that have been sent to major target audiences in the past few years. Another form of communication includes an electronic newsletter and message switching system for rapid information-sharing with the states. Also, general information is shared with member states whenever National Center staff find new items that would benefit the information base of state leaders. The consortium depends on the leadership in each state to see that the information is shared with the vocational programmes in the state.

The ABCs of Entrepreneurship (Figure 3) is a model designed by the National Center to describe the activities (A), benefits (B), and challenges (C) of the programme to build entrepreneurship education in the USA. The consortium effort can be seen as an approach to change, and it explains the National Center's role as facilitator or change agent. The six challenges — commitment, co-operation, consensus, co-ordination, collaboration and communication — describe the approach used to organize the National Entrepreneurship Education Consortium. Although still an infant organization, this consortium is actively pursuing a major change effort for the US education system that has the potential of generating more small business success than ever before.

What is entrepreneurship education?

Academics spend much time arguing about the definition of an entrepreneur. Whether entrepreneurs are only those who create something innovative, or whether they are all people who risk what they own to start a new business, is really immaterial to entrepreneurship education. Both types of new venture startups require a knowledge base to create a successful business operation — and that knowledge base can be taught in the public school system. It might be useful to see that entrepreneurship competencies could be applied to all the kinds of new ventures identified by Karl Vesper (1980). The following list was adapted from his publication *New Venture Strategies* for use in vocational programmes to expand the opportunities in the minds of young students.

1. *Self-employed individuals.* Those who perform all the work and keep all the profit. This includes everything from family-run stores, agents, repair persons, accountants, to physicians and lawyers. It can be full-time or part-time because no one else is involved.
2. *Team builders.* Those who start a business and expand as fast as possible in order to be able to hire other employees. Most of the time these additional employees have needed expertise that the owner does not have.
3. *Inventors.* Those with particular, inventive abilities who design a better product and then create companies to develop, produce and sell the item. High-technology companies of this type are a new trend.
4. *Pattern multipliers.* Those who look for an idea someone else has

already created and then create their own business based on following another's model. Franchise operations or chain stores are a form of this approach.

5. *Economy-of-scale exploiters.* Those who benefit from large volume sales by offering discount prices and operating with very low overheads.

6. *Acquirers.* Those who take over a business started by another and use their own ideas to make it successful. This often happens when there is a financial problem in the current operation. Fresh management ideas may save the business.

7. *Buy-sell artists.* Those who buy a company for the purpose of improving it before selling it for a profit.

8. *Speculators.* Those who purchase a commodity and resell it for a profit. Real estate, art, antiques, and crops are typical speculator items.

9. *Internal entrepreneurs.* Those who create new ideas and make them into a successful project within an existing business. Although they have neither the profit nor the personal financial risk of their own business, they need to use the same methods of operation.

The competencies needed to run any of these different types of business have been defined as business management skills. Unfortunately, few students have the opportunity to learn all kinds of management skills in a comprehensive course. Our educational system supports specialists who learn accounting or selling, or engineering, or carpentry. The new look currently being encouraged is to promote these business management competencies in technical training programmes through vocational education.

The National Center developed *Program for Acquiring Competence in Entrepreneurship* (known as PACE, 1983) as a way to include small business management skills in existing programmes or as a package to be used as a separate course in the public schools. PACE looks at 18 major topics that provide the management basics for any small business.

1. Understanding the nature of small business
2. Determining your potential as an entrepreneur
3. Developing the business plan
4. Obtaining technical assistance
5. Choosing the type of ownership
6. Planning the marketing strategy
7. Locating the business
8. Financing the business
9. Dealing with legal issues
10. Complying with government regulations
11. Managing the business
12. Managing human resources
13. Promoting the business
14. Managing sales efforts

15. Keeping the business records
16. Managing the finances
17. Managing customer credit and collections
18. Protecting the business.

These 18 topics can be taught in a relatively simple, definitive way for a beginning in entrepreneurship education. As such, they are the business basics that a student should know about for inclusion in a future educational plan. At this level of understanding a student would not be ready to start a business, but instead could plan an educational programme to support career plans. PACE Level 1 serves this purpose for entrepreneurship education. Level 2 of PACE is for those who have time to acquire more in-depth knowledge of the 18 major topics.

Ideally, the students will apply this knowledge to creative planning for a business to be started some time in the future. This creativity can be applied to small or big dreams, because the necessity to find capital is not a limitation to creativity in the classroom. Level 3 of PACE is for people who are ready to start a business. It assumes they have gained the expertise of the first two levels and it applies needed knowledge to the decision that must be made to get started. This level of PACE is primarily for adults who have gained the necessary technical expertise and business experience and are now ready to design their own business successfully.

This lifelong learning model is explained well by Glaser (1985) who points out that expertise is accumulated as a result of hundreds of hours of experience in a particular knowledge domain. Novices can only solve problems using the facts given them. But experts over time have organized knowledge into principles and abstractions that allow them to solve problems far beyond the literal approach of the novice. To solve problems in business by intuition and application of principles requires a knowledge base that can be built in the educational system.

Model programmes

The United States abounds with examples of the support which is being developed for entrepreneurship education. A sampling of a few model programmes follows.

☐ In Ohio a summer camp for gifted and talented vocational students offers a week-long exploration of entrepreneurship as a career opportunity.
☐ In New Jersey the Ocean County Vocational-Technical School added a special class for exceptionally talented vocational students to study entrepreneurship as an addition to their high school vocational programme.
☐ The Great Oaks Vocational School district has added a programme for all 3,000 Cincinnati area vocational students: for juniors, an

overview of entrepreneurship followed by general employability skills; for seniors, an extra period for more employability skill development and a semester of creating ideas for a business of their own.

☐ Colorado sponsored a major teacher in-service programme for both high school and two-year college instructors to learn how to use parts of the PACE curriculum at both educational levels.

☐ Illinois sponsored a year-long programme to help teachers develop expertise in teaching entrepreneurship. This was part of a programme to enhance their abilities to help community entrepreneurs in the Small Business Administration-sponsored adult counsellor programmes conducted by the Service Corps of Retired Executives (SCORE) and the Active Corps of Executives (ACE) as well as teaching future entrepreneurs in the classroom.

☐ 'Incubators' to help start up businesses in a low-cost manner have been sponsored by state governments. In Pennsylvania over 20 'incubators' have been set up, many of them in the two-year colleges. 'Incubator' operators suggest that empty schools are ideal for many types of new business startups, and partially empty schools can provide both the space and the services needed to aid economic development activities in small communities.

☐ Many states including Ohio, Minnesota and Wisconsin have full-time instructors whose vocational education responsibilities are to provide training and consulting for existing small businesses. They use a three-year assistance programme designed in Minnesota. This assistance involves classes for the entrepreneurs and on-site counselling.

In summary

Effective entrepreneurship education cannot be restricted to any one place within the educational system. It is a spirit of independence that can be nurtured by a variety of educational experiences throughout one's life. It is the understanding of innovation and change that youth can learn to expect and monitor for their own business ideas. It is an appreciation of the skills needed to be a successful entrepreneur, and the possible routes one should take to build those skills. It is practice in managing small things, such as class projects or self-employment, that builds the expertise needed for entrepreneurial success. It is the challenge of creativity provided by practice in constructive business thinking activities.

Not all vocational students will become entrepreneurs as a result of these programmes. But it seems reasonable to expect that most will have greater business expertise and become more productive employees or employers. Likewise, it seems reasonable to expect that the entrepreneurial spirit can make a difference in a nation's economy — and vocational educators have an important role to play in developing and nurturing this dynamic force.

References

Ashmore, M and Pritz, G eds (1983) *Program for Acquiring Competence in Entrepreneurship (PACE)* The National Center for Research in Vocational Education, The Ohio State University: Columbus, OH

Birch, D L (1979) *The Job Generation Process* Massachusetts Institute of Technology: Cambridge, MA

Drucker, P F (1979) *Innovation and Entrepreneurship: Practice and Principles* Harper and Row: New York

Glaser, R (1985) *The Nature of Expertise* The National Center for Research in Vocational Education, The Ohio State University: Columbus, OH

Lipper III, A (1985) Entrepreneurship education *International Council for Small Business Newsletter* **22**: 3

Monthly Labor Review (1983) November. US Department of Labor, Bureau of Labor Statistics: Washington, DC

National Center for Educational Statistics (1983) *Digest of Educational Statistics* National Center for Educational Statistics: Washington, DC

Ross, N, Ashmore, M *et al* (1984) *A National Entrepreneurship Education Agenda for Action* The National Center for Research in Vocational Education, The Ohio State University: Columbus, OH

Ross, N and Kurth, P eds (1985) *The Economic Value of Entrepreneurship Education* The National Center for Research in Vocational Education, The Ohio State University: Columbus, OH

Shapero, A (1982) *Taking Control* A commencement address at the Ohio State University: Columbus, OH

US Small Business Administration (1984) *The State of Small Business: A Report of the President* US Government Printing Office: Washington, DC

Vesper, K (1980) *New Venture Strategies* Prentice-Hall, Inc: Englewood Cliffs, NJ

13. The harambee approach to vocational education in Kenya

Henry Ayot

Summary: Harambee (self-help) village polytechnics were established in the mid-1960s as a response to the high growth in the school leaving population at the primary level, and were intended to provide vocational training for self-employment in the rural areas. The courses offered varied with the demands of each area. In 1974 a joint Evaluation Mission of the Government of Kenya and a Norwegian agency noted with satisfaction that village polytechnics offered 20 vocational courses and recommended expansion of village polytechnics round the country to mitigate rural unemployment and reduce migration into urban areas. Since that time village polytechnics have expanded greatly.

Harambee institutes of technology were established to cater for students leaving Kenyan secondary schools, and offered vocational courses at a higher level than those in village polytechnics.

The Ministry of Culture and Social Services undertakes the financial control and management of village polytechnics while the Ministry of Education, Science and Technology takes care of the harambee institutes of technology, contributing Ksh 15 million annually to supplement community resources.

By 1982 graduates from the village polytechnics and harambee institutes of technology were distributed as follows: 46.8 per cent in self-employment; 37.5 per cent in the commercial sector; and 15.5 per cent in recommended work groups. The programme has clearly succeeded in imparting technical skills to the rural population of Kenya and acted as a catalyst in the transformation of attitudes towards education. Education is no longer a passport to 'white collar' jobs and vocational training is becoming a route to self-reliance.

Introduction

Harambee is a Kiswahili word that means 'let us help each other' and was adopted as the national motto for Kenya at the country's independence in 1963. In *harambee* rallies all over the country local communities contribute money, materials or labour for specific projects.

The Kenyan formal education system comprises pre-primary level, primary level, secondary level and the university level of the education cycle. Its general structure is permeated by rigorous summative 'pencil-and-paper' examinations geared mainly towards selection for subsequent levels of education. This means that, by and large, the Kenyan formal educational system is academic and pyramidal, as many drop out after each level because places are not adequate at subsequent levels. Except for a limited number of technical schools, two government-maintained polytechnics, university faculties and some ministerial training institutions, vocational education has for a long time not received much attention in the formal education system.

Harambee (self-help) effort has made a significant contribution to the country's social and economic development. Community self-help has played a vital role in the extension of educational opportunities in Kenya through modern educational facilities. Harambee spirit, a traditional phenomenon, has manifested itself as a clear indicator of the willingness of local communities to augment government services in providing education at all levels. During the advent of Western education in Kenya, local communities showed great keenness about education and actively con- tributed to the expansion of school places by providing land and buildings for primary schools to supplement mission schools and those of local authorities. More significantly, harambee effort played a very important role in the 1960s in expanding secondary school places throughout the country when local communities built harambee secondary schools modelled on the government-maintained secondary schools. Among the results of this community self-help was a sharp rise in the number of those who had secondary schooling, but without any attendant increase in job opportunities. This state of affairs, coupled with a substantial dropout rate at primary school level, led to problems such as general unemployment among school leavers, a growing rate of exodus of youth from rural to urban areas, and consequent urban unemployment. It was perhaps partly because of these problems that a general concern about the inability of the educational system to meet the needs and aspirations of the country was aroused. From the beginning of the 1970s, there had been increased criticism of the school curriculum for its lack of a vocational component. Such criticism has led to deliberate attempts by the government to effect curricular changes such as the 'vocationalization' of the educational system embodied in the current 8-4-4 structure, which dates from January 1985.

Community self-help in Kenya is a manifestation of the willingness of local communities to supplement government provision of educational op- portunities. In the 1970s harambee effort was channelled mainly towards provision of post-primary training institutions ('village' polytechnics) and post-secondary vocational institutions (harambee institutes of technology). Unlike harambee secondary schools, these institutions were not modelled on existing vocational establishments but represented a revolutionary change in the curriculum, as indicated by the more practically oriented training programmes to be found in both the village polytechnics and the harambee institutes of technology. The following paragraphs will highlight important issues relating to the organization, financing, curriculum and achievements of these community-based institutions.

Organization, financing and staffing of the harambee vocational institutions

Organization: village polytechnics

The so-called 'village polytechnics' are community-based institutions, established in response to the high growth in the school leaving population at post-primary level in certain areas. The form which community sponsorship takes determines, to a degree, the pattern of organization.

In each village polytechnic there is a management committee elected by local people. Its key officials are the chairman and the treasurer. Usually these are elected officials who have shown interest in and commitment to the development and success of the institution; hence this mandate from the catchment community.

The project site has a manager who is in charge of the day-to-day running of the institution or project: he is what would commonly be called the principal or the institutional head. The assumption is not only that he has the relevant knowhow, but that this is capped with some administrative acumen. Often, at the initial stages of the project, he is an employee of the local community entrusted with its initiation. Later, the manager may be an *aide* to the polytechnic from the government. In such a case the move heralds a government takeover of the institution's professional executive, ie the manager assisted by his team of instructors.

Potential conflict exists in the relationship between the manager and his team on one side, and the management committee on the other. Areas of possible disagreement include local needs, local demands, personalities, aspirations and expert opinions, and so on.

Tension can also occur in the relationship between the manager and his instructors on one side and the trainees on the other. The ILO/SIDA Report recommended the establishment of trainees' councils in poly-technics in order 'that trainees can get a medium through which they can communicate with the projects' Management Committees' (ILO/SIDA, 1977, p.130).

In general the management committees have the final say in all important decisions affecting the village polytechnics.

At the national level 'village' polytechnics are under the Ministry of Culture and Social Services' Department of Social Services in the Youth Development Division. They come under the authority of the principal youth officer at the Ministry Headquarters. Below this officer are three senior youth officers in charge of administration, training and research respectively. Down the ladder, at the provincial level, are provincial youth training officers (PYTO) and district youth training officers (DYTO) at the district level.

This organization of the youth development programme is supported by the National Co-ordinating Committee on Youth; the Research and Training Committee; and the Project and Finance Committee. These supportive committees overlap and are concerned also with financing and curriculum. It is their interplay that determines the success of the whole programme.

Organization: harambee institutes of technology

Like village polytechnics, the harambee institutes of technology (HIT) are community-based institutions. They are basically a response to increased unemployment among secondary school leavers but partly also a manifestation of 'rebellion' by local communities against the 'academic' curriculum offered in secondary schools, which failed to meet the requirement of skills needed in predominantly rural Kenyan society.

Currently there are 15 institutes of technology operational, offering diversified courses of study to Kenyan youth, all under the Ministry of Education, Science and Technology, HIT Section. They are well distributed over the country. The geographical distribution strongly reflects ethnic backgrounds.

An individual institute of technology is managed by a *board of governors* on behalf of the sponsoring community. The board of governors consists of about 13 members approved by the Minister for Education, Science and Technology and must comprise representatives of the community, the government (different ministries such as Ministry of Agriculture, Ministry of Water Development, President's Office, Ministry of Education, Science and Technology, etc), non-governmental organizations and special interests. The Board's management duties include:

- ☐ day-to-day running of the institute;
- ☐ preparation of estimates and authorization of expenditures;
- ☐ appointment and payment of both teaching and non-teaching staff not employed by the government;
- ☐ monitoring community support through planning and organizing fund-raising;
- ☐ participating in all aspects of financial management for the institute;
- ☐ disciplining both staff and students.

At the national level the Ministry of Education, Science and Technology co-ordinates all matters pertaining to the harambee institutes of technology through the HIT section of the ministry. This section is manned by a senior education officer (in charge of harambee institutes of technology) who has under him two education officers. Through this section of the ministry the government co-ordinates, controls and supports all aspects of the expansion and management of these institutes.

Financing: village polytechnics

Throughout, from the drawing board to the initial takeoff of the institutions, the initiative in financing lies with the sponsors and community. This view has been confirmed by evaluation reports and by recent studies (GOK/NORAD, 1974; ILO/SIDA Report, 1977). Initially, therefore, the financing of a village polytechnic was expected to involve a large measure of self-help on the part of the immediate community. It was found, however, that the construction and operation of a polytechnic could quite often overtax the resources available within the local area. Hence harambee efforts were generally not adequate: there is an obvious need for a more regular source of funding to ensure that a village polytechnic is established and operated on a continuing basis.

From the outset, however, it is accepted that finance is an outcome of the sincerity and commitment of the local community. It is they who construct, supply and run the polytechnics. Their efforts are only supplemented by other donors like the NCCK, Kenya Association of Youth Centres, Oxfam, CARE, UNICEF, Save the Children Fund, Rotary Clubs, Lions Clubs, etc, and by the fees levied on users.

The aids and grants which are given help in meeting salaries, buildings and the cost of tools. However, despite this injection of assistance, the majority of village polytechnics 'are not financed adequately enough to provide effectively the scope and quality of training needed for profitable self-employment' (GOK/NORAD, 1974: 48).

It is for this reason that government funding is steadily pouring into the programme. Consequently, management committees are steadily becoming rubber stamps to government-initiated decisions. For example, in 1973-74 the government spent K£210,000 on the programme, while approximately K£154,000 was provided by overseas donors. This trend is currently on the increase, as witnessed by 1976-77 figures when the government spent over K£113,850 assisting about 165 of the village polytechnics. Nevertheless, the resources available cannot match the demand from local communities, although recent research has indicated that most management committees credit the government with having done well in support of their polytechnics (Orwa, 1982: 266-267).

Growing government concern with the polytechnics has been accompanied by a subtle growth in government control over them (Orwa, 1982). This in turn has had a discouraging effect on what have hitherto been active self-financing local communities. 'It appears that whenever other sources of assistance are provided the local contribution from self-help understandably tends to fall off' (GOK/NORAD, 1974: 48).

It is therefore important that for the success of the youth development programme there is need constantly and consistently to utilize the local community's financial contribution, so that it does not appear to them that all inputs will be provided by either the government or an external agency, as might be suggested by the government's circular letter DSS/3/21, Vol. V/ of 25th April, 1979, which vests financial administration in the hands of government bureaucrats. What is now being witnessed may be symptomatic of the bureaucratic embrace and its attendant dangers.

Financing: harambee institutes of technology

The initial finance for both capital and recurrent expenditure is provided entirely by the community through harambee effort. Public fundraising meetings are organized for money for the purchase of land, construction of buildings, employment of staff (both teaching and non-teaching) and to meet recurrent expenditure. In addition, voluntary contributions from co-operative societies, workers' unions, dances, raffles, and sale of badges generate considerable amounts. In preparation for public fundraising meetings, members of the community may be required to contribute either through house-to-house visits by local leadership or through a levy by the local administration.

Currently, the government plays a very significant role in financing harambee institutes of technology. It gives a per capita grant of Kshs 175 per student per month to each institute to meet recurrent expenditure. It also gives a development grant, which for the 1984-85 fiscal year was Kshs 15 million for the 15 institutes. Through the Teachers' Service Commission (TSC) the government also provides teaching staff to the institutes. In addition to this, a fee is payable for both tuition and board-ing by each student enrolling in the institute. The fee differs from one institute to another.

As well as local sources of finance, donor agencies give a substantial amount of assistance, both financial and material, to the institutes through the Kenyan government. Such agencies include the Danish International Development Agency (DANIDA), the Canadian International Develop-ment Agency (CIDA), and the United States' Agency for International Development (AID). Aid is also received from governments of other friendly countries.

Lastly, finances for running the institutes may come from institute-run enterprises. Most of the institutes own and manage agricultural farms which yield considerable income for recurrent expenditure.

Staffing: village polytechnics

Village polytechnics now number about 250 (Orwa, 1977: 134), attended by over 22,000 trainees and requiring a staff/instructor force of 1,250 or more. This projection is based on an assumption that 'there will be an average of 4 courses in each project', with each course having an average of 20 to 25 trainees (ILO/SIDA, 1977, p.134).

The administrative handling of staffing is nominally the preserve of management committees. As seen already, however, government involve-ment is on the increase. Consequently, many management committees are now discovering that government officials are becoming powerful in making decisions over such issues as expenses, recruitment, dismissals and control over managers.

The size, pattern and quality of staff in a polytechnic will normally reflect the kinds of courses offered, the time of their introduction and the levels at which they are to be offered. These matters are the responsibility of the management committees which have the legal power to hire and fire instructors and even the managers.

The 1979 circular letter, however, stripped the management committees of their powers on matters of staff recruitment:

'The responsibility for staff recruitment, which has hitherto been exercised by project committees is withdrawn and placed on the Provincial Director of Social Services who will be the Chairman of the interviewing panel.' (Department of Social Services: Circular letter DSS/3/21, Vol.V/61 of 25th April, 1979.)

This move may be one reason for a growing loss of interest by the local communities. It has seemingly done away with the community's only visible participatory leadership and involvement. Doubtless village poly-technics are being increasingly seen by their respective communities as government projects.

The maintenance of polytechnic staff is now a matter of urgency. Their interest must be sustained by way of inducements, promotions, accessibility to certification, and so on. This would require a concerted move by district, provincial and national officials. Such a move is high-lighted in the recommendations of evaluation reports as being necessary to maintain and uplift the programme, by giving it staff of the right calibre and in sufficient numbers to match local needs and variations.

Staffing: harambee institutes of technology

During the initial stages of the establishment of the institutes, both teach-ing and non-teaching staff were almost exclusively recruited and paid by their management committee and later by their boards of governors. This meant that their wages were met from revenue accruing from community contributions. Foreign assistance, however, which included both materials and technical personnel, was received by many of the institutes. Such donors included Canada, Denmark and Holland.

Towards the end of the 1970s and during the 1980s there has been a notable increase in government interest in these institutes. The government nowadays gives grants-in-aid and supplies the institutes with teachers. It also monitors foreign assistance, which includes technical assistance. By January 1985 all the institutes were receiving more than three-quarters of their teaching staff needs from the Teachers' Service Commission. The government intends to be fully responsible for staffing these institutes in future.

Range of courses offered

Curriculum and courses: village polytechnic

Courses normally last up to two years; they are subject to the needs of the geographical areas. The duration given is a maximum, otherwise it is flexible.

The fundamental premise underlying the educational strategy in all village polytechnics is that their curriculum should conform as closely as possible to the realities the trainees will face when they graduate. This has had effects on five key areas:

1. *The courses.* These are developed in response to identified needs of the locality.
2. *Technology.* It is necessary to teach the trainees technology which is appropriate to local conditions, is relatively labour-intensive, is cheap and is easy to make and repair.
3. *Training.* 70 per cent of students' time is spent in practicals and/or work. Finished work or products of work must be sold to generate revenue and provide the necessary psychological feedback — hence a vital incentive, a backdrop of relevance and realism.
4. *Certification.* Given the circumstances prevalent in the confused drive towards modernization (or is it development?), there are pressures on the village polytechnics to run their programmes on the lines of formal education. This was rightly chided by the ILO Report when it observed:

   'Harambee schools will strive to imitate conventional academic and secondary schools. Village Polytechnics will tend to become conventional vocational schools and so on. And this is unavoidable, because it is the rational thing to do as long as incentives are as at present' (ILO/SIDA, 1977: 133).

   It is good that the programme stresses the acquisition of skills first; certificates come later. Its informal character is defended.
5. *Content.* The actual curriculum reflects people's needs in a given geographical area. The GOK/NORAD Evaluation Mission gave a list of 20 different courses: commercial; agriculture; blacksmith; tinsmith; home economics; electrical; leatherwork; carpentry; motor mechanics; plumbing; baking; masonry; tailoring; handicrafts; tractor driving; technical drawing; fitting/welding; bicycle repair; taxidermy; and painting and signwriting.

   Fluctuation in the number of courses occurs in an area such as taxidermy, following the ban on the hunting of wildlife.

It is to be stressed that the training is on-the-job, with the least possible emphasis on the acquisition of certificates. Nevertheless the village polytechnics, once they have decided on the trades which they will offer, are subject to a degree of curriculum control from the Trade Test Division of the Ministry of Labour. They are also subject to periodic inspection for standards in their provision of facilities, tools/equipment and qualified instructors. This inadvertently drags in the unhealthy artificiality and competitiveness which have been such a handicap to formal education: there is a fear of their creeping into the learning-by-apprenticeship sector. It is noted by the ILO Report:

'Trainees are, for reasons of certification, exposed to Government Trade Tests which range from Grade III to City and Guilds. This is a stigma, if not a spill-over, which is a clear show of the fact that what was meant to be an informal training programme cannot be divorced from the traditional influence of examinations (trade tests).'

Curriculum and courses: harambee institutes of technology

During the early 1970s (when the harambee institutes of technology were established) the responsibility for determining what courses were to be offered in the individual institutes and how they would be taught was vested in the steering committee for a particular institute. This meant that the curricula for different institutes varied from one to the other. However, by the mid-1970s the government began to take an active interest in the expansion of these institutes, as has already been said. The government therefore took over the co-ordination of all matters pertaining to them. Centralized development and control of curriculum was placed under the direct supervision of the Ministry of Education. This ensured uniformity in the curriculum offered by institutes throughout the country. The government today assumes the responsibility of developing the curriculum, inspecting the institutes and supervising instruction, setting and administering government trade tests and certifying the graduates of the institutes.

The range of courses offered differs from one institute to another, but generally the structure of courses is similar in all institutes. They include such technical courses as building technology, engineering and textile technology, and business courses such as accounting and secretarial training. The institutes also offer general agriculture and home economics. The specific courses in the main divisions are as follows:

1. Building technology — includes carpentry and joinery, masonry and block laying and electrical installation.
2. General engineering — includes motor-vehicle mechanics, radio and TV servicing, mechanical engineering, water engineering and agricultural engineering.
3. Business studies — secretarial courses, accounting and book-keeping.
4. Textile technology — garment manufacture and textile science.
5. Home economics.

The courses are in two parts. A trainee must pass Part I before proceeding to Part II. In all the institutes the technical courses last for three years, while courses in general agriculture, business studies and home economics last for two years.

The courses are mainly practical (according to the Ministry of Education, Science and Technology, 60 per cent of the training must be practical). This is because the institutes were founded for the purpose of producing trained manpower for wage employment and self-employment. All the technical courses are organized in such a way that during the course trainees are assigned to industrial attachment as part of their practical work. In addition to this, a large part of the training in an institute consists of practical training in well-equipped workshops.

The trainees often participate in projects aimed at the expansion of facilities in their own institutes under the supervision of their instructors. This is particularly true of trainees in building technology, agricultural engineering, water engineering and general agriculture. In the majority of cases the trainees also participate in community self-help projects, offering their services at little or no cost (for example, building standard 8 class-rooms in the 8-4-4 programme).

Qualifications obtainable

Qualifications: village polytechnics

The village polytechnic was launched to prepare primary school leavers mainly for self-employment. At that time (1966) formal certification was de-emphasized. It was recommended that the programme graduates could sit for the government trade test so long as original objectives of the programme were not lost in the process. That is to say, the trade test must not become the major objective.

The same proposals were fully accepted by the government (1969) when it adopted the programme. In an attempt to formalize the de-emphasis of certification, the programme administrators introduced a 'leaver's document' to be awarded to all village polytechnic graduates. This was done, but a problem arose when employers (and, strangely enough, even programme officers) refused to recognize 'leaver's documents' and insisted on the government-recognized trade test.

The programme began to become more and more formal. By 1973, an ILO Report observed that the pressure of demand for certificates was mounting and predicted that the village polytechnics would eventually bow to the inevitable and be run as conventional technical schools. Despite a warning by the NORAD Report (1974) against this trend, studies have found that over 75 per cent of village polytechnic graduates attempted government trade tests.

Demand for the trade tests has grown to such an extent that the Directorate of Industrial Training is now organizing those tests at provincial or district Labour Centres and sometimes even at the individual village polytechnic, depending on the number of candidates. Possession of the government trade test certificate has now become one of the major objectives of the programme. Because of this development, subjects like agriculture and home economics, which were originally emphasized, are no longer popular because there is no trade test certificate for them.

Qualifications: harambee institutes of technology

Upon successful completion of training in the institutes of technology, the trainees are awarded different government certificates depending on which course was taken. For technical courses such as building technology or engineering, successful trainees are awarded government trade test certificates in their subjects.

Employment opportunities

Prospects for those who have attended village polytechnics

Graduates of village polytechnics were from the outset trained for self-employment, and to an extent for wage employment where their skills were found to be needed. The Youth Development Programme encouraged the formation of co-operatives by graduates. Such co-operatives are established by trainees as work groups while they are still on the course. The term 'graduates' happily accommodates all those who attempted trade tests, regardless of whether they passed them or not.

There has not been any reliable project, on a national scale, to follow up graduates of village polytechnics. Attempts to do this on an academic research basis have been made in 1971 by Anderson; in 1972 by Court; in 1974 by Barbra and 1980 by Orwa, but there has been only one attempt by the government, in 1973. And even the government cannot be adequately relied upon because 'as would be expected, the Government figures are inflated' (Orwa, 1982). Orwa reckons 'it seems safe to conclude that the graduates who are self-employed are about 46.8 per cent'. Graduates engaged in gainful employment can be seen to have gained entry in two other sectors: the formal sector (37.5 per cent); in the recommended work group (15.7 per cent).

It is valid to say that most village polytechnic graduates are usefully employed (63.1 per cent) in contrast to those who are unemployed (36.9 per cent). This is an encouraging pointer in that nearly 6 out of 10 village polytechnic leavers find a place in the world of work (Orwa, 1982). Orwa has also established that there is not a significant relationship between having or not having a trade test certificate and employability. He says: 'there is not much advantage in possessing a government Trade Test' (1982: 324). Such an advantage, if there was one, would have been noticed in the sphere of formal employment, but it has not been in evidence. Happily, too, informal employment shows test certificate holders to have a mere 16.9 per cent advantage over those who do not have the certificate! Indeed, quite a number of those polytechnic graduates who have managed to pass government trade tests are unemployed. Employers are more interested in work done than in paper certification.

The programme has therefore, to an extent, lived up to its expectations. It has succeeded not only in imparting the required skills but also in transforming the attitudes of trainees and their respective catchment areas. Indeed, it is worth while quoting approvingly from the ILO/SIDA (1977) Report:

'The village polytechnic programme has been one of the impressive efforts which are being made by the government to counteract the tendencies of the education system inherited from the colonial period....

the village polytechnics have become a focal point for the involvement of people in their community . . . . focal point for agricultural
extension, rural work programmes.'

Indeed their success even at an earlier stage was clearly noticed, as the
NORAD Report stated:

'The Mission is satisfied that at its present level of operation, the
programme contributes significantly to employment and rural development. It justifies the efforts undertaken by Kenyan authorities
and external support lent to it.' (GOK/NORAD, 1974: 52)

Prospects for those who have attended harambee institutes of technology

Since the ultimate aim of the colleges of technology is the training of
skilled and semi-skilled manpower in trades relevant to the needs of the
developing Kenyan economy, their products are readily absorbed into the
economy either as self-employed manpower or wage employment. It
would seem that the courses offered do reflect societal priorities in manpower needs. The methods of training in the institutes (involving ample
practical experience) prepare the trainees well for the field of work.
Employment opportunities, therefore, currently present no problem to
trainees of harambee institutes of technology, and this is likely to be the
trend for quite some time to come.

It is further to be noted that, with curricular reform in the country
necessitating the conversion of the existing technical secondary schools
into technical institutions for post-primary school leavers, the harambee
institutes' products will be eminently suitable as teachers for these technical institutions, owing to the highly practical background of the courses
they have undergone.

Self-employment has been the prospect for many trainees of the
harambee institutes, particularly those trainees in building technology and
general engineering. The government deliberately assists the trainees who
wish to establish their own enterprises, either on a co-operative basis or
individually, through parastatal lending agencies such as the Industrial
Commercial Development Corporation (ICDC). The institutes are very
keen to help such self-employed individuals or groups succeed, constantly
organizing follow-up activities for them and offering technical advice.

It can thus be concluded that the massive community input of resources
into harambee institutes of technology is yielding favourable results.
Government participation in co-ordinating funding and control of such
effort has been a major factor in its success. The products of the institutes
of technology are finding an unlimited market both for self-employment
and for wage employment.

References

Anderson, J E (1971) *The Struggle for the School* Longman Educational Books:
    Nairobi

Anderson, J E (1973) *Organization and Financing of Self-Help Education in Kenya* UNESCO: Paris

Government of Kenya and Norwegian Agency for International Development (GOK/NORAD) (1974) *The Kenya Village Polytechnic Programme* Unpublished Evaluation Report on the Kenya Village Polytechnic Programme, Nairobi

International Labour Office/Swedish International Development Authority (ILO/ SIDA) (1977) RAF/19. Unpublished report on Eastern and Southern Africa Preparation of Rural Youth Development, held in Botswana

Keller, E (1976) The role of harambee schools in education for development *Working Paper* 118, IDS, University of Nairobi: Nairobi

Kenya Education Review (1974) 1: 2 Faculty of Education, University of Nairobi: Nairobi

Kinyanjui, K (1974) *The Distribution of Education Resources and Opportunities in Kenya* (Discussion Paper 208 IDS) University of Nairobi: Nairobi

Ministry of Economic Planning and Community Affairs (Kenya) (1973) *Educational Trends* Nairobi

Ministry of Economic Planning and Development (Kenya) (1983) *Statistical Abstracts* Nairobi

Ministry of Education, Science and Technology (Kenya) (1975a) *The 8-4-4 Education System* Government Printer: Nairobi

Ministry of Education, Science and Technology (Kenya) (1975b) *Courses Offered in Institutes of Technology* Nairobi

Ministry of Education, Science and Technology (Kenya) (1985) *Courses Offered in Institutes of Technology* Government Printer: Nairobi

Ministry of Finance and Planning (Kenya) (1984a) *Development Plan 1984/88* Government Printer: Nairobi

Ministry of Finance and Planning (Kenya) (1984b) *Kericho District Development Plan, 1984/88* Government Printer: Nairobi

Office of the President, Republic of Kenya (1984) *Focus for Rural Development* Government Printer: Nairobi

Orwa, W O (1977) *in* ILO/SIDA (1977)

Orwa, W O (1982) *An Investigation of Vocational Education in Kenya with Reference to Village Polytechnic Programme* MEd thesis, University of Nairobi: Nairobi

Raju, B M (1973) *Education in Kenya* Heinemann: Nairobi

Republic of Kenya (1976) *Report of the National Committee on Educational Objectives and Policies* Government Printer: Nairobi

Reynolds, J E *et al* (1976) *Self-Help and Rural Development in Kenya* University of Nairobi, IDS: Nairobi

Thomas, B (1980) *Rural Development through Local Initiative: Observations on Kenya's Experience with Harambee Projects in Selected Rural Communities* University of Nairobi, IDS: Nairobi

14. Updating and retraining initiatives in the UK

John Twining

Summary: Two separate initiatives in the UK are starting to come together. The first is the Open Tech programme, which started as a project-based initiative with particular emphasis on technicians and supervisors and with the ethos of removing barriers for adults who wanted to enter, return to, or continue their education or training. As time went on however the burden of producing learning material came to dominate the Open Tech programme and the number of modules produced were used as a measure of its success. No national system was created, and once pump-priming finance is removed the viability of many of the projects is doubtful.

The PICKUP (Professional, Industrial and Commercial Updating) programme of the Department of Education and Science (DES) has been a systematic attempt to persuade institutions to design short updating courses specifically for industrial needs, to market the courses, to ensure that teaching staff are sufficiently expert and to charge a realistic price. Experiments with inter-institutional collaboration have taken place, one of the most successful being the Coventry Consortium, which comprises Warwick University, Coventry Polytechnic and three vocational education colleges.

Users need to be able to choose whether they want a face-to-face course or self-study. For such choice to be exercisable there has to be comprehensive availability of courses or self-study materials, a network of support and advice, and accurate and up-to-date information. The TAP (Training Access Points) initiative announced in 1986 should provide the latter by bringing information on training opportunities to places where people naturally go. The Open College of the Air initiative (also announced in 1986) may well provide an opportunity to bring together the various elements and create a comprehensive national system.

Introduction

In mid-1986 Lord Young, the British Secretary of State for Employment, launched the Open College of the Air, due to operate from September 1987. This is the latest in a series of initiatives taken in Britain to improve the opportunities for continuing vocational education and training.

Traditionally, training and post-school education have been 'front-loaded', taking place in the first years of working life, with little systematic provision for subsequent updating or retraining. Until recently, this made sense; most workers either stayed in the same trade all their lives, or progressed through it. They had to learn the essentials of their trade at the outset in order to be useful workers. It also made sense both to employer and employee that the latter should spend more time learning when his or her earning capacity and expectations were lowest.

These assumptions are no longer valid. Job requirements change far more rapidly than ever before. In many cases fewer workers are required for the same amount of output, so others have to move on. At the same time, new technologies create entirely new categories of employment: an obvious example of a common trade which hardly existed before the last two decades is television repair.

It is now widely recognized in the West that most people will change their jobs, often their career directions, several times during their working lives. This does not necessarily mean a shift from the 'front-loading' of vocational education and training. The early chapters of this *Yearbook* have shown the continuing, if not increased, importance being given to the transition from school to work, even if the length of the transition period is now less than it was in the days of six-year apprenticeships. There is, however, greater emphasis on the need for systematic opportunities for updating, retraining and career change.

These opportunities can be approached from two directions. First, there is the question of responsibilities, entitlements and payments. Some people believe that updating is the responsibility of the individual worker, sometimes formalized through requirements for, or homilies on, 'continuous professional development'. Others regard employers as responsible for updating opportunities. There is a lobby for an entitlement to paid educational leave which combines individual choice with employer support. The debate on this aspect of updating is not yet resolved in Britain, and may never be.

Second, there is the availability of the educational provision itself. The theme of this chapter is that Britain, at least, has most of the ingredients for a comprehensive system, even though the initiatives which have led to the development of these ingredients have been independent from each other and hitherto largely unco-ordinated. Two separate but potentially complementary government initiatives have started to cover a lot of the ground: the Open Tech and PICKUP.

Open Tech

Evolution of a programme

Open Tech, like the Open College, started as a political initiative. In a statement in the House of Commons on 26 November 1980, James Prior, then Secretary of State for Employment, said:

'I am convinced that we need more open opportunities for technical training. By "open" I mean that there should be no formal pre-entry educational qualifications, and that such opportunities should be available to people irrespective of whether they can join with others for structured classes at set times in working hours . . . That is why I am asking the MSC to come forward with a scheme of distance learning — what I call 'open tech' — in conjunction of course with existing technical colleges and colleges of further education' (Hansard, 1980).

Although this political initiative was based on the success of the Open University, Open Tech itself was launched in 1982 by the Manpower Services Commission (MSC) as a 'programme'. The Open University has central course structures, designs syllabuses and course material centrally, enrols its own students, and makes its own awards. The Open Tech programme, ending in March 1987, has been project-based, collaborative, developmental (providing pump-priming, not necessarily continuing, finance) and vocational (with particular emphasis on technicians and supervisors) (Tolley, 1983).

In the early days of Open Tech, great stress was laid on removing barriers for adults who wanted to enter, return to or continue their education or training. These barriers might be:

☐ geographical — travel problems, no local course available
☐ personal — domestic ties, personal disability
☐ work demands — shifts, difficulties of getting away
☐ inflexible or unsuitable course times, content etc
☐ anxieties — reluctance to return to formal study, 'I've forgotten how to study', 'I'll be shown up' (MSC, 1984).

However, as time went on, the production of learning material dominated. Many of those connected with Open Tech tended to think of it in terms of the creation of learning material. Indeed, this has been used as a measure of its success, eg 'The Open Tech programme in just 4 years produced over 1000 modules representing over 14,000 learning hours'. Of the Open Tech projects, over 100 were concerned with learning material production and only some 20 with delivery systems, with another dozen 'practical training facilities' established to provide equipment for hands-on experience (MSC, 1986).

Allama Iqbal Open University

Some critics of the Open Tech programme have suggested that it should, after all, have followed the Open University model. Such a model for vocational education does exist in Pakistan, in one of the departments of the Allama Iqbal Open University — an institution very largely modelled on the UK Open University. The department of industrial and commercial education does not operate at degree level. In the late 1970s it independently developed a course in electrical wiring, which has attracted thousands of students for each of two semesters each year. It involves learning material and 'hands-on' practical work which, in this subject at this level, can reasonably be undertaken at home with components bought in the bazaar. There are five television programmes and ten radio broadcasts in each semester. There are also frequent face-to-face tutorials, which take place at polytechnics and other educational and training institutions on Fridays, when the students who normally attend those institutions are having their day of rest. Additional pay attracts tutors to work on Fridays. The 100 or so electrical wiring study centres include a large number of schools which have the low level of equipment required.

The Allama Iqbal Open University then introduced a course in electricians' work, to which students could progress from electrical wiring. However, the hands-on practical work required for this second course not only reduced to nearly 40 the number of institutions with the necessary equipment (it eliminated the schools), but also made it impractical for the 'hands-on' work to be undertaken at home. These logistical restrictions in turn drastically reduced the number of students who could attend. In the mid-1980s courses were being developed in radio repair, basic electronics (perhaps 50 suitable study centres) and in motor vehicle mechanics work (where the specialist equipment and staffing means that only 15 to 20 study centres would be available).

The needs of the Pakistan economy, and perhaps even more the students' perception of well-paid employment, have motivated them to overcome the quite considerable difficulties in successfully undertaking the courses. Students have willingly travelled 70 miles and more each way by bus to attend electricians' work tutorials.

In the early 1970s, the head of the department drew up a 'shopping list' of technical courses for which he could see a reasonable demand. These courses covered only a small proportion of the work required within a developing economy like that of Pakistan, and were only at craft and higher craft level. Nevertheless, they were so numerous (over 70 in nine clusters) that, unless some means of accelerating normal development rates could be found, it seemed unlikely that more than a small proportion could be prepared and made available by the end of the century. If only three clusters were developed they would require a tripling of the staffing of the department of industrial and commercial education. If all nine clusters were on offer for two semesters a year, the manpower requirements in the service departments of the university (including that department which co-ordinates study centres) would also have to be increased considerably, and if the same ratio of television broadcasts were maintained about an hour a day throughout the year would be required for technical subjects alone.

Open learning for vocational education

This Pakistan experience illuminates one of the problems about open learning in vocational education as compared with the arrangements for the UK Open University. Courses offered by the latter are designed to have a 'shelf life' of five years or so, and are then replaced by new provision. If vocational open learning courses are to be of use to the economy they have to be comprehensive in coverage, and although they will need updating as technology or applications change, they need to remain available virtually in perpetuity. Provision accumulates to such an extent that it is difficult for a single institution to cope with it. The Open Tech programme was therefore justified in not trying to copy the Open University by providing a single 'open institution'.

What the Open Tech programme did was to set up a whole range of projects in different areas of industry, using different media for learning. The result has been the generation of a great deal of learning material in different media for different target groups, and with a wide variety of content. So far, however, insufficient numbers have completed the Open Tech courses for the comparative effectiveness of different approaches to have become clear. There is not the volume of knowledge that exists for more general education at the Open University. Nor has any coherent pattern developed. The viability of some of the projects is doubtful, once the pump-priming finance comes to an end.

No comprehensive network of delivery was established, even though one lay ready to hand. In 1981, a report to the Manpower Services Commission had calculated:

> 'Experimental mapping shows that if 30-40 colleges offer a subject then most of England and Wales will lie within a 30-mile radius of one of those colleges. If there are 60-70 colleges, the same will apply to a 20-mile radius, and with over 100 colleges to a 15-mile radius' (Twining, 1982).

One reason why the Manpower Services Commission ignored the college infrastructure was that in the early 1980s industry had come to regard colleges as inflexible and slow to react, with a vested interest in maintaining the status quo, which industry saw as a soft working week with long holidays. In the case of open learning, this impression of British vocational education was reinforced when both national and local representatives of teachers expressed strong, but unsubstantiated, doubts as to the wisdom of introducing open learning on a wide scale; this was seen as natural opposition to anything which might change their current way of doing things. In fact, the history of vocational education in Britain has been one of fairly constant change since the mid-1950s (see, for example, Chapter 3). Those working in colleges have made constant and successful attempts to come to terms with innovation, although there has always been some time lag. The trouble was that in the early 1980s there were so many innovations that colleges were suffering from 'indigestion'. At the same time they were being blamed for Britain's poor industrial performance, and so any doubts raised by lecturers were likely to be used as evidence against them. The climate of opinion in industry and in training at the time when the Open Tech programme was launched was not favourable to the adoption of a supporting network of colleges.

PICKUP

Using educational institutions

It was left to another initiative, sponsored and funded by a different government department, to take advantage of the infrastructure of educational institutions. The PICKUP (Professional, Industrial and Commercial Updating) programme of the Department of Education and Science was launched in May 1982 to provide post-experience vocational courses for those in employment. Delivery is through universities, polytechnics and colleges as an addition to their traditional 'front-loaded' degree, diploma or first qualification courses.

Many educational institutions in many countries have offered short courses in addition to their longer provision. The special features of PICKUP have included systematic attempts at the following:

☐ persuading institutions to design such courses specifically for industrial needs, rather than what it is convenient or interesting to offer;
☐ marketing the courses (and the ability to tailor them to client's requirements) to employers, and to a lesser extent to individuals;
☐ ensuring that staff involved are sufficiently expert both in their subject matter and in teaching adults — a somewhat different skill from that of teaching of young people; and
☐ charging a realistic price.

One rationale for the programme is that the national investment in educational resources (buildings, equipment and people) should be harnessed for the benefits of the economy. Potentially, the PICKUP programme can supply a short course in anything at any level for anyone, provided the price can be paid. I have personally arranged for one single colleague to go on a bespoke 'course' made up of elements of several different courses for a negotiated fee, which took into account that one person would be learning and using equipment, with access as required to tutors, rather than being a member of a group.

Compared to the £45 million allocated to the Open Tech programme, the PICKUP programme has been run on a shoestring, yet its achievements have been impressive. It has researched how PICKUP courses are delivered (Graham and Morris, 1984) and has used the result in a handbook for course providers (Morris, 1984). The PICKUP programme is run by a small central team with regional agents to help link institutions and local industry. A large number of special projects have been commissioned. One of these is related to the BBC and City and Guilds 'Inside Information' scheme referred to in Chapter 19.

One of the successes of the PICKUP programme has been the Coventry Consortium, which comprises Warwick University, Coventry Polytechnic and three further education colleges in the city, almost certainly the first consortium in Britain which involves these different levels of institution. Its high local profile has given industry an increasing perception of

educational institutions as an important source of training. Companies
regard educational institutions as one training resource amongst many.
They expect work to be carried out quickly and efficiently at reasonable
cost and with the minimum effort on their part. The consortium provides
this service in a business-like manner, and this is much appreciated by its
clients. The ability of companies in Coventry to use the consortium as a
'single agency' brokerage for training has been the feature which has
commended it most to local industry. As there is a fair amount of contact
between training officers the news that 'education can deliver' is likely to
spread (Graham, 1985).

A report to the Department of Education and Science suggests that the
'vital ingredients' for the success so far of the Coventry consortium are:

- the will to collaborate;
- a favourable 'mix' of partners (one university, one LEA, one polytechnic and no more than three colleges);
- co-ordinators with the patience, drive and ability to start a consortium and overcome subsequent difficulties;
- a compact area, which makes the co-ordinator's work easier;
- an industrial/commercial base, which has a considerable need for
  the PICKUP scheme and is therefore capable of generating sufficient
  income;
- the setting of clear, outward looking, achievable aims;
- the establishment of a viable central unit;
- a pump-priming grant (Graham, 1985).

Although the consortium has been successful because of its special features, it is just one example of the way in which the PICKUP programme
has started to generate a real interest in, and the excitement of, educational
institutions in the process of marketing. The British Columbia approach
described by Curtis in Chapter 15 is being repeated in Britain in many
institutions; indeed, Russ Curtis himself has had a hand in developing the
PICKUP marketing handbook (Further Education Unit, 1985).

The way educational statistics are collected in Britain does not make it
possible to provide an accurate figure of takeup, but it has been estimated
(Twining, 1985) that the *annual* throughput of students on PICKUP short
courses is in the nature of a half of a million, about 20 times the total
number who had followed Open Tech courses up to spring 1986.

Coming together

The next stage

One result has been that the MSC has changed its perception of educational institutions, and has now started to tell industrialists that they are
flexible and adaptable to the needs of the market. Indeed, the MSC
commissioned a report *Implementing Open Learning in Local Authority
Institutions* (Further Education Unit, 1986). This new perception is

making it easier to introduce the next stage of government-funded updating provision, which is likely to be an attempt to draw together the
experience of the Open Tech and PICKUP programmes into a more
comprehensive approach. A number of other national initiatives have led
to the development of self-study material or of short retraining courses.
Commercial publishers and software and courseware suppliers have also
developed materials. However, if the two main initiatives, PICKUP and
the Open Tech, can be brought together then any other initiatives can be
linked to them.

The users

Both the PICKUP and the Open Tech programmes have insisted that
course providers must start by thinking of the potential students and
their training needs. In all updating and retraining, the starting point has
to be the individual, as it is only the individual who can learn. Motivation
is essential. Britain is not yet the sort of 'learning society' which Bill Ford
in Chapter 20 so admires in Japan, nor is it likely to become so for some
time. The motivation for adults to learn may have to stem not from the
perception that it is normal to do so, but from fascination or fear. Fear of
redundancy, and of subsequent unemployment, may prove to be powerful
motivating forces in inducing adult workers to learn new knowledge or
skills. That may sound brutal, yet there is anecdotal evidence that fear can
foster fascination. When Austin Rover (as it was then called) set up a
computer-based training resource centre with retraining packages aligned
to the company's requirements, workers initially attended as a possible
insurance against redundancy. Soon, however, many became so interested
in the process of learning and in the new knowledge and skills they were
able to gain that they sought additional opportunities beyond their
employer's requirements or expectations.

Fascination with new technology is, of course, nothing new. The fields
of computing, motor vehicle maintenance and photography are examples
of subjects which can enthrall practitioners. However, many people are
innately conservative and tend to regard change in process or practice
with suspicion. For them, quite small hurdles can be used as excuses for
not starting or not persevering with learning something. The original
Open Tech ideals of removing barriers make a good starting point for all
updating provision.

In *general* adult education, the fascination with learning, and often the
social interaction associated with learning activity, may be sufficient
stimulation. It is not uncommon in parts of southern England for people
to determine to set aside a certain amount of time, perhaps at a certain
period of the day (morning, afternoon or evening) on a specific day or
days of the week, and then to see what is available at an adult education
centre to fit that pattern. This is hardly likely to happen in *vocational*
education or in retraining. The subject matter and the level at which it is
being presented is likely to be all-important, although compromises may

have to be made. It is pointless to study the latest aspects of planning law if the workplace need is for recent developments in polymers; but some categories of staff might find courses in polymer technology, plastics engineering or science of modern materials to be acceptable alternatives (Guildford Educational Services, 1986).

Some approaches to continuing professional development (eg Engineering Council, 1986) are based on a points system which requires a professional to achieve a certain number of points each year. Such approaches could make the subject matter studied of secondary importance. Normally, however, either the individual or the employer will have priorities which can be quite detailed and specific. The question then is where, if anywhere, is suitable provision available?

Linking open learning and short updating face-to-face courses is best done by starting from the viewpoint of the user, who could be:

☐ a professional who wants to keep up with the changing needs of a particular profession;
☐ an employed person who might want to change career direction, but to do so without his or her employer necessarily knowing that this is to happen;
☐ someone who is unemployed.

Users need to be able to select from the full range of opportunities the one which best suits their needs. Depending on circumstances, an individual might choose a short face-to-face course, a longer course which might lead to an additional qualification, a self-study package or something which combines self-study with hands-on practical work or considerable tutorial support at a local resource centre. For example, choice might be based on convenience (which may make self-study the most favourable mode) or an urgent need for updating of specific knowledge or skills; in the latter case a face-to-face short course is likely to be most suitable.

To have a full choice there has to be comprehensive coverage and comprehensive information about what is available. At present, the coverage is incomplete and the information about it is fragmented.

Information

Take the information systems first. The UK has three relevant national computerized databases which have developed along different lines with different aims and different funding: MARIS (Materials and Resources Information Service) is funded by the Open Tech programme to provide details of Open Tech and similar materials for self-study. It also holds data on resources which can help organizations to develop learning material. ECCTIS (Educational Counselling and Credit Transfer Information Service) is funded by the Department of Education and Science to provide information about further and higher education courses throughout the United Kingdom leading to qualifications available at individual universities, polytechnics and colleges. The PICKUP Short

Course Directory has been established under the PICKUP programme to provide details of short courses run by educational establishments and other providers. A fourth database covering the qualifications and curricula of vocational education is being developed for the Further Education Unit. The MARIS, ECCTIS and PICKUP databases can be accessed on viewdata systems. The ECCTIS, PICKUP and vocational education curriculum databases can also be accessed by microfiche. ECCTIS has experimented successfully with CD-ROM optical disc technology, and will also include the PICKUP and probably other databases on a single CD-ROM disc in the future.

At present, users have to subscribe to each service separately. The first close co-ordination was between the ECCTIS and PICKUP viewdata service, because the latter uses ECCTIS as a host and the search procedures are therefore almost identical. It was found, however, that the different levels of detail contained in the records for each database made a fully common thesaurus (a structured listing of index terms) unachievable.

A new initiative was announced by the Manpower Services Commission in 1986. Experimental Training Access Points (TAP), located in places convenient for the public at large (eg high street shops, public libraries, job centres, perhaps railway stations) bring together those databases which employers and individuals are likely to find useful in the field of training, probably including a small database on training grants.

The concept is a bold and exciting one. There are, however, a number of problems to be overcome, including the following:

☐ A cost-effective medium is needed. Although viewdata is a readily available public medium it is expensive in terms of telephone charges for the person searching. It is possible that the combination of CD-ROM for stable data and a method of broadcasting ephemeral data will provide the capability of meeting necessary requirements.

☐ All the databases concerned were originally created for use by people familiar with the vocational education and training system of the UK. This expectation of familiarity is implicit and subtle rather than obvious, but could be enough to make it difficult for the inexpert user, especially on a casual basis, to find the necessary information. It will be some time before a suitable expert system can be devised.

☐ The user needs to be able to search across the various databases without being aware of moving out of one into another.

☐ Some potential users, notably those in industrial training and running small businesses, are unlikely to come to public access points to get their information. At present they tend to phone round their normal circle of contacts, or to keep rough files of brochures, and so on. It may be that the culture will change and that they will learn to use information sources such as viewdata or to subscribe to downloaded information systems such as microfiche, floppy disc or CD-ROM.

☐ There is still a debate between government departments as to whether information about updating education and training should be a priced commodity (as financial information tends to be) or a free service to the consumer.

Nevertheless, there seems to be a convergence of technical solutions, and both the will to collaborate and adequate funding to make a comprehensive national information system available.

A comprehensive system of courses

Just as the TAP initiative looks like combining the different information systems, so there is a chance that the Open College will lead to a comprehensive pattern of updating opportunity. Although details are not available at the time of writing, it appears that the Open College will involve a network of support centres largely based on public sector institutions of vocational education. Broadcasting will mainly be used for raising public awareness and providing 'tasters' of what open learning is available; the nature of the medium makes it unsuitable for serious learning. However, as the institutions in the support network will also be providers of PICKUP or similar short courses for updating, there is a good chance that the separate programmes of Open Tech and PICKUP will come together in the same way as the information systems are likely to come together as a result of TAP.

As with TAP, however, there are problems to be resolved. Qualification courses for those in their first years out of school make different demands on the staff and physical provision of educational institutions than do short updating face-to-face courses, which in turn have different requirements from support for open learning. In theory, all three should become 'mainline'. Indeed this may eventually come to pass as 'front-loaded' education becomes more and more modular (see Chapters 4 and 18) and the same modules are used within an updating system, whether face-to-face or by self-study, or a mixture of both.

However, in order to get the Open Tech and PICKUP initiatives moving, it was at first thought necessary to treat them as being separate both from front-loaded 'mainline' provision and from each other. The realities of education themselves tend to keep the strands apart rather than bring them together. Such realities include timetabling and location of classrooms and workshops, the issues of teachers' conditions of service (eg should there be additional payment for lecturing or tutoring at evenings, weekends or other times to suit the needs of the customer?), the question of charging the customer and the different styles of teaching and tutoring required for different groups.

A secondary issue is the recognition given to updating education. Those involved in adult general education and those involved with the work-related updating of those in employment often seem to have few ideas or ideals in common. Both have argued, however, that adults do not wish to put themselves in jeopardy by being examined or otherwise assessed, and that vocational qualifications are irrelevant to them. There may be some truth in this, but if no assessments and qualifications are available then it is the providers who have made the decision rather than the learners. It is better to make such assessments available but optional. So far, however, the problem has been that the assessment and qualification arrangements of the award-making bodies have not been helpful to the field of continuing and updating education. This has partly been due to assessments being held on fixed dates, which destroys the flexibility of timing required for meeting the needs of adult learners. But even where college assessments have been accepted there has up to now been a barrier in that bodies such as the Business and Technician Education Council (BTEC) have not wished to recognize the very short courses which many people need and from whch they could accumulate a larger qualification.

This led the Birmingham Open Learning Development Unit to state in its development document (quoted in Further Education Unit, 1986):

> 'It is our perception that industry and commerce are concerned about their employees having the necessary skills for the efficient operation of their business. However, formal certification of these skills appears to have a low priority. There is much incentive to be gained by offering individuals who undertake any form of training acknowledgement of their achievements. It is unlikely that the major examinations bodies would find it attractive to provide certification for short modules but we propose to give learners some certificate.
>
> Our proposal is to use an individualised computer-managed learning system for the certification of modules. This certificate would be in the form of a profile, detailing the skills and abilities of the learner at the end of the module. Such a certificate would be created using the CAMELOT system which will also be used by the learner at other stages in the learning activity. Any learner undertaking several modules would build his or her profiles into a portfolio which could be used for accreditation within a larger course certificated by a national examination body. It is believed that such profiles validated by the City of Birmingham would be more beneficial to a learner than any certificate offered by an individual college.'

Birmingham's Open Learning Development Unit has already been overtaken by events. At the launch of its continuing education provision in July 1986, a representative of the Business and Technician Education Council expressed the council's willingness to consider how very short modules could be validated and accumulated, while (as noted by Ward in Chapter 19) assessment on disc is already being provided by City and Guilds for its 'Inside Information' Certificate, thus getting away from time constraints.

As with so much else in vocational education, modularization and information technology, hand in hand, seem to offer solutions to many of the problems which have thwarted development in the past.

References

Engineering Council (1986) *A Call to Action: Continuing Education and Training for Engineers and Technicians* Engineering Council: London

Further Education Unit (FEU) (1985) *Marketing Further and Higher Education* Longman: York

Further Education Unit (FEU) (1986) *Implementing Open Learning in Local Authority Institutions* Further Education Unit, London and Open Tech Unit, Manpower Services Commission: Sheffield

Graham, C (1985) *Developing PICKUP for Industry* Department of Education and Science: London

Graham, C and Morris, A (1984) *PICKUP Delivery Systems* Department of Education and Science (DES): London

Guildford Educational Services Ltd (1986) *The PICKUP Short Course Directory* (Microfiche version) Reissue G. Guildford Educational Services Ltd: Guildford

Hansard (1980) *House of Commons Official Report* 994,5 26 November HMSO: London

Manpower Services Commission (MSC) (1984) *The Open Tech Programme Explained* Manpower Services Commission: Sheffield

Manpower Services Commission (MSC) (1986) *Open Tech Programme News No 11* MSC: Sheffield

Morris, A ed (1984) *The PICKUP Handbook* Department of Education and Science (DES): London

Tolley, G (1983) *The Open Tech: Why, What and How?* Open Tech Paper 1 Manpower Services Commission (MSC): Sheffield

Twining, J ed (1982) *Open Learning for Technicians* Stanley Thornes (Publishers) Ltd: Cheltenham

Twining, J (1985) Flavour of the month: the response of FE *EDUCA* 55 September

15. Marketing and education

Russ Curtis

Summary: This chapter begins by discussing marketing and its potential for application by post-secondary/technical educational institutions to present-day problems of institutional adaptation.

The markets and exchange processes entered by educational institutions are described, analysed and illustrated. The complex of educational products or services and the educational institution as a service organization are compared to industrial service providers in a series of analogies.

Product differentiation, market segmentation and positioning concepts and procedures are related to vocational/technical institutions.

The chapter closes with several recommendations for implementing a marketing approach. References are made throughout the paper to the marketing efforts of the British Columbia Institute of Technology (BCIT), the second largest of five technical institutions in Canada.

Introduction

The British Columbia Institute of Technology (BCIT) is a Canadian post-secondary institution set up in 1964. During the first ten years of its existence, the institute was sustained by monthly grants from the provincial government. Then, in 1974, the institute was created by statute to serve the province's technical training needs. The institute offers two-year continuous programmes in health, business and engineering technologies.

These programmes are offered in full-time, part-time (night school) and distance learning modes. In 1985, the institute contained 4,200 students in full-time attendance, registered over 60,000 night school students (approximately 4,000 full-time equivalents), and served roughly 6,000 students at a distance.

BCIT's main campus is located in Burnaby, British Columbia. The institute also operates a smaller downtown facility in co-operation with several other post-secondary institutions, and it conducts classes during the evenings in schools and in corporate boardrooms. Several departments even conduct classes in the wilderness.

The institute is presently awaiting passage of legislation that will combine it with the nearby Pacific Vocational Institute (PVI). The resulting institution will deliver vocational, craft and technical training to students throughout the province. The new institution will be nearly twice the size of the 'old' BCIT and will operate at seven sites within a 90-mile radius.

British Columbia is Canada's westernmost province. The province is large in geography (just under 1,000,000 square km), and small in population (about 2.8 million people). The province's main industries relate to the extraction of its abundant natural resources: logging, lumber and paper production, mining and smelting, and fisheries.

Canada is a federal state and education is a responsibility of the provinces. Unlike the Federal Republic of Germany, Canada does not provide for national co-ordination of post-secondary education. Within British Columbia, there is very little co-ordination. Institutions within the post-secondary sector establish their own programmes and curriculum, in co-operation with their clients.

The province's post-secondary system consists of 15 colleges, five provincial institutes and three universities. The colleges and institutes, along with schools, are the responsibility of the provincial Ministry of Education, while the universities are part of another Ministry of the provincial government.

This chapter is about the marketing of education. It is intended not only to inform but also to stimulate discussion and debate about the role that marketing can play in the life and survival of post-secondary institutions, where attendance by students is voluntary rather than compulsory and institutions must compete for school leavers. Understanding marketing enables institutions to improve the achievement of their aims in a competitive environment.

Marketing and education

Education has its roots in the Church. Churches and religious orders were the first educators and still play a large part in education today, using various modern and traditional media in their efforts. Since the 19th century, education has become increasingly secular, and today secular educational institutions vastly outnumber religious schools. Still, modern secular education retains many vestiges of its religious past. Convocation ceremonials with academics proceeding in their hooded robes, the tapping of graduates and the convocation address (sermon) are a ritual recognition of the religious roots of education. The taking of degrees, diplomas or certificates is very much like the taking of religious orders, insofar as these documents are evidence of the bearer's membership of a special 'society'. Often, graduates are treated like novitiates, and only admitted to full membership status after some time-serving and further rites of initiation and passage. Robert Pirsig viewed university students as '. . . worshipping at the Church of Reason. . .' (Pirsig, 1979).

Modern universities still maintain indirect connections with churches through the location of theological colleges within larger university communities. The church connection with post-secondary (non-university) institutions is less direct than with universities. Still, most post-secondary teachers are university trained and bring university values and traditions to post-secondary institutions.

The roots of modern marketing are less clear. Marketing is eclectic in its origins, owing something to military tactics and strategy, scientific research, behavioural science, economics and mercantilism. Most educators would view marketing as a purely secular process. For this reason, and because education is rooted in mysticism rather than pragmatism, educators, at least until recently, have viewed marketing and its role in education with considerable scepticism. Although educators have adopted other business practices like budgeting, public relations, planning and finance, marketing has been approached, if not with reluctance, at least with considerable caution. When polled in the US, 300 college administrators whose colleges were faced with declining enrolment, rising student fees and spiralling costs, defined marketing as a combination of *selling, advertising and public relations* (Murphy and McGarrity, 1978).

When asked what marketing means, most people will reply that selling is a synonym for marketing. This is a fragmentary view of marketing, yet it is a common one, accounting for much of the resistance to the adoption of marketing as a function or process in educational institutions. Selling is a function that educators have avoided, believing that their product was a better mousetrap for which the world would beat a path to their door. Declining roles and dwindling government resources have caused an alteration to this view in recent years.

Marketing is defined by Philip Kotler as:

'The analysis, planning, implementation and control of carefully formulated programs designed to bring about voluntary exchanges of values with target markets to achieve institutional objectives. Marketing involves designing the institution's offerings *to meet the target market's needs and desires*, and using effective pricing, communication and distribution to inform, motivate, and service the markets.'

Kotler's definitions contain a number of terms which will be explained and expanded in this chapter.

Marketing offers a model to institutional managers, which will improve institutional performance if applied carefully and thoroughly. Modern educational institutions are complex organizations which are embedded in complex societies. Models are needed to ensure that educational situations can be grasped and controlled:

'No substantial part of the universe is so simple that it can be grasped and controlled without abstraction. Abstraction consists in replacing the part of the universe under consideration by a model of similar but simple structure. Models . . . are thus a central necessity of scientific procedure' (Rosenbluth and Weiner, 1979).

As suggested in Kotler's definition, the marketing model replicates, in simple form, the *exchange process* entered into by educational institutions and their various clients. An examination of the variety and complexity of educational exchanges is a first step in understanding the problems of educational marketing.

Educational exchange processes

Exchanges typically take place in a 'market'. Markets may be organized and centralized, as with securities, commodities and many tangible necessities, or they may be disorganized and decentralized. Education markets are of the latter variety. In fact, educational institutions find themselves in several markets simultaneously and in each, the nature of the exchange is different. Figure 1 illustrates the post-secondary institution in relation to its most important markets.

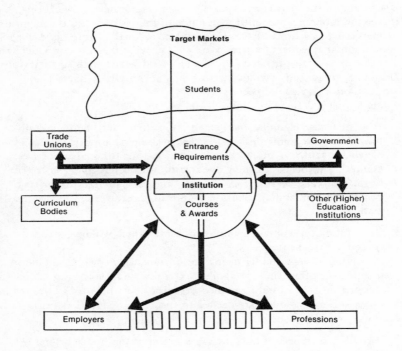

Figure 1. *Exchange processes between the post-secondary institution and its markets*

Government

Vocational and technical institutions are part of a market which also includes schools, colleges and universities, where each sector competes for diminishing state resources. This competition is a two-stage process. In the first stage, ministers of education compete with their colleagues before the treasury board, for a share of government budget. In the second stage, institutions compete among themselves for their share of their minister's budget. In the second stage, courses and academic awards seem to be exchanged for financial support. When one looks at what government measures, however, the essence of the exchange process is not academic awards but fiscal parsimony. In British Columbia, the government publishes what are called 'performance indicators' for each institution in the post-secondary system. These indicators are entirely concerned with costs (per student classroom hour) and with utilization of facilities. In each case, indicators are prepared for each institution and are compared with the average for all of the institutions in 'the system'. Our minister of education can be expected to behave as any rational consumer, and allocates his scarce resources so as to achieve the maximum economic benefit. The performance indicator reporting system encourages institutions to reduce costs and taught hours while at the same time increasing enrolments, class sizes and student-paid tuition fees. While these ends may be desirable, even necessary, they conflict with the demands made by other consumers of the institution's offerings. This is a central paradox in educational marketing, that the demands of one client can only be met at the expense of another.

Increasingly, BCIT is attempting to resolve this paradox by seeking out non-governmental sources of funding. In the past, when an institution raised funds privately, the government reduced the institution's budget, leaving the institution no better off. At the present time, the government in British Columbia is encouraging private fundraising by its institutions and allows certain types of fundraising without offsetting budget reductions. While this is an encouraging move by government, it adds yet another level of complexity to an institution's marketing effort, and places it in yet another competitive market. At the same time, the pressure to reduce costs and taught hours is in no way reduced by this alteration in government policy, and the paradox remains.

In the exchange with government, funding is exchanged for institutional efficiency and fiscal parsimony.

Students

The market potential for post-secondary institutions includes all citizens except those presently enrolled in compulsory education, and of course, pre-school children. The target market for post-secondary institutions has traditionally been the school leaver. In this exchange, institutions offer students training for work, or credit for higher education courses. In return, students pay fees, purchase books and materials, pay accommodation and commuting costs, and bear an opportunity cost in the form of lost wages or, more likely in present times, lost leisure time. (At the time of writing, overall unemployment in British Columbia is over 14 per cent and rising, and for school leavers, the rate is even higher.) This has proved to be a boon for post-secondary institutions. Not only are enrolments up across the province, but the quality of entrant is improving. In better economic times, energetic and resourceful young people entered employment upon leaving school, and earned good wages doing semi-skilled work in our resources industries. During good times, the opportunity cost of a two-year diploma was very high, indeed too high for a great many promising young people. Since 1980, many young people who would previously have gone directly to employment, have instead entered the post-secondary sector because employment was no longer a ready alternative to further education.

Despite changing patterns of enrolment in post-secondary institutions, the number of school leavers is declining, forcing institutions to redefine their market. Happily, at least for post-secondary institutions, unemployment is leading more adults to consider retraining and upgrading in order to improve their job prospects, and the age profile of our institutions is changing.

Rising unemployment in the province would seem to have more than offset the impact of declining numbers in school leavers, leading to a more mature and purposeful group of entrants to post-secondary institutions. The exchange process has been altered by this trend. When times were good, two years of attendance in an institution concluded with a diploma would have satisfied most entrants (and employers); present-day students are demanding up-to-date curricula, offered by up-to-date faculties, supported by state-of-the-industry equipment. Rapid technological change is putting pressure upon staff development aimed at keeping our faculties up to date, and upon our capital budgets. At the same time, the job market is tough for our graduates, and students insist on being thoroughly prepared for it. This *quid pro quo* is increasingly difficult to satisfy in the face of government pressure to reduce unit costs. Despite these difficulties, BCIT graduates are being taken into employment at much higher rates than either college or university graduates.

At BCIT the Canada Manpower Commission maintains a full-time placement office, funded primarily by the federal government. Most of our graduates are placed by this office. The Manpower Office also arranges part-time employment for our students during their two years at BCIT.

In summary, students offer two years of their lives, and a considerable amount of money, in exchange for up-to-date, intense job training leading to employment.

Curriculum bodies

Technical curricula and academic awards are institution-based in British Columbia. There are no bodies to set curricula and examine students such as those in Europe. Therefore, no exchange takes place; no market exists.

Professional bodies

Whereas there are no curriculum bodies in the province, professional bodies exert an active and continuing influence upon institutional curricula. This is true in all three of the Institute's generic areas, health, business and engineering. In the engineering technologies, the recently created Society of Engineering Technologists (SETBC), is exerting a growing influence in all of our engineering offerings. In addition to SETBC, other engineering professions offer credit for courses, and license engineering technologists in surveying, forestry and other disciplines. In business technologies, the accounting bodies, the real estate profession, and other commercial professional bodies credit courses and license graduates. In health, a variety of professional bodies do likewise, and some national validation and examination takes place. Relations with professional bodies are carried on principally at the department level, with the societies being represented on the advisory committees established within each department in the institute.

In the exchange process with professional bodies, the institution tailors curricula to meet professional expectations and the professional body offers graduates credit towards a professional designation, normally subject to further postgraduate training and relevant work experience. This process is not without its problems. The BC Institute of Technology was created as a 'terminal' institution, that is, without the thought that graduates would progress either to higher education (university) or to professional status. There is conflict in some departments between meeting the expectations of professional bodies and simply training graduates for direct entry into employment without regard to further education or professional standing. Conflict arises when the professional bodies alter their expectations in such a way that departments must make sudden and major alterations in curriculum.

Employers

Like professional bodies, employers are directly and actively involved in institutional affairs through representation on departmental advisory committees. Employers want graduates who are able to take up work duties immediately upon employment, with a minimum of company training and induction. Our market research has revealed an interesting aspect of employer behaviour, in that employers recruit our graduates as much for their attitude to employment as for their work skills (Venne, 1985).

Employers exchange employment prospects for curricula and methods which produce a graduate who is well grounded in entry-level technical skills, is able to work with a minimum of direction and who is highly motivated.

While the term 'employers' covers a wide range of needs and expectations, BCIT has adapted to this variety by differentiation. The Institute is divided into three schools (health, business and engineering), and has 26 teaching departments, offering diplomas in 52 specific disciplines. There are advisory committees comprising employer and professional representatives in every department and for most diplomas. There is therefore a second dimension to the exchange process between the Institute and employers, in which the Institute exchanges involvement in its decision-making processes for the employers' commitment to the Institute, its curricula and its graduates. This process deserves much credit for the Institute's growth and its ability to survive in the difficult economy of recent years in British Columbia.

Trade unions

Despite the fact that professional bodies behave like trade unions in most respects, trade unions *per se* have little or no direct involvement in Institute affairs at present. This will be changed considerably when BCIT and PVI are merged, but for the present a trade union appointee to the Institute's governing body is the extent of formal trade union involvement. Aside from this ritual exchange, then, there is little real exchange to consider at the present time.

Other (higher) institutions

Universities enjoy great independence within the total picture of education in the province. Progression or bridging from technical to university training is a matter of great difficulty. Despite the fact that certain subject offerings are identical, sometimes even taught by the same teacher, credit is seldom granted for transfer from BCIT to the province's universities. Instead, credit transfer is a matter for ad hoc arrangements between the institute and individual universities. Transfer between the colleges and the universities, and between the colleges and BCIT are, on the other hand, the subject of standing arrangements and are much simpler and therefore more common. With the merger of BCIT and PVI, progression between vocational/craft training and technical training is expected to become routine.

The exchange process, where it exists between elements in the system, involves assurances by one institution to another of curricular content and teaching and examination standards. To accomplish these arrangements, there are various institutional conferences and committees which negotiate and approve transferability between themselves on behalf of their students. Without standardization of curriculum, however, students find it difficult to move between institutions and across sectors of the system. In British Columbia's post-secondary system, much work remains to be done in the area of access through transferability.

Faculty and staff

Not only must institutions sustain relations with external groups, they must also sustain internal relations. The exchange process for educational organizations with their employees are similar to those in most organizations. Education remains labour-intensive and employer-employee relations must be satisfactory if organizational objectives are to be achieved. Post-secondary education has traditionally recruited its faculty and staff from private sector firms. Educational employment offers the inducements of relative independence, the opportunity for professional development, enhanced tenure or job security and extended vacations, in exchange for lower wages and poor work environments. In British Columbia, post-secondary teachers were organized during the early 1970s, and while wages improved to become comparable with private sector wages, since 1980 post-secondary salaries have been frozen, layoffs have been commonplace, workloads have increased and opportunities for professional development have diminished, all as a result of provincial government fiscal restraint. It is becoming increasingly problematic for institutions to sustain satisfactory relations with their employees.

The product

Philip Kotler defines 'product' as follows:

'A product is anything that can be offered to a market for attention, acquisition, or consumption; it includes physical objects, services, personalities, places, organisations and ideas.'

From the previous discussion of educational exchanges, it is clear that post-secondary institutions produce a variety of 'products' and offer them in a variety of markets. All products, educational and otherwise, have both tangible and intangible aspects. The tangible aspects of post-secondary education are courses and awards, graduates and facilities. Certainly, these tangible aspects of the educational process occupy much of the educational effort. Teaching, curriculum development and accreditation, student placement and the maintenance of the institution's fabric constitute much of what is day-to-day life in academic institutions. But are our consumers really buying our tangible product?

Charles Revson of Revlon Cosmetics said of his enterprise: 'In the factory we make cosmetics, in the drugstore we sell hope'. Revson understood that his product had both tangible and intangible properties, and he also understood that his consumers purchased the intangible ones.

Similarly, the Xerox Corporation sells office copiers, yet its sales force is trained to sell intangible benefits of the product (convenience, overall cost, productivity, simplicity and quality) (Xerox, 1967).

Ostensibly, students seem to buy courses and awards, whereas actually they are buying a set of intangibles which might include status, career advancement or change, fulfilment, success and even hope.

Government buys efficiency. Employers buy attitudes and values in graduates which are consistent with the firm's attitudes and values. Professional bodies buy teaching quality and examination standards.

Clearly, it is the intangible aspects of the education product that are being evaluated and purchased by all of the consumers of education in all the markets where it is offered. Yet these intangible aspects receive little attention from educators when communicating with their audiences. College calendars (prospectuses) contain many pages of extravagant prose describing the curriculum, entrance requirements, examination dates, lists of faculty names complete with accompanying 'alphabet soup', and the occasional photograph of the fabric — as if the institution were selling its buildings.

The consumers of education are buying its intangible product. Courses, awards and facilities are simply tangible means which serve intangible ends. As such, education is in the service sector, and has much to learn from industrial service firms about selling its services.

Making the intangible tangible

When marketing a service, the provider makes the intangible aspects of the service tangible by using metaphors. An architect will sell his building concept using renderings (sketches) of the completed product. These renderings are not precise replicas of the finished product, nor are they detailed. When people are sketched in the architect's rendering, they are often depicted at leisure and always appear happy and relaxed, as if the architect's building will, by virtue of its design, produce these happy results. Neither the architect nor the client really believe that the building will produce happiness and leisure, but the metaphor is used nevertheless, to aid the exchange.

Automobiles are shown in advertising being driven with great skill and at high speed on empty highways, or parked in front of mansions draped with elegant ladies dressed in furs. No one believes that buying the car will make rush-hour traffic disappear and make the owner rich and famous. The advertisement is a metaphor that helps to make tangible the intangible attributes that the manufacturer is selling his audience. Service firms also attempt to make tangible their intangible products, and use metaphors to do this. Conversely, industrial firms selling tangible products stress their intangible aspects.

College registrars will hasten to point out that the calendar or prospectus is a legal contract between the institution and its clients, that details of courses, curricula and credit are mandatory. But that is not what is suggested in the industrial analogies above. Look again at the examples used. Following the presentation of his renderings, the architect and his client agree to proceed with the project, and having agreed to proceed, detailed drawings are produced and approved. Automobile brochures do contain detailed specifications and performance ratings, but in small print and on the back cover of the brochure. Owners' manuals are provided with each vehicle, and these contain detailed tangible product specifications, warranties, maintenance schedules, and so on.

In selling a service, therefore, the metaphor precedes the detailed product specification. Put another way, industrial service providers sell the intangibles first, using metaphors to do so, and only then follow with detailed product specifications. Educational institutions seem to have this process backwards. Calendars, the detailed specification of the tangible product are offered first, while selling the intangibles is either left to chance or ignored completely. When communicating with government, institutions stress quality and academic standards, when what the government is really buying is fiscal parsimony and efficiency. We send employers transcripts of syllabuses studied by students which say nothing of the values and attitudes that our institution's approach to its curriculum encourages and fosters in its graduates. It isn't so much that post-secondary education isn't doing what its consumers want it to do, rather it is that it says the wrong things in communicating with its audiences. In the halcyon days of the 1960s and 1970s, institutions got away with ignorance of effective marketing. The 1980s have brought declining numbers in our traditional recruitment pools, dwindling government resources and the occasional closure of post-secondary institutions. In this environment, effective marketing by educational institutions is critical to institutional survival.

Remindering

(*Remindering* is a term used in marketing to describe the process in which a tangible reminder is left on the scene of an intangible service.) If education is part of the service sector, then there is another lesson to be learned from our industrial counterparts. Industrial service providers have long understood that services are only noticed by consumers when they are absent. Consumers notice when a queue forms at the bank or at a MacDonald's restaurant, but when the queue isn't there, the consumer takes the service for granted. This means that consumers must be reminded when a service has been rendered. Reminding consumers that they have been well served is most often done interrogatively. For example, in a decent restaurant, the customer is asked often whether he is enjoying the meal. The waiter or maitre d'hotel knows before the question is asked that the customer is satisfied; the question simply serves as a reminder that the service has been excellent. How often do educational institutions ask their clients about the service that has been rendered?

At BCIT School of Business there is a department which teaches marketing. Each year, under the direction of faculty, students carry out a large market research project in which 25,000 questionnaires are mailed to employers, professional bodies, former students, present students, faculty and government departments. These questionnaires serve several purposes. Questionnaires returned are analysed, the results interpreted and action is taken to correct any deficiencies revealed. Equally important is the fact that these questionnaires serve as a reminder to our clients that the Institute is rendering a service to them and that it cares enough about what it does (and how it does it) to ask for feedback from its customers.

In the same vein, in 1980 BCIT funded the establishment of an Alumni Association to serve graduates of the Institute. Again, the Institute had several objectives in mind for its Alumni Association, not least of which was a remindering objective. The Institute understands that graduates eventually become employers, professionals, even politicians, and sees the need to remind this audience of the service rendered them by the Institute.

The annual cost to the Institute of sustaining the Alumni Association is about $25,000. In 1985, the Alumni has raised over $700,000 for the Institute in a fundraising exercise. Education is part of the service sector. As such, it must render tangible its intangibles by using metaphors. This process precedes detailed product specification to the client.

As a service provider, the institution must remind its clients that a service has been rendered or the service will be taken for granted (or only noted when it is absent). Neither of the aspects of servicing seem to be well understood by educators.

Product differentiation

In industrial marketing, product differentiation is a consequence of market segmentation. In the early 20th century, industrialists saw that the key to profit maximization was the development of a single product which could be mass-produced and mass-marketed. This strategy took maximum advantage of standardization and simplification, which in turn reduced unit costs and prices. By producing goods at low cost, market potentials were enlarged. The best example of this strategy is the Ford Motor Company's Model 'T' automobile. Using an assembly-line technology and a highly developed mass-distribution system, Henry Ford made the automobile available to everyone.

Seeing prices decline, other automobile manufacturers saw the necessity of product differentiation and began producing automobile models which had features, style and quality aimed at meeting the needs of a particular part of the market or market segment. It is important to note here that these manufacturers, unlike Ford, did not begin with a product and then bring it to market. On the contrary, manufacturers seeking to differentiate their products began by studying the market, identifying parts of the market which had specific, unmet needs and then created a product to meet these needs. The man who conceived this strategy, Alfred P Sloane, and his firm, General Motors Corporation, came to dominate the North American automobile market in less than a decade and has been dominant ever since.

It is also important to note that Sloane's conception of product differentiation arose as a matter of necessity, even survival. In differentiating products (and by merging a number of small, specialist firms into a larger organization), Sloane was adapting to competition in order to survive.

Educational offerings in the post-secondary, vocational/technical sector are highly differentiated. In institutions which are not dedicated to a single specialism, for example maritime and agricultural colleges, differentiation enables the identification and exploitation of market opportunities, fine adjustments to curriculum in adapting to changes in market needs, and better allocation of resources in order to achieve overall institutional effectiveness.

Educators have recognized, as Sloane recognized, that in order to achieve these ends a large-scale organization is required. In the UK in recent years, the trend has been to combine specialist colleges under single administrations. The BCIT/PVI merger of 1986 is a Canadian example of a similar trend. In order to take maximum advantage of product differentiation, vocational/technical institutions are consequently being scaled up and rationalized. This process is both a response to the need for differentiation and a product of earlier specialization. Under present conditions of rapid sociotechnical and economic change, characterized by sudden and sharp discontinuities in the nature and patterns of employment, the survival of monotechnic or sole purpose institutions is in jeopardy. Institutional rationalization is both a survival reflex and a strategic adaptation.

Education is somewhat more complex than the car business in that institutions find themselves in the middle of a means-end chain. The differentiation of courses and awards recognizes reality at the output end of the educational process, while ignoring important trends and changes at the input stage. Course offerings and entrance requirements are targeted primarily at school leavers or at adults in employment who wish to change careers. The school-leaving segment has been declining in recent years due to demographic changes arising from declines in the birth rate. Coincidentally, there has been significant growth in another segment, the single female head of family. Sadly, as the rate of family breakdown accelerates in Western societies, this is becoming a rapidly growing market segment. Single mothers seek employment opportunities, and training for access to work as an alternative to dependency on welfare. Neither in British Columbia nor in the UK have vocational/technical institutions recognized this market segment, nor have they developed differentiated offerings and support systems to meet its needs.

Another neglected market segment is the mid-career employee in a traditional vocation who has been displaced and made redundant as a result of technological change or economic decay. While there have been some notable examples of offerings to this segment in the UK (Sheffield and Coventry, for example), in British Columbia the post-secondary sector is notable only for its ignorance of this important and growing market segment.

Thus, while vocational/technical training has offered a differentiated product, differentiation has focused more upon the output end of the educational process and has not paid sufficient attention to the input stage.

Nothing is simple, of course, and while vocational/technical education has been highly differentiated, the trends are moving away from differentiation both as a result of rapid technological change and in response to market needs. Technological change has brought about a decline in traditional apprenticeships and crafts. The 'new' technologies in production systems rely much less upon skilled workers (de-skilling), and have given rise to 'multi-skilled' technical positions. This trend is (slowly) being reflected in more generic forms of technical training in which a specialism is not established in curriculum until the third or fourth level or stage in a technician's training. This trend responds not only to employer needs, it also responds to that segment of the student intake which is unsure about vocational interests when commencing training.

Production differentiation is a marketing concept that has been taken up, at least partially, by the vocational/technical sector. Unlike schools, and to a lesser degree universities, the vocational/technical sector has always been highly differentiated in its curriculum. As technological and social change accelerates, however, new differentials must emerge if institutions are to be responsive. Traditional craft distinctions are rapidly becoming meaningless in light of new technologies. New and different sectors of society both need and are seeking training and retraining. A much greater commitment by institutions to a marketing approach will assure rational responses and adaptation to social and technological change.

Positioning

Many of the models used to understand organizations are primarily descriptive in nature. The marketing model uses its own set of descriptors in interpreting organizational activity. Some of these descriptors have been defined and used in this chapter. But the marketing model is not only descriptive, it is also an action model which enables adaptation.

Positioning is a marketing procedure which attempts to measure products in relation to other products using a two-factor analytic procedure, originated at Boston College in the US. Using this approach, an institution can locate itself or its courses in relation to alternatives. Once this is accomplished, a desired position is defined and a plan made to move the institution towards the desired position. Consider the hypothetical analysis of an engineering department's courses as shown in Figure 2. The institution's strengths and weaknesses can be appraised using a variety of institutional assessment procedures (Curtis, 1983). Similarly, the environmental situation can also be assessed. It should be noted here that the procedures used for sizing up an institution or its offerings need not be sophisticated (ie expensive and time-consuming). Informal procedures can produce sufficiently accurate results for the institution to proceed rationally to the next stage.

In the hypothetical case, two new and recently established courses have been identified as opportunities. They are both institutionally weak by virtue of being small in size and staff, and are underequipped. The equipment required for these courses is extensive and costly. Resources must be allocated to these courses so that they can proceed from infancy towards maturity, and strength.

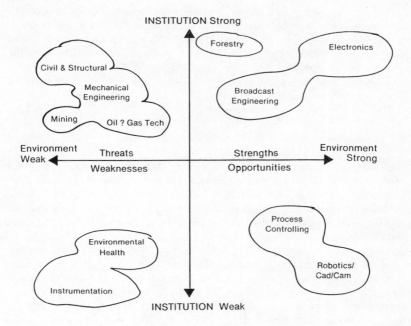

Figure 2. *Analysis of courses offered by a hypothetical engineering department*

Three courses have been identified as strengths. Two of the courses are very strong while the third (forestry) borders on weakness as far as its environment is concerned. The two strong courses require maintenance, while forestry would seem to require further analysis to establish its valence (ie positive or negative position) along the environmental continuum. If further environmental erosion is predicted, then the course will require contraction and staff will need retraining and redeployment. If, on the other hand, the valence is positive, then some expansion may be desirable.

Four courses have been identified as threatened. These courses are being offered in areas where employment is declining, using outmoded equipment, and taught by a large and ageing faculty complement. Resources must be directed toward staff retraining and redeployment in this area in the short run, and away from these courses in the medium term. These courses should be contracted, but not necessarily abandoned.

Two courses have been identified as weaknesses. Staff must be redeployed, and the courses abandoned. Patterns of employment and technological change have made both courses redundant.

The illustrations above portrayed the application of the Boston College matrix to the analysis of courses within a department of engineering. The technique can be applied as well to larger or smaller components of the institution and it can be used to relate one institution as a whole to other institutions in a system. The application of this marketing technique need not require sophisticated research and analytic techniques. Periodic reviews of institutional offerings using this technique should produce a more responsive institution and will enable more effective allocation of resources to courses and programmes.

Making marketing happen in educational institutions

Marketing is a process in which providers identify consumer needs and develop and deliver products to meet these needs. It is at the same time a corporate function. In industrial organizations, the marketing function is carried out by a specialist group within, often headed by a vice-president. A great many corporate chief executive officers come up the organization through the marketing function.

Education organizations have not as yet recognized marketing as a distinct function deserving a separate place and a clear role in the institution. Instead, educational marketing activities are fragmentary and decentralized, seldom integrated and often occur only as a survival reflex. In view of government's aim at controlling expenditure on education, it is unlikely that a marketing establishment would be approved in an educational institution. Other means must therefore be found to regularize the marketing function, means which recognize the complexity of educational marketing.

Earlier in this paper, a number of educational exchanges were described in which education was related to a variety of client groups. A first step in regularizing the marketing function is to arrange for periodic and purposive contact with representatives of the institution's clients. Advisory committees which are established for each course offered by the institution, and which are empowered with decision-making authority, can regularize contact with employers, alumni and professional bodies. These committees must be more than cosmetic, however, if they are to fulfil a marketing function. They must be given significant decision-making authority. Advisory committees can be asked to approve curricula, for example, or be authorized to approve the number of places to be offered in a course. In granting such authority to an advisory committee, an institution ensures that it is being responsive to its employer and professional markets. At the same time, as advisory committee members are involved in institutional decision-making, they are reminded of the service provided by the institution to the markets that the committee members represent.

BCIT has recently fostered the establishment of an Alumni Association. Our former graduates, by their involvement in this association, are reminded of the service which has been rendered them by the institution. Alumni are now an important source of information regarding the efficacy of the institution's curriculum, methods and support systems, which can be reached and researched at minimal cost.

Faculty and staff will only be committed to institutional change if they are fully involved in the decision-making that leads to change. Provision must be made, therefore, for the involvement in institutional decision-making by organizational members. Academic boards and senates must be empowered to make decisions, not simply asked to approve the decisions of others in the organization. This is not an argument for more democracy in post-secondary institutions. It is a long-accepted principle of organization that people who are properly involved in decision-making are more committed to the outcome than people who are not involved. BCIT's Educational Council recently suspended its operation while the institute examined a more effective mechanism for involving faculty and staff in institute decisions.

The exchange with government, education's paymaster, is more problematic. The religious roots of education seem to argue for a separation of Church and State. Yet in ancient times, when the separation argument was first made, the Church had independent means and sought to preserve its wealth from government's avarice. In modern times, education depends almost entirely upon government funding. The separation argument is medieval and not currently useful to educational institutions. Either institutions must find independent (private) means, or they must achieve partnership with government. The basis for this partnership, from government's point of view, is a willingness in educational institutions to deliver their product at increasingly lower cost, to increasingly large numbers of students. Institutions must become more responsive to society's educational needs as perceived and defined by government. Better yet, these needs should be perceived and defined by institutions and pointed out to government, and accompanied with effective programmes to satisfy the needs defined. Only a commitment by institutions to a marketing approach can accomplish this.

Press, media and public relations must be regularized in educational institutions. This need not be a costly procedure. The media need to fill space in their offerings to the public. Education news will seldom make the front page, but consistent attention paid to media relations will promote regular exposure of institutional events. The media do not charge for news items. Press releases issued by institutions to media are a form of free advertising for the institution, and serve to remind institutional audiences of the service being rendered. A minimum of training will prepare faculty and staff to write press releases. Delegating the media relations function to an existing member of staff can be a zero-cost method of starting a programme. At BCIT, we are fortunate in teaching broadcasting, for which we have a licensed FM radio station and a TV studio, while our staff includes a group of experts in this area. Institutions without a broadcasting resource can still achieve effective media relations at minimum cost in time and money.

The front line of the institution to the student public is the admissions office. Does your admissions office sell the institution and its programmes to students? Can students easily get reliable advice about courses at the admissions desk? Can your admissions area be easily located by students coming on to the campus for the first time? The admissions area often makes that important first impression not only on students, but also on other visitors to your institution. When was the last time your institution reviewed and improved its admissions area? When the phone rings in your admissions office, what image does the person answering give to the caller? The admissions office is an important element in the marketing effort of the institution. It requires periodic review and assessment by senior administration and regular relations with the teaching function to ensure that communications at this location in the institution are accurate, complete and effective.

The printed matter of the institution, brochures, institutional letter-heads, prospectuses and other printed offerings establish an image of the institution for users of this material. A committee of the institution, with outside professional assistance, must be asked to review periodically the institution's printed materials and their use, to ensure consistency in message and image. Some means other than the calendar or prospectus must be used as the initial message to potential clients: a means which stresses the intangible benefits of attending the institution. Detailed specifications, such as prospectuses, are a second-level communication and should follow up a commitment to purchase the service.

Continuing institutional assessment is necessary in order to assure that clients' needs are being met. BCIT is committed to a form of continuing assessment within a five-year period. On a rotating basis, each course, programme and department is assessed using both internal and external personnel in the process. The first such assessment was concluded in 1985 with a report to the Board of Governors by an external team of assessors. The recommendations of this report were being carried out in the institution during 1986.

Where marketing is a decentralized function, some form of institutional assessment is necessary and performs an integrating function. Institutional assessment, if it takes a marketing perspective, not only assures the institution that marketing is taking place, but also assures consistency and effectiveness in marketing efforts.

Conclusion

Post-secondary vocational/technical institutions have always marketed their product, albeit to a narrow and traditional market segment. When modern post-secondary education was begun in the 1960s, it was a government response to a public need. Since the inception of post-secondary institutions, however, public needs for technical/vocational training have evolved and changed, yet institutions have been slow to adapt to changes in its public and have continued to service traditional market segments. The adoption of a marketing approach will produce more responsive institutions, new curricula and new delivery methods aimed at meeting public needs.

References

Curtis, J R H (1983) *Institutional Assessment: A Canadian Example* The Further Education Staff College: Blagdon, Bristol

Kotler, P (1979) *Marketing Management, Analysis, Planning and Control* Prentice-Hall Inc: Englewood Cliffs, NJ

Murphy, P E and McGarrity, R A (1978) Marketing universities: a survey of student recruiting activities *College and University* Spring 1978: 249–61

Pirsig, R (1979) *Zen and the Art of Motorcycle Maintenance* Morrow: New York

Rosenbluth, A and Weiner, N (1979) *in* Kotler (1979)

Venne, R (1985) *Annual Research Project* BCIT School of Business Marketing Management Department: Vancouver

Xerox Corporation (1967) *Professional Selling Skills Seminar* Xerox National Sales Development Centre: Fort Lauderdale, FL

16. Technical teacher training in the Western Region of India

Narendra Banthiya

Summary: Staff development including teacher training, carrying out educational reforms at the grass root level, disseminating and sustaining educational innovations — all these are difficult propositions for any institution. This chapter records some experiences of the Technical Teachers' Training Institute, Bhopal (TTTI Bhopal) over the last 20 years, in which it has changed from a straightforward technical teachers' training institute to an external change agent for the technician education system in India. It also describes changes in the form and content of teacher training over the years. TTTI's contribution to curriculum development work in the technician education system is discussed. A few innovations — planned change, design and development of a laboratory course known as the engineering experimentation course, and introduction of a comprehensive scheme of assessment have been taken as examples to bring out the various aspects which influence the process of change. Change strategies adopted by TTTI are also described. It was necessary that TTTI itself should have a structure conducive to working as an external change agent. Structural changes in TTTI to achieve this end are also described.

Introduction

Polytechnics in India mainly provide facilities for the education and training of technicians. Technicians are employed in a broad spectrum of occupations lying between craftsmen at one end and professionals or technologists at the other. There are about 600 polytechnics in India, offering diploma courses of three years' duration in engineering disciplines such as civil, electrical, mechanical, electronics, chemical and textiles, after ten years of schooling. Some polytechnics also offer post-diploma courses in specialized fields. Courses are also offered in foodcraft, home science, pharmacy, commercial practice, and so on by some polytechnics. About 150 polytechnics are situated in the western region of India, in the states of Gujarat, Maharashtra, Madhya Pradesh (MP) and the union territory of Goa, Daman and Diu. These western region polytechnics have about 32,000 students on their rolls and employ about 4,000 teachers. The administrative and academic control of polytechnics is under the respective State Directors of Technical Education (DTE) and Boards of Technical Education (BTE). The government of India has no direct control over the polytechnics. Polytechnic teachers are usually degree holders in engineering, science, mathematics or English, or diploma holders in engineering. Most have not undergone any pre-service teacher training. The Indian polytechnic scene over the years is described in Chandrakant (1971), the Damodaran Committee Report of the Ministry of Education and Social Welfare (1971) and Ministry of Education and Culture (1979).

During the expansion of polytechnic education in the early 1960s, a severe scarcity of technical teachers was felt. Four Technical Teachers' Training Institutes (TTTIs) were established by the government of India at this time, one for each region of the country, located at Bhopal (Western), Calcutta (Eastern), Chandigarh (Northern) and Madras (Southern).

In 1970 to 1971, under the Indian government's quality improvement programme, Curriculum Development Centres (CDCs) were established at all TTTIs to undertake curriculum development work on scientific lines. As a result, the TTTIs became involved with the systems and faculty in those states which showed interest in the curriculum development work. At present TTTIs are not only technical teacher training institutions, but also institutions which help the state governments in their regions to improve the technician education system. Thus, in addition to teacher training, they undertake staff development work related to various educational projects and innovations introduced in the states, and work as external change agents. They also assist the government of India in policy formulation and implementation of technician education system together with its monitoring. TTTIs' working was influenced by the Kelkar Committee Report, Ministry of Education and Social Welfare (1976) for some time. Now a national guide document on TTTIs by the Ministry of Education (1983) is available. TTTI Bhopal's activities, including various projects, thrusts and innovations undertaken by it and their changing pattern, are described in Saran (1976) and Technical Teachers' Training Institute Bhopal (1975a, 1983, 1984).

Long-term technical teacher training

At TTTI Bhopal the form, duration and content of long-term teacher training has been undergoing changes in line with the needs of the system. These changes have occurred in three distinct phases.

First phase

This phase covers the period from 1966 to 1970. The training for both diploma and degree holders consisted of one semester of education content, including teaching practice, and two semesters of industrial training. Diploma holders were, in addition, required to undertake courses in engineering and sciences for two semesters. Thus the duration of training was long: one and a half years for degree holders and two and a half years for diploma holders. The trainees were mainly pre-service students. For some of them, the training was perhaps a stopgap arrangement. Some of these trainees eventually did not join the teaching profession.

Second phase

This covers a period from 1971 to 1978. In 1971, the TTTIs became completely in-service institutions, training only those who were sponsored by their employers. The training duration was also reduced to one year for degree holders and one and a half years for diploma holders. At Bhopal, changes were gradually made in the programme content and processes to bring about the integration of different elements. Figure 1 shows the model of training used around 1975-76. The two main integrating elements

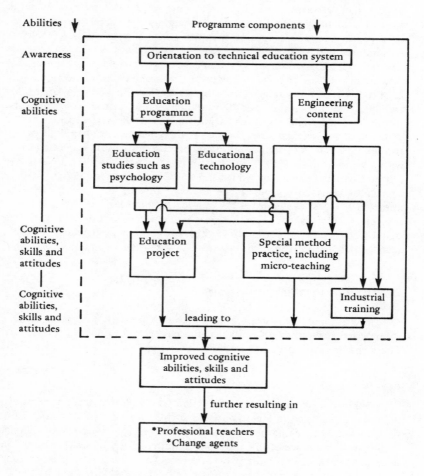

Figure 1. *Technical teacher training model, incorporating integrating elements*

were special methods practice and an education project. In the special methods practice, the teaching of psychology, educational technology and engineering content were integrated during 'micro-teaching' sessions. In the education project, every trainee was required to produce a programmed text, a laboratory manual or some similar task.

Third phase

Due to a severe shortage of teachers in the institutions and in the absence of any training reserves, sponsoring authorities started finding it difficult to sponsor trainees for long-term teacher training. The sponsored teachers also found it difficult to stay away from their homes for long periods. In addition it was felt by both trainee teachers and TTTI faculty that the training programme was imposing a straitjacket rather than catering for individual needs. More flexibility was needed.

As a result of thinking about these problems the TTTI Bhopal faculty opted for teacher training based on the concept of competency-based teacher education (CBTE). The development work related to this approach began in November 1976 and the first set of 41 CBTE modules was ready by August 1978, when the first batch of teacher trainees was admitted for a 12-week modular programme. Figure 2 gives the steps in the CBTE development at TTTI Bhopal. For details, see Saran (1979), Saran and Chandran (1979) and Technical Teachers' Training Institute Bhopal (1976a, 1978, 1980a).

At present, the approach to teacher training is quite flexible, suiting the needs of the clients. The teachers, who can come to TTTI for training for one year at a stretch or in periods of three months at different times, are provided with training in the four components: CBTE phase I competencies, CBTE Phase II competencies, content updating and industrial training.

Although most of the states in the country feel that TTTI training is a very useful qualification for polytechnic teachers, very few states have taken steps to recognize it for faculty recruitment and promotion. No monetary incentives have been provided. Thus there is frustration among those who qualify for TTTI, and untrained teachers are not attracted to seek admissions in TTTIs on their own initiative. There is an urgent need to plan faculty development at the state level and to link it up with some incentive or career development prospect.

Although the TTTIs began primarily as technical teachers' training institutes, their field of activity started expanding from 1970 onwards. It was realized that merely training a few teachers would have no impact on the total system. People at all levels in the technician education system (eg directors of technical education and other administrators, principals, heads of departments, lecturers and even laboratory assistants and office staff) must be involved in the change processes. Conferences, seminars, workshops and short courses were organized to suit the different clientele and the objectives to be achieved in each programme. To influence the

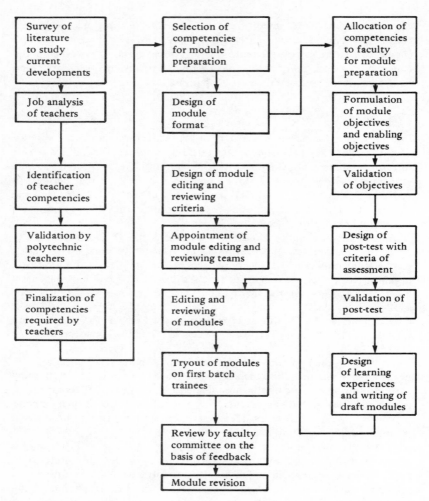

Figure 2. *Steps in competency-based teacher education (CBTE)*
development at TTTI Bhopal

total system and bring about necessary changes, projects and activities
were undertaken to meet the needs and demands of the people at various
levels in the system. Many of these needs are voiced during conferences
and workshops. (See, for example, Technical Teachers' Training Institutes,
1976 and Technical Teachers' Training Institute Bhopal, 1976b, 1976c.)
TTTI Bhopal thus got involved in a variety of activities and projects, some
of which have succeeded and others which have been less successful. A few
of these projects are discussed in this chapter as examples. Others (not
discussed) include the autonomous polytechnics project of Maharashtra,

community polytechnics, a distance learning polytechnic, a master's degree in technical education, a national testing service including an item bank, a software tryout, production of educational films and videos, production of multimedia learning packages, institutional evaluation and vocational education. Brief references to these and other projects are available in Technical Teachers' Training Institute, Bhopal (1975c, 1975e, 1983, 1984).

Curriculum development

There had been persistent criticism by industry of abilities possessed by polytechnic graduates. An urgent need for curriculum development was felt. This task was started by all the TTTIs in their regions from 1970 to 1971 and continues today. At TTTI Bhopal, a model was used to frame the curricula of the civil, electrical and mechanical engineering diploma. Details about this work are available in Technical Teachers' Training Institute, Bhopal (1971, 1975b, 1975e).

Later curriculum development work, especially for the post-diploma courses in refrigeration and air conditioning (Banthiya, Jain and Saksena, 1979) and production technology (Saksena, Banthiya and Jain, 1979) and diploma courses in textile technology (Jain, Banthiya and Saksena, 1979) used a similar model. The main features of the model are:

1. The course structure, content and objectives were derived from an analysis of needs of the industry and functions performed by technicians in the industry. During the job analysis survey in 1970–71, about 1,400 diploma holders were contacted, in addition to employers.
2. Specialists from field and industry were consulted for topic validation.
3. The curriculum was spelled out in terms of behavioural objectives (both general and specific). Curriculum documents also contained content analysis and suggestions for teaching and learning.
4. Orientation programmes, content updating courses and courses for developing professional skills were organized at Bhopal and at individual polytechnics.
5. The work of developing instructional resources based on the new curriculum was undertaken. This included development of textbooks, workbooks, learning packages, sample test items and questions, slides, film strips, OHP transparencies, etc.
6. In all the efforts related to curriculum development, from the survey for job analysis through writing objectives to developing instructional resources, polytechnic teachers participated actively.
7. Short courses were also organized in educational management for senior polytechnic faculty and administrators, so that they could influence the system in internalizing this massive change, and other changes which were to follow in its wake.

The new curriculum was implemented in the state of MP in 1972 and in Gujarat in 1975, in the first-year classes and successively every year in other classes. Curriculum evaluation was carried out in MP during 1975–77 (Verma, Dharap, Kapse, Shah and Banthiya, 1977). This study looked at aspects of learning strategies, teaching strategies, the examination system, curriculum support material, resources and institutions. Curriculum evaluation was undertaken in Gujarat during 1980-81 (Mukhopadhyaya, Jain, Banthiya and Halani, 1982). This study examined the aspects of objectives and contents, teaching-learning strategies and resource needs and utilization.

Curriculum revision work was undertaken in MP in 1981 and the processes related to it began in Gujarat immediately after the curriculum evaluation report was published in 1982. Some of the issues related to curriculum development and implementation are as follows:

1. Directorates of technical education and boards of technical education of the states are the only administrative bodies which can implement any curriculum changes and provide necessary resource support to the polytechnics. TTTI, depending on necessity, sometimes plays an active and sometimes a passive role in persuading state authorities to implement necessary changes. Either way, it does not always succeed.
2. In spite of the massive involvement of teachers at all stages of curriculum development, the general teacher population saw the new curriculum as the one prescribed by TTTI. With the passage of time and with active involvement of more and more teachers in curriculum development and other related activities, there has been a considerable reduction in this feeling.
3. Shortage of staff and resources in the polytechnics are chronic problems. These created pressures which were not conducive to change.

The issues discussed above were not peculiar to curriculum development. The same or similar problems are being faced during the implementation of other projects and innovations.

Planned change

The movement for planned change began in 1976 and 1977 in the polytechnics of MP and Gujarat after a study conference for polytechnic principals (Technical Teachers' Training Institute Bhopal, 1976b). Eight key areas for development were identified with priorities in this order: improvement of laboratory instruction, use and preparation of inexpensive teaching aids, use of appropriate teaching-learning methods, improving subject competence of teachers, staff appraisal, development of student-centred learning materials, improving institutional management and provision of reprographic facilities. The polytechnics chose a cluster of areas from these for their developmental planning. The planned change project had a very short tenure of two to three years in the MP polytechnics, although it is still continuing in Gujarat polytechnics. The continuance of the project in Gujarat is due to the support given by top administrators there.

From the project's early stages a senior faculty member was designated as a change agent in each polytechnic. Change agents are being trained and retrained. Their functions include diagnosing problems, difficulties and barriers; encouraging, counselling and helping people involved in the change process; isolating resisting forces, and overcoming them through persuasion.

Action plans are being prepared by project polytechnics. These plans are sent to the directorate for information and administrative support. Nowadays the plans are prepared on the basis of critical success factors (CSF) instead of key areas. CSF used are social tone, cost-effectiveness, course development and implementation, corporate reputation, investment in human capital, development of physical facilities, student relations, employee relations and public responsibility. The output targets are defined in terms of performance indicators for the elements of various critical success factors.

In Gujarat polytechnics, where the project has been continuing for the last eight to nine years, it has been observed that:

1. there is a lot of awareness of the planning process, and by and large planning occurs regularly;
2. work has become more systematic;
3. there is a shift towards participative management;
4. innovations and innovators are being supported.

Engineering experimentation course (EEC)

During the 1976 Principals' Conference, the improvement of laboratory instruction was identified as the key area with top priority. In a later workshop, senior polytechnic teachers identified problems connected with traditional laboratory teaching, some of these being:

1. lack of well-defined aims for laboratory work
2. lack of relevance of laboratory experiences to the technicians' job functions
3. lack of motivation, challenge and scope for creative working for the students
4. over-emphasis on written reports.

After diagnosing the problems, these teachers identified aims of laboratory work and also suggested some strategies for improvement.

A monograph discussing the possible approaches for improvement in laboratory instruction was prepared by TTTI faculty (Rao, Balu and Chandran, 1981). This was discussed during a seminar in April 1977 at TTTI Bhopal in which directors of technical education, other senior administrators, principals and senior polytechnic teachers participated. The composite approach to laboratory instruction was accepted by the Gujarat group for implementation in that state. The course designed on this approach is called the 'Engineering Experimentation Course (EEC)'. It has been designed and implemented jointly by the TTTI faculty, polytechnic teachers and some UK consultants. The special features of this course are that:

1. the laboratory experiences are designed to achieve the identified aims. The aims which emphasize the development of skills and attitudes related to technician's job functions are given priority over aims connected with reinforcement of theoretical work;
2. proper organization of laboratory work is recognized as a key factor in ensuring that students are able to achieve the stipulated aims;
3. the project work is an important element in the course. Even at the first-year stage, students are expected to do an individual mini-project;
4. the laboratory teaching is primarily an inter-disciplinary activity. Except for special techniques related to major engineering disciplines, all the core experiences are implemented by the joint faculty teams. The complete course is co-ordinated by an inter-disciplinary task group;
5. the course consists of lectures on the approach and philosophy of EEC, experimental skills and project work.

For further details see Rao, Jain and Dharap (1981).

The EEC was introduced in two polytechnics in Gujarat in 1977. The first cycle of implementation was completed in these pilot polytechnics during 1979—80 session. A series of orientation programmes for the teachers and monitoring visits to the polytechnics were organized during all three years. The results of this experiment were encouraging, and EEC was implemented in three more polytechnics in 1980, and then in 1981 in all the other polytechnics of Gujarat.

Staff training and monitoring visits to polytechnics have been inbuilt components of this project. Initially, monitoring visits used to be by TTTI faculty, assisted sometimes by UK consultants. During the monitoring visits, the emphasis was on identifying problems of implementation, and resolving these. (For guidelines about conducting monitoring visits, see Technical Teachers' Training Institute Bhopal, 1980b.) When it was felt that the problems faced by teachers and institutions were common and related to lack of human and material resources and other administrative constraints, monitoring teams were expanded to include officials of the directorate, principals of polytechnics and senior polytechnic teachers. This has resulted in better appreciation of the institutional problems by the directorate, and many problems are being resolved. The participation of teachers in these visits has worked as a catalyst for change and a source of information diffusion from one polytechnic to the other.

Some other measures which have helped in internalizing the innovation are:

1. training of senior polytechnic teachers for conducting orientation programmes and monitoring visits and using them for this purpose.
2. training of supporting staff, including laboratory assistants and workshop staff, who were being neglected in the initial stages of the project.
3. developing in the polytechnics an infrastructure conducive to EEC implementation.
4. the recent formation of a state-level high-power EEC co-ordinating committee. This committee has a policy-making role, in addition to ensuring that the EEC is implemented properly and related problems are resolved. It is envisaged that, within a year or so, the EEC project will be completely looked after by this committee, and TTTI's role will be to assist only if requested to for a specific task.

Comprehensive scheme of assessment (CSA)

Assisting states in designing proper student assessment systems and carrying out examination reforms became an important activity of TTTI after the new curricula were introduced. The emphasis initially was on improving terminal examinations. Some of the steps undertaken for this purpose were as follows (see Technical Teachers' Training Institute Bhopal, 1975d):

☐ workshops to train teachers in writing objective-type items and good quality subjective questions of other kinds;
☐ the development of specification tables for setting of question papers;
☐ the establishment of an item bank at TTTI Bhopal in which pre-tested items are stored;
☐ assistance to boards in setting question papers from the item bank.

These steps brought about increased awareness and improvement in state student assessment systems. However, some adverse consequences also followed: for example, some boards decided on an ad hoc basis to have a specific proportion of objective-type items in each question paper. Very few teachers had by then attained competence in writing good objective items, and they were not necessarily the same teachers as are traditionally chosen to set papers. The rates of payment to paper-setters remained unchanged from the rates paid when long essay-type questions were used. There was also no change in the rules for administering papers consisting of objective items, which resulted in a regular complaint by the teachers that students used some kind of sign language for copying. As a result a stage has now been reached when objective items are no longer used in the boards' examinations. However, question papers now being set use a large number of short answer and/or structured questions. Also, specification tables are being widely used.

The validity, reliability and comparability of internal assessment were being closely questioned by the teachers and administrators. The comprehensive scheme of assessment (CSA) was developed (see Verma, Dharap, Kapse, Shah and Banthiya, 1977) to assess the stipulated abilities in the students by proper sampling during and at the end of the course. The main aims of this scheme are:

☐ to ensure content validity, reliability and comparability in the assessment.
☐ to improve learning by feedback to students.
☐ to improve teaching processes by the use of appropriate methods.

TTTI faculty explored the possibility of introducing CSA in some polytechnics. In informal discussions, principals of two polytechnics became interested in introducing this innovation. They were requested to take their faculty into their confidence about it. When the faculty at these two polytechnics became convinced of the advantages of the scheme, TTTI faculty visited these polytechnics in July—August 1980 to assist them in preparing schemes of assessment, instead of calling the teachers at Bhopal (Banthiya, Dharap, Haider and Vyas, 1980). At present, the scheme is in operation in six polytechnics. Under the scheme, subject group teachers prepare assessment schemes for their subjects, the work being facilitated by TTTI faculty. The assessment scheme includes course work, assessed course work and assessment instruments. All the teachers in the group agree to operate on the same scheme. By now a number of reports have been published concerning the work done in these polytechnics. More details about CSA are available in Banthiya (1985) and Kapse and Shrivastava (1985). Important points which have been observed are:

1. To a large extent, the spirit of CSA has been internalized. When a group has started operating on a scheme prepared by it, it continues to operate the scheme by making changes on the basis of operational experience. Teachers own the schemes prepared by them and are motivated to see that the CSA project succeeds.
2. Whenever a new faculty member joins or the composition of the group changes, new entrants are oriented to the method of working and the scheme remains in operation.
3. A scheme is prepared by a group consisting of the teachers teaching that subject. There is evidence of regular meetings of the group. However, there is very little evidence of meetings between different groups, although CSA co-ordinators are functioning in all the institutions.
4. There is systematic and complete coverage of the curriculum during the semester, resulting in content validity of the assessment.
5. Most of the faculty members stick to the scheme prepared by their group, thus working towards inter-marker reliability.
6. Due to continuous and regular assessment, the work does not pile up towards the end of the semester. Also as the schemes are designed to be practicable, there is no undue increase in workload.

7. Record keeping has improved considerably.
8. Feedback to students is now a regular feature.

Change strategies adopted by TTTI Bhopal

TTTI Bhopal has been taking the role of an external change agent for the state polytechnic systems in its region. In Chin and Benne's terminology (1970) TTTI has primarily adopted a normative re-education strategy with the administrators and managers of the state systems, and it has continued a normative re-education with a rational-empirical strategy with the general teacher population. As TTTI is external to the state polytechnic systems, there is no question of its using a power-coercive strategy. Administrators and managers have usually attended conferences organized by TTTI Bhopal away from their actual work settings. During these conferences, which emphasized group working, problems have been identified, possible solutions have been discussed and future actions have been decided. Most of the innovations and changes in which TTTI has assisted the state systems have been agreed to in such conferences.

Once an educational innovation has been accepted by the administrators and managers, to a certain extent they have used a power-coercive strategy to introduce the innovation at grass roots level. In addition, they have also given the green signal to TTTI to involve polytechnic teachers. Whenever this co-operation has stopped, the progress in the implementation of an innovation has come to a standstill. The TTTI faculty has influenced the polytechnic faculty by involving them from the inception of an innovation. All the curricula, instructional materials, laboratory experiences and assessment schemes have evolved during group working. A very healthy system linkage has been established between individual polytechnics, their teaching faculty and TTTI. Where a fairly large segment of the total system has been involved in implementing an innovation, it has been observed that changes have occurred from the top down and not from the bottom up. The key role in initiating or resisting innovations has been played by the top administrators in the states.

Many teachers who have undergone courses and workshops at TTTI Bhopal have introduced changes in their classes and institutions. These changes usually remain isolated and do not spread to other institutions because no forum is available. However, when visiting institutions, faculty from TTTI keep their eyes and ears open, and try to bring such changes to the attention of others, thus aiding diffusion. They also recruit these innovators as guest faculty for TTTI's short courses and workshops, so that the message percolates to others at the grass-root level.

TTTI structure and faculty roles

When TTTI Bhopal started, its primary role was teacher training and even in this the emphasis was on content teaching. As it graduated from a teacher training institute to a staff development institute and then on to an external change agent for the technician education system, its initial structure, based on traditional departments and pyramidal organization, started to crumble. Today TTTI still has traditional departments like civil engineering, electrical engineering, mechanical engineering, science, education, training and placement, but over the years a number of new departments and facilities have been created as the needs arose. These are curriculum development, education management, educational research, a national testing service, multimedia learning packages, film production and computers and rural development.

When the institute started, classroom teaching and supervising the industrial training of trainees were the only roles expected of faculty members. With the beginning of curriculum development activity in 1970-71, faculty members became involved with this activity also, whether they had been recruited for curriculum development work or not. The advent of planned change identified key areas in which assistance was required by polytechnics. This resulted in the development and involvement of TTTI faculty in these key areas, for example audiovisual aids, laboratory innovations, student evaluation and education of management. A dual faculty structure consisting of traditional departments and task groups was formalized during 1975—76. Each faculty member was expected to be member of two task groups. Task groups worked as think tanks in their areas and organized activities connected with those areas, which could be projects, conferences, short courses, workshops or research projects. A task group leader was chosen, usually for a one-year term, by the group members. The task group leader was not necessarily the most senior faculty member in the group. Task groups functioned quite effectively, co-existing with the departments, for a number of years. As the number of activities at TTTI increased further, faculty members were recruited, transferred or promoted to newly formed departments. For most of the faculty members in these newly formed departments, department and task group activities were one and the same. These faculty members could thus devote much more time for a particular type of work. For faculty members associated with traditional departments, but working for task groups, a lack of role clarity began to emerge. Simultaneously, due to the enhanced involvement of TTTI in a wide range of activities, some project groups were formed to look after specific project activities. Sometimes a project activity which would normally come under a task group was carried out by a project group independent of the task group. Some project groups, however, maintained linkages with the parent task groups. Thus a third dimension was superimposed on the already existing dual structure of departments and task groups. Sometimes this lack of role clarity and lack of communication between a project group and related task group created problems, and the need to evolve a new internal structure for TTTI was felt. Faculty consultations continued for a long period of time, and by consensus opinion, in place of task groups, small-size project groups were recently mooted to undertake specific projects or activities within a set schedule. A group consisting of five faculty members was also formed to co-ordinate various activities.

Initially, as in other institutions, TTTI had a pyramidal faculty structure, with very few positions at the top, and most of the positions at middle or lower rungs. But over the years, the pyramid has been turned upside down. Today most of the positions at TTTI are at professor level, and very few at the assistant professor and lecturer levels. Such a structure reflects its role across the whole spectrum from top administrators to laboratory instructors.

Conclusion

Technical Teachers' Training Institutes are serving a very useful purpose as external change agents and as staff development institutes for the technician education system in India. No such institutes have been established for engineering colleges and universities. Due to the existence and growth of TTTIs, the technician education system has undergone much more profound changes than the university technical education system. In the technician education system, there is wider use of innovative teaching-learning methods and valid and reliable assessment instruments. Curriculum development work is carried out much more scientifically. Decisions and actions are based on educational research. Management is becoming much more participative. Many of the innovations have been internalized within the system. Innovations are being diffused to a wider audience.

References

Banthiya, N K (1985) *Design of Assessment Schemes under Comprehensive Scheme of Assessment* TTTI: Bhopal

Banthiya, N K, Dharap, K P, Haider, S Z and Vyas, K D (1980) *Report on Pilot Introduction of Comprehensive Scheme of Assessment* TTTI: Bhopal

Banthiya, N K, Jain, P C and Saksena, S C (1979) *A Survey for Job Analysis: Post Diploma in Refrigeration and Air Conditioning* TTTI: Bhopal

Bennis, W G, Benne, K D and Chin, R eds (1970) *The Planning of Change* (second edition) Holt, Rinehart and Winston: London

Chandrakant, L S (1971) *Polytechnic Education in India* D B Taraporevala: Bombay

Chin, R and Benne, K D (1970) General strategies for effecting changes in human system *in* Bennis, Benne and Chin (1970)

Jain, P C, Banthiya, N K and Saksena, S C (1979) *A Survey for Job Analysis: Diploma in Textile Technology* TTTI: Bhopal

Kapse, V M and Shrivastava, K K (1985) *CSA Project in Gujarat: Impact Study at Porbandar, Rajkot, Patan Polytechnics* TTTI: Bhopal

Ministry of Education (1983) *Technical Teachers' Training Institutes: National Guide Document on their Role and New Perspectives* Ministry of Education, Government of India: New Delhi

Ministry of Education and Culture (1979) *Technical and Vocational Education: India* Country Report for Unesco Regional Seminar on Technical and Vocational Education (Singapore — November 1979) Ministry of Education and Culture, Government of India: New Delhi

Ministry of Education and Social Welfare (1971) *Report of the Special Committee on Reorganization and Development of Polytechnic Education in India 1970-71* (Damodaran Committee) Ministry of Education and Social Welfare, Government of India: New Delhi

Ministry of Education and Social Welfare (1976) *Report of the Review Committee for the Technical Teachers' Training Institutes* (Kelkar Committee) Ministry of Education and Social Welfare, Government of India: New Delhi

Mukhopadhyaya, M, Jain, P C, Banthiya, N K and Halani, D M (1982) *Gujarat Polytechnic Curriculum Evaluation Project* TTTI: Bhopal

Rao, G N N, Balu, S A and Chandran, G S (1981) *Laboratory Instruction in Polytechnics: Approaches Monograph LTG 1* (second edition) TTTI: Bhopal

Rao, G N N, Jain, P C and Dharap, K P (1981) *Laboratory Innovation for Polytechnics: Engineering Experimentation Course Monograph LTG 2* (second edition) TTTI: Bhopal

Saksena, S C, Banthiya, N K and Jain, P C (1979) *A Survey for Job Analysis: Post Diploma in Production Technology* TTTI: Bhopal

Saran, Y (1976) India: a strategy to improve technician education *Prospects 6* **2**: 245-53

Saran, Y (1979) *Technical Teacher Training — Towards a New Initiative* Working paper for the international workshop for the In-service Training of Technical Teacher Educators, Turin, Italy TTTI: Bhopal

Saran, Y and Chandran, G S (1979) *CBTE at TTTI Bhopal: A Case Study of an Innovation in Teacher Education* TTTI: Bhopal

Technical Teachers' Training Institute (TTTI), Bhopal (1971) *A Survey for Job Analysis: A Report on a Survey Conducted to collect Data for Preparing Technician Curricula* TTTI: Bhopal

Technical Teachers' Training Institute (TTTI), Bhopal (1975a) *TTTI: Questions and Answers* TTTI: Bhopal

Technical Teachers' Training Institute (TTTI), Bhopal (1975b) *Curriculum Development — Monograph 2* TTTI: Bhopal

Technical Teachers' Training Institute (TTTI), Bhopal (1975c) *Educational Projects — Monograph 3* TTTI: Bhopal

Technical Teachers' Training Institute (TTTI), Bhopal (1975d) *Examination Reforms — Monograph 4* TTTI: Bhopal

Technical Teachers' Training Institute (TTTI), Bhopal (1975e) *Interaction with Industry — Monograph 5* TTTI: Bhopal

Technical Teachers' Training Institute (TTTI), Bhopal (1976a) A rational approach to technical teacher education. Paper presented at *Second Inter—TTTI Faculty Conference Madras* TTTI: Bhopal

Technical Teachers' Training Institute (TTTI), Bhopal (1976b) *Planned Change: A Monograph based on the Proceedings of the Study Conference for Polytechnic Principals, Western Region* TTTI: Bhopal

Technical Teachers' Training Institute (TTTI), Bhopal (1976c) *Country Course on Institution Building Processes: A Monograph* TTTI: Bhopal

Technical Teachers' Training Institute (TTTI), Bhopal (1978) *Modular Approach to Technical Teacher Training: Competency Based Teacher Education.* Paper presented at Third Inter-TTTI Faculty Conference Chandigarh TTTI: Bhopal

Technical Teachers' Training Institute (TTTI), Bhopal (1980a) *Competency-Based Teacher Education: A New Dimension in Teacher Training* TTTI: Bhopal

Technical Teachers' Training Institute (TTTI), Bhopal (1980b) *Engineering Experimentation Course: Guide Lines for Organising and Conducting Monitoring Visits* TTTI: Bhopal

Technical Teachers' Training Institute (TTTI), Bhopal (1983) *Technical Teachers' Training Institute — An Overview* TTTI: Bhopal

Technical Teachers' Training Institute (TTTI), Bhopal (1984) *Over the Years: TTTI Bhopal* TTTI: Bhopal

Technical Teachers' Training Institutes (1976) *Report on the Study Conference for Senior Administrators on Technician Education Held at Simla (11-16 October, 1976)* Sponsored by the ISTE and the four TTTIs TTTI: Bhopal

Verma, L N, Dharap, K P, Kapse, V M, Shah, B C and Banthiya, N K (1977) *Curriculum Evaluation Project: Final Report (September 75—August 77)* TTTI: Bhopal

Acknowledgements

The author sincerely thanks Professor Y Saran, Ex-Principal, Technical Teachers' Training Institute, Bhopal and Professors S A Balu, V M Kapse and S Z Haider, his colleagues at Technical Teachers' Training Institute, Bhopal for their comments on the draft of this chapter.

17. The developing interaction between research and teacher training

D Ian McCallum

Summary: This chapter suggests that changes in technology, the very high levels of unemployment, uncertainty in commerce and industry regarding the nature of education and training and indifference on the part of successive governments, place new responsibilities on the current generation of teachers. Not only do they have to design and justify courses for students who may have no clear employment prospects, but they also need to be able to survey possible local needs and to respond to the particular learning requirements of the older worker seeking retraining. The importance of these elements is highlighted by evidence of serious skill shortages alongside very high levels of unemployment. The new technology both poses a challenge and offers opportunities to teachers: courses need to take account of the changes which the new technology is bringing about in industry and commerce, and new technology enables new and powerful teaching methods. Research techniques which can contribute to our understanding of the learning process are of particular value to the innovator and are now available to teachers with quite modest computing resources. These factors, together with the speed of technological change, emphasize the important role which a new style of teacher training could play in equipping teachers to respond to the responsibilities which have been thrust upon them.

Introduction

Forecasts of the impact of the new technology on society are well documented. It was well known that advances in microelectronics in particular would offer industry and commerce highly efficient means of production, communication, information gathering and processing, together with the opportunity to reduce labour costs. In spite of this foreknowledge, many companies which formerly led the high technology field have been outstripped by their Japanese competitors. One British company was reported to have found it necessary to send production line supervisors, in addition to more senior staff, to Japan in order to provide them with adequate training (Bridge and Hewitt, 1983). They contrasted the day-release opportunities for training in Britain with the full-time training on offer up to the age of 22 in Japan. They also expressed the view that technical advances in their company had outstripped the currently available expertise among technical college staff.

The decline of the traditional heavy engineering industries, mirrored by a corresponding reduction in dependent lighter industries together with technological changes in the means of production, has dramatically reduced the need for a large workforce with traditional skills. It has also contributed to the creation of a large pool of unemployed men and women, many of whom are well beyond the traditional age at which skills training takes place. Uncertainty about future requirements for skilled labour has contributed to the growth in the policy of industry and commerce of seeking special skills in the marketplace in preference to the more costly alternative of providing systematic 'in-house' training.

Unemployment and the pattern of study

In Great Britain the combined effects of the increase in unemployment, which by 1985 had risen to three and a quarter million, and the reduction in the willingness or ability of industry and commerce to provide or support training, is reflected in government statistics. These show that between 1978 and 1982 the number of part-time and day release students in the 16-18 age range who were enrolled on vocational courses had decreased by 27 per cent. During the same period the number of students enrolled on full-time (including sandwich) courses had increased by 50 per cent. For students aged 21 and over there is some evidence of a reverse trend, with full-time enrolments having fallen by 15 per cent and part-time enrolments rising by 2 per cent.

The changing clientele

Changing patterns of post-school study suggest that unemployment has led to a reduction in the traditional employer-based training with close links to part-time further education, and an increase in the attractiveness of full-time education as an alternative to unemployment and as a preparation for a more competitive labour market. Among older workers seeking retraining there is a preference for part-time courses and forms of learning which enable them to remain in employment whilst, presumably, acquiring skills to meet its changing requirements.

Matching technical training and jobs

Great Britain, in common with other developed countries, has a major unemployment problem and, with approximately 16 per cent of the workforce unemployed, it has become particularly important that the training provision meets the nation's requirements. In these circumstances it is disturbing to note from the Confederation of British Industry's (CBI) industrial trends survey of April 1986 that 13 per cent of companies throughout the country predicted that output over the following four months would be restricted by shortages of skilled labour (Confederation of British Industry, 1986). The most striking feature of the findings of this survey relate to the very high proportion of companies in certain fields for whom shortage of skilled labour is an important factor. The following table shows responses from selected industries.

Table 1. *Percentage of companies identifying shortage of skilled labour as a factor likely to limit output over 'the next four months'*
(Source: CBI, 1986)

Pharmaceuticals and consumer chemicals	0%
Man-made fibres	1%
Metal manufacture	1%
Electrical industrial goods	10%
Mechanical engineering	12%
Shipbuilding	17%
Engineers' small tools	26%
Textiles	28%
Instrument engineering	28%
Metal working and machine tools	29%
Office machinery and data processing equipment	34%
Electrical and instrument engineering	37%
Electronic industrial goods	74%

In the circumstances of record unemployment, these figures provide a particularly damning indictment of society's ability to match the provision of training opportunities to the needs of industry.

Future training needs and sources of training

A survey by interview of randomly selected companies in East and West Sussex and Kent (McCallum *et al*, 1984) established that a majority of companies considered that the introduction of new technology would lead to an increase in the skill content of each category of employee in their workforce during the next three years. It was considered that this would be the case even among craftsmen and skilled operatives, although little indication could be given of the nature of the skills likely to be sought. Three-quarters of the companies considered that greater skills would be required by managers and 84 per cent expressed a similar belief with regard to clerical and related staff. This view was held most strongly by those companies which had already introduced elements of the 'new technology' into their work. However, less than 10 per cent saw the local college as a means of providing new skills. In-house training, with support from equipment suppliers, was reported to be the preferred means of meeting future training needs. Early recipients of such training would be expected to train other staff in return for their own 'favoured treatment'. Specialist technical needs were expected to be met by recruitment in the 'marketplace'. A very strong preference was however expressed for distance learning materials, with most companies stating their willingness to invest resources in order to enable their employees to acquire new skills. This was seen as an economic way of providing training, with the added advantage that, in order to ensure that it met their specific needs, the content could be approved in advance of any commitment.

If these views are indicative of future trends in the form of acceptable training provision, it has important implications for teachers, for the skills which they will need to acquire, and for the nature of the training which they must receive.

Less job-specific vocational training

The very serious economic decline and rapid increase in unemployment associated with the 1980s has provided the motivation for the government to take a series of unprecedented steps to make some form of vocational training available to all unemployed school leavers, to encourage retraining to meet the demands of the 'new technology' and to explore alternative, and less labour-intensive, methods of teaching. The large pool of unemployed people of 18 or younger, which has increased from less than 4 per cent in 1973 to over 25 per cent in 1982 (Department of Employment, 1985), has provided both a major opportunity and an incentive for the provision of training opportunities. The introduction of training schemes provides a mechanism for removing young people from the register of unemployed. Because no one can be certain what job opportunities will be available after training, it also provides a challenge to educators (traditionally only marginally involved in determining training policy) in designing and evaluating courses which must have the widest possible job relevance, and in which the long-term interests of the student can have a greater influence than has been the case in the past.

The current generation of teachers is faced with the responsibilities of identifying such training needs as may exist or develop in their region and then designing appropriate courses. Teachers are also expected to negotiate for course approval and to incorporate adequate monitoring, evaluation and certification. Additionally, some of them are required to ensure appropriate work experience placements which include some systematic 'on-the-job' training. The problems which teachers face in deciding which of the competing models provided by different government agencies has been well documented by Seale (1984).

The new technology and the curriculum

Teachers of subjects which included mathematical or statistical components had, until the mid-1970s, experienced great difficulty in providing students with tasks which would contribute to the development of insights into the basic principles of the subject in their completion. The advent of the cheap electronic calculator enabled the teacher and student to focus their attention upon the subject principles, without the distraction of long periods spent on arithmetic calculations. It also provided correct answers very soon after tackling the problem, so that students could acquire a 'feel' for the order of answer which they should expect. The advent of the cheap microcomputer enabled this approach to be greatly extended; more complex problems could be simulated and solved and students could be presented with graphical information and hard copy. It thus became possible for experiments or incidents to be simulated with a high degree of realism.

By 1985, the availability of microcomputers with mass storage devices and medium-resolution colour monitors for about £1,000 facilitated the introduction of students on a wide range of courses to four major commercial computer applications — word processing, spreadsheets, graphics and database management. These microcomputers could also be used to emulate the most widely used features of the much larger, more sophisticated and expensive equipment used in industry and commerce. Subsequent reductions in the cost of hardware have brought the cost of the personal computers made by several major manufacturers to little more than that of those produced for the home and educational markets. The dramatic reduction in the cost of computer memory has enabled programmers to incorporate extensive 'help' facilities which have contributed to the development of 'user-friendly' programs which are relatively easy to use. Many of these programs, whilst retaining their advanced capabilities, are more straightforward in use, at comparable levels, than their 'educational' equivalents. Their general availability has important implications for the teaching profession, for the training of teachers and for their skills as innovators and evaluators.

Young students, who may be working at quite a modest level of subject matter, can be introduced to important concepts, ideas, procedures and techniques which are identical with those which are likely to be encountered at work. Not only can the relevance of these be perceived by the students, but they can be provided with a range of experiences, impossible before the advent of the computer, which may be planned to develop those insights considered to be relevant and of value. If teachers are to perform these functions effectively, there are several important prerequisites. They must have a thorough understanding of the teaching opportunities provided through the currently available software and of its potential value to industry and commerce; they must also develop appropriate teaching material which, whilst emulating the real world, offers the students experiences which will develop relevant concepts.

As has been shown, few companies can give a clear indication of their probable future training requirements. They have little incentive to assume training responsibility, preferring either to compete in the open market for the necessary skills or to take advantage of the training schemes offered by the companies retailing the new technology. In these circumstances, added responsibilities for assessing which skills and insights are likely to be required by employers and which will have lasting value to employees, falls to the teacher and to the teacher trainer, who must also endeavour to monitor and evaluate the courses which are introduced to meet these ill-defined requirements.

The teachers are also presented with an opportunity to take advantage of computing resources in the form of word processing packages, as an effective means of producing teaching/learning materials, database management programs and spreadsheets to aid record keeping and record maintenance. A much greater opportunity and challenge is offered by the computer-aided learning 'framework' packages into which teachers can incorporate their own material. Advanced packages in this form enable the user to present textual material in a variety of typestyles and colours, with high quality graphics and, in some programs, animated diagrams. Students may be directed through the learning material in a manner which depends upon their responses to multiple-choice questions. Learning programmes may be constructed which record the time taken to respond to each question, the response made and, if required, the marks earned. Such facilities offer teachers unique opportunities to develop independent learning materials suited to their own subject specialisms and, perhaps more importantly, the chance to experiment with alternative methods of presenting learning material and to monitor and evaluate it with minimum difficulty. It is essential that teachers are familiar with the resources which they can tap and also that they have the necessary knowledge of the techniques for the evaluation if it is to be an effective feature of their work.

Alternative learning modes

Pressure to provide inexpensive opportunities for workers to update their knowledge and to retrain has led to the introduction of distance and open learning material. This is designed to give students all the information they need without making them dependent upon the active participation of teachers. Such material must be stimulating, self-evidently relevant and easily understood, and it must include any practical components needed to support the textual material. Some fairly minimal tutorial support is usually a feature of distance learning material and, even if not engaged as authors, tutors must be provided with opportunities to update the subject matter in the packages. The short shelf life of much of these materials makes this task particularly difficult. The cost-effective production, marketing and management of distance learning materials imposes a requirement that the next generation of teachers acquire skills not currently considered essential. Additionally, if they are to write distance learning material, their training must include reference to the particular problems associated with this work and with the problems experienced by the older worker returning to study.

Equipping teachers to undertake research/evaluation

Just as the arrival of the new technology has presented opportunities to revolutionize the curriculum, so it presents the teacher with the opportunity to apply sensitive statistical techniques during both the construction of valid measures of attainment and the evaluation of teaching materials and methods. As late as the 1970s teachers who wished to apply such techniques were only able to do so if they could obtain access to computers and to software usually only available in university and polytechnic computing departments. Item and factor analysis programs which can be run on microcomputers have been available for some years: the advanced and widely used Statistical Package for the Social Sciences (SPSS) is currently available for use on some of the larger personal computers and it will only be a matter of time before some of the specialist techniques, perhaps including some of the most mathematically complex methods of item analysis, will also become available. If teachers are to be equipped to take advantage of these new resources for research, their training must include suitable components.

Some of the most valuable statistical procedures used widely in educational and sociological research come under the general name of factor analysis. Their particular value lies in the fact that they provide an objective means of describing how the variance observed in a large number of variables may be accounted for by relatively few underlying factors. This requirement is common to many types of research but is of particular importance to work in social and psychological fields in which, almost invariably, the researcher is faced with interpreting data on a scale which makes this task extremely difficult.

Work in which factor analysis has been of particular value include the development of ideas on the nature of intelligence and the extent to which it could be considered to account for differences in performance observed among children undertaking complex learning tasks. Similar procedures have been widely used in subsequent studies which sought to examine concepts related to personality, creativity, teaching and learning strategies and subject-specific abilities. They have also proved to be of particular value in attempts to determine the extent to which these and other such concepts could be considered not as vague abstractions, but as 'real entities', of importance in contributing to an understanding of human behaviour and the learning process. Until computing resources capable of applying advanced statistical methods became available to teachers, it was difficult if not impossible for them to challenge many of the ideas which depended upon these methods and which were propounded by theorists.

Evidence regarding the value of factor analysis was provided soon after it became available, when market research companies were prepared to meet what were then substantial computer charges in order to gain an understanding of behavioural and other characteristics which could be associated with particular spending patterns. Other quite different applications have been found in such diverse tasks as studies of the relationships between different body measurements used by the clothing industry for the design of garments, and also for the provision of information which can be used as an aid to production quality control in a variety of industries. Factor analysis thus embraces a well-established range of valuable statistical methods which, until quite recently, were unfortunately available only to those with access to substantial and expensive computing resources. The development of the microcomputer not only makes these methods available to those with much more limited resources, but also enables the latter to use features which have generally been considered to be too expensive of time for widespread use. For example the 'Jack-knife' method proposed by Pennell (1972) for calculating confidence intervals for factor loadings, involving the re-analysis of ten or more very large data sub-samples, is unlikely to be attractive commercially, but would offer considerable advantages to the teacher/researcher prepared to spend an extra hour or so to seek evidence to justify confidence in research findings.

Another, perhaps equally important, advantage of helping teachers to undertake this work is that they can apply alternative statistical procedures very quickly and efficiently. This provides them with the experiences needed to acquire insights into these and other less advanced methods which, otherwise, they could only develop over a long period of time spent in educational research.

As recently as the 1970s there was, for example, considerable emphasis in the literature on the nature of the measurement scales employed in educational research, the need to correct for non-normal distributions and the most appropriate methods for calculating correlation coefficients and undertaking factor analysis. Although these issues are of importance, it was impossible for the non-statistician to participate in the debates, or to come to an understanding of the likely scale of error if the complex issues remained unresolved. Such influential authors as Cureton (1971), Gorsuch (1974), Cattell (1971) and Thurstone (1969) were concerned with interpreting the principles laid down by pioneers in the field which included Guttman (1954), Kaiser (1960) and Lawley and Maxwell (1971). Many of the issues with which they were concerned could never be completely resolved and many of the rules which they laid down were qualified with judgements which were essentially subjective and dependent upon the skills which had been developed with the aid of the computing departments to which they had access. Now, however, the skills which previously could only be developed by these privileged few can be acquired very much more readily with the aid of a modest microcomputer, a suitable database and an element of guidance and tuition. The teacher of the future can therefore be equipped to undertake evaluative studies, or other forms of educational research, and to evaluate statistical analyses in a way which was previously only available to the specialist.

When computing time was expensive and the researcher was unable to interact directly with the computer, detailed decisions about the nature of the analyses required had to be taken in advance and resources did not often allow alternative procedures to be tried. It is now possible for the researcher to examine the stability, and hence estimate the significance of factor loadings, by methods that would have been considered relatively recently as unacceptably extravagant of computer time. It is of greater importance that, in addition to applying the conventional tests, the researcher may undertake confirmatory analyses which can generate greater

confidence than the solely theoretical basis on which decisions had formerly to be based. The skills which these activities generate can improve the
ability to interpret reports of research. It is interesting to conjecture
whether the ideas propounded by psychologists like Vernon and Guilford
regarding the structure of human abilities would have been interpreted
more cautiously if readers had possessed a clearer insight into the extent to
which details of some findings can be sample-specific. The introduction of
a complex, but potentially valuable, method of item analysis which
facilitated the production of 'equal interval' scales might have evoked less
hostility if the opponents to its introduction had been able to evaluate it
in practical, rather than purely theoretical, terms. The advent of the
relatively inexpensive microcomputer which is capable of supporting the
mathematical procedures demanded by these techniques has considerable
implications for teachers and, of course, for those engaged in training
them.

The measurement of intelligence has, for a considerable time, proved to
be a source of controversy. The advent of computerized automated testing
on inexpensive microcomputers may intensify this controversy, but it also
offers some advantages to the teachers who are concerned with the interaction of intelligence, or other psychological factors, with other characteristics of relevance to education.

The microcomputer can maintain control over the presentation, timing,
recording and scoring of tests at a level which teachers find difficult to
achieve. Such tests are already available and by 1985, for an outlay of
£13.00, teachers could purchase a computerized Cattell IQ test for use on
a microcomputer selling for about £100. This development does of course
offer new opportunities for the teacher to embark on particular styles of
research, but it also introduces dangers which must be considered during
training. The teacher must be made aware of the manner in which changes
in the relationship between tester and testee may influence the outcomes,
and of the deficiencies of the standardizations currently available, which
are based on traditional methods and likely therefore to be inappropriate.

The development of computer-aided learning systems is probably too
demanding a task for the ordinary teacher and would not therefore be an
appropriate topic for an initial teacher training course. Recently, however,
programs for use on personal computers have become available which
enable the user to create adaptive electronic books. Authors with a little
computing knowledge can construct books which extend the features
currently available in conventional programmed texts.

Such books enable the author to produce a variety of text styles, to
present diagrams which may be animated, to time learner response rates,
to award and record marks and to adapt learning routes in the light of
responses made. The production by teachers of electronic books which
meet local needs has clear merit: it enables students to study independently and also enables the teacher to obtain precise monitoring information which can be invaluable in the study of learning difficulties or styles.
The use of electronic book authoring programs greatly simplifies the task

of the author, but student teachers need to be provided with initial training in their use.

Programs which enable teachers to generate electronic books can also be used to provide interactive 'self-tests', although for this purpose much less complex programs would suffice. These offer the teacher the ability to evaluate their own test items, to monitor student progress and to maintain records of progress and identify learning weakness.

Considerable attention has recently been devoted to profiling in response to what is perceived as the weakness of current normative assessment procedures when applied to a proportion of unemployed young people. Nuttall and Goldstein (1984) draw attention to the issues involved in establishing a technique which may not be sufficiently challenged on its reliability and validity by teachers. They express the fear that the potential of profiling may not be realized, because too ready an acceptance of a technically weak system may lead to its subsequent unjustified rejection. Macintosh (1985) provides further grounds for this fear by drawing attention to the 'woefully inadequate' nature of this aspect of current teacher training.

Conclusion

The new technology, coupled with the growth in unemployment, has serious long-term implications for teacher training, for teachers and for the abilities which will be demanded of them. Lack of positive national commitment towards the provision of technical training and uncertainty in industry and commerce have provided an element of freedom to develop less syllabus-bound courses. Such freedom does impose additional responsibilities, and teachers must acquire the skills needed to identify local needs, to respond to individual student needs, and to be capable of monitoring and assessing the provision, in some instances, without the support of examining boards.

Teachers must be enabled to keep abreast of technological changes and to develop and experiment with the new materials and teaching methods which these facilitate, in order that their teaching may be relevant and responsive to changing student needs. It is during teacher training that the most economic opportunities can be provided for them to learn to use these new resources, to evaluate them and to monitor the learning of their students.

If teachers are to be equipped to assume these new responsibilities, some radical rethinking of the traditional teacher training course is essential, with careful consideration given to the need to develop skills previously considered to be necessary only for the professional researcher.

References

Bridge, W A and Hewitt, C L (1983) *Report of a Survey of Industrial Demand for Open Tech Provision in the South-East* Southtek: Brighton

Cattell, R B (1971) *Handbook of Multivariate Experimental Psychology* Rand McNally & Co: Chicago, IL

Cattell, R B (1984) *Cattell IQ Test* Sinclair Research Ltd: Cambridge

Confederation of British Industry (CBI) (1986) *Industrial Trends Survey 100* Confederation of British Industry: London

Cureton, E E (1971) Communality estimates in factor analysis of small matrices *Educational & Psychological Measurement*, **31** 2 (Summer)

Department of Employment (1985) *Employment Gazette* July 1985 HMSO: London

Gorsuch, L R (1974) *Factor Analysis* W B Saunders Co: Philadelphia, London, Toronto

Guilford, J P (1964) *The Nature of Human Intelligence* McGraw-Hill: New York, NY

Guttman, L (1954) Some necessary conditions for factor analysis *Psychometrika*, **19** 2

Kaiser, H F (1960) *Relating Factors between Studies based upon Different Individuals* unpublished manuscript, University of Illinois

Lawley, D N and Maxwell, A E (1971) *Factor Analysis as a Statistical Method* (second edition) Butterworths: London

McCallum, D I et al (1984) *Changing Technology and its Impact on Training — A Report of a Survey of Companies in Sussex and Kent* (Unpublished) Garnett College: London

Macintosh, H G (1985) *Assessment in Education and Training 14-18: Policy and Practice. A Review of Current Initiatives, drawing upon a Conference held at Stoke Rochford in December 1984* National Institute for Careers Education and Counselling: Cambridge

Nuttall, D and Goldstein, H (1984) Profiles and graded tests: the technical issues *Profiles in Action*, FEU: London

Pennell, R (1972) Routinely computable confidence intervals for factor loadings using the 'Jack-knife' *British Journal of Mathematical and Statistical Psychology* **25** 107-111

Seale, C (1984) FEU and MSC: Two curricular philosophies and their implications for a youth training scheme *in The Vocational Aspect of Education* (YTS Special Edition) **36** 93 May 1984

SPSS (1984) *Statistical package for the Social* Sciences/PC. SPSS UK Ltd: Richmond

Thurstone, L A (1969) *Multiple Factor-Analysis: A Development and Expansion of the Vectors of the Mind* The University of Chicago Press: London

Vernon, P E (1961) *The Structure of Human Abilities* Methuen: London

Wells, W (1985) The relative pay and employment of young people *Department of Employment Research Paper Series* **42** Department of Employment: London

18. Modular structures: their strengths and weaknesses

Iolo Roberts

Summary: The introduction of the EITB's modular system for the training of engineering craftsmen in 1968 heralded an approach to industrial training which is now recognized worldwide. However, during recent years the modular approach has also grown in importance within education in general and vocational education in particular. Indeed in both areas its introduction is seen as a vital step in the progressive move towards credit transfer.

The development of modularization within both industry and education is outlined, and following a detailed analysis of terminological issues an attempt is made to present a working definition which can provide the basis for a greater understanding of the central concept. Subsequently the dangers inherent in moving too rapidly into wholesale modularization before the possible pitfalls have been identified are highlighted and discussed.

Introduction — the growth of modular provision

Since the mid-1960s the UK has seen a number of major initiatives aimed at improving the education and training of its workforce, many of which involve a substantial element of modularization. Following the Industrial Training Act of 1964, the Engineering Industry Training Board (EITB) established in 1968 its modular system for the training of engineering craftsmen, thus initiating a system which had by 1986 been adopted in many other industries.

In 1974, the Technician Education Council (TEC) announced its plans for a unitary structure leading to TEC certification to replace the dual system of course programmes leading either to a City and Guilds of London Institute (CGLI) Technician Certificate or to Ordinary and Higher National Certificates. This approach has subsequently been endorsed by the Business and Technician Education Council (BTEC).

More recently the present government, working through the Manpower Services Commission (MSC), has initiated an even more radical attempt to develop 'a coherent approach to work related education and training' (MSC, 1985) through developments such as the Technical and Vocational Education Initiative (TVEI), the Youth Training Scheme (YTS) and the Adult Training Strategy. To this end it established a Review of Vocational Qualifications Group (RVQ) to review existing examining and qualification models and make recommendations concerning an improved structure of accepted and recognized vocational qualifications. One such model is that based on the Scottish Action Plan arising from the 1983 announcement by the Scottish Education Department (SED) that it was moving to a new modular system of study. As a consequence, the Scottish Vocational Education Council (SCOTVEC) has taken a quantum leap and introduced a single national certificate based on combinations of modules selected from a national catalogue of some 1,600 modules (Scottish Vocational Educational Council, 1985).

Not surprisingly, in spite of the claims made by advocates of the modular approach to education and training, many educationists are wary of going too far along this particular route before all the possible pitfalls have been identified and ironed out. The purpose of the rest of this chapter is therefore to analyse selected modular schemes representative of developments in the United Kingdom, Europe and the United States, in the hope of providing a basis for further discussion of the strengths and weaknesses of modular provision.

The nature and rationale of modular schemes

The Engineering Industry Training Board module and module segment systems for the training of engineering craftsmen

The Engineering Industry Training Board system, as originally conceived, is based on the concept of a series of building blocks which clearly define the craft skills of a number of skill areas, along with the training and experience needed to acquire them. Towards the end of their period of basic engineering training, all trainees select a minimum number of modules to form an agreed programme of training, which also has a built-in release to a college of further education for a matching course of theoretical study.

The main advantages of the system are:

1. Its flexibility. The system ensures that individual trainee craftsmen receive training to an adequate level of attainment in a defined range of skills. It also provides a sound basis for further training as and when required.
2. The length of training is based on what has to be taught and the rate of learning of the individual trainee. This means that there is an incentive for trainees to become qualified as soon as possible.
3. Standards of performance are set and recognized by certification when they have been reached.
4. The attainment of approved standards is measured by a system of regular tests, which are used with training records and log books as the basis for the Certificate of Craftsmanship.

In 1984, the Board announced that its module system was being developed into the *module segment* system, each segment being based on a cluster of related craft skills approximating to one-third of the content of a typical module. Each segment is standards-based and, as in the case of modules, the time taken to achieve the required standard depends on the ability of an individual trainee to develop the skills in accordance with requirements.

Segments fall into three categories, viz:

□ a common core segment which contains only the skills common to all the modules in that particular skill area, eg safety, standards and procedures;
□ a key segment which contains common skills which naturally lead to the development of skills in groups of free-standing segments;
□ a free-standing segment or group of related skills which form an identifiable package.

A typical training programme will consist of a common core segment plus at least one key segment plus four free-standing segments.

The module segment system, whilst retaining all the advantages of the module system, is considered to be more flexible and adaptable (Engineering Industry Training Board, 1982). Additionally it will be much easier to revise the new system, since individual segments can be updated more rapidly than modules.

Courses leading to BTEC National and Higher National qualifications

In contrast to the EITB system, where the modules and segments specify the craft skills within a training programme, approved Business and Technician Education Council (BTEC) programmes are now based on what have come to be referred to as *units of study* (Business and Technician Education Council, 1984, 1986).

A unit constitutes a self-contained, significant component of a programme of study leading to an employment-related qualification for which a separate assessment grade is awarded. Units, which are categorized as standard units (planned and designed centrally) or centre-devised units (planned and designed by the staff of a centre in conjunction with local employers and validated by the council), normally require between 60 and 90 hours of learning support. Furthermore, it is customary to attribute levels to units, with units which are part of a National Certificate originally designated either as level I, II or III, but now as N.

Normally a programme of study or course leading to a BTEC qualification will be a collection of a specified number of core, other essential and optional units either taken as a package or accumulated over a period of time.

The growth of modular provision within the secondary school sector

At the time of writing there are many instances where fourth and fifth form courses in our secondary schools are being restructured into shorter units or modules. In at least two instances, such changes are a direct outcome of major reports such as the Munn Report on *The Structure of the Curriculum in the Third and Fourth Years of the Scottish Secondary School* (Scottish Education Department, 1977) and the Hargreaves Report on *Improving Secondary Schools* within the Inner London Education Authority (1984).

The curricular arguments advanced for modular schemes include the following:

☐ the aims and objectives of modular units provide clearly defined goals to which pupils can relate closely;
☐ the use of modular units allows pupils to renegotiate their curriculum pathways periodically.

Understandably, it has been necessary to rethink assessment procedures to accommodate such changes. Stimulated by the apparent success of the modular approach which is now an integral part of the TVEI initiative at Ysgol Emrys ap Iwan, Abergele, the Welsh Joint Education Committee (WJEC) approved in principle modular schemes for examinations at both 16 plus and Advanced Level (Welsh Joint Education Committee, 1985).

Terminology

Before proceeding further it is important that we should at this point seek an agreed definition of the term 'module'. This can best be done by a more detailed analysis of various modular and unitary schemes.

The EITB's definitive booklet on *The Training of Engineering Craftsmen* (Engineering Industry Training Board, 1981) includes the following statements:

'22. For module training the Board provides:
    a) A Skill and Training Specification for each module which:
        i) indicates the range of skill to be developed during training and the standards to be reached at its completion
        ii) sets out details of the training to be given
    b) An Instruction Manual for each module which:
        i) indicates methods of developing each element of skill contained in the training specification
        ii) provides a set of sample phase tests which indicate the range of skills to be completed successfully during the progress of the training
    c) A Log Book in which the trainee records the training received.
23. Training in the chosen module proceeds in accordance with the appropriate training specification and to the standard prescribed by the skill specification . . . Close attention must be given to such matters as:
    i) quality
    ii) accuracy
    iii) time

iv) safe working practice

v) periodic testing (phase testing) in accordance with the prescribed standards.

24. Module training may take place on or off-the-job, but in all cases it is a requirement for recognition of approved training that the trainee is responsible to a supervisor who has been trained in the techniques of instruction including the use of Instruction Manuals and testing procedures...

27. The length of time spent on each module depends on individual attainment. It is important that the full breadth of the Training Specification is covered and that the approved standard of performance is reached in all the elements of skill within the module.'

Whilst the EITB's approach to modularization has been absolutely consistent from the outset, BTEC has, possibly for good reason, taken much longer to clarify its policies. Thus, whilst the Technician Education Council adopted a unitary approach defining a *unit* as 'a self-contained and significant component of a course or programme' (TEC, 1974) the Business Education Council used the term *module*, which it defined as 'a significant teaching/learning component of a course, not necessarily a subject or discipline', adding the comment:

'BEC wishes to encourage colleges to consider ways of meeting course objectives without necessarily using an entirely subject-based approach, and it is for this reason the "module" rather than "subject" has been chosen' (Business Education Council, 1976).

However, since the merger of the two Councils in 1983, the term 'module' has been progressively phased out as a matter of policy.

Thus the first Joint Policy Statement (Business and Technician Education Council, 1984) includes the following section:

'Studies for BTEC National and Higher National Qualifications

44. Students will gain a BTEC qualification by achieving the intended outcome of an approved course...

46. Courses are likely to be structured in one of two ways:
  * unit-based: a combination of units of study, with progression through the course depending on success in each unit and with credit being given for each unit achieved — whether or not the whole course is completed;
  * grouped: the elements grouped in successive stages, with progression to each stage normally depending on success in the previous stage.

Units

51. Units of study will be designed around the knowledge and skills which the student must attain; this continues the practice of BEC and TEC. In the light of experience, the BTEC Boards will review the way in which the required knowledge and skills

are described, with a view to improving the description of units.

52. Units will have a notional design range of 60-90 hours' formal study for a "whole" unit. Multiple and half units will be available to students, subject to review by BTEC Boards.

53. The former TEC practice of attributing levels to units will be maintained at levels I, II and III where it has proved useful.'

Some 18 months later, BTEC published a further document amplifying the policies as already outlined in which it defines units as follows:

'A self-contained, significant component of a programme of study for which a separate assessment grade is awarded.

(a) Each unit successfully completed as part of a programme of study counts towards a student's award.

(b) A unit specifies the student's knowledge, understanding, competence and skills which are to be developed and assessed, and the learning activities and assessment strategies which are to achieve this.

(c) Units normally require between 60 and 90 hours of learning support depending on the nature of the course and/or an individual student's background. The learning support for a unit is more commonly 60 hours in respect of a part-time course (where it is complemented by work-based experiential learning) with up to 90 hours' learning support being more usual in full-time courses.

(d) Units may be classified as core units, essential units (necessary for the completion of a particular qualification) or option units.'

At this point it is illuminating to compare (b) above, with the following extracts taken from a slightly earlier document, entitled *BTEC General Award in Business Studies Course Specification:*

'3.2 Core Modules are the compulsory section of the course and are intended to develop basic knowledge, understanding and skills necessary for all students who have recently entered, or are about to enter, business or public administration . . . The detailed aims and objectives of these core modules are given in Sections 5 to 8.

3.3 . . . Option modules fall into three main categories as follows:

3.3.1 those dealing with more specific knowledge and skills relevant to a particular type of employment occurring within a number of business sectors.'

(Business and Technician Education Council, 1983)

As a consequence one cannot but surmise that what has actually happened in practice is that BTEC, having built on and further developed the original BEC concept of modules in preference to the TEC concept of a unitary structure is now, for purely political reasons, using the term 'unit' to describe what used to be referred to by BEC as a module. Whatever the reasons for this change in terminology it is one which is regrettably likely to cause curricular confusion in the long term.

Another document which seeks to define the term *module* is the Scottish Education Department's (SED) Action Plan (Scottish Education Department, 1983). Here are some relevant extracts:

'*A NEW FRAMEWORK*

This analysis has implications for overall curriculum design. In order to make provision for all the potential participants and in order to ensure optimum use of resources, it will be necessary to design curriculum components, or modules, which are sufficiently flexible to be built into individual programmes in a large variety of ways, and by a process of negotiation.

A general module may be part of a mainstream linear course progression, or an element required to service other disciplines, or an optional component related to mainstream activities, or may offer opportunities for the development of personal interests or leisure pursuits . . . The length of each module has to be governed by two considerations: it must be long enough to offer a worthwhile unit of study and yet must not be so long that it exceeds the time available to part-time users. Anything less than 20 hours will not satisfy the former consideration and a unit of more than 100 hours' duration will be unsatisfactory for the latter. It is suggested that the optimum is of the order of 40 hours, or multiples of this unit, providing a full-time student with at least 20 modules in a year, and there is already some experience of this approach in further education, although not across all courses . . .

It is important that the content of modules is not interpreted as only the acquisition of knowledge, since this view commonly leads to a didactic approach to teaching and learning. Each module should incorporate a specification of its objectives as well as the content which will act as a vehicle for these objectives. In some cases the objectives may focus to such an extent on certain skills, such as planning or problem-solving, that the particular content chosen is relatively unimportant. In other cases the objectives may be integrative, drawing together the knowledge and skills already acquired, or may be concerned with the application of certain knowledge and skills and related to work experience. A wide variety of approaches to teaching will therefore be required in order to cover the range of objectives listed in each module. It will also be necessary to provide descriptors for each module stipulating the objectives, content, levels of attainment required on entry and anticipated on exit, techniques of assessment, and suggestions for methodology and resources . . .'

Clearly in spite of the fact that the statements above have been taken from three different sources, there is a substantial element of agreement about the meaning of the term, whether it be defined as a module or in BTEC terms as unit. Briefly stated the term may be defined as *a self-contained package that includes a planned series of learning experiences designed to help the student master specified objectives* (Goldschmidt and Goldschmidt, 1972; Russell, 1974).

At this point it may be useful to make two further comments. Firstly, some authors (Finch and Crunkilton, 1979) would also suggest that in some instances it may be useful to include 'individualized' in the above definition. Secondly it will be noted that as stated above the definition omits any reference to the notion of the nominal time factor associated with some modular schemes. Both these points will be returned to later.

To accommodate such additions we must therefore amend the above definition to read as follows:

A module is a self-contained package that includes a planned series of (individualized) learning experiences designed to help a student master specified objectives (within a given nominal time range of X hours of formal study or learning support).

The strengths and weaknesses of modular systems

As one would anticipate, the moves towards the progressive adoption of modules are a reflection of the perceived advantages of introducing such a system. These advantages may be summarized as follows:

1. As modules are self-contained, credit, accumulation and transfer are facilitated. In an economic climate such as that of the UK in the mid-1980s, young people must take jobs as and when they arise. The modular system offers a great variety of entry and exit points and furthermore enables credit to be given for participation in a recognized scheme irrespective of its nature or location.

2. a. As modules are of a relatively short duration, student motivation is enhanced. An interesting example of this is to be found in Gareth Newman's comments on the introduction of a modular system into the TVEI programme at Einrys ap Iwan School, Abergele in North Wales.

   [After a year's experience] 'We are even more convinced that learning by doing and individual resource-based learning programmes are the answer to many of the serious problems facing educational establishments today.

   * Pupils value the relationships (particularly with teachers) that the new courses generate more than the equipment now available to them.

   * Teaching in small units of 40 hours and encouraging students to renegotiate their options at the end of each module helps to counteract the harmful influences of sex stereotyping evident in traditional two-year courses.

   * Pupils learn effectively and rapidly in these conditions and in new technological subjects they learn faster than their teachers.

* The renegotiation of courses certainly appears to be improving behaviour and attendance at least at the end of this fourth year.' (Newman, 1984)
    b. The need to state both short-term and more specific objectives is beneficial in that they can be shared with the students. This enables students to work towards defined goals.
    c. The inbuilt systematic review of student progress can lead to a more positive attitude towards learning.
3. Modular systems can facilitate curriculum change because
    a. new curricular areas can be developed without totally displacing existing areas.
    b. evaluation and subsequent revision — should that be necessary — can take place fairly rapidly.
    In a rapidly changing technological age, both of these features are extremely important in the context of vocational programmes. This aspect of modular provision is strongly reflected in the EITB's move, referred to earlier, towards a further division of modules into modular segments.
4. Modular systems are much more flexible and adaptable than traditional schemes. This enhances student choice and furthermore allows programmes to be prepared to suit the actual requirements of an individual student or the company.
5. A modular course structure enables part-time students, be they on schemes for young people or on an adult retraining scheme, to participate in existing full-time provision. This has distinct advantages in terms of its resource implications and also the resultant learning environment.
6. Finally, the undoubted success of modular systems in the vocational training context is illustrated by the continuing growth of industrially based schemes both in the UK and elsewhere. Thus the International Labour Office has developed what it refers to as 'a universal and flexible concept of vocational training called *Modules of Employable Skills* (MES)'. These are self-contained instructional booklets, each covering a specific learning objective, and there are some 600 MES learning elements covering six major occupational areas, viz: automative engineering, building and construction, electrical engineering, mechanical engineering and plumbing and pipe fitting. Whilst such learning elements are being developed initially in English, provision is also being made for their translation into other languages, including French, Spanish and Arabic (International Labour Office, 1985). In 1984, a Working Party of the Hotel and Catering Industry Training Board also recommended a system of 'craft proficiency recognition' to be followed by specialist proficiency and supervisory modules (HCITB, 1984).

However, whilst modular structures clearly have strengths, they can also be extremely problematic in a number of respects. At the risk of oversimplifying, I will now differentiate between intrinsic issues arising from the nature of modules, and issues which are essentially organizational in character, which can thus be progressively overcome with experience and adequate planning.

Intrinsic issues

Whilst there are obvious advantages in specifying objectives, there are also substantial dangers in such an approach.

a. Considerable difficulties arise when the objectives model is adhered to in situations in which personalized responses to learning situations are encouraged, or where the emphasis is on the development of affective characteristics in addition to cognitive and/or psychomotor skills (Stenhouse, 1975; Heathcote *et al*, 1982).

   Indeed, there is substantial evidence from the school sector to suggest that the objectives model is generally associated with subject-centred curricula and that its use is particularly in evidence in 'linear subjects' where the subject matter involves hierarchical ordering of concepts, as in most mathematics, academic science and modern language curricula. Interestingly the organizers of Somerset's modular TVEI scheme have decided that

   'All technical and vocational areas of the curriculum will be provided in modular form as will most other areas, except those which have a linear structure such as English, Mathematics and Foreign Languages. Even in these areas some modules are under consideration' (Henderson, 1985).

b. There appears to be an inconsistency between the existence of an overall intention that all students should attain specific objectives and standards and the notion of a nominal time equivalence which has come to be associated with many modular systems. Whilst the EITB, as we have seen, stresses that 'the length of training is based on the rate of learning', BTEC on the other hand in its latest policy statement reiterated (Business and Technician Education Council, 1984) the view first expressed in the Technician Education Council's original policy statement that 'the expectation is that a student who is recruited with integrity to the course should with diligent study and application attain a qualification'.

c. Another problem relating to the notion of time is that it would seem to suggest that all subjects and subject areas can be broken down into roughly 'equivalent' units; this is unlikely to be the case. Indeed, as indicated by Cassells and Johnstone (1984) it may be necessary in some subjects such as chemistry to envisage a module as built up of various small parts or units, a type of system which is very much akin to the modular sciences which have been developed in Australia and the USA.

d. Finally, as previously indicated, in their purest form, modules must be seen as competence-based curricular units. A crucial factor in the assessment of such units is a move away from norm-referenced systems to criterion-referencing. However, such developments are not easy. For example,

1. there are problems associated with the development of the General Certificate of Secondary Education (GCSE). Whilst the new syllabuses at 16 plus are being introduced in 1986, it is unlikely that appropriate criterion-referenced assessment procedures will be available before the 1990s.
2. the unsatisfactory nature of certain aspects of the City and Guilds of London Institute grid profiles is indicative of the difficulties which still lie ahead. Here again, many of the statements used would seem to be based on norms rather than criteria.

Further discussion of some of the issues arising may be found in the Further Education Unit's brief but well-presented technical statement *Towards a Competence-Based System* (Further Education Unit, 1984). It explains 'the task of coming to grips with a training/education philosophy that is concerned with competence rather than time serving'.

Organizational aspects

The purpose of this section is to deal with the issues of cohesion, progression and interrelationships, problems which normally dog modular systems but which can be alleviated by careful planning at both the developmental and implementation stages.

Undoubtedly our starting point must be the care with which individual modules are conceived and presented. Possible guidelines (Scottish Education Department, 1983; Spencer, 1984) include the need

a. to ensure that each module is accompanied by 'descriptors stipulating the objectives, content, levels of attainment required on entry and anticipated on exit, techniques of assessment, and suggestions for methodology and resources';
b. to indicate, by the use of appropriate terminology, the possible relationships between individual modules. In practice this can be achieved in two ways:
   i. by the use of terms such as general, specialist, complementary and sequential;
   ii. by the articulation of modules to ensure sequence and continuity. In this instance it is customary to specify progression by attributing levels to each module, eg Technology 1, Technology 2 and Technology 3.

Once the individual modules have been written and suitably categorized, the next stage in the process is the planning of a coherent modular structure or programme. Here again there are two complementary aspects to be considered — firstly, the possible institutional inputs, and secondly the student requirements. The former relate to perceived need and the availability of resources, whilst the latter require student negotiation and guidance. In practice both aspects are extremely complex tasks which need to be carried out with care and respect for the views of the students and staff involved.

The third and final stage is the implementation of the agreed programme, and here again there is substantial evidence to suggest that a satisfactory outcome is extremely difficult to achieve, especially in cross-boundary situations. To start with, as Bernstein (1971) has pointed out, in England and Wales in particular there is a very strong subject loyalty which is not easy to overcome. This view is endorsed by the continuing battle which BTEC was still fighting with respect to improving the quality of cross-modular assignments (CMAs) in the context of Awards in Business and Related Studies some ten years after such programmes were first established.

'In the opinion of both lecturers and students, cross-modular assignments are perhaps the most interesting and successful part of the course. On the evidence of the review, though, the quality of CMAs was not substantially different from the assignment work done on the rest of the course.' (Business and Technician Education Council, 1985)

Conclusion

Between the time this chapter was written and the need to go to print, the final report of the Review of Vocational Qualifications Group has appeared. As indicated in our introduction, the Review Group were expected to pronounce on modular systems. The following extract is taken from the final report.

'6.18 . . . The advantages of a modular approach are well recognised. In particular, the value of modularisation in offering flexible provision of education and training has been established. Modularisation may also contribute to the motivation of learners and to acceptability to employees and may help to sharpen the objectives of education and training programmes. Modular programmes may be particularly helpful in meeting the needs of adult learners and as a basis for cumulative credit. In seeking flexibility it is inevitable and proper that modular approaches will be used and further developed. But it is unlikely in our view that a single pattern of modular provision will satisfy all requirements that have to be met within the national framework. Whatever the pattern of provision adopted by bodies accredited by the National Council, it is vital that there should be full opportunity for individuals to accumulate credit for achievement in the component parts of awards.' (Manpower Services Commission, 1986)

It is to be hoped that full discussion of the issues which have been raised in this chapter will contribute to the means through which credit transfer becomes much more widely acceptable than is currently the case.

References

Bernstein, B (1971) On the classification and framing of educational knowledge *in* Young, M F D (1971)

Business and Technician Education Council (BTEC) (1983) *BTEC General Award in Business Studies Course Specification* BTEC: London

Business and Technician Education Council (BTEC) (1984) *Policies and Priorities into the 1990s* BTEC: London

Business and Technician Education Council (BTEC) (1985) *Review of BTEC National Awards in Business and Related Studies: Report on the Council's Programme of Consultation and Research* BTEC: London

Business and Technician Education Council (BTEC) (1986) *Circular 15. BTEC Qualifications and Certificates of Achievement: The Framework* BTEC: London

Business Education Council (BEC) (1976) *Policy Statement* BEC: London

Cassells, J R T and Johnstone, A M (1984) Modules and 'H' grade chemistry *in* Spencer (1984)

Engineering Industry Training Board (EITB) (1981) *The Training of Engineering Craftsmen* Engineering Industry Training Board. London

Engineering Industry Training Board (EITB) (1982) *The Training of Engineering Craftsmen* (revised edition) Engineering Industry Training Board: London

Finch, C R and Crunkilton, J R (1979) Individualised, competency-based packages *in Curriculum Development in Vocational and Technical Education: Planning, Content and Implementation* Allyn and Bacon Inc: London

Further Education Unit (FEU) (1984) *Towards a Competence-Based System: An FEU View* FEU: London

Goldschmidt, B and Goldschmidt, M (1972) Modular instruction: principles and applications in higher education *Learning in Higher Education* 3

Heathcote, G, Kempa, R and Roberts, I (1982) *Curriculum Styles and Strategies* Further Education Unit (FEU): London

Henderson, J M (1985) *The Somerset TVEI Project: A Summary* TVEI Office: Chard

Hotel and Catering Industry Training Board (HCITB) (1984) *Craft Proficiency Recognition, Specific Modules and Sample Programmes* HCITB: Wembley

Inner London Education Authority (ILEA) (1984) *Improving Secondary Schools* (The Hargreaves Report) ILEA: London

International Labour Office (1985) *Modules of Employable Skill: An Approach to Vocational Training. Catalogue of Learning Elements and Related Materials* (Fourth edition) ILO Publications: Geneva

Manpower Services Commission (MSC) (1985) *Education and Training for Young People* Cmnd 9482 HMSO: London

Manpower Services Commission (MSC) (1986) *Review of Vocational Qualifications in England and Wales* (Joint Manpower Services Commission/Department of Education and Science Working Group Report) HMSO: London

Newman, G (1984) Taking the initiative *TVEI Insight* 1: 5-6 MSC, London

Russell, J D (1974) *Modular Instruction* Burgess Publishing Company: Minneapolis

Scottish Education Department (SED) (1977) *The Structure of the Curriculum in the Third and Fourth Years of the Scottish Secondary School* (The Munn Report) HMSO: Edinburgh.

Scottish Education Department (SED) (1983) *16-18s in Scotland: An Action Plan* HMSO: Edinburgh.

Scottish Vocational Education Council (SCOTVEC) (1985) *The National Certificate* SCOTVEC, Glasgow

Spencer, E *ed* (1984) *Modules for All: Discussion Papers on New Proposals for the Education of 16-18s* Scottish Council for Research in Education, Edinburgh

Stenhouse, L (1975) *An Introduction to Curriculum Research and Development* Heinemann Education Books Ltd, London

Technician Education Council (TEC) (1974) *Policy Statement* TEC: London

Welsh Joint Education Committee (WJEC) (1985) *Guidelines for the Use of Modular Schemes of Assessment* WJEC: Cardiff

Young, M F D *ed* (1971) *Knowledge and Control* Collier Macmillan, London

19. Qualifications and assessment of vocational education and training in the UK

Christine Ward

Summary: After giving a brief history of recent vocational education and training in the UK, this chapter looks at some current trends: broadening assessment to cover a wider range of skills, including the idea of 'competence'; the continuing trend to greater professionalism in assessment; division of both education and training programmes into relatively short 'modules', and the growing recognition of the need to update the skills and knowledge of the workforce. There is a discussion of some current issues, including the need to assess process skills, transfer of knowledge and skills and core skills, demand for mutual recognition of qualifications by awarding bodies and the practical uses of norm- and criterion-referencing. The chapter then identifies the assessment methods most used for different levels of cognitive, communication, psychomotor and affective skills, and methods of assessing competence in an occupation or range of tasks. Methods of reporting results, including profiling, are surveyed. Implications of information technology for recording results and for assessing candidates 'on demand' are described. Throughout the chapter there are references to the implications of the *Review of Vocational Qualifications* and the extension of the Youth Training Scheme (YTS).

Introduction

In the United Kingdom, the division between vocational education and training was emphasized by the 1964 Industrial Training Act, which put the responsibility for industrial training on to a series of Industrial Training Boards and resulted in the removal of some of the practical elements from college-based educational courses (see Lang, 1978).

Education for work in the UK can be divided according to academic level. Those aspiring to professional status commonly take a university degree, which may be vocationally related (eg for engineers) or may be followed by part-time professional education and training, (eg for accountants or bankers). In the business area, access to professional qualifications is usually also available to suitably qualified 18 year-old school leavers who may study for the examinations of the relevant professional body. Below professional level, and particularly in the technical area, there is a division in education and training between the more academic 'technician' stream and the less academic 'craft' stream. This stems in particular from the 1961 government White Paper *Better Opportunities in Technical Education*

(Ministry of Education, 1961) and was intended to reduce the high failure rates on the more academic college courses.

In engineering, construction and other practical subject areas, students below professional level normally aim at one of the qualifications of the Business and Technician Education Council (BTEC), City and Guilds of London Institute (CGLI) or one of the six regional examining bodies which offer qualifications similar to CGLI. In business and commercial subjects qualifications are available from BTEC, the Royal Society of Arts, Pitman Examinations Institute and London Chamber of Commerce and Industry.

In technical education, the late 1960s and early 1970s were a time of greatly increased interest in assessment matters. (For a description of assessment techniques and discussion of the issues involved see Ward, 1980, 1981a, 1981b; Hudson, 1973; Macintosh, 1974; Thyne, 1974.) The emphasis at the time was on the very necessary task of improving the reliability of assessment and this was achieved by the extension of the use of multiple-choice questions and by improvements in the methodology and statistical analysis of more traditional questions requiring written, drawn or calculated responses from the candidate ('constructed-answer' questions). However, the discussion of the issues raised in making exam-inations more reliable also led to attempts to make them more valid, both in the spread of syllabus coverage and in the nature of the abilities being assessed. This led to an increase in the use of coursework assessment to give better sampling of the abilities assessed and also to the use of projects, assignments, case studies and open-book examinations in order to make assessment more realistic and relevant to the skills needed in industry. These developments were accompanied by changes in result determin-ation and reporting rules, particularly in the separate reporting of results obtained in different subjects. There followed an increased interest in stating the syllabus in terms of learning objectives so that teachers, exam-iners and students all had a clearer idea of what the student should be able to do at the end of the course (Mager, 1984).

The setting up of the Industrial Training Boards, with responsibility for fostering training and setting industry-based practical tests, had the effect of extending this interest in assessment methods to the assessment of practical skills. The end-of-course practical tests marked in percentage terms, which had been common before the Industrial Training Act, were superseded by other methods such as 'phased tests' (set at intervals during the course) or the use of assessment on the job. Marking became more closely related to objectives and usually was carried out by reference to a checklist of criteria. The criteria were based not only on the end product ('Was dimension A within the stated tolerances?') but also on the process involved, thus requiring the examiner or assessor to observe the candi-date at work on the test ('Did the worker wear the correct protective clothing?'). The time taken to perform the task now became more signifi-cant in the assessment process, as employers were concerned to know whether the trainee had achieved the speed of a skilled worker.

In this general trend towards increased professionalism in assessment of both education and training, some organizations were left behind. The professional bodies in particular, more closely linked to the academic world than other institutions, have continued to examine their candidates almost exclusively by means of formal written examinations, often of the essay type, with perhaps the addition of a vague requirement for a given number of years of relevant experience.

The setting up of the Youth Training Scheme (YTS) and its extension to a two-year programme from April 1986 have focused attention on the need for further changes in assessment and certification arrangements. Trainees include many young people who would not previously have received systematic training and who are working in jobs for which no recognized qualification exists. The published objectives of two-year YTS include such qualities as personal effectiveness and ability to 'transfer' skills to new situations, which have not previously been assessed as part of vocational qualifications. A YTS certification board has been established under the Manpower Services Commission (MSC) to determine ways of assessing and certifying trainees' achievements within YTS.

The need to provide adequate recognition of success on YTS was one factor leading to the establishment of the Working Group for the Review of Vocational Qualifications in April 1985. The Working Group reported in April 1986 (Manpower Services Commission, 1986) and its recommendations included the establishment of a national framework for vocational qualifications, the categorization of qualifications at four or five levels, the setting up of a National Council for Vocational Qualifications and the accreditation of existing and new qualifications by the National Council. The report listed the objectives for an improved system of qualifications (comprehensibility, relevance, credibility, accessibility and cost-effectiveness) and the three elements required in any vocational qualification (assessment of knowledge, skills and performance of relevant tasks).

One of the more controversial aspects of the report is the proposal to categorize all vocational qualifications by level, the level definitions ranging from I ('occupational competence in performing a range of tasks under supervision') through II and III ('. . . satisfactory responsible performance in a defined occupation or range of jobs') to IV ('. . . design and specify defined tasks. . . and accept responsibility for the work of others'), with one or possibly two levels above IV. Although this framework of levels has the advantage of relating closely to the requirements of particular occupations rather than attempting to judge occupations by the academic standard needed, it may be too far from existing thinking to gain acceptance. It implies, for example that a milkman or postman may well be performing at level III whereas a new chemistry graduate entering industry may start at level I.

At the time this chapter was written, the full details of the implementation of the report had not yet been announced, but it was clear that the review would have a major impact on the assessment and certification of vocational education and training.

Development of new assessment methods in vocational education and training was paralleled in secondary education during the 1960s and 1970s by an increase in the use of multiple-choice and structured questions and coursework assessment in the General Certificate of Education and the Certificate of Secondary Education. These two certificates are to be combined into a single General Certificate of Secondary Education (GCSE) with first examinations in 1988, and the Secretary of State for Education has requested that the new examination should eventually be criterion-referenced (Secondary Examinations Council, 1984 and 1985). However, this is not without its problems, and development of this aspect of the GCSE is still in its early stages.

Current trends and issues

Modularization

There is an increasing tendency to divide courses of training into 'modules' which may be taken in different combinations according to the needs of the individual worker and his employer. This has considerable advantages in providing flexibility and giving the opportunity for easy updating of skills if an employee changes jobs or if the work available within the firm changes. Disadvantages are that the resulting pattern may appear confusing and that it may be difficult for colleges to provide suitable matching education.

There is a parallel trend for educational courses to be divided into 'units'; these do not necessarily match directly with the training modules, and indeed it is doubtful whether they should do so. Modular further education courses enable colleges to meet the needs of a wider range of students within the overall course framework and enable students to accumulate the 'credits' required for a qualification over a period of time. They can also facilitate updating of knowledge and transfer from one route to another. The trend to modules seems likely to be accelerated by the results of the Review of Vocational Qualifications, but at the same time there is increasing pressure from educationists for course integration, particularly for the under-20 age group. Schools and colleges offering courses with a modular structure are exhorted to weld the modules into a coherent whole and to emphasize the interrelationship between elements of the course.

Updating

There is a growing recognition of the need for constant updating of the workforce in all sectors of business and industry in view of changing technology. Updating courses for mature people in employment may be offered in-house or in college, and may be based on a selection of the modules available to younger students (particularly in technical subjects), on specially devised adult modules (particularly in the business and management field) or on highly specific college-devised short courses.

Short courses may also be run to cope with particular short-term needs, such as the introduction of new technology or new legislation or regulations; the examining bodies need to respond with the provision of assessments to meet these needs. A recent example in the UK has been the introduction of new Regulations for Electrical Equipment of Buildings, and the requirement for all electrical contracting employees to undertake courses and assessment on the new regulations. Many short courses are offered without assessment or certification, sometimes because they are not tied to a nationally-validated syllabus, sometimes because an examination is not offered at the time of year when the course finishes. Pitman Examinations Institute, which offers a range of secretarial and commercial examinations, has offered all its examinations 'on demand' for several years, drawing its test papers from a bank which continues to increase in size. Other award-making bodies have been slow to follow suit, but a gradual increase can now be detected in frequent and on-demand examinations. Developments in information technology described later in this chapter offer the scope for more flexible examination arrangements.

If, as seems likely, one effect of the *Review of Vocational Qualifications* is to heighten awareness of the value of formal qualifications, there will be an increased demand for certification of short courses and for certification recognizing the knowledge and skill of existing 'unqualified' workers.

In some industries, particularly where there are high risks, regular re-testing of the same skills may be required. In welding and aviation, for example, it is necessary for employees to repeat their skills tests and renew their licence to practise at regular intervals. Certificates of competence in these industries do not remain in force indefinitely because it is recognized that skills may decay if unused. There are some indications that the concept of a 'limited shelf life' may be spreading to other occupational qualifications.

Assessment of a broader range of skills

A significant trend in the assessment of vocational education and training is the increased recognition that what is currently being assessed does not cover the whole spectrum of what needs to be assessed. The attempt to improve the reliability of assessment has tended to concentrate attention on individual and low-level skills which are more easily defined and measured. For example, in the cognitive area it is now possible to make reliable assessment of candidates' recall of facts and understanding (comprehension). Although the examining bodies concerned have consistently expressed an interest in assessing candidates' ability to apply their knowledge to novel situations, only a limited proportion of assessment has in practice been devoted to application. The need to assess such skills as planning and report-writing has been recognized, but perhaps underrated in practice.

In the psychomotor domain, the purely manual skills have been reliably assessed, but there has been less emphasis on the use of these skills in practical situations and on the more advanced skills such as fault diagnosis. Almost no attention has until now been given to the need to assess attitudes ('affective domain'), largely because of the extreme difficulty of making reliable assessments of these skills and the danger that assessment will be influenced by subjective personal consideration (Goodlad, 1985). However, the inclusion of 'personal effectiveness' as one of the objectives of the revised Youth Training Scheme (Manpower Services Commission, 1985c) makes it urgently necessary at least to attempt to tackle this issue.

The concept of 'competence'

It is now increasingly recognized that assessment should cover the higher cognitive and psychomotor skills, and also the candidate's ability to combine all the necessary skills in order to carry out his job satisfactorily. This may be used as a loose definition of 'competence'. No generally agreed definition of vocational competence exists, but a convenient definition is 'minimum acceptable performance evidenced by outcome', which relates the idea of competence to the level of performance required for the particular job in question, and also to the observable and measurable skill of the candidate. 'Competence' also appears to equate to the third area of assessment required by the Review of Vocational Qualifications, assessment of the ability to use skills and to apply knowledge and understanding to the performance of relevant tasks. In addition, there are those who argue that any definition of competence must cover not only the candidate's ability to perform to a satisfactory level in his job, but also to cope with his life outside employment — the so-called 'life skills' (Further Education Unit, 1984).

The idea of 'competence' can be illustrated by listing the type of function which might be carried out by a skilled worker in a maintenance job, which could be in an engineering or process industry. The skilled worker would be expected to work largely without supervision on a given task, which might involve

- ☐ planning the work
- ☐ assembling the tools, instruments and materials required
- ☐ as part of the above, reading systems literature and drawings, making rough drawings and plans, carrying out related calculations, looking up tables and referring to statutory and other regulations
- ☐ taking appropriate safety measures, including ensuring the safety of others working in the same building
- ☐ carrying out the job
- ☐ testing that the system now works satisfactorily
- ☐ undertaking any fault-finding and repair functions
- ☐ tidying up, restoring electrical supply etc, returning tools and unused material to store

☐ reporting on work undertaken (orally or in writing), filling in any necessary work schedules or time sheets, reporting on any further work which needs to be undertaken.

The above will involve the combination of a range of cognitive and psycho-motor skills. The worker will be unable to perform satisfactorily without an understanding of the equipment or installation concerned.

The task also has an affective dimension; for example, a skilled and knowledgeable worker will be an unsatisfactory employee without an appropriate attitude to safety.

Process skills and transfer

One of the issues raised from time to time is that of transfer of skills. Because of the rapid change of technology it is generally recognized that employees are now unlikely to remain in the same job throughout their working lives. If they do remain in nominally the same occupation, their actual functions will change considerably as a result of the changes in technology, and it is therefore argued that they need a broader education and training which will enable them to adapt to change. From this is developed the argument that it is more important to teach 'process' skills such as planning and fault-finding than to teach technology, which is liable to change (Ward, 1984; Further Education Unit, 1985).

Further education can go part of the way in teaching these 'process' skills but it needs to be recognized that there is a limit to the extent to which young people can be expected to acquire transferable skills. Most young trainees need to see the immediate relevance of the education and training which they are receiving, and to be able to relate the skills they are learning to their immediate job situation. Any attempt to teach skills in the abstract will lead to a reduction in motivation. This fact is most pronounced amongst the low achievers (eg the craft and below craft streams) and in the earlier years of a further education course.

Ideas on the validity of assessments when the worker transfers to new situations have not been fully developed. A hypothesis which may prompt further discussion is that 'process skills' may be transferred, but only if the employee is also equipped with the theoretical and practical knowledge relevant to the new situation. For example, a worker who has shown ability in fault-finding in one type of equipment is likely to be capable of fault-finding in another type of equipment, but only after acquiring the necessary knowledge and experience of that type of equipment.

One of the four intended outcomes of the Youth Training Scheme is to foster in young people the ability to transfer their skills to different situations. This focuses attention on the need to teach, assess and report on skills of transfer. Although much work remains to be done in this area, and the theoretical foundation is still undeveloped, it seems clear that trainees need to be shown at the time of learning skills that these skills can be applied in different contexts. They also need an awareness of their own skill and opportunities to transfer their skill to new situations. Any reporting of their ability to transfer must relate to actual examples of the exercise of that ability and should be regarded, at best, as rather 'weak' evidence.

Core skills and work-based learning

In addition to the vocational skills which are specific to a particular occupation, it is increasingly recognized that there is a range of 'core skills' which are fundamental to success in almost any occupation. The Core Skills project, based on the Further Education Staff College (Coombe Lodge) and jointly funded by the Manpower Services Commission and the European Social Fund, has identified 103 core skills under the broad headings of number, communication, problem-solving and practical, plus a range of skills relating to the use of, and awareness of, information technology (Manpower Services Commission 1984, 1985a, 1985b). Acquisition of these skills forms one of the objectives of the two-year YTS.

In the light of awareness that formal school education has bored and alienated many of the lower achievers, much emphasis is placed on the acquisition or improvement of these skills through practical and relevant work-based projects. The Core Skills team have drawn up a range of work-based projects which can be used to foster specific core skills, supplementing the experience which young people gain from their training and work placements. There naturally follows a demand for trainees' achievements in the core skills to be measured and certificated on the basis of their employment or work-based projects. This has the advantage that it relates the core skills directly to practical applications and demonstrates that the trainees can actually use their skills in realistic situations, but it entails considerable problems of reliability. Many of the core skills are expressed in general terms and are capable of being interpreted at a number of different academic levels. Their application will depend very considerably on the ability of the trainee and the nature of his work placement, so that it will be difficult to compare the achievements of different trainees.

At the other end of the scale, dissatisfaction with the arithmetic and English skills of school learners, including some with passes in the General Certificate of Education, has prompted the setting up by the Associated Examining Board, one of the GCE boards, of a range of basic tests, covering such subjects as arithmetic, English and computer literacy. These are formal tests, using mainly multiple-choice and short-answer questions, concentrating on basic knowledge and skills which often appear to be overlooked by schools pursuing broader educational aims.

Testing of basic vocational knowledge and skills

Although the need to assess a combination of skills and abilities and their application to the working situation has been noted earlier, it is important not to lose sight of the need to assess basic vocational knowledge and skills. These may be tested more in the earlier years of the course, and are needed for the following reasons:

a. As a foundation on which the higher skills can be developed. For instance, the worker needs both practical skill and knowledge of the technology before he or she can exercise planning or fault-finding functions.

b. As terminal assessment in its own right for some categories of workers who will not progress to broader or higher skills. For example, within the motor vehicle trade some workers will be employed only on the replacement of exhaust systems or of tyres, and do not need to progress to a broader motor vehicle maintenance course.

c. As a motivating factor, to give the satisfaction of achieving some measure of recognition to young trainees who may not have achieved any degree of success in their school curriculum.

For this reason, there is an emerging trend towards assessing trainees at the end of their first year of training, which may be partly or wholly off-the-job. The next major assessment takes place at about the end of the third year, after which they should have reached the standard normally expected of a skilled worker within the industry. After that the worker may proceed to a more detailed study of a particular aspect of technology, to a study of a wider range of technical options, or to studies preparatory to a supervisory or planning role.

Increased use of professional assessment methods

Two recent developments have given additional impetus to the trend towards greater professionalism in assessment.

The New Training Initiative published by the Manpower Services Commission in December 1981 required industrial training boards and non-statutory training organizations to move towards a 'standards-based' system in which successful completion of apprenticeship would be made dependent upon attainment of the required standard rather than on time-serving. This has led to the definition of the standards required and the setting up of assessment systems in industries which have not previously had formal assessment schemes. Work is still continuing, particularly in minority occupations.

One recommendation of the *Review of Vocational Qualifications* is the accreditation of bodies offering assessment and certificates; a condition for accreditation could well be the establishment of more professional assessment and result reporting methods where needed.

Norm- and criterion-referencing

There has been continuing debate amongst educational experts about the relevant merits of norm- and criterion-referencing (Ward, 1980). There is a general assumption that criterion-referencing is 'good' and that norm-referencing is not, but this is a simplistic view which overlooks the effects of sampling. Criterion-referencing is probably best suited to practical skills which can more easily be demonstrated and which require a relatively long period of training and practice for each objective. Assessment, particularly if it is undertaken throughout the course or training period, can therefore cover all the objectives which the trainee is required to meet, and provided that the standards and conditions can be specified with sufficient accuracy, the assessment can be truly criterion-referenced.

For cognitive skills it is much more difficult to assess all the possible objectives because of the large number of facts which may be imparted during a course. Traditional examinations can only sample the knowledge to be tested, and coursework assessments, because they are undertaken in different conditions, do not necessarily test the students' retention or comprehension of facts. As far as application of knowledge is concerned, the essence of this is to assess the students' ability to apply their knowledge to a situation which is novel to them, and it is therefore impracticable to specify or to publish assessment questions for all the possible applications of their knowledge. It becomes necessary to sample their ability to apply their knowledge to a range of problems typical of those which they may experience later in their careers, and to use statistical and essentially norm-referenced measures to compare the difficulty of the assessment questions with which they have been presented with the difficulty of those set in other areas or to other groups of students. This immediately introduces an element of norm-referencing into the assessment, even though the aim of these measures is to maintain the standard of the examination. It seems almost impossible to escape from norm-referencing in an educational context.

A further complication is introduced by the fixed length of many educational courses. There is an increased emphasis in training programmes on training to a particular standard of competence, with the length of training determined by the trainee's progress rather than any predetermined ideas about course length. On reaching the required standard, each trainee can undertake the final assessment and if successful receive a certificate to indicate completion of the training programme. No equivalent to this 'standards-based' approach exists in the corresponding educational courses, which are normally of fixed length. All students attend for the same one or two years of full-time or part-time study, at the end of which there is naturally a considerable spread in the standard of their attainment.

Mutual recognition

Another issue being raised by the *Review of Vocational Qualifications* is that of mutual recognition of assessments and certification (MSC, 1985). The UK system has become a maze of overlapping qualifications, each developed to meet a perceived need, and this is particularly true where a large number of bodies are involved. At professional level there is obvious scope for rationalization and indeed some professional bodies are beginning to work together on common syllabuses and mutual recognition.

At lower levels, co-ordination is more difficult to achieve. A survey of the skills assessment procedures of some of the main sectors of British industry which I undertook in 1985 indicated that industry's current needs are for the assessment of employees in tasks which are strictly relevant to their present occupation. It was emphasized that workers doing apparently similar jobs in different industries work under different conditions, and must be assessed in conditions relevant to their industry. For example, a chainsaw operator working for the Forestry Commission will draw a chainsaw from the stores and return it for a replacement if it becomes faulty. A chainsaw operator working on a farm will be expected to do basic maintenance on the one available saw, and maintenance is therefore included in the relevant test of the National Proficiency Testing system for Agriculture. Similarly, the standards of accuracy required in different industries may vary, and adverse working conditions (eg out of doors or in hazardous environments) may affect the level of skill required. It therefore seems essential that part of the industrial assessment should be closely related to the conditions of the industry in which the worker is currently employed, even though there is a need for recognition of comparable skills between different industries.

What and how to assess

This section summarizes the different skills which need to be assessed in a vocational education and training programme, not necessarily all at the same time or all in the same way, and indicates the assessment methods most commonly used for each.

Lower-level cognitive abilities

These include recall and comprehension of facts, some degree of application of knowledge to particular situations, comprehension of drawing and other technical communications and simple calculations. Multiple-choice questions remain the most reliable and often the most valid method of assessing these abilities, but if candidate numbers do not justify their use, or if it is essential to test a student's ability to draw or to calculate, then short-answer or structured questions may be used as an alternative. Despite reliability problems, work-based projects are also being used for these skills.

Higher-level cognitive skills

These include some measure of application of knowledge to given situations, evaluation, planning, design and fault-finding. They must be related to the practical working environment in which candidates will find themselves, but they can often be assessed by some version of paper and pencil tests. Although structured examination questions may be suitable, the best assessment method is often a form of project or assignment undertaken over a period of time and requiring students to organize their work and to consult relevant sources of information. Assessment criteria may include the student's ability to plan a project, to assemble the relevant information, to perform necessary calculations or to include appropriate safety precautions.

Communication skills

Comprehension of communications can be tested reliably and adequately by means of multiple-choice questions, but if it is necessary to test the candidate's ability to communicate, whether verbally, in writing or by means of drawings, then the assessment must involve communication of this form. Usually the most appropriate method will be to conduct the assessment during the course either with reference to coursework or to a series of planned assignments or projects.

Reliable assessment of oral communication, including the use of the telephone, presents some problems but is increasingly recognized as important. There is also a growing awareness of the need for foreign language skills, with the emphasis on oral and reading skills.

Basic psychomotor skills

These skills include use of specific tools and machinery and the capability to work to specified standards and tolerances, usually in the workshop or in a favourable environment. Assessment may be undertaken either during the course or training period, or by means of more formal tests towards the end of the training period.

Psychomotor skills on site

These skills are a development of those in the previous section, but involve trainees in demonstrating their skills in a practical environment which may involve unfavourable working conditions (for example a muddy field or a hazardous environment), and may involve the use of complex machinery or plant. Occasionally it may be possible to provide simulations of large plant or equipment, but it is usually necessary to undertake assessment of this type of skill in the working environment, and the timing of the assessment may have to be determined by the prevailing conditions and the work available at the time. To take the simplest example, it is only possible to assess a candidate's operation of a combine harvester at the appropriate time of year. Some fault-finding tasks may only be capable of assessment when a suitable fault arises in the plant.

Affective skills

Candidates' attitudes can only be assessed in the working environment and over a long period of time. A trainee may well be able to answer theoretical questions about safety precautions, but it is only by observation that the assessor will be able to say whether he or she takes the precautions in practice. For 'caring' occupations there needs to be observation of the trainee's attitude to clients and empathy with them.

For all occupations, affective skills include the establishment of satisfactory working relationships with colleagues and supervisors and the display of appropriate levels of reliability, perseverance and initiative. Related considerations, sometimes grouped with these qualities under the general heading of 'personal effectiveness', include appropriate standards of dress and appearance and skills of study and career development.

Any assessment of affective skills needs to include safeguards against the possible bias of the assessor. Ideally, at least two people should be involved in the assessment.

'Competence'

In addition to separate assessments of the basic cognitive and psychomotor skills, there is a requirement for an overall assessment of 'competence' which assesses the trainee's ability to use the knowledge and skill to perform practical, work-related tasks in his working environment. Together with knowledge and skills, this is one of the three essential elements of a vocational award identified by the Review of Vocational Qualifications. Assessment of competence will almost invariably be undertaken on the job, even though it will draw on the training which may have been received off the job and the education which will have been received in a college course. Assessment may be by means of a set examination or task, or may sometimes be based on observation of the trainee's work during employment.

Evidence of experience

A number of professional organizations within the UK require evidence that applicants for membership have had a given period of relevant training and experience. In some cases there is a list of subject areas in which experience must have been obtained. This is probably an unnecessary addition to a systematic assessment of competence. If it is to be retained, it needs thorough monitoring in order to achieve validity and reliability.

Reporting and use of results

Separate grades

One of the outcomes of the critical appraisal of assessment in the 1960s and 1970s was the realization that the results of several different assessments could not meaningfully be reported by means of a single grade.

Exceptional performances on a practical assessment could not be used to mitigate poor performance in a written paper and high marks in one subject could not be used as an argument for passing a candidate who was clearly below the required standard in another. Therefore, although the rules for the award of a certificate continued to require passes in a specified range of subjects, no attempt was made to combine results on these separate subjects into a single 'grade' or 'class'. Increasingly, however, awarding bodies tended to provide more information, often by reporting a grade for each separate 'component' of the assessment.

Many organizations now allow passes in the various subjects required for a certificate to be accumulated over a period of time, although professional bodies may set a time limit during which all passes must be achieved. Other organizations require students to attempt all 'components' initially but they may be 'referred' in any which they fail, ie they do not need to retake components which they have already passed.

Demand by students, lecturers and employers for more information has led to other experiments, including printing the syllabus on the back of the certificate, but perhaps the major current development is in profiling.

Profiles

A number of awarding bodies are experimenting with this method of reporting course results. Profiles can indicate the candidates' achievements in each of a large number of skills or subject areas and can be used to indicate affective as well as psychomotor and cognitive skills. They can therefore give a much more comprehensive picture of the student's achievements than can be conveyed in a single component grade.

A profile of a student's performance, particularly in basic skills, can be of interest to a potential employer who may be more concerned with the student's competence in specific limited areas (eg can he/she use the telephone, can he/she cope with calculations relating to money?) than with a global assessment of his/her ability. During the course, profiles can have a formative function, highlighting the student's deficiencies and giving lecturer and student an opportunity to remedy them before the end of the course.

However, the provision of greater information has disadvantages if it is not both clear and reliable. Potential users need to read the profile carefully and in detail — which they may not feel they have time to do. Prospective employers also need to be aware that the profile system can be manipulated to give a false overall picture of the student, by omitting to mention subject areas failed or the higher levels of skill aimed at but not attained.

Despite their appearance of greater precision, profiles are only as valuable as the assessment strategy upon which they are based (see, for instance, Mitchell, Perfect and Boyd, 1985 and Hitchcock, 1986). If the assessment is not reliable, then the profile will be misleading. Profiles may be issued on the basis of student achievement in different subject areas on the basis of formal tests, but their use in this way may be suspect if the number of subdivisions profiled is large and the judgement on each is based on only a very small sampling of ability. For example the temptation to produce profile results based on a five-, or even ten-question section of a multiple-choice test should normally be resisted, because the subtest is too small to be reliable.

Where the profile reports are based on criterion-referenced judgements they are a more comprehensive and useful indicator of the candidate's achievements. However, it is important to ensure that the criteria are very precisely defined so that they will be interpreted in the same way by all those making the assessments and by all users. Where complex or affective skills are involved, training of lecturers or examiners may be necessary.

A further potential disadvantage of profiling is that if the profile is issued once and for all at the end of a course of education and training it will appear to have lasting validity. In fact the student's abilities may continue to develop (or indeed to decline) so that after a few years the profile will no longer be a reasonable indication of his/her skills.

Use of certification

It is clear that old ideas of certification are becoming outdated. It is no longer possible to say that the particular mix of skills and subject knowledge required by a worker in a given occupation can be summarized in a single grade and represented on a single piece of paper issued once and for all. In fact workers will need a mix of skills, and the subject areas in which they require knowledge will change as their careers develop and they transfer from one employer to another.

Paradoxically, despite the trend to more detailed information as represented by modularization and profiles, there is an increasing trend to require evidence of competence in employees by means of a joint single certificate of education, training and experience. An emerging pattern in the construction industry is the certificate of craft competence, which draws together evidence of success in the vocational education examination, evidence of success in practical skills tests and proof of relevant experience in the industry. Similar joint certification is being introduced for engineering craftsmen.

In construction, possession of the joint certificate is likely to become a condition of employment in the appropriate trade and this enormously enhances the value of the certificate. Similar recognition may follow in other industries, but is the exception rather than the rule at present.

The impact of information technology

Rapid advances in information technology enable award-making bodies to streamline their record-keeping and results processing. With increasing modularization of education and training courses, record-keeping becomes more important.

A more significant impact of information technology, however, is in the opportunity it offers for individualized and self-paced learning and assessment. Already a joint scheme entitled 'Inside Information' has been produced by the City and Guilds of London Institute and the British Broadcasting Corporation (described in Twining, 1986). The total package includes BBC radio programmes about information technology, audio cassettes which hold an edited version of the broadcasts, computer software which gives the user introductory 'hands-on' experience, a book, and a City and Guilds assessment. Additional material for tutors is being produced. The novel feature of the City and Guilds assessment is that the bank of multiple-choice questions is held on a microcomputer floppy disc which is issued to registered examination centres. Whenever one or more candidates are ready to take the test the centre arranges for each to have the use of a microcomputer, provides a room and sufficient invigilation to safeguard the security of the questions. The test is taken at the keyboard. The programme presents the candidates with 24 questions selected randomly from the bank held on the disc. The candidates may go back to earlier questions to check or revise their answers. When they indicate that they have finished (there is no time limit) the computer marks the answers and reports the result and any areas of weakness on a printout for each candidate. The centre applies for certificates for successful candidates. Information about each candidate's answers are recorded on the floppy disc which can be recalled by City and Guilds to enable the performance of the questions to be analysed.

The total 'Inside Information' package is significant because of its assessment methodology, its individualization of assessment and its integration of learning material and assessment. It could well herald significant advances in several directions. Indeed, a whole range of new developments, and even concepts of assessment, are likely to depend on information technology.

References

Further Education Unit (FEU) (1984) *Towards a Competence-Based System: An FEU View* FEU: London
Further Education Unit (FEU) (1985) *Core Competencies in Engineering* FEU: London
Goodlad, S ed (1985) *Studies in Higher Education* **10** 2 Carfax Publishing Co: Abingdon
Hitchcock, G (1986) *Profiles and Profiling* Longman: Harlow
Hudson, B ed (1973) *Assessment Techniques, an Introduction* Methuen: London
Lang, J (1978) *City and Guilds of London Institute Centenary 1878-1978: An Historical Commentary* City and Guilds of London Institute: London
Macintosh, H G (1974) *Techniques and Problems of Assessment: a Practical Handbook for Teachers* Edward Arnold: London
Mager, R F (1984) *Preparing Instructional Objectives* Pitman Learning Inc: Belmont, CA

Manpower Services Commission (MSC) (1984) *Core Skills in YTS Part I: YTS Manual* MSC: Sheffield

Manpower Services Commission (MSC) (1985a) *Core Skills in YTS Part II: Computer and Information Technology: YTS Manual* MSC: Sheffield

Manpower Services Commission (MSC) (1985b) *Work-Based Projects in YTS: YTS Manual* MSC: Sheffield

Manpower Services Commission (MSC) (1985c) *The Development of the Youth Training Scheme: Report, July 1985* MSC: Sheffield

Manpower Services Commission (MSC) (1986) *Review of Vocational Qualifications in England and Wales* Joint Manpower Services Commission/Department of Education and Science Working Group Report HMSO: London

Ministry of Education (1961) *Better Opportunities in Technical Education* Cmnd 1254 HMSO: London

Mitchell, A, Perfect, H and Boyd, J (1985) Scope for profiling: computer support for teachers in developing profiled reports *Programmed Learning & Educational Technology* **22**: 4

Nuttall, D S and Wilmott, A S (1972) *British Examinations: Techniques of Analysis* NFER: Slough

Secondary Examinations Council (SEC) (1984) *Annual Report 1983-4* SEC: London

Secondary Examinations Council (SEC) (1985) *The Development of Grade Criteria for the GCSE* SEC: London

Thyne, J (1974) *Principles of Examining* University of London Press: London

Twining, J (1986) Inside information: a door to the future? *International Review of Education* **32** 3: 295-311

Ward, C (1980) *Designing a Scheme of Assessment* Stanley Thornes (Publishers) Ltd: Cheltenham

Ward, C (1981a) *Preparing and Using Constructed Answer Questions* Stanley Thornes (Publishers) Ltd: Cheltenham

Ward, C (1981b) *Preparing and Using Objective Questions* Stanley Thornes (Publishers) Ltd: Cheltenham

Ward, C (1984) Hargreaves — a progress report *EDUCA* **42**: 14-16

20. A learning society: Japan through Australian eyes*

Bill Ford

Summary: The international economic success of Japan challenges much of the conventional wisdom of skills formation and work organization held by unions, management, governments and educators in Australia. Japan is a 'learning society' in which the financial, technical, human and organizational capital are not developed in isolation from one another. Management education, for example, is predominantly integrated into Japanese organizations' general skill formation programmes. The Japanese have achieved an adaptable and innovative workforce because they have adopted a wider sharing of formal and informal opportunities for learning at the workplace.

By contrast, in Australia there is a general belief among corporate executives that technical and managerial education is a public responsibility. The nineteenth-century class concepts of unskilled, semi-skilled and skilled employees tend to mask the importance of making all workers skilled, while the rigid division of workers into operation and maintenance is another handicap to skill formation and the organization of learning. Australian organizations seldom provide incentives for process workers to update, upgrade or broaden their skills. This is true both of management and of many traditional craft unions. The 1985 Kirby Report contained 86 recommendations which could break the mould of the past and help overcome the cultural barriers to make Australia a learning society. Unfortunately, most of the early follow-up has concentrated on youth traineeships and not on the need for lifelong learning. Yet Australia is a multi-cultural society with a potential to follow examples from anywhere in the world.

Introduction

In the post-World War II period, Japan has developed a remarkably adaptive, innovative and productive economy. I suggest that all those who still believe that the Japanese are only copiers and cannot innovate look more closely at what has happened to the Swiss watch industry or the American car and electronics industries or the Australian steel industry. All of these were once leaders in their field. Now they are learning from

*Note This chapter is an edited combination of parts of two papers by Professor Ford. These are Learning from Japan: The Concept of Skill Formation: paper given at the International Conference on Employment and Training, held at Perth, Western Australia, September 1985; and Japan as a learning society: Work and People 9 (1).

Japanese innovation in production processes and products. However, the central theme of this chapter is the necessity to learn also about the *Japanese concepts of skill formation and work organization.*

If Australia is to learn from Japan, then it is necessary to clearly understand that Japan is first and foremost *a long-term learning society.* Most of us are familiar with the high levels of participation in formal education in Japan. What is less well known is the commitment of Japanese organizations (management and unions) to continual skill formation and innovation at all levels of the organization, and the importance of this to the so-called 'Japanese economic miracle'.

Barriers to understanding skill formation in Japan

Very few Western observers have shown any interest in, let alone studied, the nature and significance of enterprise-level skill formation in Japan. Why is this? I suggest it is because what people see often depends on what they want to see or what they have been conditioned to see. To illustrate this, I propose to look briefly at some of the preconceptions and visions that six influential Western interest groups take to and from Japan. The six groups are Western critics of Japanese employment systems, Western economists, Western technologists, Western managers, Western management consultants and Western vocational educators.

1. *Western critics* of Japanese employment systems, from both the left and the right of the ideological spectrum, tend to concentrate their vision on employment discrimination against women, part-time, temporary and minority group employees; or on the pressure put by large and powerful organizations on their smaller suppliers; or on plant unions which ignore the interests of non-unionized employees. Critics also note that the predominant view of Japanese employment systems relates only to full-time career employees in large organizations. All of this criticism is basically correct. But Western critics of Japan often ignore the fact that many of the above criticisms are also appropriate for their own countries. Certainly, after 40 years of working and researching in Australian industry, I believe that we cannot be proud of some of the conditions and practices that still exist in employment in Australia.

2. *Western economists'* perceptions of Japan are often influenced by their assumptions about the supposed virtues of free-flowing external labour markets. But major Japanese organizations are more concerned with the innovative use of internal labour markets for the development and utilization of their human resources. In economic terms, they are concerned to develop and retain their investment in human capital. They do not rely on uncontrollable markets to meet their skill needs.

As part of my Japanese research, I studied the establishment of two new plants. A noticeable feature was that the establishment planning did not require the recruitment of skilled people from other organizations. The physical and human resources of each plant were seen in terms of an

integrated development process. The Japanese manager responsible did
not rely on other people to provide him with an appropriately skilled
workforce.

In Japanese organizations, the financial, technical, human and organizational capital are *not* developed in isolation from one another. This was
emphasized on a national scale during the first and second oil crises, when
Japanese enterprises shifted their financial and their human resources in
tandem into new projects and industries. For instance, I asked one chief
executive why a new fabrication plant was being located in the same area
where his company was dismantling a relatively new smelting plant. He
answered immediately in terms of the location of the company's committed and skilled workforce. He emphasized their importance in terms of
organizational capital. Unfortunately, in Australia, many large organizations concentrate on the financial and technical aspects of new projects
and expect the labour market to solve their skills needs. (A notable exception to this is Lend Lease Corporation.) In boom periods, this results in
volatile labour markets characterized by high turnover and industrial
conflict.

3. *Western technologists'* visions of Japan are often focused on masses
of robots, automated systems of production and more recently on office
automation. Our mesmerized engineers tell stories of how these technologies work the night shift without lights or people, how they do not
take leave and how they result in large savings in energy and wages. We
rarely, if ever, read of the innovative skill formation processes and work
organization systems that encourage the development, utilization and
maintenance of these new technologies. We hear even less of the 'down-
time' in these technologies when they are transferred to Western organizations which have not developed appropriate skill levels and mixes and
work organizations to match their new technologies. We never hear how
some Japanese organizations have developed policies and practices to
ensure that the introduction of new technology does not endanger their
traditional systems of individual and organizational learning.

4. *Western managers'* visions of Japan are often focused on what they
see as a highly disciplined workforce and compliant or co-operative
enterprise unions. They rarely attempt to understand the basis for this
co-operation and commitment, part of which relates to both management
and union concern for the development of an adaptable, multi-skilled and
innovative workforce. The formal and informal learning opportunities and
processes that are available to management in Western organizations tend
to be more widely distributed throughout Japanese organizations. I have
found more real egalitarianism in learning opportunities in Japanese
organizations than I have experienced in Australian organizations. The
establishment of a second elite national school of business administration
in Australia is in sharp contrast to Japan, where management education is
predominantly integrated into an organization's general skill formation
programme.

5. *Western management consultants* (academic and commercial — these

are often indistinguishable) tend to concentrate their visions of Japan on what they believe will be easily marketable practices in their own country. Their orientation is towards finding a new management tool which will sustain rather than challenge the role of management in Western organizations. They rarely try to challenge their Western clients with the need to innovate in terms of the complex interrelations between new technologies, skills, skill formation, work organization, organizational participation and learning. The Japanese concern for an adaptable and innovative workforce means a wider sharing of formal and informal opportunities for learning at the workplace.

6. *Western vocational educators'* visions of Japan have been concentrated on the formal public systems of training. This is understandable, as such people have been conditioned to look at concepts such as teaching, training, curriculum, and so on. The Japanese government also provide excellent publications setting out the structure of the formal public vocational training systems, and Japanese public institutions welcome international visitors. But the public vocational training system is not the key to understanding the *innovation in skill formation in Japan.* It is in the large enterprises and their affiliates that the innovations in informal and formal learning occur. Unfortunately, it is becoming increasingly difficult for Western observers to develop an understanding of these innovations. As one senior Japanese executive from a large electronic group once said to me, 'We now understand that the way we develop and organize our workforce is our competitive advantage over Western organizations, so from now on that is the top corporate secret'.

The Japanese have developed what I call 'catwalk' tours of Japanese production establishments. That is, Western observers are taken on tours that allow them to observe the production processes from above. They can look down on the innovative technologies but they are rarely encouraged to focus on the innovative interrelationships between the development of new technology, skills, work organization and organizational participation. To understand these concepts it is necessary, for example, to be able to see and discuss multi-skilling charts, job rotation processes, group project material (in crib rooms and on walls), small group activities and other participative practices. These are not understandable if one is restricted to the formal training systems and the catwalks.

Unfortunately, with the rare exception of people like Professors Kazuo Koike and Kazutoshi Koshiro, Japanese scholars have not developed an interest in detailed plant-level observations. Much of Japanese scholarly analysis does not go beyond the large-scale survey of human resource policies. It is interesting to note that Professor Koike and his colleagues are now involved in long-term detailed plant-level studies of the transfer of Japanese skill formation process to Malaysia and Thailand. I know of no other similar research project being carried out by Western scholars. Australian research on the transfer of knowledge in the Asian pacific region concentrates on surveying graduates of Australian formal education systems who have returned home. This example of different perspectives illustrates that it is important to understand that the individuals' views of indigenous or other cultures is influenced by education, experience, interest and values; by whether the reference group is managers, men, women or minorities, and so on, and by their access to information and observation at different levels of organizational life. In discussing another culture, it is particularly important for people firstly to try to make the factors that influence their perspective explicit and secondly to state clearly the focus of their analysis.

A different Australian perspective

My perspective on employment is strongly influenced by my experiences as an early school leaver, who spent many years as a low-skilled worker employed by different organizations in a variety of industries in Australia. My concern as a scholar has been primarily to understand cross-cultural differences in employment at the level of production. My value orientation has been towards improving the employment opportunities and quality of working life for people in industrial organizations. It is these experiences, interests, values and reference groups that have influenced my perspective and research on Japanese employment and employee relations.

The focus of my research on employment in industrial organizations in Japan and Australia has been on understanding the development and organization of human resources and the implications for technological change, organizational participation and learning. My research, like that of most other scholars in Japan and elsewhere, has been restricted to large organizations.

I believe that Japan's favourable terms of trade and balance of payments with other advanced technological nations of Europe and North America is now determined primarily by her favourable *balance of skills* (Ford, 1982). A highly skilled and participative workforce now gives Japan a 'natural advantage' over her competitors.

A general concern for continual skill formation and development at all levels of an organization clearly differentiates major Japanese and Australian organizations. An understanding of these differences is fundamental to understanding the differences in technological change, employment, skills, work organization, organization participation, organizational learning, industrial relations and innovation in the two countries.

Australia has prospered by the exploitation of readily available physical resources. In comparison to Australia, however, Japan's physical resources are minute. *Japan has prospered by the development and participation of a highly educated, skilled, adaptable, flexible and innovative workforce.* This, I believe, is central to understanding the difference in each nation's ability to sustain comparatively orderly technological, employment, and industrial change in the face of turbulent and discontinuous multidimensional changes in the world's economies.

Plant-level skill formation in Japan

To understand the concept of 'skill formation' it is necessary to realize first that it is *not* the Japanese equivalent, interpretation or translation of the Western concepts of 'vocational training' or 'skills training' or 'technical education'. The Japanese concept of skill formation embraces the ideas of education, training, experience and personal development. It is a holistic concept that does not fragment human development in terms of the vested interests of traditional institutions. It is based on a realization that adaptive and innovative productive organizations cannot rely on fragmented policies or practices which do not integrate the processes of technological change, skill formation, work organization and organizational participation. The outcome of this integration is that the development of new technologies in Japan is often related to a firm's work organization and skills. However, a failure to realize these new interrelationships has led to increasing problems of technology down-time in Australian industry. Again, the importation of good technology is not good enough.

In the Japanese organizations that I have studied, there is considerable variation in their skill formation policies and practices. There is certainly no one Japanese model. For example, they often differ considerably in their emphasis or mix of *off-the-job formal training* and *on-the-job learning*. Notice I use the concept of 'on-the-job learning', rather than the traditional Western concept of 'on-the-job training'. I believe Japanese skill formation processes are best understood in terms of broad-based processes of learning, rather than the more narrow didactic concept of 'training'.

In addition to the wide variety of on-the-job learning practices, some large Japanese organizations maintain major formal educational establishments. For instance, Mitsubishi Heavy Industries has five technical institutes which are continually developing people to sustain the corporation's comparative advantage. Similarly, Hitachi has three technical institutes to support its recurrent learning systems. Members of the Hitachi workforce have a wide range of opportunities to develop formally, update, upgrade and expand their skills. For example, production workers who have graduated from high school and who have a minimum of two years' work experience, may be given the opportunity to undertake a 15-month full-time intensive engineering training course. While I was visiting one of these institutes I was told of a 35-year-old worker who had been selected to participate in such a course. Although these organizational qualifications are not officially recognized by tertiary education institutions, arrangements have been made for graduates of an Hitachi Institute to audit graduate work at some universities.

Such enterprise establishments are not isolated educational or training institutions staffed by permanent teachers. Learning, like research and development, is not seen as a discrete function in Japanese organizations but as part of an integrated human and organizational development plan. Such learning systems are one of the important reasons for the lifetime commitment of people to large organizations in Japan.

It is rare for large organizations in Australia to develop their own skill centres. There is a general belief among corporate executives that technical and managerial education at all levels is a public responsibility. Unfortunately, this tends to isolate formal tertiary education from organizational life. It also means that many large organizations contribute little, if anything, to the development of formal learning in Australia. This has added to the perennial skill shortage in Australia and the reliance on immigration to meet recurring skills shortages. In recent years, this situation has worsened with the rapid changes in technology and the availability of international air travel. Some organizations in Australia (private and public) now rely on skilled people to be flown in on a regular or ad hoc basis to provide essential maintenance on imported high technology. Consequently, Australia is an increasingly vulnerable technological society (Ford, 1984).

However, it is the *innovations in on-the-job learning* which provide the greatest challenge to Australia's ability to learn from Japan. We must first go through a process of systematic unlearning to rid ourselves of many outmoded forms of classification and work organization.

It is still popular in Australia to classify employees by using the nineteenth-century class concepts of unskilled, semi-skilled and skilled. Consequently, there is little concern in Australia for the skill formation of the majority of people classed as unskilled or semi-skilled.

For comparative purposes, some writers classify the Japanese industrial workforce in terms of unskilled, semi-skilled and skilled. However, my plant-level studies of Japanese organizations in Japan and Australia indicate that such classification does not reflect the view within Japanese organizations. Japanese managers whom I have interviewed regard workers as skilled or *under*skilled. That is, there is a clear recognition that all workers need to develop skills and that it is the responsibility of managers, section heads, foremen and subforemen to see that there are no underskilled workers in their area of responsibility.

The rigid division of workers into operation and maintenance in Australia handicaps skill formation and organization of learning further. This dichotomy has been institutionalized by long-standing industrial relations custom and practice. Such divisions are being increasingly blurred in advanced technology organizations in Japan and Germany.

The tendency in Australia to see skills predominantly in terms of traditional trades has meant that the skill needs of the majority of Australian workers tend to be ignored. This is perhaps best seen in the 'underskilling' of process operators in Australia. A high technology society involves sophisticated processing of material, products and information. Employees involved in process work often need conceptual skills to understand the process to avoid major losses, technical skills to make adjustments to the technology and managerial skills to co-ordinate the process with other aspects of the organization's activities. A skilled process worker can contribute to the improvement of the process and the product. In one modern steel plant I visited in Japan, they were recruiting their new operator trainees from the general education stream of high school graduates, while their new maintenance trainees came from the lower vocational stream — what will happen when this plant's technology is transferred to Australia?

Skilled process workers in factories and offices can significantly reduce the down-time on new process technologies. This can be illustrated with reference to the productivity of a particular process technology in plants in Japan, Australia and the United States. In an interview, the production manager of a plant in Northern Japan explained that the operation ran at 98.5 per cent of capacity. This compared most favourably with the 80 per cent capacity achieved in an identical plant that he had worked at in the US and one that he had visited in Australia. He was very emphatic that the difference could be attributed to the higher skills of the Japanese process workers. To illustrate this difference, he highlighted how Japanese workers were skilled at cleaning their equipment. He emphasized that such skills were not respected in non-Japanese plants and therefore ignored.

The failure to understand the need for broadly skilled process workers in Australia is highlighted by the narrow skilling and work organization of people operating word processing equipment. By contrast, one large Japanese insurance organization, before introducing office automation, set down a rule that no one worked at a keyboard for more than three hours a day. They did not want the new technology to narrow the learning of their staff.

The different assumptions underlying the concept of 'job rotation' in Australia and Japan also highlight different approaches to work organization and skill formation. In Australia, 'job rotation' developed as a personnel management gimmick to offset problems of boredom and monotony, employees being rotated between boring and monotonous jobs in the belief that this would somehow relieve the boredom and monotony. In Japan, job rotation is primarily a method of multi-skilling an organization's workforce and thus increasing individual and organizational adaptability, flexibility, innovation and participation.

Similarly, concepts such as the 'over-educated worker' ignore the different opportunities people have to contribute and to learn in Australian and Japanese organizations. This can be seen in the different approaches to research and development (R&D). In Australia, R&D tends to be the province of narrow groups of specialists in universities and government and industry research laboratories. This isolation of R&D from the production processes and workforces limits the opportunity for skill formation and broader participation in industrial organizations. In Japan, a considerable amount of R&D is done at the place of production. People are encouraged to contribute at all levels of the organization to improving production processes. Regular, incremental and participative change is an important characteristic of individual and organizational learning in Japan. Consequently, Australian and Japanese industrial employees with similar levels of formal education have different opportunities to be involved in stimulating organizational activity and continual learning.

Rewarding continuous skill formation

Unlike Japan, key industrial workers in large organizations in Australia generally do not have career-based employment, learning and reward systems. Employment systems in Australia rarely reward on-the-job learning or provide incentives for large groups of process workers and tradespeople to update, upgrade or broaden their skills. The discriminatory division of employees into wages (paid hourly or weekly) and staff (paid fortnightly or monthly) is a major barrier to skill formation in Australia. In general, wages employees are not rewarded in either income or security for their on-the-job learning. However, it is not unusual for staff employees (public and private) to have their on-the-job learning rewarded by upgrading.

It is interesting to note that state and national governments in Australia have been developing equal employment opportunity policies to reduce discrimination in terms of sex, age, ethnicity, religion and disablement. However, they have ignored the class division of employees into wages and staff. Yet this archaic classification, inherited from Britain, discriminates against equal employment opportunity for large numbers of industrial employees. The emerging concept of 'equal worth' might one day be applied to reward the on-the-job learning of all employees.

Also, by not generally recognizing experiential learning, traditional craft union wages policies in Australia do not provide income incentive for individuals to update, upgrade or broaden the qualifications gained through their apprenticeship. An important exception to this is the Electrical Trades Union (ETU) policy of developing award classifications which recognize the use of 'additional knowledge'.

Demarcation as a barrier to learning

In Japan, the development of plant unions, lifetime employment and wage systems which recognize continual skill formation and seniority have meant that demarcation issues have not been a significant area of industrial conflict. In Australia however multi-union plants, the lack of employment security and tradition-based work organizations and wage relativities have meant constant demarcation and jurisdictional disputes. Such disputes provide major barriers to on-the-job learning. In the short run, demarcation disputes may be merely irritating and disruptive. However, in the long run, they may confine people to such narrow groups of skills that they will become more vulnerable to technological, economic, social and industrial change.

Technological change in Japan

The relatively smooth adoption and development of technology in Japan provides a good example of Japan as a learning society. We often hear people ask such questions as 'How has Japan sustained rapid technological change without social and organizational disruptions?' But of course Japan has not avoided social disruptions. The extremely violent history of Tokyo's Narita International Airport is an ever present reminder that the Japanese have also made very costly mistakes in their attempts to push the pace of change.

However, it is true that the questions about the human aspects of technological change which concern people in the West, such as redundancy and deskilling, are rarely issues of broad concern, let alone dispute, in Japan. Why?

To understand why this is so, it is necessary to understand initially the historic Japanese concern for the process of transition. This can be seen when one observes the care, effort and time taken to move a shrub from one part of a garden to another. In contrast, many Western managers tend to focus on the end product rather than the process of achieving the end product. This is clearly seen in the Japanese/American competition, from cars to semiconductors.

National goals

The development or purchase of new technology in Japan is normally based on a long-term view of the needs of the nation or organization and relies heavily on appropriate learning systems. At the national level, this is clearly evident in the document published in 1980 by the Ministry of International Trade and Industry (MITI), *The Vision of MITI Policies in the 1980s*. Among the stated new national goals are:

☐ economic security through technological innovation and
☐ maintaining the vitality of society along with an improved quality and comfort of life.

The following quote from the document shows that Japanese bureaucrats understand the ability to achieve these goals is dependent on key social and institutional traditions:

'Japan's unique problem-solving capability is supported by the industriousness of its people, the high standard of education, the narrow income differentials and the relatively stable labor-management relations. Therefore we belive that these long-term national goals, encompassing the 1980s and beyond, are attainable with the people's efforts.'

Note that the critical emphasis is on human resources and human arrangements, rather than narrow reliance on physical resources or technology to solve national problems.

Knowledge and skills

In the development of new technology in Japan, particularly process technology, a wide range of the available knowledge and skills is utilized.

For example, it is not unusual for process workers to be seconded to a design group who are working on a new assembly or process line. Similarly, line workers will be involved in the installation of new equipment. These are part of the organizations' learning and development systems. (Given such utilization of non-research specialists, it is probable that the level of research and development expenditure in Japan has been seriously underestimated, particularly by non-Japanese scholars.)

In the introduction of technology, Japanese organizations give priority to developing appropriate skills and preserving employment security. Deskilling often takes place in Western organizations because workers have not been given an adequate opportunity to expand and develop their skills. In one steel mill in Japan, all the production workforce were trained to the next level of technology before it was installed, and therefore showed no concern about the introduction of the new technology.

The security of employment issue is one which is central to the policies of plant unions. The fiercest industrial disputes in Japan are often related to employment security. The violence which occurred during the closure of Japanese coal mines in the early 1960s is still a vivid reminder to Japanese management and unions that they must strive to achieve continuity of employment.

Action for Australia

I was a member of the Committee of Inquiry into Labour Market Programs which in early 1985 produced the Kirby Report. This contained 86 recommendations, many of them aimed at making major changes in Australian vocational education and training. Taken together, these could yet break the mould of the past and help overcome the cultural barriers to make Australia also a learning society (Committee of Inquiry into Labour Market Programs, 1985).

Unfortunately, the early government follow-up of the Kirby Report concentrated on the proposals for youth traineeships which, although the centrepiece of the report, were contained in only one of the 12 chapters and five of the 86 recommendations. A cultural breakthrough in skill formation needs a more thorough-going acceptance of the other recommendations, including those on

☐ industrial democracy and participation
☐ further training and retraining for adults
☐ research into skills formation
☐ the privatization of knowledge.

The last concept is sufficiently new internationally to be worth expanding.

During the course of the Kirby Committee Inquiry, we were continually made aware that a considerable amount of knowledge, particularly in the technical areas, was no longer a part of the public domain in Australia. That is, the knowledge being developed within large private organizations was seen as part of their capital and therefore often not available to public educational institutions. Thus public programmes for skill formation now have only limited access to new technologies and skills. This privatization of knowledge increases the dependency and vulnerability of small economies such as that of Australia. In this respect, Australia could well learn from Singapore, where negotiations with overseas organizations have led to the establishment of a number of public skill formation centres. These new centres have negotiated access to private education technologies and materials.

An issue related to the privatization of knowledge is the multicultural origin of much of the new technology that comes into Australia. I take up this issue at some length in a commissioned paper (Ford, 1986) which I have prepared as one of the supporting documents for the Australian government's discussion paper on industrial democracy. The paper deals with the need to understand the multicultural origin of new technologies that are being transferred into Australia, and the implications of culturally specific technologies for skills, skill formation, work organization, organizational participation and workplace innovation.

Conclusion

Japan has rapidly incorporated new knowledge, new technologies and new industries within its unique culture. By doing so it has challenged much of the conventional wisdom of skills formation and work organization held by unions, managements, governments and educators in Australia. Unfortunately, many people mistakenly believe they can avoid the challenge by claiming Japan is a vastly different culture. That claim is, of course, very true. But it did not stop the Japanese from systematically learning from what were for them, equally vastly different cultures. Is multicultural Australia in reality more ethnocentric than Japan?

References

Committee of Inquiry into Labour Market Programs (1985) *Report of the Committee of Inquiry into Labour Market Programs* (The Kirby Report) Australian Government Publishing Service: Canberra

Eastwood, J et al eds (1984) *Labour Essays* Drummond: Melbourne

Ford, G W (1982) Human resources development and the balance of skills *Journal of Industrial Relations*, September 1982: 443—53

Ford, G W (1984) Australia at risk: an underskilled and vulnerable society *in* Eastwood (1984)

Ford, G W (1986) The transfer of culturally-specific industrial technology to Australia *in* Ford and Tilley (1986)

Ford, G W and Tilley, L eds (1986) *Diversity, Change and Tradition: The Environment for Industrial Democracy in Australia* Australian Government Publishing Service: Canberra

21. Information technology: its impact on work, education and training

Harry Knutton

Summary: This chapter looks at the ways in which the subjects of communications, computing and microelectronics are developing and producing an expanding global resource. This is already having an effect on many human activities comparable with the eighteenth-century industrial revolution. The new technologies involved with it offer enormous savings in cost and improvements in performance over conventional methods. The versatility and power of the devices associated with information technology are enabling some representation of human intelligence to be incorporated in them with increasing rapidity, thus permitting the control of events in a quasi-human way. The data handling capacity of future computing and communication systems is becoming both massive and flexible. Such advances are bound to have a profound effect on our social and economic environment; these are examined in order to try to predict the nature of work at the beginning of the 21st century, and the ways in which human society might adapt to it. This leads to an identification of the ways in which the vocational education and training services should respond to meet individual and community needs.

Introduction

When Marconi established wireless telegraphic communication across the Atlantic at the beginning of the 20th century, it was said that 'he turned the world into a village'. This did not mean, as even a present-day villager will testify, that a state of perfect universal intercommunication was about to exist. Nevertheless it was a major technological advance, to be supplemented later by voice and television links forming a worldwide network of receiving and transmitting stations in every country, together with countless mobile versions throughout land, air, sea and space.

Mankind's earliest number scripts, whether for counting sheep or recording the positions of stars, bear the impress of our ten fingers. For centuries, people have used analogue devices of various kinds for computation, including the abacus and successive machines using gears, cams and clutches such as mechanical cash registers. However, computing as we know it today started with the introduction of digital methods of representation using binary arithmetic, when 40 years ago the first programmable electronic computer, based on thermionic valves, was put into operation. The advent of the transistor soon afterwards led to smaller machines with increased capabilities and enormously reduced cost. Then the ability to incorporate a number of transistors into an integrated circuit within a chip of material based on silicon led to the introduction of the microcomputer, now used by millions throughout the world.

The rapid development in both communication and computing technology stems from the rapid advances in electronics over this period. These have led to the creation of a wide variety of relatively cheap techniques for processing and storing data and transferring it elsewhere through various input and output devices. Electronic devices now challenge the paper-based methods of data storage and transfer used for centuries by scholars, couriers, commerce, governments and the general public.

This convergence of interest between electronics, computing and communications is now denoted by the phrase 'information technology'. Information is a marketable commodity; it can be sold to others, and its possession can enhance the authority of its holder. The saying 'knowledge is power' was attributed to the Chinese over 2,000 years ago. The ability to gather, record, organize, analyse, transfer and exploit information has grown in importance over the years. The recent enormous advances in technology seem likely to make this ability a dominant factor in the future development of human society. Consequently it is bound to have a significant effect on future patterns of work and on vocational education and training.

The information revolution

The development of information technology may be compared with the development of mechanical power in the industrial revolution of the 18th century. The steam engine enabled man to pump water, mine coal extensively, provide rotary power, make artefacts in large numbers and generate electricity, resulting in an enormous increase in productivity. This brought wealth and power to some but social disruption and unwelcome employment changes to many others. The adverse effects were not due to the technology itself but to the inability of the economic and social systems of the day to react quickly and fairly to them. In seeking to determine the effect of burgeoning information technology on future work, and hence on vocational education and training, we must therefore consider economic and social factors as well as technological developments.

Some economists explain the large-scale changes which have taken place in society over the last two centuries in terms of cycles lasting 50-60 years, called Kondratiev long waves. The first of these is said to have started about 1780 with the advent of the steam engine; the second coincided with the building of railroads, and the third cycle was linked to the introduction of electric power and the automobile, lasting until the Second World War. Each wave can be divided into two stages; the first is when the new technology attracts investment and provides big profits for those exploiting it. This is followed by a second phase when the benefits of new technology are disseminated through the economy, producing greater competition and increasingly affecting markets and jobs; individuals and industries have to change their methods and products radically, and economic depressions may result, like those of the 1930s, 1870s and 1820s. Since the mid-1950s most advanced countries have participated in what could be regarded as a fourth Kondratiev wave, associated with the development of microelectronics and information technology. Superimposed on this broad description of events are changes brought about by wars, famines and political decisions affecting the free movement of goods, services and information. Let me look in turn at the main factors of technology, society and economics.

Technology

Microelectronics is arguably the most powerful tool yet developed by mankind. Complex devices can be mass-produced with negligible consumption of the world's limited resources. Computer hardware has in the last 40 years moved from mechanical components to very large-scale integration of circuits with the equivalent of hundreds of thousands of components mounted on a single silicon chip having a maximum dimension of less than one centimetre and costing less than £1. The effect has been to improve the cost/performance ratio of such equipment by a factor of over 100 million times in this period, and to make computers much more usable. The price of complete data processing systems has been dropping by 30 per cent per year for over a decade, and this trend is continuing.

Compared with hardware, the cost of current software is inordinately high. This is a potential brake on progress and is likely to be removed by developing a greater degree of operability between different hardware systems as a result of incorporating a compatible range of general purpose programs or other matching devices. Furthermore such devices will offer greater enhancement by enabling information to be transferred in and out of a computer system not just as alphanumeric data through manually operated keyboards but also by voice and graphics.

Current computers handle data by following the rules of arithmetic in sequential stages. The next major step, dubbed 'the fifth generation' will almost certainly allow complex problems to be tackled rapidly in parallel and enable information to be processed by logical inference or heuristic (trial-and-error) methods. Such systems can be made to embody some of the knowledge of an expert as well as the relevant and necessary facts together with the required processing programs. Such a network of associations, intuitions, inferences and data will allow an intelligent decision to be made by the computer itself, rather than the human expert. The knowledge base in these systems will be capable of interpreting the data presented to it and processing the appropriate conclusions in situations within its scope. The results of such actions can also be used to augment the knowledge base itself, so that in effect it will 'learn' from experience.

The software for such expert systems is quite different from traditional languages such as Fortran or Cobol, which have a highly developed syntax but make little or no use of semantics. In future, we will use languages such as Prolog which permit the development of rule-based relationships and networks, based on possibilities and inferences.

Greater use is being made of the higher frequencies of the electromagnetic spectrum. Optical fibres are replacing copper cable in many communication links, and offer big improvements in cost and capacity, as well as reducing the demand for copper. The use of lasers and infra-red devices as sensors for checking movements of all kinds and for monitoring inventories is reducing the human effort previously needed for such activities. The introduction of robots will replace many repetitive human activities, will enable fewer people to control more machines and will allow people to carry out operations in hazardous environments. These devices can also speed up the process of design and control the efficient integration of manufacturing or servicing operations.

The combination of computers and telecommunications enables business to be conducted between individuals and organizations without direct human involvement or traditional paper methods. This results from the growing number of so-called 'value-added networks' offering facilities for home banking, ticket purchasing, facsimile, stock control, traffic-flow monitoring and so on.

Looking ahead another 20 years, it may well be that the current pace of information technology development will slow down as computer and communication suppliers try to maintain revenues from their current products with only second-order improvements to existing systems. Even if the wider application of existing technology is all that investment restraints and social forces will permit, it is inescapable that there will be improvements in the accuracy, reliability, cost, flexibility and ease of operation of the information technology systems which have already entered public, industrial, commercial and domestic domains. These systems will increasingly control most human activities.

Indeed the advantages offered by information technology are likely to result in increased competition for their application.

Society

Most modern countries have now experienced a decline in labour-intensive work. In the last decade, unemployment in some industrial areas has increased sixfold; this is perhaps a manifestation of the second phase or downwave of the fourth Kondratiev cycle. It can be compared with the massive shift in agricultural employment in an earlier cycle as workers moved to manufacturing and mining industries in towns. In recent years, as manufacturing productivity has improved, there has been a steady shift in employment from many traditional occupations to the service industries.

We can already see that information technology has the capability to permeate almost all spheres of industrial and domestic activity, to control resources more efficiently, to replace many human actions and hence to exert a powerful influence on the economics of all related operations. As more applications of information technology are introduced, there will be the facility for more people to work from home at flexible times, giving them greater leisure time. The need for factories, office blocks and large public transport systems may, therefore, diminish. Hence the basic character of the traditional working life for the last hundred years could be changed, with a substantial reduction in the time spent travelling to, from or at work, or in the number of those required to work in urban areas. It may be anticipated that some people may attempt to resist such developments and hence put a brake on technical progress. However, many communities may take up such new possibilities with enthusiasm and achieve a comparatively higher standard of living; this happened for example when Japan increased its economic strength by the vigorous exploitation of British and other inventions in the period 1950-1980.

A number of social questions, therefore, need to be answered. Will people be content to work at home in physical isolation from their colleagues? Will they forego the conventional work ethic for a life of comparative idleness? Will they share the amount of work available with their fellows? Will they willingly accept retraining for new occupations at intermediate stages in their working lives? Will current competence be the main criterion for wages and salaries rather than obsolescent academic achievement or previous work experience? We don't yet know the answers but there are some indications. People don't like being unemployed through no fault of their own, nor having to live at a markedly low level of subsistence. However they are naturally competitive and do not willingly accept lower standards of living. Changing the nature of work through an all-pervasive and radical new technology will require for many the acquisition of new skills, knowledge and attitudes to work; these attributes will require updating at intervals. Whether the new technology can be widely introduced as soon as new applications are proven will depend critically on the speed at which human society adapts to accommodate the concomitant changes in its traditional values and structure. While there will be increased demands for leisure, travel and education, this may not result in increased happiness for all.

Economics

Information technology clearly has the potential to affect the economic performance of individuals, corporations and countries by enabling the more efficient use of resources. There is, however, the likelihood of a conflict of interest between investment in it and maintaining existing employment opportunities for those displaced or likely to be displaced from previous or current work. Information technology can, however, be regarded as a new resource comparable to the three dominant resources described by Adam Smith as land, labour and capital. This implies that there is a risk to any country which fails to introduce microelectronics, particularly through communications and computing, into its products and services; the efficient use of its human and material resources will undoubtedly lag behind its competitors. As the new 'world village' becomes more integrated through better and more rapid flows of information, and more efficient use is made of its resources, there should be overall material benefits for all, even though there are bound to be some inequalities between individuals and corporations, particularly in the periods of transition between successive applications of new technology. The economics of everyday local life will become more and more integrated on a global scale, particularly between the leading industrial nations at comparable stages of development, as information and new knowledge is dispensed rapidly throughout a universal communications network.

As some of the old labour-intensive manufacturing and mining industries continue to run down and the large numbers of 'shop-floor' workers are reduced, the human resources for the exploitation of information technology should become available and, provided investment is directed towards appropriate education and training, there is no reason why this occupational shift should not happen successfully. Current experience suggests that modern industry needs to spend 10-20 per cent of its turnover on training if it is to compete in world markets.

The nature of future work

Mankind's basic physical needs will ensure that human work will continue to produce food, clothes and shelter. Many long-established crafts will therefore remain; the extent to which they are supplemented or replaced by new technology will depend on the economic strength and mode of living of individuals and communities. World resources appear to be sufficient to sustain a higher standard of life and greater sophistication for many. A natural desire for knowledge and health will provide a universal motivation for greater intercommunication and better control of indigenous resources. Knowledge and technology cannot easily be prevented from crossing national frontiers. Capital and trade will also move across the world to wherever they can be most effectively used. Large-scale production of artefacts or services will take place where costs are low, either because of cheap labour and basic materials or through the efficient control of all resources and clever marketing.

As information becomes more accessible, the boundaries between many established trades and professions will break down. Events in any one part of the world are now quickly known in many places elsewhere. A global system of information for business, pleasure or propaganda already exists and shows every sign of expanding. Thus the insurance broker in London will have virtually the same access to information as a banker in Chicago or Singapore. The same will be true for the carpenter and the builder, the plumber and the electrician, the civil and the mechanical engineer, the

farmer and the fisherman, the tailor and the upholsterer, the motor mechanic and the crane driver and so on. All occupations have the potential to
use information technology; many do so already and this facility will
increase as the value of access to knowledge and the efficient use of
resources are recognized. Many routine jobs are more effectively carried
out wholly or partially by computers or computer-controlled devices, and
new applications of information technology are constantly being developed. Furthermore, the marketplace is increasingly global in character,
hence industrial competition will not decrease. Many firms and organizations no longer have to employ large numbers of production workers
nor every conceivably useful type of artisan. They tend to work in smaller
multidisciplinary teams able to manage flexible, automated systems
turning out large numbers of products or smaller numbers of more complex artefacts and services, but all under strict cost and quality control.
They seek greater flexibility to meet market demands and tighter resource
criteria; this flexibility can be met by subcontract work, by automation
and by using temporary or part-time labour and overtime.

The result is a core of permanent staff able to control and service
variable outside resources, made up of specialist firms or individuals who
are more likely to be paid for the actual work done — for their competence in contributing to a multiskilled team effort — rather than for
the time spent at the workplace decided previously in accordance with
nationally negotiated wage levels for ill-defined classes of workers.

Skills and their areas of application will need matching to market needs,
and many people will have to change careers as well as jobs at various
times. Flexibility will be regarded as a valuable attribute in terms of
individual and group expertise, location, time spent and the hours worked.
The concept of a long apprenticeship, followed by a job for life and little
or no subsequent retraining, is already defunct. Indeed, we may have
to recognize that employment is only one form of work, that leisure
activities may be just as useful and that we may have to develop new ways
of distributing money incomes. Thoroughly modern competitive production and service sectors of a national economy may have to be balanced by
structured community and leisure programmes for society as a whole if it
is not to disintegrate. Hence the social skills pertaining to industrial and
community relations will continue to be in demand. In business as a whole
operating in an increasingly competitive environment with fast-flowing
information, there will be an increasing need for adaptive and creative
individuals with the intellectual capacity to experiment with and to operate in high-risk, high-return and flexible roles. The mediocre staff often
produced by the 'old boy network' of recruitment is likely to be replaced
by individuals with demonstrable competence, flexibility and motivation.

Vocational education and training

The general prospects for work and society outlined in the previous paragraphs present a formidable challenge for the education and training services. The task of achieving an efficient economy and a stable society during the transformation being brought about by information technology will depend on national cultures and attitudes. The natural human desires for a significant economic improvement will require the transfer of resources from other activities and their redeployment to maximum effect. If the will to do this can be established, the vocational preparation of students and trainees must be modified along the following lines:

a. The school curriculum must move away from its traditional concentration on the accumulation of knowledge towards the acquisition of some technical or professional skills, social and life skills, the development of creativity and expertise in team-working. Beyond the age of about 14, students should be able to develop vocational skills according to their bent rather than be made to concentrate unwillingly on traditional academic studies. The transfer from full-time study to work could take place at any age up to about 23.

b. The top industrial countries already ensure that about 90 per cent of their young people receive full-time education or training up to the age of 18. It is clear that others who aspire to economic parity must reach a similar standard, either by this method or by providing better part-time facilities up to almost any age.

c. Many occupations already use information technology of some kind, and this trend will certainly increase. The ability to use network or robotic terminals will be essential for the great majority of 21st century workers, together with an understanding of common peripheral devices.

d. Vocational education and training are integral parts of the lifelong learning process, and should no longer be separated rigidly from each other, either in terms of the general curriculum, or its delivery and the way in which national systems are organized. Learning centres can be located in educational institutions and industrial or commercial training centres. Their facilities and financial support can be co-ordinated on a local, regional or national basis where appropriate together with the necessary arrangements for work experience and employment opportunities. Indeed it is not difficult to envisage a worldwide network of learning resources accessible to any student using the increasingly cheap tools of information technology; this facility already exists within and across some national frontiers.

e. The length and depth of initial vocational education or training will continue to vary according to individual and employment needs, but all workers face the prospect of retraining at several stages in their working lives. It follows therefore that the range of courses offered by learning centres will not decrease and may well increase. There will, however, be a trend towards shorter courses with limited objectives, towards distance learning and towards a stronger tutorial, rather than didactic, role for teachers.

f. Computer-aided learning, a flexible method of study which can be paced according to individual progress, seems certain to expand; it can also incorporate computer-based assessment for cognitive and for some practical skills. All distance learning can, however, be boring and sometimes unhelpful unless reinforced by the stimulus of an enterprising teacher or instructor. It is significant that in the British Open University, student numbers have remained roughly steady over the last two decades; this may be due to the difficulties of learning in this way coupled with the current cost of doing so. Falling costs of information technology and the developing facilities for students to gain access to learning centres through public communication networks will offer opportunities for growth, provided that the learning centres concerned pool their resources and offer good tutorial help.

g. Such a comprehensive system will be expensive and difficult for many countries to operate and develop. It could however be funded by a variety of methods such as interest-free loans, tax remissions and subsidized scholarships and traineeships. As national productivity is increased, this task will become easier, but considerable personal and corporate motivation will be needed in the transition period.

h. The dominant mode of assessment for vocations must shift from one based on the recall of knowledge towards competence, made up of criterion-referenced skills, of understanding of the subject with particular emphasis on system analysis and management, of attitude to the kind of work involved and of experience. This assessment must inevitably be task-based and made available at different times and locations to meet employment requirements.

It is not suggested that all forms of education should develop in this way. The humanities and the arts will undoubtedly continue to be studied in traditional ways; these will however be facilitated by greater accessibility of information.

Conclusion

The new 'world village' of the 21st century will not be perfect. People will continue to be rich or poor, simple or clever, weak or strong, independent or gregarious. Their expectations and determination to achieve them will vary enormously. Information technology has the potential to improve or disrupt standards of living just as other major innovations have done. The way in which it is implemented will depend very largely on how the vocational education and training services react to this challenge and the way in which national cultures provide the necessary investment. The flow of information throughout the world will increase in quantity and in speed. The opportunities for intercommunication and trading will encourage both standardization and competition within information technology itself and in many other human activities. Individual and corporate demands for knowledge, and hence for power, are most unlikely to diminish.

Bibliography

The bibliography is divided into three sections. The first covers published chapters and articles in books, including the whole books, and booklets by individual authors, the second lists publications (books and documents) issued by official and corporate bodies, and the third includes articles, periodicals and working papers. These three sections include all the references cited in individual chapters.

Section I: Books and pamphlets

Aarts, J F M C (1985) Features of specializations in higher education: a problem definition (Kenmerken van studierichtingen in het hoger onderwijs: een probleemstelling) *in* Aarts and Wijnen (1985)

Aarts, J F M C, and Wijnen, W H F W *eds* (1985) *Specializations in Higher Education (Studierichtingen in het Hoger Onderwijs)* Swets and Zeitlinger: Lisse

Andel, S I van (1984) On the grass between the tiles (Over het gras tussen de tegels) *Higher Vocational Education in Variety by Context (Hoger Beroepsonderwijs in Verscheidenheid naar Samenhang)* HBO-Raad/VUGA: The Hague

Anderson, D S *et al* (1980) *Schools to Grow In: An Evaluation of Secondary Colleges* Australian National University Press: Canberra

Anderson, J E (1973) *Organization and Financing of Self-Help Education in Kenya* UNESCO: Paris

Anderson, J E (1970) *The Struggle for the School* Longman Educational Books: Nairobi

Ashmore, M, and Pritz, G (1983) *Program for Acquiring Competence in Entrepreneurship (PACE)* The National Center for Research in Vocational Education, The Ohio State University: Columbus, OH

Banthiya, N K (1985) *Design of Assessment Schemes under Comprehensive Scheme of Assessment* TTTI: Bhopal

Banthiya, N K, Dharap, K P, Haider, S Z and Vyas, K D (1980) *Report on Pilot Introduction of Comprehensive Scheme of Assessment* TTTI: Bhopal

Banthiya, N K, Jain, P C and Saksena, S C (1979) *A Survey for Job Analysis: Post Diploma in Refrigeration and Air Conditioning* TTTI: Bhopal

Bennis, W G, Benne, K D and Chin, R *eds* (1970) *The Planning of Change* (2nd edn) Holt, Rinehart and Winston: London

Benor, D, Harrison, J and Baxter, M (1984) *Agricultural Extension: The Training and Visit System* World Bank: Washington, DC

Berg, R van den and Vandenberghe, R (1981) *Educational Innovation in Shifting Perspective (Onderwijsinnovatie in Verschuivend Perspectief)* Zwijsen: Tilberg

Berger, M, Delancey, V and Mellenchamp, A (1984) *Bridging the Gender Gap in Agricultural Extension* International Centre of Research on Women: Washington, DC

Berkel, H J M van, Bax, A E and Holleman, J W *eds* (1985) *Quality of Higher Education: Control and Improvement (Kwaliteit van Hoger Onderwijs: Bewaking en Verbetering)* Versluys: Amsterdam

Bernstein, B (1971) On the classification and framing of educational knowledge *in* Young, M F D (1971)

Bettles, F M (1980) *Women's Access to Agricultural Extension Services in Botswana* Women's Extension Unit, Ministry of Agriculture: Gaborone

Bevers, J A A M, Bouhuis, P A J and Gobbits, R (1981) *Results of the preliminary investigation: Te verwachten mutanten in de vraag naar c.q. het aanbod van hoger onderwijs in de komende decennia (Expected changes in the demand for and supply of higher education in the coming decades)* Staatsuitgeverij: The Hague

Birch, D L (1979) *The Job Generation Process* Massachusetts Institute of Technology (MIT): Cambridge, MA

Boyer, E (1983) *High School: A Report on Secondary Education in America* Harper and Row: New York, NY

Brannen, P (1975) *Entering the World of Work* HMSO: London

Bridge, W A and Hewitt, C L (1983) *Report of a Survey of Industrial Demand for Open Tech Provision in the South-East* Southtek: Brighton

Brine, J, Perrie, M and Sutton, A *eds* (1980) *Home, School and Leisure in the Soviet Union* George Allen & Unwin: London

Bronneman-Helmers, R (1984a) Developments and outlooks (Ontwikkelingen en vooruitzichten) *in* Bronneman-Helmers (1984b)

Bronneman-Helmers, R (1984b) *The Job Market for Higher Education Graduates (De Arbeidsmarkt voor Hoger Opgeleiden)* SCP: Rijswijk

Brook, D and Race, P (1978) *Aspects of Educational Technology XII* Kogan Page: London/Nichols Publishing: New York, NY

Cassells, J R T and Johnstone, A M (1984) Modules and 'H' grade chemistry *in* Spencer (1984)

Catherwood, V (1985) *Young People, Education and Employment* Planning Paper 23 NZ Planning Council: Wellington

Cattell, R B (1971) *Handbook of Multivariate Experimental Psychology* Rand McNally & Co: Chicago, IL

Cattel, R B (1974) *Cattell IQ Test* Sinclair Research Ltd: Cambridge

Chandrakant, L S (1971) *Polytechnic Education in India* D B Taraporevala: Bombay

Chin, R and Benne, K D (1970) General strategies for effecting changes in human system *in* Bennis, Benne and Chin (1970)

Christiaans, H H C M (1985) Features of university education and higher vocational education in technical higher education (WO en HBO-kenmerken in het technisch hoger onderwijs) *in* Aarts and Wijnen (1985)

Drucker, P F (1979) *Innovation and Entrepreneurship: Practice and Principles* Harper and Row: New York

Duncan, J G (1982) A marketing perspective *in* Squires (1982)

Duncan, J (1984) *Options for New Zealand's Future* Victoria University/ANZ Bank: Wellington

Eastwood, J *et al eds* (1984) *Labour Essays* Drummond: Melbourne

Ford, G W (1964) Australia at risk: an underskilled and vulnerable society *in* Eastwood (1984)

Ford, G W (1986) The transfer of culturally-specific industrial technology to Australia *in* Ford and Tilley (1986)

Ford, G W and Tilley, L *eds* (1986) *Diversity, Change and Tradition: The Environment for Industrial Democracy in Australia* Australian Government Publishing Service: Canberra

Frissen, P (1985) The government and quality control in higher education (De over-heid en kwaliteitsbewaking in het hoger onderwijs) *in* van Berkel *et al* (in press)

Frissen, P and Hoewijk, P M T van (1985) University education organization: envir-onment and policy (De universitaire onderwijs organisatie: omgeving en beleid) *in* Frissen, van Hoewijk and van Hout (in press)

Frissen, P, Hoewijk, P M T van and Hout, J F M J van eds (1986) *The University: an Effective Educational Organization? (De Universiteit: een Adequate Onderwijs-organisatie?)* Het spectrum: Utrecht/Antwerp

Garforth, C (1982) Reaching the rural poor: a review of extension strategies and methods *in* Jones and Rolls (1982)

Garforth, C (1986) Universities, educational research and the development of media for non-formal education: lessons from agricultural projects in Africa and SE Asia *in* Smawfield (1986)

Glaser, R (1985) *The Nature of Expertise* The National Center for Research in Vocational Education, The Ohio State University: Columbus, OH

Goodlad, J (1984) *A Place Called School: Prospects for the Future* McGraw-Hill Book Company: New York, NY

Goodlad, S ed (1985) *Studies in Higher Education* 10 2 Carfax Publishing Co: Abingdon

Gorsuch, L R (1974) *Factor Analysis* W B Saunders Co: Philadelphia, London, Toronto

Graham, C (1985) *Developing PICKUP for Industry* Department of Education and Science (DES): London

Graham, C and Morris, A (1984) *PICKUP Delivery Systems* Department of Edu-cation and Science (DES): London

Guilford, J P (1964) *The Nature of Human Intelligence* McGraw-Hill: New York, NY

Hargreaves, D (1983) *The Challenge for the Comprehensive School: Culture, Curriculum and Community* Routledge and Kegan Paul: London

Heathcote, G, Kempa, R and Roberts, I (1982) *Curriculum Styles and Strategies* Further Education Unit (FEU): London

Henderson, J M (1985) *The Somerset TVEI Project: A Summary* TVEI Office: Chard

Heywood, J ed (1980) *The New Technician Education* Society for Research in Higher Education Surrey University: Guildford

Higgins, K M (1984) *Curriculum Development and Citizen Education: A Case Study of a Farmer Training Programme for Women in Botswana* Institute of Adult Education, University of Botswana: Gaborone

Hitchcock, G (1986) *Profiles and Profiling* Longman: Harlow, Essex

Hout, J F M J van, Frissen, P and Hoewijk, P M T van (1985) eds *The University: an Effective Educational Organization? (De Universiteit, een Adequate Onder-wijsorganisatie?)* Symposiumverslag: Nijmegen

Hudson, B ed (1973) *Assessment Techniques, an Introduction* Methuen: London

Husén, T (1979) *The School in Question: A Comparative Study of the School and its Future in Western Society* Oxford University Press: Oxford

Imrie, B W (1984) *Technical Education and Training, AAVA Policy: Current Topics and Future Development* Invited paper presented at the Biennial Conference of the NZ Institute of Draughtsmen: Wellington

Imrie, B W (1985) *Vocational Options for School Leavers in New Zealand* Papers of the Fourth World Conference on Co-operative Education: Edinburgh

Jain, P C, Banthiya, N K and Saksena, S C (1979) *A Survey for Job Analysis: Diploma in Textile Technology* TTTI: Bhopal

Jones, G E ed (1986) *Investing in Rural Extension: Strategies and Goals* Elsevier Applied Science Publishers: London

Jones, G E and Rolls, M R eds (1982) *Progress in Rural Extension and Community Development, vol 1: Extension and Relative Advantage in Rural Development* John Wiley and Sons: Chichester

Kapse, V M and Shrivastava, K K (1985) *CSA Project in Gujarat: Impact Study at Porbandar, Rajkot, Patan Polytechnics* TTTI: Bhopal
Kemenade, J A van ed (1981) *Education: Management and Policy (Onderwijs: Bestel en Beleid)* Woltes-Noordhoff: Groningen
Knip, H (1982) *Organization Studies in Education (Organisatiestudies in het Onderwijs)* SVO: Harlingen
Kotler, P (1979) *Marketing Management, Analysis, Planning and Control* Prentice-Hall Inc: Englewood Cliffs, NJ

Lang, J (1978) *City and Guilds of London Institute Centenary 1878-1978: An Historical Commentary* City and Guilds of London Institute: London
Lawley, D N and Maxwell, A E (1971) *Factor Analysis as a Statistical Method* (2nd Edn) Butterworths: London
Lieshout, W C M van (1984) The time is ripe (De tijd is rijp) *in* Lieshout (1984a)
Lieshout, W C M van (1984a) *Higher Vocational Education in Variety by Context (Hoger Beroepsonderwijs in Verscheidenheid naar Samenhang)* The Hague
Lisovsky, V (1983) *Soviet Students: Questions and Answers* Novosti Press Agency Publishing House: Moscow
Longden, J (1986) *Learning with Profit. The Application of the Tradec System to the Youth Training Scheme and Beyond* Yorkshire and Humberside Association for Further and Higher Education: Leeds
Lunacharsky, A (1981) *On Education: Selected Articles and Speeches* Progress Publishers: Moscow

McCallion, H and Britton, G A (1978) *A Survey of Engineers in New Zealand Engineering and Manufacturing and Processing Industry* Technical Manpower Training Committee
McCallum, D I et al (1984) *Changing Technology and its Impact on Training — A Report of a Survey of Companies in Sussex and Kent* (Unpublished) Garnett College: London
McDaniel, O C (1985) The structure of higher education and the criteria for the future (De indeling van het hoger onderwijs en de criteria voor de toekomst) *in* Aarts and Wijnen (1985)
Macintosh, H G (1974) *Techniques and Problems of Assessment: a Practical Handbook for Teachers* Edward Arnold: London
Macintosh, H G (1985) *Assessment in Education and Training 14-18: Policy and Practice. A Review of Current Initiatives, drawing upon a Conference held at Stoke Rochford in December 1984* National Institute for Careers Education and Counselling: Cambridge
Mager, R F (1984) *Preparing Instructional Objectives* Pitman Learning Inc: Belmont, CA
Marshall, M (1983) *The Compulsory Secondary School: Adolescents and the Curriculum* Report to the Standing Conference of European Ministers for Education, Thirteenth Session: Dublin
Marx, E C H (1975) *The Organization of School-Groups from a Pedagogical Viewpoint (De Organisatie van Scholengemeenschappen in Onderwijskundige Optiek)* Tjeenk Willink: Groningen
Miller, R M ed (1971) *Technician Training* Report of the National Study Conference, Massey University
Morris, A ed (1984) *The PICKUP Handbook* Department of Education and Science (DES): London
Mukhopadhyaya, M, Jain, P C, Banthiya, N K and Halani, D M (1982) *Gujarat Polytechnic Curriculum Evaluation Project* TTTI: Bhopal

Naisbitt, J (1984) *Megatrends* Warner Books: New York, NY
Nuttall, D S and Wilmott, A S (1972) *British Examinations: Techniques of Analysis* NFER: Slough

Odell, M J ed (1977) *Group Formation: Senior Agricultural Officers' Workshop. Final Report and Course Materials* Ministry of Agriculture: Gaborone
Offenberger, H (1979) *The Making of a Technician A study of New Zealand Certificate Holders* New Zealand Council for Educational Research: Wellington
Orwa, W O (1977) *in* ILO/SIDA (1977)

Perraton, H (1983) Mass media, basic education and agricultural extension *in* Perraton, Jamison, Jenkins, Orivel and Wolff (1983)
Perraton, H, Jamison, D T, Jenkins, J, Orivel, F and Wolff, L (1983) *Basic Education and Agricultural Extension: Costs, Effects and Alternatives* World Bank: Washington, DC
Pirsig, R (1979) *Zen and the Art of Motorcycle Maintenance* Morrow: New York
Power, C (1983) *Satisfaction With High Schools* Flinders University: South Australia

Raju, B M (1973) *Education in Kenya* Heinemann: Nairobi
van Rensburg, P (1974) *Report from Swaneng Hill: Education and Employment in an African Country* Dag Hammarskjold Foundation: Uppsala
Reynolds, J E *et al* (1976) *Self-Help and Rural Development in Kenya* University of Nairobi, IDS: Nairobi
Richard, P (1985) *Indigenous Agricultural Revolution. Ecology and Food Production in West Africa* Hutchinson: London
Roling, N (1982) Alternative approaches in extension *in* Jones and Rolls (1982)
Romiszowski, A J (1985) Applying the new technologies to education and training in Brazil *in* Rushby and Howe (1986)
Romiszowski, A J and Machado, N H S (1978) Developing a large-scale modularized training system for Brazilian telecommunications *in* Brook and Race (1978)
Rosenbluth, A and Weiner, N (1979) *in* Kotler, P (1979)
Ross, J A (1985) *Implications of the Removal of the University Entrance Examination from Form 6* First Report of the Committee of Inquiry into Curriculum, Assessment, and Qualifications in Forms 5 to 7 Department of Education: Wellington
Ross, N and Ashmore, M *et al* (1984) *A National Entrepreneurship Education Agenda for Action* The National Center for Research in Vocational Education, The Ohio State University: Columbus, OH
Ross, N and Kurth, P *eds* (1985) *The Economic Value of Entrepreneurship Education* The National Center for Research in Vocational Education, The Ohio State University: Columbus, OH
Rushby, N and Howe, A (1986) *Aspects of Educational Technology XIX* Kogan Page, London/Nichols Publishing, New York, NY
Russell, J D (1974) *Modular Instruction* Burgess Publishing Company: Minneapolis
Russell, J A A (1986) Extension strategies involving local groups and their participation, and the role of this approach in facilitating local development *in* Jones (1986)

Saksena, S C, Banthiya, N K and Jain, P C (1979) *A Survey for Job Analysis: Post Diploma in Production Technology* TTTI: Bhopal
Saran, Y and Chandran, G S (1979) *CBTE at TTTI Bhopal: A Case Study of an Innovation in Teacher Education* TTTI: Bhopal
Sizer, Theodore (1984) *Horace's Compromise: The Dilemma of the American High School* Houghton Mifflin Company: Boston, MA
Smawfield, D ed (1986) *International Academic Interchange and Cooperation in Higher Education* International Education Unit, University of Hull: Hull
Smith, Sir Swire (1877) *Educational Comparisons: Remarks on Industrial schools in England, Germany and Switzerland* Simpkin, Marshal & Co: London

Spencer, E *ed* (1984) *Modules for All: Discussion Papers on the New Proposals for the Education of 16-18s* Scottish Council for Research in Education: Edinburgh

Squires, C *ed* (1982) *Innovation through Recession* Society for Research in Higher Education: Guildford

Stenhouse, L (1975) *An Introduction to Curriculum Research and Development* Heinemann Education Books Ltd: London

Studt, F E (1971) New Zealand's requirement for science technicians *in* Miller (1971)

Swan, D and McKinnon, K (1984) *Future Directions of Secondary Education: A Report* New South Wales Education Department: Sydney

Taylor, J B C (1980) *The Supply of and Demand for Technician and Professional Engineers (1967-82)* Technical Report 22 Department of Mechanical Engineering, University of Canterbury: Canterbury, NZ

Thomas, B (1980) *Rural Development through Local Initiative: Observations on Kenya's Experience with Harambee Projects in Selected Rural Communities* University of Nairobi IDS: Nairobi

Thurstone, L A (1969) *Multiple Factor-Analysis: A Development and Expansion of the Vectors of the Mind* University of Chicago Press: London

Thyne, J (1974) *Principles of Examining* University of London Press: London

Tolley, G (1983) *The Open Tech: Why, What and How?* Open Tech Paper 1 Manpower Services Commission (MSC): Sheffield

Twining, J *ed* (1982) *Open Learning for Technicians* Stanley Thornes (Publishers) Ltd: Cheltenham

Vaughan-Evans, R H and Mandebvu, F G (1986) Group activity and involvement of peasant farmers in disseminating technology in the Gweru Region of Midland Province, Zimbabwe *in* Jones (1986)

Veld, R J in't (1985) Opening of the symposium (Opening van het symposium) *in* Hout, Frissen and Hoewijk (1985)

Verma, L N, Dharap, K P, Kapse, V M, Shah, B C and Banthiya, N K (1977) *Curriculum Evaluation Project: Final Report (September 1975-August 1977)* TTTI: Bhopal

Vernon, P E (1961) *The Structure of Human Abilities* Methuen: London

Vesper, K (1980) *New Venture Strategies* Prentice-Hall Inc: Englewood Cliffs, NJ

Ward, C (1980) *Designing a Scheme of Assessment* Stanley Thornes (Publishers) Ltd: Cheltenham

Ward, C (1981a) *Preparing and Using Constructed Answer Questions* Stanley Thornes (Publishers) Ltd: Cheltenham

Ward, C (1981b) *Preparing and Using Objective Questions* Stanley Thornes (Publishers) Ltd: Cheltenham

Weaver, K (1981) *Russia's Future* Praeger Special Studies: New York, NY

Weir, A D (1980) A context for technician education *in* Heywood, J (1980)

Willett, A B J (1981) *Agricultural Group Development in Botswana* (4 vols) Government Printer: Gaborone

Young, M F D *ed* (1971) *Knowledge and Control* Collier Macmillan: London

Zajda, J (1980) *Education in the USSR* Pergamon Press: Oxford

Section II: Official and corporate publications

Academic Council (Academische Raad) (1983) *A Convergent Model for Higher Education (Een Convergent Model voor het Hoger Onderwijs)* Staatsuitgeverij: The Hague

Association of Teachers in Technical Institutes (ATTI) (1984) *Development Policies* Annual Conference of the NZ Association of ATTI

Authority for Advanced Vocational Awards (AAVA) (1983) *The AAVA 'National' Qualifications* Authority for Advanced Vocational Awards: Wellington

Beazley, K *Chairman* (1984) *Education in Western Australia* Government Printer: Perth

Blackburn, J *Chair* (1985) *Ministerial Review of Post-compulsory Schooling: Report, volumes 1 and 2*: Melbourne

Bund-Länder Commission for Educational Planning and Research Promotion (Bund-Länder-Kommission fur Bildungsplänung und Forschungsförderung (1985) *Short- and Medium-Term Possibilities to Secure Training Places (Kurz-und mittelfristige Möglichkeiten zur Sicherung von Ausbildungs-platzen)* BLK: Bonn

Bund-Länder Commission for Educational Planning and Research Promotion (Bund-Länder-Kommission fur Bildungsplänung und Forschungsförderung) (1985a) *Future Job Prospects of Graduates (Kunftige Perspektiven von Hochschulabsolventen im Beschäftigungs-system)* BLK: Bonn

Business and Technician Education Council (BTEC) (1983) *BTEC General Awards in Business Studies Course Specification* BTEC: London

Business and Technician Education Council (BTEC) (1984) *Policies and Priorities into the 1990s* BTEC: London

Business and Technician Education Council (BTEC) (1985) *Review of BTEC National Awards in Business and Related Studies: Report on the Council's Programme of Consultation and Research* BTEC: London

Business and Technician Education Council (BTEC) (1986) *Circular 15. BTEC Qualifications and Certificates of Achievement: The Framework* BTEC: London

Business Education Council (BEC) (1976) *Policy Statement* BEC: London

Colombo Plan (1982) *Aspects of Curriculum for Technician Education* Colombo Plan Staff College for Technician Education: Singapore

Committee of Inquiry into Labour Market Programs (1985) *Report of the Committee of Inquiry into Labour Market Programs* (The Kirby Report) Australian Government Publishing Service: Canberra

Committee on Higher Education (1963) *Higher Education* (The Robbins Report) HMSO: London

Confederation of British Industry (CBI) (1986) *Industrial Trends Survey 100* Confederation of British Industry: London

Constitution of the Union of Soviet Socialist Republics (1984) Novosti Press Agency Publishing House: Moscow

Consultative Committee on the Curriculum (1983) *An Education for Life and Work: Report by the Planning Committee of the Education for the Industrial Society Project* HMSO: Edinburgh

Department of Education (1984) *Education Statistics of New Zealand* Department of Education: Wellington

Department of Education and Science (DES) (1963) *Half Our Future: Report of the Central Advisory Council for Education (England)* (The Newsom Report) HMSO: London

Department of Education and Science (DES) (1964) *Day Release: Report of a Committee set up by the Minister of Education* (The Henniker-Heaton Report) HMSO: London

Department of Education and Science (DES) (1969) *Report of the Committee on Technician Courses and Examinations* (The Haslegrave Report) HMSO: London

Department of Education and Science (DES) Inspectorate of Schools (1979) *Curriculum 11-16: Working Papers by HM Inspectorate — A Contribution to Current Debate* 1st edn reprint with additions. DES: HMSO: London

Department of Education and Science (DES) (1980) *Education for 16-19 Year Olds: A Review undertaken for the Government and the Local Authorities Association* Chairman: N Macfarlane HMSO: London

Department of Education and Science (DES) (1981) *Curriculum 11-16: A Review of Progress* HMSO: London

Department of Education and Science (DES) (1983) *Curriculum 11-16: Towards a Statement of Entitlement* HMSO: London
Department of Employment (1981) *A New Training Initiative: A Programme for Action* Cmnd 8455 HMSO: London
Department of Employment (1985) *Employment Gazette* July 1985 HMSO: London
Department of Labour (1984) *Engineering Industry (A Study of Trends in the Future Demand for Skilled People)* Department of Labour: Wellington

EMBRATEL (1982) *Projeto Ciranda: A Primeira Comunidade Teleinformatizada do Brasil* EMBRATEL, Ministerio de Comunicacoes: Rio de Janeiro
EMBRATEL (1983) *Unindo Esforcos: Empresa e Escola (Convenio Embratel/Centro Educacional de Niteroi)* Embratel, Ministerio de Comunicacoes: Rio de Janeiro
Employers' Federation (1984) *Employer Approach to Vocational Training* NZ Employers' Federation: Wellington
Employers' Federation (1985) *Tertiary Education and the Path to Work* NZ Employers' Federation: Wellington
Engineering Council (1986) *A Call to Action: Continuing Education and Training for Engineers and Technicians* Engineering Council: London
Engineering Industry Training Board (EITB) (1981) *The Training of Engineering Craftsmen* EITB: London
Engineering Industry Training Board (EITB) (1982) *The Training of Engineering Craftsmen* (Revised edition) EITB: London

Further Education Unit (FEU) (1984) *Towards a Competence-Based System: An FEU View* FEU: London
Further Education Unit (FEU) (1985) *Core Competences in Engineering* FEU: London
Further Education Unit (FEU) (1985) *Marketing Further and Higher Education* Longman: York
Further Education Unit (FEU) (1986) *Implementing Open Learning in Local Authority Institutions* Further Education Unit, London and Open Tech Unit, Manpower Services Commission: Sheffield

Gardner, D P *Chairman* (1983) *A Nation at Risk: The Imperative for Educational Reform* United States Government Printer: Washington, DC
Government of Kenya and Norwegian Agency for International Development (GOK/NORAD) (1974) *The Kenyan Village Polytechnic Programme* Unpublished Evaluation Report on the Kenya Village Polytechnic Programme. Nairobi, Kenya
Guildford Educational Services Ltd (1986) *The PICKUP Short Course Directory* (Microfiche version) Reissue G. Guildford Educational Services Ltd: Guildford

Hansard (1980) *House of Commons Official Report* 994,5 26 November HMSO: London
HBO Council (HBO-Raad) (1984) *HBO Council's View of the Green Paper on Scale Expansion, Specialization and Concentration in HBO (Standpunt HBO-Raad over Nota Schaalvergroting, Taakverdeling en Concentratie in het HBO)* HBO: The Hague
HBO Council (HBO-Raad) (1984-1985) *Scale Expansion/Specialization/Concentration Reports: various issues (Schaalveergroting-Taakverdeling-Concentratie-Berichten)* HBO: The Hague
HBO Council (HBO-Raad) (1985) *Almanac 1985 (Almanak 1985)* HBO: The Hague
Hotel and Catering Industry Training Board (HCITB) (1984) *Craft Proficiency Recognition, Specific Modules and Sample Programmes* HCITB: Wembley
House of Lords Select Committee on the European Communities (1984) *Youth Training in the EEC* Report HL 282 HMSO: London
Her Majesty's Inspectors of Schools (1977) *Curriculum 11-16: Working Papers: A Contribution to Current Debate* HMSO: London

International Labour Office/Swedish International Development Authority (ILO/ SIDA) (1977) *RAF/19* Unpublished report on Eastern and Southern Africa Preparation of Rural Youth Development, held in Botswana

Inner London Education Authority (ILEA) (1984) *Improving Secondary Schools* (The Hargreaves Report) ILEA: London

International Labour Office (ILO) (1985) *Modules of Employable Skill: An Approach to Vocational Training. Catalogue of Learning Elements and Related Materials* (4th Edn) ILO Publications: Geneva

Joint Board for Pre-Vocational Education (1984) *The Certificate of Pre-Vocational Education* City and Guilds of London Institute and Business and Technician Education Council: London

Karmel, P *Chairman* (1985) *Quality of Education in Australia: Report of Ministerial Review Committee* Australian Government Publishing Service: Canberra

Keeves, J *Chairman* (1982) *Education and Change in South Australia: A Final Report* Government Printer: Adelaide

Kenya Education Review (1974) 1 2 Faculty of Education, University of Nairobi: Nairobi

Manpower Services Commission (MSC) (1984) *The Open Tech Programme Explained* MSC: Sheffield

Manpower Services Commission (MSC) (1984) *Core Skills in YTS Part I: YTS Manual* MSC: Sheffield

Manpower Services Commission (MSC) (1985) *Review of Vocational Qualifications in England and Wales: Interim Report of Joint Manpower Services Commission/ Department of Education and Science Working Group* MSC: Sheffield

Manpower Services Commission (MSC) (1985a) *Core Skills in YTS Part II: Computer and Information Technology: YTS Manual* MSC: Sheffield

Manpower Services Commission (MSC) (1985b) *Work-Based Projects in YTS: YTS Manual* MSC: Sheffield

Manpower Services Commission (MSC) (1985c) *The Development of the Youth Training Scheme: Report, July 1985* MSC: Sheffield

Manpower Services Commission (MSC) (1985d) *Education and Training for Young People* Cmnd 9482 HMSO: London

Manpower Services Commission (MSC) (1986) *Open Tech Programme News No 11* Manpower Services Commission: Sheffield

Manpower Services Commission (MSC) (1986a) *Review of Vocational Qualifications in England and Wales* Joint Manpower Services Commission/Department of Education and Science Working Group Report HMSO: London

Ministerio de Educacao e Cultura (MEC) (1983) *Projeto 'EDUCOM'* MEC: Brasilia

Minister of Education (1984) *Education, the Economy and Social Equity* Address to the Economic Summit Conference Wellington

Minister of Education (1985) Address to the Annual Conference of Association of Teachers in Technical Institutes (22 May 1985): Upper Hutt

Ministers of Education, Employment and Maori Affairs (1985) *Skills for Young People* A discussion paper on transition education and training, Ministers of Education, Employment and Maori Affairs: Wellington

Ministry of Economic Planning and Community Affairs (Kenya) (1973) *Educational Trends* Nairobi

Ministry of Economic Planning and Development (Kenya) (1983) *Statistical Abstracts* Nairobi

Ministry of Education (1961) *Better Opportunities in Technical Education* Cmnd 1254 HMSO: London

Ministry of Education (1983) *Technical Teachers' Training Institutes: National Guide Document on their Role and New Perspectives* Ministry of Education, Government of India: New Delhi

Ministry of Education and Culture (1979) *Technical and Vocational Education: India*
Country Report for Unesco Regional Seminar on Technical and Vocational
Education (Singapore — November 1979) Ministry of Education and Culture,
Government of India: New Delhi

Ministry of Education, Science and Technology (Kenya) (1975) *The 8-4-4 Education System* Government Printer: Nairobi

Ministry of Education, Science and Technology (Kenya) (1975) *Courses Offered in Institutes of Technology* Nairobi

Ministry of Education, Science and Technology (Kenya) (1985) *Courses Offered in Institutes of Technology* Nairobi

Ministry of Education and Social Welfare (1971) *Report of the Special Committee on Reorganization and Development of Polytechnic Education in India (1970-71)* (Damodaran Committee) Ministry of Education and Social Welfare, Government of India: New Delhi

Ministry of Education and Social Welfare (1976) *Report of the Review Committee for the Technical Teachers' Training Institute* (Kelkar Committee) Ministry of Education and Social Welfare, Government of India: New Delhi

Ministry of Finance and Planning (Kenya) (1984) *Development Plan 1984/88* Government Printer: Nairobi

Ministry of Finance and Planning (Kenya) (1984) *Kericho District Development Plan 1984/1988* Nairobi

Ministry of Science and Education (Ministerie van Onderwijs en Wetenschappen) (1975) A possible long-term development and first moves in the coming years (Een mogelijke ontwikkeling op lange termijn en aanzetten in de komende jaren) *Higher Education in the Future (Hoger Onderwijs in de Toekomst)* Staatsuitgeverij: The Hague

Ministry of Science and Education (Ministerie van Onderwijs en Wetenschappen) (1983) *Scale Expansion, Specialization and Concentration in Higher Vocational Education (Schaalvergroting, Taakverdeling en Concentratie in het Hoger Beroesonderewijs)* Staatsuitgeverij: The Hague

Ministry of Science and Education (Ministerie van Onderwijs en Wetenschappen) (1984a) *More about Management (Meer over Management)* Staatsuitgeverij: The Hague

Ministry of Science and Education (Ministerie van Onderwijs en Wetenschappen) (1984b) *Towards a New Funding System for HBO (Naar een Nieuw Bekostigingssysteem voor het HBO)* Staatsuitgeverij: The Hague

Ministry of Science and Education (Ministerie van Onderwijs en Wetenschappen) (1985) A different administrative method (Een andere besturingswijze) *Higher Education: Autonomy and Quality (Hoger Onderwijs: Autonomie en Kwaliteit)* Staatsuitgeverij: The Hague

Monthly Labor Review (1983) November US Department of Labor, Bureau of Labor Statistics: Washington, DC

National Center for Educational Statistics (1983) *Digest of Educational Statistics* National Center for Educational Statistics: Washington, DC

National Research Advisory Council (NRAC) (1984) *A Strategy for Science and Technology* Discussion Paper NRAC 84 257: Wellington

Office of the President, Republic of Kenya (1984) *Focus for Rural Development* Government Printer: Nairobi

Organization for Economic Co-operation and Development (OECD) (1983) *The Future of Vocational Education and Training* OECD: Paris

Report on Vocational Training (Berufsbildungsbericht) (1985) *Grundlagen und Perspektiven für Bildung und Wissenschaft* Nr. 7 Der Bundesminister für Bildung und Wissenschaft: Bonn

Republic of Kenya (1976) *Report of the National Committee on Educational Object-ives and Policies* Government Printer: Nairobi

Schmitt, R J *et al* (1984) *Vocational Training Systems in the Member States of the European Community: CEDEFOP Guide* European Centre for the Development of Vocational Training: Berlin

Schools Commission Project (1984) *Schooling for 15 and 16 Year Olds* Launceston Teachers Centre: Launceston, Australia

Schwarz, B (1981) *The Integration of Young People in Society and Working Life* Report for the Prime Minister of France, Paris. English version published by the European Centre for Vocational Training: Berlin

Scottish Education Department (SED) (1963) *From School to Further Education* HMSO: Edinburgh

Scottish Education Department (SED) (1977) *The Structure of the Curriculum in the Third and Fourth Years of the Scottish Secondary School* (The Munn Report) HMSO: Edinburgh

Scottish Education Department (SED) (1983) *16-18s in Scotland: An Action Plan* HMSO: Edinburgh

Scottish Vocational Education Council (1985) *The National Certificate* SCOTVEC: Glasgow

Secondary Examinations Council (SEC) (1984) *Annual Report 1983-1984* SEC: London

Secondary Examinations Council (SEC) (1985) *The Development of Grade Criteria for the GCSE* SEC: London

SPSS (1984) *Statistical Package for the Social Sciences/PC* SPSS UK Ltd: Richmond

Steinle, J *Chairman* (1983) *The Challenge of Change: A Review of High Schools in the ACT* Australian Government Publishing Service: Canberra

Technical Teachers' Training Institute (TTTI), Bhopal (1971) *A Survey for Job Analysis* a Report on a survey conducted to collect data for preparing technician curriculae TTTI: Bhopal

Technical Teachers' Training Institute (TTTI), Bhopal (1975a) *TTTI: Questions and Answers* TTTI: Bhopal

Technical Teachers' Training Institute (TTTI), Bhopal (1975b) *Curriculum Develop-ment — Monograph 2* TTTI: Bhopal

Technical Teachers' Training Institute (TTTI), Bhopal (1975c) *Educational Projects — Monograph 3* TTTI: Bhopal

Technical Teachers' Training Institute (TTTI), Bhopal (1975d) *Examination Re-forms — Monograph 4* TTTI: Bhopal

Technical Teachers' Training Institute (TTTI), Bhopal (1975e) *Interaction with Industry — Monograph 5* TTTI: Bhopal

Technical Teachers' Training Institute (TTTI), Bhopal (1976a) A rational approach to technical teacher education. Paper presented at *Second Inter-TTTI Faculty Conference Madras* TTTI: Bhopal

Technical Teachers' Training Institute (TTTI), Bhopal (1976b) *Planned Change: A Monograph based on the Proceedings of the Study Conference for Polytechnic Principals, Western Region* TTTI: Bhopal

Technical Teachers' Training Institute (TTTI), Bhopal (1976c) *Country Course on Institution Building Processes: A Monograph* TTTI: Bhopal

Technical Teachers' Training Institute (TTTI), Bhopal (1978) *Modular Approach to Technical Teacher Training: Competency-Based Teacher Education.* Paper presented at Third Inter-TTTI Faculty Conference Chandigarh TTTI: Bhopal

Technical Teachers' Training Institute (TTTI), Bhopal (1980a) *Competency-Based Teacher Education: A New Dimension in Teacher Training* TTTI: Bhopal

Technical Teachers' Training Institute (TTTI), Bhopal (1980b) *Engineering Experi-mentation Course: Guidelines for Organising and Conducting Monitoring Visits* TTTI: Bhopal

Technical Teachers' Training Institute (TTTI), Bhopal (1983) *Technical Teachers' Training Institute — An Overview* TTTI: Bhopal

Technical Teachers' Training Institute (TTTI), Bhopal (1984) *Over the Years: TTTI Bhopal* TTTI: Bhopal

Technical Teachers' Training Institutes, Bhopal (1976) *Report on the Study Conference For Senior Administrators on Technician Education held at Simla* (11-16 October, 1976) Sponsored by ISTE and the four TTTIs TTTI: Bhopal

Technician Education Council (TEC) (1974) *Policy Statement* TEC: London

Trainee Statistics (Lehrlingsstatistic) (1985) Deutsches Handwertesblatt **10** Bonn

Training Services Agency (TSA) (1976) *Technicians: A Possible Basis for a TSA Programme* TSA: London

United Nations Educational, Scientific and Cultural Organization (UNESCO) (1974) *Revised Recommendations Concerning Vocational Education adopted by The General Conference of United Nations Educational Scientific and Cultural Organisation (UNESCO)* UNESCO: Paris

US Small Business Administration (1984) *The State of Small Business: A Report of the President* US Government Printing Office: Washington, DC

Vocational Training in the Federal Republic of Germany (Berufsbildung in der Bundesrepublik Deutschland) (1984) Bundesinstitut für Berufsbildung: Berlin

Vocational Training in the USSR (1982) Novosti Press Agency Publishing House: Moscow

Vocational Training — Investment for the Future The Dual Training System in the Federal Republic of Germany (1983) Carl Duisberg Gesellschaft eV: Cologne

Welsh Joint Education Committee (WJEC) (1985) *Guidelines for the use of Modular Schemes of Assessment* WJEC: Cardiff

Xerox Corporation (1967) *Professional Selling Skills Seminar* Xerox National Sales Development Centre: Fort Lauderdale, FL

Yorkshire and Humberside Association for Further and Higher Education (1982) *The Principles and Practice of Trades Education* YHAFHE: Leeds

Section III: Articles, periodicals and working papers

ABT (1983) *Working paper for the discussion group on computers in education at the 1983 Seminar on Educational Technology of the Brazilian Association for Educational Technology* Associacao Brasileira de Tecnologia Educacional (ABT): Rio de Janeiro

ABT (1985) *Working paper for the discussion group on computers in education, at the 1985 Seminar on Educational Technology of the Brazilian Association for Educational Technology (ABT)* ABT: Rio de Janeiro

Acherman, J A, Brons, R and Kuhry, B (1981-1982) The development of student numbers in university education (De ontwikkeling van het aantal studenten in het wetenschappelijk onderwij) *Universiteit en Hogeschool* **28** 6: 321-339

Alex, L (1983) Education and qualified labour demand (Ausbildung und fachkräftebedarf) *Berufsbildung in Wissenschaft und Praxis* December 1983: 181

Arce, J F and Romiszowski, A J (1985) Using a relational database as a means of integrating instructional and library materials in a computer managed course *Proceedings of the 26th ADCIS International Conference* Association for the Development of Computer-Based Instructional Systems, Western Washington University, Bellingham: Washington

Bates, D B (1980) Important innovations introduced by agricultural extension to the tribal farmer over the last twenty years *The Zimbabwe Science News* **14** 7: 187-190

Beeby, C E (1956) Address to the Senate of the University of New Zealand *in* Offenberger (1979) p 280 loc cit

Bembridge, T J (1972) *Extension in a Rhodesian Purchase Land Area* Unpublished MSc dissertation Reading University: UK

Byram, M and Garforth, C (1980) Researching and testing non-formal education materials: a multi-media extension project in Botswana *Educational Broadcasting International* December: 190-194

Chirambo, S (1985) *Factors Affecting the Rate of Adoption of Agricultural Innovations with Special Reference to Northern Malawi* Unpublished Msc dissertation Reading University: UK

Cohen, M D, March, J G and Olsen, J P (1972) A garbage can model of organizational choice *Administrative Science Quarterly* **17** 1: 1-25

Collins, and Hughes, P W (1982) Where junior secondary schools are heading *The Australian Education Review* **16** Australian Council for Educational Research: Melbourne

Cureton, E E (1971) Communality estimates in factor analysis of small matrices *Educational and Psychological Measurement* **31** 2 (Summer)

Curtis, J R H (1983) *Institutional Assessment: A Canadian Example* The Further Education Staff College: Blagdon, Bristol

Finch, C R and Crunkilton, J R (1979) Individualised, competency-based packages *in Curriculum Development in Vocational and Technical Education: Planning, Content and Implementation* Allyn and Bacon Inc: London

Ford, G W (1982) Human resources development and the balance of skills *Journal of Industrial Relations* September: 443-43

Fortmann, L (1984) *The Performance of Extension Services in Botswana* Network paper no 20, Agricultural Administration Network, Overseas Development Institute: London

Gevers, J K M (1984) Of visionary administration and paternal management (Van visionair bestuur en vaderlijkbeheer) *in Higher Vocational Education in Variety by Context (Hoger Beroepsonderwijs in Verscheidenheid naar Samenhang)* HBO-RAAD/VUGA: The Hague

Goldschmidt, B and Goldschmidt, M (1972) Modular instruction: principles and applications in higher education *Learning in Higher Education* 3: 8

Grip, A de (1984) Education and job market (Onderwijs en arbeidsmarkt) *Intermediair* **20**: 21

Gorsuch, L R (1974) *Factor Analysis* W B Saunders Co: Philadelphia, London, Toronto

Guttman, L (1954) Some necessary conditions for factor analysis *Psychometrika* **19** 2

Horn, R E (1974) *Course Notes for Information Mapping Workshop* Information Resources Inc: Lexington, MA

Hover, C (1983) Scale expansion: more people, more problems, more costs (Schaalvergroting: meer mensen, meer problemen, meer kosten) *HBO-Journaal 6* 2: 34-37

Imrie, B W (1984) *AAVA Assessment of Student Performance* M Circular 84/4 Authority for Advanced Vocational Awards: Wellington

Imrie, B W, Blithe, T B and Johnston, L C (1980) A review of Keller Principles with reference to mathematics courses in Australasia *British Journal of Educational Technology* **11**: 2

Imrie, B W, McCallion, H and Thomas, R F March (1985) *Providing Technicians for Research and Development* Paper prepared for the National Research Advisory Council: Wellington

Kaiser, H F (1960) *Relating Factors between Studies based upon Different Individuals* Unpublished manuscript, University of Illinois

Keller, E (1976) *The role of harambee schools in education for development* Working Paper No 118 IDS University of Nairobi: Nairobi

Keller, G (1983) The management revolution in American higher education *Academic Strategy*

Kennan, P B (1980) Agricultural extension in Zimbabwe, 1950-1980 *The Zimbabwe Science News* 14: 7: 183-186

Kickert, W J M (1985) Quo vadis, higher education? Present-day policy developments and possible future explorations (Quo vadis, hoger onderwijs? Huidige beleidsont-wikkelingen en mogelijke toekomstverkenning) *Bestuur* 4 4: 14-25

Kingshotte, A (1979) *The Organisation and Management of Agricultural Extension and Farmer Assistance in Botswana* Discussion Paper 1, Agricultural Adminis-tration Unit, Overseas Development Institute: London

Kinyanjui, K (1974) *The Distribution of Education Resources and Opportunities in Kenya* (Discussion Paper No 208, ID) University of Nairobi: Nairobi

Kodde, D A (1984) Who's for higher education? (Wie kiest er voor hoger onderwijs?) *Research Memorandum 8401* University of Nijmegen

Lawrence, P R and Lorsch, J W (1967) Managing differentiation and integration *Organisation and Environment* Harvard University Press: Boston

(1983) Learning a skill: training young workers in the USSR *Socialism: Theory and Practice* 7: 73-78

Lima, M C M de A (1984a) Informatics and education (Informatica e educacao) *Tecnologia Educacional* 56 January/February ABT: Rio de Janeiro

Lima, M C M de A (1984b) A informatica educativa no contexto do Ministerio de Educacao e Cultura *Tecnologia Educacional* 59 July/August ABT: Rio de Janeiro

Lipper III, A (1985) Entrepreneurship education *International Council for Small Business Newsletters*, 22: 3

McBride, E F and Imrie, B W (1985) Technician training — on the right track *New Electronics:* October

Maimbo, P (1982) *An Analysis of the Training and Visit System as an Additional Approach to Agricultural Extension in the Central Province of Zambia* Unpub-lished Diploma dissertation, Reading University: UK

Marsh, D T (1984) *Vocational Training in the USSR: Further Education Staff College Information Bank 2023g* Bristol

Mertens, F J H (1981) The practical year in higher technical education (Het prak-tijkjaar van het hoger technisch onderwijs) *Practical Periods in Vocational Education (Stages in een Beroepsopleiding)* PhD Thesis, Amsterdam

Mitchell, A, Perfect, H and Boyd, J (1985) Scope for profiling: computer support for teachers in developing profiled reports *Programmed Learning & Educational Technology* 22: 4

Mungate, D T (1983) *Agricultural Extension: Philosophy and Practice, with Special Reference to the Small-Scale Commercial Areas of Zimbabwe* Unpublished MSC dissertation, Reading University: UK

Murphy, P E and McGarrity, R A (1978) Marketing universities: a survey of student recruiting activities *College and University* Spring 1978: 249-261

Newman, G (1984) Taking the initiative *TVEI Insight* 1: 5-6 MSC: London

Nuttall, D and Goldstein, H (1984) Profiles and graded tests: the technical issues *Profiles in Action* FEU: London

Orwa, W O (1982) *An Investigation of Vocational Education in Kenya with Reference to Village Polytechnic Programme* MEd thesis, University of Nairobi: Nairobi

Peixoto, M do C L (1984) O computador no ensino de segundo grau no Brasil *Tecnologia Educacional* **60** September/October ABT: Rio de Janeiro

Pennell, R (1972) Routinely computable confidence intervals for factor loadings using the 'jack-knife' *British Journal of Mathematical and Statistical Psychology* **25**: 107-111

Plowes, D C H (1980) The impact of agricultural extension in the eastern tribal area of Zimbabwe *The Zimbabwe Science News* **14**: 7: 197-200

Putten, M J T A van der (1981) Developments in educational policy and how the higher technical education school supervision functions (Ontwikkelingen in het onderwijsbeleid en het functioneren van het Rijksschooltoezicht Hoger Technisch Onderwijs *Policy and Supervision (Beleid en Toezicht)* Nijmegen

Rao, G N N, Balu, S A and Chandran, G S (1981) *Laboratory Instruction in Polytechnics: Approaches Monograph LTG 1* (2nd Edn) TTTI: Bhopal

Rao, G N N, Jain, P C and Dharap, K P (1981) *Laboratory Innovation for Polytechnics: Engineering Experimentation Course Monograph LTG 2* (2nd Edn) TTTI: Bhopal

Ritzen, J M M (1982) Higher education graduates in a spot (Hoger opgeleiden in de knel) *Research Memorandum 8205* University of Nijmegen

Ritzen, J M M (1983) No work for higher-education and further-education graduates? (Geen werk voor hoger en semi-hoger opgeleiden?) *Hoger Onderwijs* **1** 2: 43-46

Romiszowski, A J (1983a) Introduction to an annotated bibliography on computers in education (Computador na educacao: o que ha para ler?) *Tecnologia Educacional* **54** September/October ABT: Rio de Janeiro

Romiszowski, A J (1983b) The computer in education: how to get started on a shoestring (Computador na educacao: como comecar com o minimo de recursos) *Tecnologia Educacional* **55** November/December ABT: Rio de Janeiro

Saran, Y (1976) India: a strategy to improve technician education *Prospects* **6** 2: 245-53

Saran, Y (1979) *Technical Teacher Training — Towards a New Initiative* Working paper for the international workshop for the In-service Training of Technical Teacher Educators, Turin, Italy (17-22 Sept 1979) TTTI: Bhopal

Seale, C (1984) FEU and MSC: Two curricular philosophies and their implications for a youth training scheme in *The Vocational Aspect of Education* (YTS Special Edition) **36** 93: May 1984

SENAI (1984) *Comunicacao/SENAI* **58** July/August Newsletter describing the 16 electronics training projects developed in 1983-85

Shapero, A (1982) *Taking Control* A commencement address at the Ohio State University: Columbus, OH

Soviet Weekly (1984-1986) 2204-2308 May 1984-May 1986: London

Twining, J (1985) Flavour of the month: the response of FE *EDUCA* **55**

Twining, J (1986) Inside information: a door to the future? *International Review of Education* **32** 3: 295-311

Venne, R (1985) *Annual Research Project* BCIT School of Business, Marketing Management Department: Vancouver

Ward, C (1984) Hargreaves — a progress report *EDUCA* **42**: 14-16

Wells, W (1985) The relative pay and employment of young people *Department of Employment Research Paper Series* **42** Department of Employment: London

Wieringen, A M L van (1976) An investigation into the role and position of higher vocational education in the Dutch school system (Een onderzoek naar de taak en plaats van het hoger beroepsonderwijs in hete Nederlandse schoolwezen) *in The Identity of Higher Vocational Education (De Identiteit van het Hoger Beroepsonderwijs)* Tjeenk Willink: Groningen

Biographical notes on contributors and editors

Catherine Ashmore (Chapter 12) received her MA from Ohio State University and her PhD from the University of Michigan. After working as a high school distributive education teacher in Columbus, Ohio and Ashland, Kentucky, she became Director of the Distributive Education Materials Laboratory at Ohio State University in 1973. There she developed competency-based job training materials for use in vocational education.

In 1980 she became the marketing director of the National Center for Research in Vocational Education at Columbus, becoming Entrepreneurship Program director in 1983. In that post she has provided leadership in developing entrepreneurship education initiatives for high school and two-year college programmes nationwide. She has organized a consortium of study directors of vocational education to support state-wide leadership in supporting entrepreneurship in all vocational programmes. She is vice-president for entrepreneurship education for the US affiliate of the International Council for Small Businesses. She has written numerous articles and developed curriculum materials in support of new programmes.

Henry O Ayot (Chapter 13) is the chairman of the Department of Educational Communications and Technology at Kenyatta University College. Born a Kenyan and educated in Kenya, Britain and the USA, he graduated BA in history at Lincoln University, Pennsylvania in 1966; MA in Educational Communications and Technology in 1967 at St Joseph's College, Philadelphia; and PhD in Social Studies at the University of Nairobi in 1973. He taught at Kenyan secondary schools between 1968 and 1974 before joining the University of Nairobi as a lecturer in Education in 1974.

Professor Ayot has travelled widely and represented his country in international seminars and forums on education. He has been UNESCO and Commonwealth Secretariat consultant in workshops and projects.

He has undertaken wide research on education and has many publications in the field of education. Among them are: *Topics in East African History* (1976, EALB, Nairobi); *Historical Texts of the Lake Region of East Africa* (1978, EALB, Nairobi); *A History of Luo Abasuba of Western Kenya* (1979, EALB, Nairobi); (Ed) *Language for Learning* (A Methodology Book for English Language Learning in Secondary Schools) (1984, MacMillan Kenya Ltd); *New Approach in the Teaching of History* (1980, KLB, Nairobi); *Primary Social Studies*, Pupils' Books 1-3 (1980, MacMillan Educational Ltd); contributions to educational journals both as editor and as co-author.

Narendra K Banthiya (Chapter 16) has a Bachelors degree in mechanical engineering from Birla College of Engineering, Pilani, a Masters degree in refrigeration and air-conditioning from Indian Institute of Technology, Kharagpur and a doctorate degree in Heat Transfer from Indian Institute of Technology, Kanpur. During his professional career spanning 29 years, he has taught undergraduate and postgraduate engineering students for 16 years at Birla Institute of Technology, Mesra, Ranchi, before taking up the position as Professor of Mechanical Engineering at the Technical Teachers' Training Institute (TTTI), Bhopal during 1976. In 1986, on deputation from the government of India, he has taken up Associate Professorship of Mechanical Engineering at the University of Al-Fateh, Tripoli, Libya. He has published a number of research papers in Heat Transfer in international journals. As a teacher trainer at TTTI Bhopal, he co-ordinated the introduction of Competency Based Teacher Education (CBTE). He also worked as task group leader for student evaluation and distance learning task groups. He has co-ordinated a number of projects and programmes in the above areas and in teaching-learning, curriculum development, curriculum evaluation, and laboratory innovations. Many of the projects with which he has been associated have had a profound impact on the technician education system in India.

Russ Curtis (Chapter 15) graduated from the University of British Columbia with honours in Industrial Engineering 1964. Thereafter he worked in Sales and Marketing Management with the Ford Motor Company, Xerox of Canada Limited and Pro Sports Marketing Incorporated, prior to joining the faculty of the British Columbia Institute of Technology in 1973. While at BCIT he earned an MBA at Simon Fraser University, served upon a ministerial task force which examined management systems in the post-secondary sector, and has served on BCIT's Board of Governors (Audit, Education and Governance Committees). He has held a post as sessional lecturer in the MBA Program at Simon Fraser University, lecturing in Accounting and Management Systems.

He was recently appointed as Director, Learning Resources Division, BCIT. In this position he is responsible for providing support services to innovative learning materials development and production.

Since 1981, he has also held a post as Associate Tutor, The Further Education Staff College, Blagdon, Bristol.

Previous publications include a number of papers written for the Coombe Lodge Information Bank on the subject of academic staff performance appraisal.

Dorothee Engelhard (Chapter 5) has been with the Bund-Länder-Kommission für Bildungsplanung und Forschungsförderung since 1971. There she has been responsible for educational planning duties at the federal level. Since then she has dealt mainly with elementary education, immigrant children, handicapped children and vocational education. In 1970 she graduated from the University of California, Riverside. In 1980 she has the opportunity within a Fulbright Scholarship, of investigating problems concerning bilingual education, aspects of pre-school education and the education of the handicapped in USA. Resulting publications are:

— Aspekte vorschulischer Erziehung in den USA (1983), Sozialpädagogische Blätter, Heft 2
— Bundesgesetze und ihre Auswirkungen auf das Bildungssystem in den Vereinigten Staaten (1984), Recht der Jugend und des Bildungswesens, Heft 1.

Bill Ford (Chapter 20) is Professor in the Programme of Organizational Behaviour in the University of New South Wales. After leaving school at the age of 15, he was employed for over seven years in a variety of industries and occupations. He then returned to formal education at Sydney Technical College and the University of Sydney. Following a short period of high school teaching, he went to the United States as a Fulbright scholar to continue his studies at the Universities of Illinois and California.

Professor Ford has written and edited a number of books and articles in the fields of technological transfer/change, employment, unemployment, skill formation, recurrent education, organizational learning and participation, unions, industrial relations and industrial democracy. He has also served in a variety of government positions in Australia; in 1986 he was a consultant to the South Australian Ministry of Technology, the Western Australian Technology Directorate and the Australian Bureau of Labour Market Research.

He has held visiting positions at Warwick University (UK), Stanford University (US), and Keio University (Japan). He has also held senior research positions and consultancies with intergovernmental organizations, including the International Labour Office in Geneva and the government and the university of Papua New Guinea. In 1985-6 he was a member of the Organization of Economic Cooperation and Development (OECD)'s international team for the Human Resources Project on technological change, work organization and skill formation.

His current research focus is on enterprise level, cross-cultural studies of technological transfer/change, work organization and human resource development, organizational learning and participation, with particular emphasis on Australia, East Asia, Germany and the Nordic countries.

Paul Frissen (Chapter 10) studied public administration and pedagogy in Nijmegen. In 1982 he worked at the Public Administration Department of Nijmegen University. From 1983 to 1985 he worked in the Social Sciences Faculty of Nijmegen University and as a consultant to the management of a department of the Ministry of Education and Science. Since 1986 he has been a university teacher in public administration at the Faculty of Law, Department of Public Administration, of Tilburg University. Publications include articles on the inspectorate in education and higher education policy, and a book on the organization of universities.

Chris Garforth (Chapter 11) became interested in agricultural extension while he was conducting fieldwork in Nigeria for a PhD thesis on land tenure and agricultural land use. From 1977 to 1980 he worked as an Action Research Officer within the Agricultural Information Services of the Botswana Ministry of Agriculture, developing formative research procedures for the design and testing of educational and advisory materials. Since January 1980 he has been a lecturer in the Agricultural Extension and Rural Development Centre (AERDC) at Reading University (UK) where he teaches communication and extension methods on short courses and on the one-year postgraduate courses. Advisory visits and consultancies undertaken in recent years include work in Malawi, Uganda, Nepal, the Philippines and Thailand. Research interests include the communication of crop protection information to farmers and the use of communications technology to support agricultural extension. With Dr Peter Oakley, a colleague at the AERDC, he has written a Guide to Extension Training for FAO.

Phillip Hughes (Chapter 1) is currently Professor of Education at the University of Tasmania. He has had substantial experience in education, in teaching, in administration, in research and in policy development. He has taught in secondary schools, technical colleges, universities, has been superintendent of a curriculum branch, principal of a teachers college and is a former Deputy Director-General of Education in Tasmania. He was the founding chairman of the first new schools authority for over 100 years and has been active in UNESCO, particularly in Asian and Pacific regions. His major interests are in curriculum and in policy development.

Bradford Imrie (Chapter 9) is a previous Director of the Authority for Advanced Vocational Awards. After training as a professional mechanical engineer with Babcock and Wilcox Ltd (UK) he held teaching positions at Paisley College of Technology, Leeds University, the Open University (part-time) and Victoria University of Wellington, where he was a Senior Lecturer in the University of Training and Research Centre.

He is author of *Compressible Fluid Flow* and co-author of *Assessing Students, Appraising Teaching*. He has published some 40 papers on aspects of engineering and of teaching and learning in higher education. His current interests are professional development of staff, student development, assessment of student performance and the development of vocational education.

In March 1986, Brad Imrie took up the position of Deputy Principal (Academic) at the Central Institute of Technology, Heretaunga, New Zealand.

Ron Johnson (Chapter 2) runs his own consultancy company (Ron Johnson Associates Limited) which specializes in manpower matters and in helping individuals and groups of people to become more effective. He acts as a manpower consultant to regional, national and EEC bodies.

Up until early 1981, Dr Johnson was Director of Training at the Manpower Services Commission (Training Services Division), a post he held for seven years. He was responsible for a national programme of research, development and advisory services in management development and vocational training, and also represented the United Kingdom in Europe and the MSC on various education and training bodies.

His early career included seven years as a scientist in the food industry and a number of academic posts, including a lectureship at the University of London and head of the Food Science Department at the Polytechnic of the South Bank. Dr Johnson became head of the training department of the Food, Drink and Tobacco Industry Training Board before joining the MSC in 1974. He currently chairs the Employee Development Working Party of the Institute of Personnel Management.

Harry Knutton (Chapter 21) spent his formative years as an artillery officer and parachutist in the Second World War. He qualified afterwards as a chartered electrical engineer, and was concerned for many years with the development and production of advanced defence equipment for the British Army, in which he rose to the rank of Major-General. He was also responsible for a number of joint engineering projects with other countries. He was a lecturer in control engineering at the Royal Military College of Science and has taught computing science in a secondary school. From 1976 to 1985 he was Director-General of the City and Guilds of London Institute. He is deputy chairman of the Standing Conference for Schools, Science and Technology, a fellow of the College of Preceptors and a governor of Imperial College of Science and Technology.

Kurt Kreuser (Chapter 5) has been General Secretary of the Bund-Länder-Kommission für Bildungsplanung und Forschungsförderung since 1976. Before that he was Under-Secretary in the Department of Education, Science and Art in Bremen, which is one of the 11 states in the Federal Republic of Germany. In addition, he is chairman of the Deutsche Gesellschaft für Bildungsverwaltung and represents the Federal Republic in the Steering Committee of the European Forum on Educational Administration. Further appointments include Vice-President of the Deutsche Bibliotheksverband and Vice-Chairman of the governing body of the Deutsche Institut für Internationale Pädagogische Forschung.

Jack Longden (Chapter 3) recently retired as Principal, Keighley Technical College. He has worked in further education and training since 1946, and was formerly head of engineering at the Mid-Warwickshire College. Before that, he worked in public transport engineering, in various positions with Ferranti Ltd, and was superintendent of the Preston NPL Gauge Testing Centre.

He has been a member of the Central Training Council, the Carpet Industry Training Board, and Committees of the Engineering Industry Training Board, the Technician Education Council, the City and Guilds of London Institute, the National Advisory Council for Education in Industry and Commerce, the Pilkington Committee on use of Technical College Resources, the Advisory Committee on the Supply, Education and Training of Teachers, and other public committees. For over 25 years he acted as curriculum developer and Chief Examiner to the City and Guilds of London Institute, West Midlands, and Yorkshire Council Examination Boards. He has been chairman of trades principles development for the Yorkshire and Humberside Association for Further and Higher Education. He is a past president of the Association of Teachers in Technical Education. He has visited the USSR, the German Democratic Republic, Spain, France, and USA on educational missions. He is the author of various publications on curriculum and staff development.

Ian McCallum (Chapter 17) is currently Director of the Research and Development Unit at Garnett College of Education (Technical). His introduction to teaching occurred during service as a technical officer in the Royal Air Force. After obtaining a first degree in mathematics and qualifying as a teacher, he obtained a Masters Degree in Education at the University of Leicester and a doctorate at the University of Sussex. He has taught in a variety of institutions and has a major interest in the assessment of factors which can be associated with the way in which the understanding of technical subjects may be developed.

Derek Marsh (Chapter 6) read English at the University College of Wales, Aberystwyth (1951-1954), and served with the RAF Education Branch until 1966, spending the last five years at the RAF College, Cranwell. After a period as head of department in a public school he joined the Civil Service (Home Office) in 1970, lecturing in management development and training systems, and then in September 1978 the Further Education Staff College. He obtained the Diploma in Advanced Studies in Education in 1978 at Bristol University and in 1984 graduated MEd for research into the cognitive strategies of managerial problem-solving. His main professional interests include the management of the public sector of further and higher education and its qualitative development, organizational development, and inter-personal skills. His interest in comparative studies of vocational education have taken him to Ireland, Israel, the Federal Republic of Germany, Canada, the German Democratic Republic, and the USSR.

Jacquetta Megarry (Series Editor) is an author and training consultant. After a first degree in maths and psychology at Cambridge University she trained and practised as a teacher in Glasgow. She took an MEd degree in 1972 and became a lecturer in education first at Glasgow University, then at Jordanhill College of Education (1973-1980), where she also produced distance learning materials in a variety of media. From 1973 to 1986 she was a leading figure in the UK Society for the Advancement of Games and Simulations in Education and Training, having been its chairman, general editor, vice-president and editor of its journal *Simulation/Games for Learning* (1975-80). She was a regular visiting lecturer at Concordia University, Montreal, from 1975 to 1981.

Since 1981 she has worked freelance, specializing in computers, educational technology and information technology. Recent books include *Computer World* (Pan/Piccolo Factbook, 1983), *Computers Mean Business* (Kogan Page and Pan, 1984) and *Inside Information: Computers, Communications and People* (BBC Publications, 1985). She writes regularly for such newspapers as the *Times Educational Supplement* and various computing periodicals. She has also published extensively in academic periodicals such as *Educational Analysis* and has written chapters of academic serials including *Aspects of Educational Technology* (Kogan Page), *Perspectives on Gaming and Simulation* (Kogan Page/SAGSET) and the *International Encyclopaedia of Education: Research and Studies* (Pergamon). She was series editor of the *World Yearbook of Education* from its revival in 1979 to the present volume.

She has acted as a consultant to the Manpower Services Commission (MSC), the Department of Trade and Industry, the British Broadcasting Corporation's Computer Literacy Project, the Council for Educational Technology (CET) (UK), the Bologna Children's Book Fair, the British Council in India, OECD/CERI and the European Commission's Delta Project, as well as to various companies with training needs. She has been actively involved in developing education and training systems using interactive videodisc.

Stanley Nisbet (Series Editor) retired from the Chair of Education at the University of Glasgow in 1978. Starting his professional life as a classics teacher, he was caught up in the vigorous psychometric activity at Moray House in Edinburgh under Godfrey Thomson, and his early work was in this field. After five years of wartime service in the RAF, part of the time in its training research branch, and a short spell in the University of Manchester, he became professor of education in Queen's University, Belfast, and was involved in some of the post-war educational developments in Northern Ireland. From 1951 to 1978 he was professor of education in the University of Glasgow, holding various administrative posts in the University (eg Dean of Faculty of Arts, 1965-7) and serving on many bodies outside the University, such as the Scottish Council for Research in Education. His teaching was mainly on educational theory, curriculum study (in 1957 he wrote one of the earliest books in this field) and comparative education, with a special interest in Germany and the USSR. Much of his writing has consisted of contributions to official publications. Since his retirement he has participated in projects on a number of subjects, including home-school co-operation in the EEC countries, and the monitoring of in-service courses for primary school teachers.

Frank Pignatelli (Chapter 4) is now Deputy Director of Education, Strathclyde Region. He has been involved in the education of young people as teacher and administrator for the past 16 years. In 1978 he became Education Officer in Strathclyde, with responsibilities for schools/further education liaison, schools/industry liaison, the careers service, the community education service and the introduction of the Youth Opportunities Programme. He has been heavily involved in the introduction of the Technical and Vocational Education Initiative (TVEI) in Scotland, as chairman of the Scottish advisory group and as a member of the UK national steering group. In addition, he is centrally involved in implementing the wide-ranging and innovative post-compulsory education policy which has been adopted by his authority in response to economic, educational and social pressures in the Strathclyde area. He has spoken and written extensively on the education of 14-18 year olds, and in 1985 acted as consultant to the Egyptian Ministry of Education on the introduction of vocational education into their system.

Marijke van der Putten (Chapter 10) first took a higher vocational course in social and cultural work. She then studied pedagogy in Nijmegen and specialized in organization theory and public administration. From 1981 to 1985 she has worked for Interstudie: School Organization and Educational Management in Arnhem. Since 1986 she has been head of the Education and Training Department of Postbank NV in Arnhem.

Publications include articles on the inspectorate in education, innovative capacities of schools and school amalgamations.

Iolo Roberts (Chapter 18) taught within secondary and further education before moving to the University of Keele, Staffordshire, to specialize in science education and further education. Having retired from a senior lectureship in education, he is now a Fellow of the University.

His continued involvement in the FE scene at regional and national level has enabled him to make a substantial contribution to the growth of research into further and vocational education. He is also co-author of *Further Education in England and Wales*, Routledge, 2nd Edn 1972, and *Further Education Today: a critical review*, Routledge, 3rd Edn 1986, which are recognized as standard texts on the development of the sector in the post-war era.

A J Romiszowski (Chapter 7) originally studied engineering, followed by educational psychology, a combination that led to an early involvement with the design of training systems and an interest in the newly developing field of educational/training technology. Since the mid 1960s he has worked as a consultant and practitioner in most aspects of educational technology and in every type of educational and training context.

After several years as director of the Learning Systems Unit of the Middlesex Polytechnic in London, he spent some time as a United Nations Consultant, working on projects in Spain, Italy, India, Hungary and Brazil, most of these in the field of adult education. His activities ranged from media development and production to the planning of national curricula and distance education systems.

He has published several books on aspects of instructional design and educational technology, as well as some 200 papers and articles. Research interests include media utilization, distance education, individualization, CAL and artificial intelligence.

He has also taught at several universities and colleges in the UK, Canada, and Brazil and is currently at Syracuse University, New York State, pursuing research interests, writing, and acting as a freelance consultant.

John Twining (Guest Editor, Introduction and Chapter 14) joined the City and Guilds of London Institute (Britain's major technical examining body) in 1963, following an earlier career in the Uganda Civil Service. He was Head of the City and Guilds Engineering Branch from 1965-1973, when he was appointed leader of the City and Guilds staff team which serviced the Technician Education Council at its initial establishment. He was deeply involved in the design of a major modular system for technician education.

In 1978 he left to found his own companies, one of which, Guildford Educational Services Ltd, specializes in vocational education and training. Specific activities have included consultancy in Open Learning in the UK, India and Pakistan, and in qualifications and assessment. John Twining and Christine Ward (Chapter 19) wrote the majority of the background papers for the Review of Vocational Qualifications. Other activities have included the design and maintenance of major computerized databases, including the Short Course Directory for the PICKUP programme of the Department of Education and Science.

He is Editor of *EDUCA*, the Guildford Educational Services digest for vocational education and training, and has written a large number of articles on various aspects of vocational education. In 1982 he wrote *Open Learning for Technicians*, published by Stanley Thornes (Publishers) Ltd.

Ian Waitt (Chapter 8) has written widely on education, and technical education in particular. He has contributed many articles to UK journals and the educational press, as well as in various international publications. His major published work is *College Administration* (NATFHE, 1980), which he edited as well as contributing two-thirds of the text. This book is the standard guide to public sector further and higher education in England and Wales, and was commended by the UK Library Association in 1981 as 'one of the reference books of the year'. He edited (with L S Gray) and contributed to *Simulation in Management and Business Education*, Kogan Page/Nichols Publishing, 1982, and also jointly edited and contributed to an environmental studies textbook for schools. Dr Waitt has worked extensively in Asia in technical education consultancy, and in the preparation, definition and execution of a variety of major projects. His experience includes work in India, Singapore, Thailand, Hong Kong, South Korea, Malaysia, Thailand, Egypt and the USA. He currently directs the Management and Education Projects Office at the North East London Polytechnic.

Christine Ward (Chapter 19) is employed at Guildford Educational Services Ltd (GES) as assistant editor of *EDUCA* and on a wide range of consultancy projects relating to further education, training and assessment. She has worked on reports prepared by GES for the Review of Vocational Qualifications and on setting up a database of UK Further Education qualifications. Her earlier career was at City and Guilds of London Institute (1965-1974), first as a subject administrative officer and then in research and development, with particular involvement in assessment methodology. She is author of three books in the *Handbooks for Further Education* series published by Stanley Thornes (*Designing a Scheme of Assessment* 1980, *Preparing and Using Constructed Answer Questions* 1981, and *Preparing and Using Objective Questions* 1981) and has edited a number of books of multiple-choice questions on nursing, catering and food service.

Index